Arab-Islamic Groups And Organizations

(From Muhammad to the present)

Saul Silas Fathi

Ingram / Lightningsource.com

Arab - Islamic groups and organizations

(From Muhammad to the present)

Copyright 2013 by Saul Silas Fathi

Library of Congress Number: 2013904829

ISBN#: 978-1-62620-377-8   Trade paper

Book Design: Fran Padro

Cover design: Daniel Middleton

Image/art: Shutterstock # 101389795

All rights reserved. No part of this book may be reproduced or transmitted in
any form or any means, electronic or mechanical, including photocopying,
recording, or by any information storage and retrieval system, without permission in writing from the copyright owner.

This book was printed in the United States of America

Books by Saul Silas Fathi:
1. Full Circle: Escape from Baghdad and the return ISBN# 978-0-9777117-8-9
2. History of the Jews and Israel ISBN# 978-0-9777117-3-4
3. Islamic leaders, their biographies & accomplishments ISBN# 978-0-9777117-5-8
4. Glossary of Arabic terms ISBN# 978-0-9777117-4-1
5. Arab-Islamic groups and organizations ISBN# 978-1-62620-377-8

ACKNOWLEDGEMENT

I owe deep gratitude to Fran Padro for her assistance in typing, editing and researching this manuscript; for her patience, her valuable advice and dedication to this project.

***

Author/Lecturer: Saul Silas Fathi

Saul Silas Fathi was born to a prominent Jewish family in Baghdad, Iraq. At age 10, he was smuggled out of Baghdad through Iran and eventually reached the State of Israel. He began writing a diary at age 11 and had several stories published in Israeli youth magazines. In 1958, he worked his way to Brazil where he nearly starved. In 1960, he came to the U.S. on a student exchange visa. After Basic Training in Fort Benning, Georgia, he was sent to helicopter school at Fort Bragg, North Carolina, and there enrolled at the University of Virginia.

Within a few months, Saul was shipped to South Korea where he served with the 1st Cavalry Division, 15th Aviation Company, the famed helicopter division in the Vietnam War. Saul retired in 2003 and began writing his memoirs, Full Circle: Escape from Baghdad and the return. Today, he lives in Long Island, New York, with his wife Rachelle. He is a certified linguist, fluent in English, Hebrew, Arabic, and Portuguese.

Mr. Fathi has lectured at 160+ organizations since 2006, and authored 5 books.

www.saulsilasfathi.com / fathi@optonline.net

***

T.O.C.: Arab-Islamic groups and organizations

Inside front cover, documentations..................................2
Acknowledgement 3
About the author, Bios..4
Table of Contents..5
Introduction: History of Islam...........…...................…......6
Arab-Islamic groups & organizations: A~Z.......................12
Caliphs and Caliphates (section #1)............................194
Muslim empires & Dynasties (section #2).....................249
Islamic Divisions (section #3)...................................262
Muslim population by country (section #4)................. 267
Rightly-Guided Caliphs (section #5)...........................275
Ruling families (section #6).................................... 278
Twelver Shi'ah (section #7)....................................…280
Islam's great accomplishments (section #8)..................299
Islamic Charities (section # 9).................................…319
Bibliography, Recommended reading (section #10)..........332
Fathi's books 356

***

Introduction: A brief history of Islam

Dear reader: In this book you will be introduced to hundreds of Arabic terms, an extensive Islamic Dictionary. They are presented in alphabetical order.

History of Islam:
In less than a century after Muhammad's death Islam swept through Asia, Africa and Europe, dominating an area larger than that of the Roman Empire at its peak. Today, one in 5 people on the face of this earth is a Muslim. A total of 1.6 billion people; the second largest religion in the world and the fastest-growing.

For a period of 400 years, from the Eighth to the Twelfth Century, the achievements of this synthesized culture were unsurpassed. In fact, much of the science and literature of the European Renaissance was inspired by Islamic models. I urge everyone to learn about it.

Islam (=Submission): Is the monotheistic religion articulated by the Qur'an, a text considered by its adherents to be the verbatim word of God (Arabic: *Allāh*), and by the teachings and normative example (called the *Sunnah* and composed of *Hadith*) of Muhammad, considered by them to be the last prophet of God. An adherent of Islam is called a *Muslim*.

God (Allah): Muslims believe that God is one and incomparable and the purpose of existence is to worship God. Muslims also believe that Islam is the complete and universal version of a primordial faith that was revealed at many times and places before, including through Abraham, Moses and Jesus, whom they consider prophets. They maintain that previous messages and revelations have been partially changed or corrupted over time, but consider the Qur'an to be both the unaltered and the final revelation of God.

Islam's most fundamental concept is a rigorous monotheism, called Tawhid. God is described in chapter 112 of the Qur'an as: "Say: He is God, the One and Only; God, the Eternal, Absolute; He begetteth not,

not is He begotten; and there is none like unto Him." **(Qur'an 112:1-4)** Muslims repudiate the Christian doctrine of the Trinity and divinity of Jesus, comparing it to polytheism, but accept Jesus as a prophet. In Islam, God is beyond all comprehension and Muslims are not expected to visualize God.

Muslims believe that creation of everything in the universe is brought into by God's sheer command "'Be' and so it is." and that the purpose of existence is to worship God. He is viewed as a personal God who responds whenever a person in need or distress calls Him. There are no intermediaries, such as clergy, to contact God who states "We are nearer to him than (his) jugular vein" *Allāh* is the term with no plural or gender used by Muslims and Arabic-speaking Christians and Jews meaning the one God.

Holy Qur'an: It is divided into 114 suras, or chapters, which combined contain 6,236 *āyāt*, or verses. Muslim jurists consult the H*adith*, or the written record of Prophet Muhammad's life, to both supplement the Qur'an and assist with its interpretation. The science of Qur'anic commentary and exegesis is known as T*afsir*. To Muslims, the Qur'an is perfect only as revealed in the original Arabic; translations are necessarily deficient because of language difference, the fallibility of translators, and the impossibility of preserving the original's inspired style.

Predestination: In accordance with the Islamic belief in predestination, or divine preordainment (*al-qadā wa'l-qadar*), God has full knowledge and control over all that occurs. For Muslims, everything in the world that occurs, good or evil, has been preordained and nothing can happen unless permitted by God. According to Muslim theologians, although events are pre-ordained, man possesses FREE WILL in that he has the faculty to choose between right and wrong, and is thus responsible for his actions.

Five Pillars of Islam
The Pillars of Islam (A*rkan al-Islam*; also *Arkan ad-din*, "pillars of religion") are five basic acts in Islam, considered obligatory of all believers. The Quran presents them as a framework for worship and a sign of commitment to the faith. They are (1) Shahadah (Creed), (2)

daily prayers (Salat), (3) Almsgiving (Zakah), (4) Fasting during Ramadan (Sawm), and (5) Pilgrimage to Mecca (Hajj) at least once in a lifetime. The Shi'a and Sunni sects both agree on the essential details for the performance of these acts.

1. **Testimony** (*Shahadah*)
   The Shahadah, which is the basic creed of Islam that must be recited under oath with the specific statement: " *'ashadu 'al-lā ilah illā-llāhu wa 'ashadu 'anna Muhammadan rasūlu-llāh*", or "I testify there are no deities other than God alone and I testify that Muhammad is the Messenger of God." Muslims must repeat the S*hahadah* in prayer, and non-Muslims wishing to convert to Islam are required to recite the creed.

2. **Prayer** (*Salah*)
   Ritual prayers, called Ṣalāh or Ṣalāt, must be performed five times a day. Salah is intended to focus the mind on God, and is seen as a personal communication with Him that expresses gratitude and worship. Salah is compulsory but flexibility in the specifics is allowed depending on circumstances. The prayers are recited in the Arabic language, and consist of verses from the Qur'an.

   - **Mosque (Masjid)**
     A mosque is in place of worship is a place of worship for Muslims, who often refer to it by its Arabic name, M*asjid*. The word M*osque* in English refers to all types of buildings dedicated to Islamic worship. Although the primary purpose of the mosque is to serve as a place of prayer, it is also important to the Muslim community as a place to meet and study. Shi'a Islam permits combining prayers in succession.

3. **Fasting** (*Sawm of Ramadan*)
   Fasting, from food, drink and sex must be performed from dawn to dusk during the month of Ramadhan. The fast is to encourage a feeling of nearness to God, and during it Muslims should express their gratitude for and dependence on Him, atone for their past sins, and think of the needy. But missed fasts usually must be made up

quickly. The fasting ends daily at sun-down and continues for 30 days.

4. **Alms-giving** (*Zakat and Sadaqah*)
   "Zakat" is giving a fixed portion of accumulated wealth by those who can afford it to help the poor or needy, and also to assist the spread of Islam. It is considered a religious obligation (as opposed to voluntary charity) that the well-off owe to the needy because their wealth is seen as a "trust from God's bounty". The Qur'an and the Hadith also suggest a Muslim give even more as an act of voluntary alms-giving (*Sadaqah*).

5. **Pilgrimage** (*Hajj*)
   The pilgrimage, called the H*ajj* during the Islamic month of *Dhu al-Hijjah* in the city of Mecca. Every able-bodied Muslim who can afford it must make the pilgrimage to Mecca at least once in his or her lifetime. Rituals of the Hajj include walking seven times around the Kaaba, touching the black stone if possible, walking or running seven times between Mount Safa and Mount Marwah, and symbolically stoning the Devil in Mina.

Jihad and the Military: Jihad means "to strive or struggle" (in the way of God) and is considered the "Sixth Pillar of Islam" by a minority of Sunni Muslim authorities. Jihad, in its broadest sense, is classically defined as "exerting one's utmost power, efforts, endeavors, or ability in contending with an object of disapprobation. Jihad, when used without any qualifier, is understood in its military aspect. Jihad also refers to one's striving to attain religious and moral perfection. Some Muslim authorities, especially among the Shi'a and Sufis, distinguish between the "greater jihad", which pertains to spiritual self-perfection, and the "lesser jihad", defined as warfare.

Within Islamic jurisprudence, jihad is usually taken to mean military exertion against non-Muslim combatants in the defense or expansion of the Ummah. Others have argued that the goal of Jihad is global conquest. Jihad is the only form of warfare permissible in Islamic law and may be declared against terrorists, criminal groups, rebels, apostates, and leaders or states that oppress Muslims or hamper proselytizing efforts.

Under most circumstances and for most Muslims, jihad is a collective duty (*Fard Kifaya*): Its performance by some individuals exempts the others. For most Shi'as, offensive jihad can only be declared by a divinely appointed leader of the Muslim community, and as such is suspended since Muhammad al-Mahdi's occultation in 868 AD.

Muhammad (610-632): Muhammad (570–June 8, 632) was a trader later becoming a religious, political, and military leader. However, Muslims do not view Muhammad as the creator of Islam, but instead regard him as the last messenger of God, through which the Qur'an was revealed. Muslims view Muhammad as the restorer of the original, uncorrupted monotheistic faith of Adam, Abraham, Moses, Jesus, and other prophets.

For the last 22 years of his life, beginning at age 40 in 610 CE, Muhammad started receiving revelations that he believed to be from God. The content of these revelations, known as the Qur'an, was memorized and recorded by his companions. During this time, Muhammad preached to the people of Mecca, imploring them to abandon polytheism. After 12 years of preaching, Muhammad and the Muslims performed the Hijah ("emigration") to the city of Medina (formerly known as *Yathrib*) and the Meccan migrants (*Muhajirun*), Muhammad established his political and religious authority. By 630 Muhammad was victorious in the nearly bloodless Conquest of Mecca, and by the time of his death in 632 (at the age of 63) he untied the tribes of Arabia into a single religious polity.

Rise of the caliphate and civil war (632–750):
With Muhammad's death in 632, disagreement broke out over who would succeed him as leader of the Muslim community. Umar ibn al-Khattab, a prominent companion of Muhammad, nominated Abu Bakr, who was Muhammad's companion and close friend. Others added their support and Abu Bakr was made the First Caliph.

- **The Rashidun (Rightly-Guided Caliphs):**
  Abu Bakr's death in 634 resulted in the succession of Umar ibn al-Khattab as the caliph, followed by Uthman ibn al-Affan, Ali ibn Abi Talib and Hasan ibn Ali. The first 4 caliphs are known as *al-khulafa' ar-rāshidūn* ("Rightly Guided Caliphs"). Under them, the territory under Muslim rule expanded deeply into Persian and Byzantine territories. When Umar was assassinated in 644, the election of Uthman as successor was met with increasing opposition. In 656, Uthman was also killed, and Ali assumed the position of caliph. After fighting off opposition in the first civil war (the "First Fitna"), Ali was assassinated by Kharijites in 661. Following this, Mu'awiyah seized power and began the Umayyad dynasty, with its capital in Damascus.

Islamic Accomplishments:
Islamic civilization flourished in what is sometimes referred to as the "Islamic Golden Age". Public hospitals established during this time, are considered "the first hospitals" in the modern sense of the word, and issued the first medical diplomas to license doctors of medicine. The Guinness World Records recognizes the University of Al Karaouine, founded in 859, as the world's older degree-granting university. An important pioneer in this, Ibn al-Haytham is regarded as the father of the modern scientific method and often referred to as the "world's first true scientist." Discoveries include gathering the data used by Copernicus for his heliocentric conclusions and Al-Jahiz's proposal of the theory of natural selection. Rumi wrote some of the finest Persian poetry and is still one of the best selling poets in America. Legal institutions introduced include the trust and charitable trust (Waqf).

***

Arab - Islamic groups and organizations
(From Muhammad to the present): A~Z

Abushiri Revolt: (August 1888-89) Arab revolt against German traders on the East African coast north of Zanzibar. The Arab leader Abushiri (Abu Bashir ibn Salim al-Harthi) united local hostility to German colonization at Pangani when in August 1888 the Germans hauled down the Sultan of Zanzibar's flag and hoisted their own.

African National Congress: (ANC) A South African political party. It was established in Bloemfontein in 1912 as the South African Native National Congress by a Zulu Methodist minister, J.W. Dube. The first multiracial elections, held in 1994, were won by the ANC and Mandela became President. Violence has been prevalent, both before and after the transition to majority rule, between ANC supporters and adherents of the mainly Zulu Inkatha Freedom Party, especially in Inkatha's power-base, eastern region of KwaZulu/Natal. In December 1997 Thabo Mbeki succeeded Mandela as president of the ANC.

Aghlabids: Tunisian Arab dynasty. Islamic dynasty in Tunisia; established in 868.

Ahabish: The Taqif of Taif and the tribe of Abd Manat.

Ahad: literally "one". Islamically ahad means One Alone, unique, none like God. Al Wahid is one of the names of God.

Ahadith (singular, Hadith): news, reports. Documented traditions of the teachings and actions of the Prophet Muhammad, which were not in the Quran but which were recorded for posterity by his close companions and the members of his family.

Ahd (dar al): land of contractual peace in Islamic doctrine; zone where Muslims can live in peace in a non-Muslim state. (Covenant): in

2: 27, for instance, refers to the command issued by God to His servants. This ahd consists of God's eternal command that His creatures are obligated to render their service, obedience and worship to Him alone.

Ahkam: rulings and orders of the Qur'an and Sunnah. Five kinds of orders: Wajib, Mustahab, Muharram, Makruh and Halal.

Ahl al Bayt: "People of the house of Muhammad" Members of Muhammad's household. Also known among Shi'a as the Ma'sumin (infallibles, spiritually pure)

Ahl al Fatrah: people who live in ignorance of the teachings of a revealed religion, but according to the Fitra, the natural religion innate to human nature as created by God.

Ahl al-Bayt: "People of the House," referring to the members of the Prophet's family; descendants of the Prophet's son-in-law 'Ali. The household of the Prophet; those Muslims loyal to the Prophet's immediate family, specifically 'Ali, his wife, Fatimah, and their two sons, Hasan and Husayn; Shi'ites, defining themselves apart from, and over against, dominant Sunni Muslims.

Ahl al-Dhimmah (or **Dhimmis**) are the non-Muslim subjects of an Islamic state who have been guaranteed protection of their rights – life, property and practice of their religion, etc. – by the Muslims. are the non Muslim subjects of an Islamic state who have been guaranteed protection of their rights, life property and practice of their religion.

Ahl al-Hadith refers to the group of scholars in Islam who pay relatively greater importance to 'traditions' than to other sources of Islamic doctrine such as **qiyas**, and tend to interpret the traditions more literally and rigorously. The term has also come to be used lately for a group of Muslims in the Indo-Pakistan subcontinent who are close to the Hanbali school in theology, and claim to follow no single school on legal matters. Hadith People. A school of thought which first appeared during the Umayyad period, which would not permit jurists to use **ijtihad**

(q.v.) but insisted that all legislation be based upon valid **ahadith** (q.v.)

Ahl al-Kitab: People of the Book. The Qur'anic term for people, such as Jews or Christians, who adhered to the earlier scriptures. Since the Prophet and most of the early Muslims were illiterate, and had very few – if any – books, it has been suggested that this term should more accurately be translated: "followers of an earlier revelation." Those who acknowledge God as creator, guide and judge of humankind; Jews, Christians, and others who have a Book that was revealed by God before the final Book, the Qur'an. Also refers to the followers of divine revelation before the advent of the Prophet Muhammad

Ahl I Haqq (Ahl- I Haqq): a branch of Shiite Islam with strong esoteric leanings and centered in Kurdistan

Ahl: people of . . .

Ahlaf: The Confederates

Ahlil Bayt: People of the house

Ahmadiyyah: A mission (Qadiani); founded in Punjab, India by Ghulam Ahmed. A movement; began in the 19th century in Punjab, India by Mirza Ghulam Ahmed, who claimed to be the messiah.

Al Aqsa Intifada: see Second Intifada

Al Asharatu Mubashsharun bil Jannah: or just Asharatu Mubashsharah (Arabic Mubashshirune bil Jannah): the ten companions of Muhammad who were promised paradise only in Sunni Islam

Al Daaqa al Islamiya (Iraq): see al Daawa

Al Daawa (Iraq) Arabic the Call: Iraqi political party Official title: Hizb al Daawa al Islamiya, the Islamic call Party. Following the secular Ba'athists seizure of power in Iraq in July 1968, the government censored religious publications, closed several Islamic institutions and began to harass Shi'a clergy. In 2002 al

Daawa formally split from SAIRAI when the latter decided to cooperate with US sponsored Iraqi opposition groups.

Al Ferdose: A graveyard for all the martyrs of Iran in war with Iraq

Al Gamaat al Islamiya (Egypt) Arabic the Islamic groups, Egyptian Islamic movement. After carrying out a coup against the leftist Ali Sabri and his followers in the ruling Arab Socialist Union in May 1971, President Anwar Sadat instructed Abdul Munim Amin, an army general with pro Muslim Brotherhood sympathies, to establish, train and arm 1,000 Islamic Groups al Gamaat al Islamiya in universities and factories to fight atheist Marxism. The October 1973 Arab Israeli War described as a victory for Egypt by the authorities, produced a lull in al Gamaat's activities, but the economic crisis that followed the war and Egypt's step by step rapprochement with Israel, created conditions conducive to the rise of Islamic fundamentalism. In early 1999 al Gamaat leaders declared a unilateral cease fire that was endorsed by Shaikh Abdul Rahman Omar serving a life sentence in an American jail. The government released over 5,000 al Gamaat members out of an estimate 20,000.

Al Gamaat al Muslim in (Egypt): see al Takfir wal Hijra (Egypt)

Al Hashem clan: Jordan's ruling dynasty, named after Hashem ibn Abdul Manaf, the great grandfather of the Prophet Muhammad, the Banu Hashem clan was part of the Quraish tribe of Arabia. In 1893 Sultan Abdul Hamid II exiled Sharif Hussein ibn Ali al Hashem, the thirty seventh in line of descent from the Prophet Muhammad, through his daughter, Fatima and her husband Imam Ali and their son Hassan by forcing him to live in Constantinople. His exile ended when the sultan was deposed in 1909 by the Young Turks. In 1916 during the First World War, Sharif Hussein, allying with Britain against the Ottoman Turks, led the Arab revolt with the help of his sons, Ali, Abdullah Faisal and Zaid.

Al Husseini clan: prominent Palestinian family Based in Jerusalem since the nineteenth century al Husseinis have been religious and political leaders of the Arab community in the city, holding the offices of grand mufti and mayor. His son Faisal al Husseini emerged as the chief spokesman of the Palestine Liberation Organization on the West Bank in the late 1980s.

Al Jihad al Islamic: Egyptian Islamic organization The Egyptian authorities discovered the existence of Al Jihad al Islamic, often called Al Jihad in 1978 during Muslim Copt riots. Its leadership council included Ismail Tantawi; Shaikh Omar Abdul Rahman; Muhammad Abdul Salam Faraj an Islamist ideologue; Abbud Abdul Latif Zumur a colonel in military intelligence who headed the groups operational wing and Ayman Zawahiri a young surgeon. In his books, Al Jihad: The forgotten pillar and the absent obligation. Faraj argued that a true Muslim is obliged to struggle for the revival of the Islamic Ummah and that Muslim groups or leaders who have turned away from the Sharia are apostates. Al Jihad now calling itself the New al Jihad, revived. It concentrated on assassinating high officials, such as ministers, but its two such attempts in 1993 failed. Government repression followed, including trials by military courts. By Early 1997 these courts handed down eighty seven death penalties to Islamic extremists. In 1999 al Jihad's military leader Adim Sigam, was killed, and 107 AJ members were tried for attempting to overthrow the government. Nine were given capital punishment. In early 2000 the leadership called on its followers to cease military activities and focus their attention on liberating Jerusalem from the Zionists. The government released a few hundred AJ detainees. radical fundamentalist group established in Egypt that spread to many Muslim countries, such as Palestine and others.

Al Khalifa dynasty: Bahraini ruling dynasty, following the migration of the Al Khalifa clan of the Utaiba tribe of the Anaiza tribal federation from the Arabian Peninsula to the offshore islands of Bahrain, in 1783 the clan succeeded in wresting control of the islands from Iran then Persia. After Sheikh Isa I ibn Ali was deposed by the British in 1923 his son Hamad (1873-1942) became the ruler. During his rule, oil was discovered in 1932, with output reaching 19,000 barrels a day in 1940.

al Nahda :Renaissance; the name of an Islamic political party in Tunisia

Al Qaida: Arabic The base: The extremists Islamist organization Al Qaida grew out of the Maktab al Khidmat established by Abdullah Azzam in Pashawar, Pakistan, in 1984 At the Inter services Intelligence US CIA training camps established on both sides of the Afghan Pakistan frontier, the non Afghan Mujahedin underwent military training based on the manuals used by the US defender Department and the CIA and translated into Persian Arabic and Urdu as well as political education which emphasized nationalism and Islam. Their leader was Osama Bin Laden he declared the departure of the Soviet troops from Afghanistan in February 1989 as a victory for the anti Soviet jihad.

However by early 2003 the remnants of Al Qaida inside Afghanistan had established an underground network to carry our guerilla actions and assassinations and set up a radio station. Its strength was back to where it was before the Pentagon's Afghanistan war. With Aref dead and bin laden and al Zawahiri rendered virtually inoperative in their secret hideouts, the task of planning future attacks fell on Khalid Shaikh Muhammad who had played an important role in the 9/11 terrorists strikes. His arrest in Pakistan in March 2003 was a great setback to the organization.

Al Sabah clan: *Kuwaiti ruling clan* the al Sabah clan is part of the Amarat tribe of the Anaiza tribal federation. After settling on the shores of Kuwait in 1710, the Anaizas developed trading facilities under the suzerainty of the Ottoman Turks. In 1899 Shaikh Mubarak I al Sabah (r. 1986-1915) signed a secret treaty with the British whereby, for an annual subsidy of £1500, the Kuwaiti ruler accorded Britain the right of exclusive presence in Kuwait and control over its foreign policy. Shaikh Mubarak I was followed briefly by his older son, Shaikh Jaber II (b. 1865, r. 1915-17), who was deposed by the British for suspected pro-Ottoman sympathies during the First World War, and then by his younger son, Shaikh Salim I (b. 1875, r. 1917-21). In 1965— four years after Kuwaiti independence—the title of the ruler was changed from *Shaikh* to *emir* (*Arabic: ruler/commander*).

Al Saud clan: *see* House of Saud.

Al Sawa al Islamia: The Islamic Awakening, the term sometimes used to refer to the political Islam phenomenon

Al Takfir wal Hijra (Egypt) *(Arabic: The Denunciation/Repentance and the Migration): Egyptian Islamic group* A clandestine group established in 1972, al Takfir wal Hijra came to light during the January 1977 rioting that followed the withdrawal of subsidies on daily necessities, when its members attacked nightclubs and bars in Cairo. The subsequent repression led to the trial of 465 members by military courts. Of these, five, including Mustafa, were executed. Many of its members then joined the al Gamaat al Islamiya. However, in the mid-1990s the party revived, and 245 of its members found themselves behind bars in 1996.

Al Thani dynasty: The progenitor of the al Thani dynasty was Shaikh Thani ibn Muhammad, who belonged to the Bani Tamim tribal confederation's Mudari tribe of Wahhabi persuasion, which had migrated to Qatar in the eighteenth century. In a bloodless coup in 1972 Shaikh Ahmad was replaced by his first cousin, Shaikh Khalifa ibn Hamad al Thani. The al Thani clan was about 1,500 strong in the late 1990s.

Alam al-Arwah: (A) the world of pure souls, where all souls are performing **Tasbih**, or prayers of praise to God. ... the world of the spirits, contrasted with the world of the bodies; often called Malakut

Alam al-Mithal: the world of pure images. A realm of the human psyche which is the source of the visionary experience of Muslim mystics and the seat of the creative imagination.

Alam: Association of Latin American Muslims

Alawis (Arabic followers of Ali): Islamic sect also known as Alawites. The term Alawi came into vogue in Syria during the French mandate replacing the earlier terms: 1) Nusayri derived according to some scholars from the name of the first theologian of the sect. Muhammad ibn Nusayr who in 245 AH AD 857 proclaimed himself back to the tenth Shi'a. Imam Ali Naqi and of his son, Muhammad, who died before him, and Ansariya, the name of the mountain range where they lived. Imam Musa al Sadr an eminent Twelver Shi'a theologian based in Lebanon, ruled in 1974 that Alawis were part of the Shi'a school of Islam. Most present day Alawis are settled as peasants, mainly in the mountainous region around Latakia a port city in Syria, where they constitute 12 to 15 percent of the national population. The best known Alawi politician is Bashar Assad president of Syria. The name of a sect of the Shi'a, chiefly represented in Turkey and in Syria, where they were long known by the name Nusayri. The Alawis are regarded as deviants alike by the mainstream Shi'a, the Ismailis and of course most of all the Sunnis. They nevertheless form an important population group in both countries.

Al-Ghurabaa: English Jihadist group

Ali bin el Kharij: Shiite Jihadist group (one who goes out; Exiter).

Alianza Islamica: Islamic organization

Al-Jahiliyyah: the "time of ignorance" or period of Arab paganism preceding the revelation of Islam.

Almohad Dynasty (1196-1465): (from the Arabic *al-Muwahhidun,* Unitarian) A Berber dynasty that originated in the Atlas Mountains of North Africa c.1121. The founder, Ibn Tumart, claimed to be Mahdi (the divinely guided one), whose coming was foretold by Muhammad, and he preached an extreme puritanical form of Islam. His successor, Abd al-Mumin, seized all North Africa and then southern Spain from the Almoravids in 1145. The Almohad empire was a great Islamic and Mediterranean power. the dynasty survived in Marrakesh until 1269.

Almoravid: (from the Arabic *al-Murabitun*, 'member of a religious group') A Berber dynasty that originated in North Africa (1061-1145), and in Spain from 1086. It originated among the Lamtuna Tuareg, whose extreme Islamic faith compelled even men to wear veils. The founder, Abu Bakr, built Marrakesh in 1070, and his cousin, Yusuf ibn Tashfin, conquered all of north-west

Africa, and then Spain, to which he was invited in 1086 by al-Mu'tamid of Seville. His Berber army defeated Alfonso VI of Leon at Zallaqah, near Badajoz, in 1086. In 1088 he returned to Spain and began his new campaign by taking Granada. He took Seville and Cordoba in 1091, Badajoz in 1094. Valencia in 1102, and Saragossa in 1110, but he failed to overcome Alfonso VI, or to take Toledo. The end of the dynasty came in 1145, with a further Berber invasion under the Almohads, who succeeded to the conquests of the Almoravids.

Al-Mu'minum: The believers

Al-Mushrikun: Idolaters, polytheists, disbelievers in the oneness of Allah; pagans.

Al-Muwaiddun: Al-Mohads, a powerful politico-religious movement, founded by Abu Abdullah Muhammad ibn Abdullah ibn Tumart in Morocco

Al-Qa'ida: literally, a base; title of the terrorist organization led by Osama bin Laden.

Al-Rashidun: The rightly-guided caliphs (the first four caliphs: Abu Bakr, Omar, Uthman and Ali).

Al-Sawa al-Islamia: the "Islamic Awakening"; the term sometimes used to refer to the political Islam phenomenon.

AMAL: (Arabic acronym of Afwaj al Muqawama al Lubaniya, The Lebanese Resistance Detachments): Lebanese militia, Amal was formed in July 1975, a few months after the outbreak of civil war in Lebanon, as the armed wing of the Movement of the Disinherited, which had been established in February 1973 by a radical Shi'a leader, Imam Musa al Sadr. It was popularly known as Amal. After the disappearance of Al Sadr in August 1978 during his visit to Libya, Amal came under the leadership of Shaikh Muhammad Mahdo Shams al Din and Hussein Husseini, who forged strong links with Iran after an Islamic revolution there in early 1979. It continued to function as political party and contested parliamentary polls, with its leader Berri being elected parliamentary speaker. In the 2000 general election it allied with Hezbollah and together they won all of the twenty three seats in the governorate of South Lebanon. Lebanese resistance squads A Shi'a militia group "the Lebanese Resistance Squads".

American hostages in Iran: On 4 November 1979 militant Islamist students in Tehran occupied the embassy and took hostage sixty seven American diplomats. The US administration, under President James Carter, immediately froze Iran's large reserves in the United States, severed diplomatic relations and together with the European Community, imposed economic sanctions against Iran. Its attempt to rescue the hostages in April 1980 failed. Along with the sluggish US economy, the hostage issue was instrumental in the defeat of Carter by Ronald Reagan in the November 1980 presidential poll. In line with a secret deal between Iran and the US, brokered by Algeria, the American hostages now reduced to 52 due to earlier individual releases were freed in Algiers after 444 days of captivity within minutes of President Carter handing over the office to Reagan on 21 January 1981.

Ammoweyeen: Part of the Quraysh tribe

Anaiza tribal federation: Also spelled Anaza. Anaiza is one of the 25 major tribal federations in the Arabian Peninsula. It is considered noble because of its claim to lineal descent from Yaarab, the eponymous father of all Arabs. Its origins can be traced back to the 15th century and the territory around the town of Diraiya in the Najd region. The House of Saud belongs to the Masalikh clan of the Ruwalla tribe of the Anaiza federation. The ruling al Sabah clan of Kuwait is part of the Amarat tribe of the Anaiza federation.

Anbiya: (A) prophets.

Ansar e Islam: (Kurdish Persian Helpers of Islam): Iraqi Kurdish Islamists group it was one of three recently established Islamists groups in Irtaqi Kurdistan opposed to the draft agreement between representatives of the Iraqi Kurdistan Front and the Baghdad government in June 1991 that led to the formation of the Islamic Movement of Kurdistan the others being the Kurdish Hezbollah and the Kurdish Mujahedin. Unable to overpower Ansar e Islam insurgents the PUK put it about in the summer of 2002 that the Islamists organization, fortified by the arrival of about 100 Al Qaida fugitives from Afghanistan, was now led by Abu Mussab Zaraqi, a Jordanian operative of Al Qaida who was allegedly in touch with the government of Baghdad.

Ansar: means 'the Helpers'. In Islamic parlance the word refers to the Muslims of Madina who helped the **Muhajirun** of Makka in the process of the latter's settling down in the new environment. The Medinese Muslims who became the "helpers" of the Prophet by giving the first Muslims a home when they were forced to leave Mecca in 622, and assisted them in the project of establishing the first Muslim community.

Arab Baath Party: Michel Aflaq and Salah al Din Bitar established a study circle in Damascus in 1940 called the Movement of Arab Baath. They published pamphlets in which they expounded revolutionary, socialist Arab nationalism and were committed to achieving Arab unity as the first step. It stood for a representative and constitutional form of government as well as freedom of speech and association within the bounds of Arab nationalism.

Arab Baath Socialist Party: see Baath Socialist party

Arab cooperation Council (1989-90) a regional Arab organization, consisting of Egypt, Iraq, Jordan and North Yemen, the Arab Cooperation Council ACC was formed in Baghdad in February 1989. It brought together those Arab countries outside the Gulf cooperation council that had aided Iraq during its war with Iran from 1980-88. In April the ACC urged the comprehensive removal of all weapons of mass destruction in the Middle East. Iraq's invasion of Kuwait in August 1990 resulted in the disintegration of the ACC, with Egypt allying with the United States to forge an anti Iraq alliance.

Arab Democratic Party: Israeli political party formed in 1988 in Nazareth the Arab Democratic Party aimed to unify Israeli Arabs behind a three point program: recognition of the Palestinian people's right to self determination, recognition of the Palestine Liberation Organization PLO as their sole representative, and the withdrawal of Israel from all the Occupied Arab Territories. It won seat in the 1988 election and two in 1992. On the eve of the 1996 poll it merged with another group to form the United Arab list which secured four seats.

Arab Deterrent Force: Arab league peacekeeping force in Lebanon, October 1976 to July 1982 The Arab league summit of October 1976 ordered the deployment, for an initial period of six months of a peacekeeping force called the Arab Deterrent Force ADF-to maintain the cease fire in the Lebanese Civil War which had broken out in April 1975. Its 30,000 troops were drawn from Syria (25000), Saudi Arabia (2000). Sudan (1,000), South Yemen (1000), Libya (600) and the United Arab Emirates (500) The ADF's mandate ended in July 1982.

Arab East: Arab East is the term applied to the Arabic speaking Middle East excluding Arab North Africa (Algeria, Libya, Mauritania, Morocco, and Tunisia), Djibouti, Somalia and Sudan. It includes Bahrain, Egypt, Iraq, Jordan, Kuwait, Lebanon, the Occupied Arab Territories, Oman, Qatar, Saudi Arabia, Syria the United Arab Emirates and Yemen.

Arab higher Committee: The killing of Shaikh Izz al Din Qassam, a popular Arab leader, by the British in an encounter in November 1935, and the discovery of an arms cache in a cement consignment for a Jewish builder in Jaffa, led the different Arab factions to form the Arab Higher Committee in early 1936 under the leadership of Haajj Muhammad Amin al Husseini. With the formation of the Palestine Liberation Organization in 1964 the AHC became redundant.

Arab Jews: Jews originating in Arab countries see also Oriental Jews and Sephardim.

Arab League Summits: Arab league members are normally represented by their foreign ministers at the meetings of the Arab League Council of Ministers, but from 1964 the member states started meeting at the head of state level. First summit: January 1964 in

Cairo it resolved to struggle against the robbery of the waters of Jordan by Israel. Second summit: September 1964 in Alexandria. It welcomed the establishment of the Palestine Liberation Organization to liberate Palestine from Zionist imperialism. Third summit: September 1965 in Casablanca. It renounced ultra Arab Hostile Propaganda. Fourth summit: 29 August 1 September 1967 in Khartoum. Held in the wake of the June 1967 Arab Israeli War it reaffirmed Palestinians rights in their own country and declared No negotiations with Israel no treaty no recognition of Israel. Fifth summit: December 1969 in Rabat. It called for the mobilization of all Arab states against Israel.

Sixth summit: November 1973 in Algiers. Held in the wake of the October 1973 Arab Israeli War it set down strict conditions for talks with Israel. Seventh Summit: 30 October 2 November 1974 in Rabar. It declared the PLO to be the sole and legitimate representative of the Palestinian people, "with the right to establish the independent state of Palestine on any liberated territory. Eighth summit: October 1976 in Cairo it approved the formation of the Arab Deterrent Force for peacekeeping in the Lebanese Civil War. Ninth summit: November 978 in Baghdad it condemned the Camp David Accords of September 1978 between Egypt and Israel and decided that pan Arab sanctions against Egypt, including suspension of its League membership and severance of diplomatic relations would go into effect when it signed a peace treaty with Israel.

Tenth summit: November 1979 in Tunis. It deliberated over continued Israeli occupation of southern Lebanon following Israel's invasion of Lebanon in March 1978. Eleventh summit: November 1980 in Amman it adopted a strategy for join Arab economic action dealing with pan Arab development until 2000. Twelfth summit: November 1981 in Fez after sharp disagreement over a peace plan drafted by Saudi Crown Prince Fahd which implied de facto recognition of Israel the meeting was suspended after a few hours so the September 1982 meeting in Fez became the 12th summit. Resulting in a Palestinian state in the West Bank and Gaza strip with east Jerusalem as its capital; interim UN supervision of the West Bank and Gaza; and the guaranteeing of peace for all the states in the region by the UN Security Council.

Thirteenth summit: August 1985 in Casablanca; boycotted by Algeria, Lebanon, Libya, South Yemen and Syria. It failed to back the agreement between the PLO and Jordan envisaging talks with Israel on Palestinian rights.

Fourteenth Summit: November 1987 in Amman. It endorsed UN security council resolution 598 of July 1987 on a cease fire in the Iran Iraq War and criticized Iran for prevaricating over its acceptance of the resolution. It also declared that the resumption of diplomatic links with Egypt was an issue to be decided by individual members. Fifteenth summit: June 1988 in Casablanca. It decided to fund the PLO to continue the six month old Palestinian uprising in the Israeli occupied territories. Seventeenth summit: May 1990 in Baghdad It condemned the recent large increase in the migration of Soviet Jews to Israel. Eighteenth Summit: August 1990 in Cairo Twelve members out of the twenty present condemned Iraq for its invasion and annexation of Kuwait and accepted the request of Saudi Arabia and other Gulf states to dispatch troops to assist their armed forces.

Nineteenth summit: June 1995 in Cairo held after an unprecedented gap of nearly five years this summit was also notable for the absence of an invitation to Iraq twentieth summit: October 2000 in Cairo. This emergency summit was convened to debate the Second Intifada of the Palestinians against Israeli occupation. Twenty first summit: March 2001 in Amman it was heed in the aftermath of the election of hawkish Ariel Sharon as the Israeli prime minister. It decided to appoint Amr Mousa the League's new secretary general. Twenty second summit: March 2002 in Beirut it adopted a peace plan of Saudi Crown Prince Abdullah offering Israel total peace with all the league members in exchange for its total withdrawal from all of the Occupied Arab Territories it rejected exploitation of war on terrorism to threaten any Arab country and use of force against Iraq.

Twenty third summit: March 2003 in Sharam al Shaikh, Egypt. Describing an invasion of Iraq as a threat to Arab security, it declared that its members will not participate in any such war. This however allowed them room to let the United States use their military bases to invade Iraq. **Arab nationalism:** Nationalism in the Arab world was defined in opposition to foreign rule, first by Ottoman Turkey and then by Britain and France. In the 19th century, Egyptians were in the forefront in rebelling against their Ottoman masters. Muhammad Ali as viceroy of Egypt in 1805 signified the special place the Ottomans were prepared to assign Egypt. In time Cairo became a haven for non Egyptian Arab intellectuals who clashed with their Ottoman rulers. In 1990 Arab nationalism received a severe blow when Iraq a proponent of Baathism, invaded and annexed Kuwait, the first instance since the founding of the Arab League of a member state acting so aggressive toward another.

Arab League: Organization of twenty Arab states, officially formed on March 22, 1945; addresses, mediates, and improves cooperation on Arab social, political, economic, and military issues. (League of Arab States) An organization of Arab states, founded in Cairo, Egypt in 1945. In 1991 its members were: Algeria, Bahrain, Comoros, Djibouti, Egypt, Iraq, Jordan, Kuwait, Lebanon, Libya, Mauritania, Morocco, Oman, Palestine, Qatar, Saudi Arabia, Somalia, Sudan, Syria, Tunisia, United Arab Emirates, and Yemen. ... Opposition to the state of Israel and the demand for the establishment of a Palestinian state have been central to the policies of the League. The organizations headquarters were transferred to Tunis during the suspension of Egypt from the League because of President Sadat's peace agreement with Israel's Prime Minister Begin in 1978 (see Camp David Accord). Egypt was readmitted in 1989 and in 1990 Cairo once again became the League's headquarters. ...The League supported the peace accord between Israel and the PLO (1993) but decided to uphold the boycott of Israel until it withdrew from all the occupied territories. In 2000 the total population of the Arab League states was 280 million.

Arab Nationalist movement: pan Arab political party The Arab nationalist Movement came into being in 1952 as a result of the merger of two groups, composed chiefly of the students and staff of the American University in Beirut. George Habash, Nayif Hawatmeh and Ahmad Khatib were among the founders of the ANM, whose main slogan was Unity of Arabs Liberation of

Palestine, Revenge against Zionist state. The Arab defeat in the June 1967 Arab Israeli War finally destroyed the ANM's confidence in the Egyptian and Syrian regimes and led to the pan Arab body being divided into individual sections in different countries. In December 1967 the Palestinian section of the Arab Nationalist Movement, along with its armed affiliates, combined with the Syria based Palestine Liberation Front to form the Popular Front for the Liberation of Palestine. In the early 1960s in North Yemen the Arab Nationalist Movement backed Gamal Abdul Nasser but later, following the reconciliation between Nasser and the Saudi monarch in the wake of the June 1967 Arab Israeli war when the local Nasserites tried to reach a compromise with the royalists the ANM opposed the move. The subsequent arrest of 200 conspirators, followed by scores of executions destroyed the party.

Arab socialism: Originating as Egyptian socialism the term was transformed to Arab socialism when Egypt and Syria merged in 1958 to form the United Arab Republic. Its leading proponent was Egyptian President Gamal Abdul Nasser. Also objecting to attaching an ethnic or nationality label to socialism the Marxists in Egypt preferred to express their belief in an Egyptian path to socialism.

Arab Socialist Party of Egypt: Following the decision of President Anwar Sadat to introduced a multiparty system in Egypt, a joint commission of the ruling Arab Social Union and parliament decided in May 1976 to license three forums: right, left and center. After threatening to birch anybody who tried to disrupt his course of action, he announced the formation of the National Democratic Party under his supervision. With 275 ASPE parliamentarians rushing to join the NDP even before it had announced its program, the ASPE collapsed.

Arab Socialist party: The Arab Socialist Party was founded by Akram Hourani, a lawyer from Hama in January 1950. By participating in the anti French armed struggle after the Second World War, he had gained popularity with the officer corps of independent Syria. Following his advice, the government decided to disregard the social background of the applicants to the country's only armed forces in Homs. Sharing their opposition to the doctorial regime of Col. Adib Shishkali, the leaders of the ASP and the Baath party decided in September 1953 to form the Arab Baath Socialist Party and did so six months later.

Arab Socialist Union: In May 1962 a National Congress of the Popular forces, attended by trade unions, professional syndicates, and other voluntary groups, adopted the Charter of National Action. Besides explaining Arab socialism it specified the political structure upon which it was to be built. In August 1978 Sadat's invitation to Mustafa Khalil, the ASU secretary general to head his newly announced party, the NDP formally ended the ASU.

Arab West: The Arab West included all the countries of Arab North Africa: Algeria, Libya, Mauritania, Morocco, and Tunisia. It is separated from the Arab East by the Libyan desert.

Arabs or Arabians: The nomads of the steppe land of Arabia. The Arabian peninsula was a dwelling place for various tribal and nomadic groups. The first biblical passage which refers to the inhabitants of Arabia is the table of the nations in Genesis 10.

Arabs: People who claim descent from Ismail and Ishmail, Prophet Abraham's son by Hagar, appear frequently in the Bible as Ishmaelites. In the Old Testament the second book of Chronicles alludes to some Arabs bringing 7,700 sheep and 7,000 goats as a present to King Jehosophat of Judah, the term describing nomadic people from the eastern bank of the Jordan River. Later Islam took hold in the world of Arabs who became its leading proselytizers. In modern times an Arab means someone who speaks Arabic. In 2003 there were an estimated 291 million Arabs living in twenty two member states of the Arab League.

Artuqids: The Turkish rulers of the Diyarbekir area in SE Turkey from the late 11th to the early 15th century. They controlled major copper and iron mines and were important in the trade between Iraq and the Caucasus which was only marginally affected by The Crusades and Muslim counter Crusade in the 12th and 13th centuries. Their copper coins bear many ruler portraits, signs of the zodiac or planets and heraldic animals. They were considerable patrons of the arts, in particular al Jazari's famous Book of Automata, which probably describes machines he had made, written in 1205 for the ruler of Diyarbekir.

Ash'ari: Orthodox theological school founded by Abu'l Hasan al Ash'ari (873-74 to 935-36) combining the literal reading of the Koran of the Hanbalis with rational argument (kalam), an approach developed by later theologians. Its most important political consequence was the doctrine that a Muslim remained a believer even when in a state of grave sin, hence that even a wicked caliph must be obeyed.

Ashab **(A):** Companions of Prophet Muhammad

Ashab al Suffah: consisted of about three or four hundred Companions who spent most of their time in the company of the Prophet. They acquired knowledge and had dedicated themselves wholly to serving Islam.

Ashab al-A-'raff: (Heights) will be the people who are neither righteous enough to enter Paradise nor wicked enough to be cast into Hell. They will, therefore, dwell at a place situated between the two.

Ashraf **(sing.** *Sharif***):** descendants of the Prophet Muhammad

Assassins (Hashasheen): The assassins (Persian/Arabic: Ḥashashin, also Hashishin, Hassassin, or Hashashiyyin) were an order of Nizari Ismailis, particularly those of Persia (and Syria) that existed from around 1092 to 1265. Posing a strong military threat to Sunni Saljuq authority within the Persian territories, the Nizari Ismailis captured and inhabited many mountain fortresses under the leadership of Hassan-i Sabbah. The modern word 'assassin' is derived from their name. The name 'Assassin' is often said to derive from the Arabic Hashishin or "users of hashish", to have been originally derogatory and used by their adversaries during the Middle Ages. According to texts that have come down to us from Alamut, Hassan-i Sabbah liked to call his disciples Asasiyun, meaning people who are faithful to the Asas, meaning 'foundation' of the faith. This is the word, misunderstood by foreign travelers that seemed similar to 'hashish'". The Masyaf branch of the Assassins was taken over by the Mamluk Sultan Baibars in 1273. The Mamluks however, continued to use the services of the remaining Assassins: Ibn Battutah reported in the 14th century their fixed rate of pay per murder. In exchange, the higher authorities allowed them to exist. The mention of Assassins were also preserved within European sources, such as the writings of Marco Polo, in which they are depicted as trained killers, responsible for the systematic elimination of opposing figures.

Origins: The origins of the Assassins trace back to just before the First Crusade around 1080. Most sources dealing with the order's inner working were destroyed with the capture of Alamut, the Assassins' headquarters. However, it is possible to trace the beginnings of the cult back to its first Grandmaster, Hasan-i Sabbah. A passionate believer of the Isma'ili beliefs, Hasan-i-Sabbah was well liked throughout Cairo, Syria, and most of the Middle East by other Isma'ili, which led to a number of people becoming his followers. Using his fame and popularity, Sabbah founded the Order of the Assassins. His motivation for political power probably came through what he thought to be dealings with other Muslims in the Middle East, particularly Sunnis, but because of the unrest in the holy land caused by the Crusades, Hasan-i-Sabbah found himself not only fighting for power with other Muslims, but also with the invading Christian forces. After creating the Order, Sabbah searched for a location that would be fit for a sturdy headquarters and decided on the fortress at Alamut in what is now northwestern Iran. After laying claim to the fortress at Alamut, Sabbah began expanding his influence outward to nearby towns and districts, using his agents to gain political favor and intimidate the local populations. Sabbah was never to leave his fortress again in his lifetime. He had established a secret society of deadly assassins, one which was built in a hierarchical format. Below Sabbah, the Grand Headmaster of the Order, were those known as "Greater Propagandists", followed by the normal "Propagandists", the Rafiqs ("Companions"), and the Lasiqs ("Adherents"). It was the Lasiqs who were trained to become some of the most feared assassins, or as they were called, "Fida'i" (self-sacrificing agent), in the known world. It is, however, unknown how Hassan-i-Sabbah was able to get his "Fida'i" to perform with such fervent loyalty. One theory, possibly the most well known but also the most criticized, comes from the observations from Marco Polo during his travels to the Orient. He describes how the "Old Man of the Mountain" (Sabbah) would drug his young followers with hashish, lead them to a "paradise", and then claim that only he had the means to allow for their return. Perceiving that Sabbah was either a prophet or some kind of magic man, his disciples, believing that only he could return them to "paradise", were fully committed to his cause and willing to carry out his every request. With his new weapons, Sabbah began to order assassinations, ranging from politicians to great generals. Assassins rarely would attack ordinary citizens though and tended not to be hostile towards them. Although the "Fida'i" were the lowest rank in Sabbah's order and only used as expendable pawns to do the Grandmaster's bidding, much time and many resources were put in to training them. The Assassins were generally young in age giving them the physical strength and stamina which would be required to carry out these murders. To get to their targets, the Assassins had to be patient, cold, and calculating. They were generally intelligent and well read because they were required to possess not only knowledge about their enemy, but his or her culture and their native language. They were trained by their masters to disguise themselves, sneak in to enemy territory and perform the assassinations instead of simply attacking their target outright. As tensions in the Middle East grew during the Crusades, the Assassins were also known for taking contracts from outside sources on either side of the war, whether it was from the invading Crusaders or the Saracen forces, so long as the assassination fit in to the Grandmaster's plan.

Etymology: The Assassins were finally linked by the 19th century Orientalist scholar Silvestre de Sacy to the Arabic hashish using their variant names assassin and assissini in the 19th century. The first known usage of the term Hashishi has been traced back to 1122 CE when the Fatimid caliph al-Amir employed it in derogatory reference to the Syrian Nizaris. This label was quickly adopted by anti-Ismaili historians and applied to the Ismailis of Syria and Persia. By the 14th century CE, European scholarship on the topic had not advanced much beyond the work and tales from the Crusaders. In 1603 the first Western publication on the topic of the Assassins was authored by a court official for King Henry IV and was mainly based on the narratives of Marco Polo from his visits to the Near East. According to texts that have come down to us from Alamut, Hassan-i Sabbah liked to call his disciples Asasiyun, meaning people who are faithful to the Asas, meaning "foundation" of the faith. This is the word, misunderstood by foreign travelers that seemed similar to "hashish". It is unlikely that the austere Hassan-i Sabbah indulged personally in drug taking. ...there is no mention of that drug hashish in connection with the Persian Assassins – especially in the library of Alamut ("the secret archives").

Timeline: Their support and involvement with a series of killings of famous scholars, Imams and other noble personalities has given them title of one of the very first terrorist organizations in the world. Some of the famous killings and events in those dark centuries by Assassins included the following:

1. 1092: The famous Seljuq vizier Nizam al-Mulk was murdered by an Assassin in Baghdad. He becomes their first victim.
2. 1094: Al-Mustansir dies, and Hassan does not recognize the new caliph, al-Musta'li. He and his followers transferred their allegiance to his brother Nizar. The followers of Hassan soon even came at odds with the caliph in Baghdad too.
3. 1113: Following the death of Aleppo's ruler, Ridwan, the Assassins are driven out of the city by the troops of Ibn al-Khashab.
4. 1110's: The Assassins in Syria change their strategy, and start undercover work and build cells in all cities around the region.
5. 1123: Ibn al-Khashab is killed by an Assassin.
6. 1124: Hassan dies in Alamut, but the organization lives on stronger than ever. — The leading Qadi Abu Saad al-Harawi is killed by an Assassin.

After the death of Hassan some notable events included the following:

1. 1126 November 26: Emir Porsuki of Aleppo and Mosul is killed by an Assassin.
2. 12th century: The Assassins extend their activities into Syria, where they could get much support from the local Shi'i minority as the Seljuq sultanate had captured this territory.
3. The Assassins capture a group of castles in the Nusayriyya Mountains (modern Syria). The most important of these castles was the Masyaf, from which the "The Old Man of Mountain", Rashideddin Sinan ruled practically independent from the main leaders of the Assassins.
4. 1173: The Assassins of Syria enter negotiations with Amalric I, King of Jerusalem, with the aim of converting to Christianity. But as the Assassins by now were numerous and often worked as peasants, they paid high taxes to local Christian landlords, that Christian peasants were exempted from. Their conversion was opposed by the landlords, and this year the Assassin negotiators were murdered by Christian knights. After this, there was no more talk of conversion.
5. 1175: Rashideddin's men make two attempts on the life of Saladin, the leader of the Ayyubids. The second time, the Assassin came so close that wounds were inflicted upon Saladin.
6. 1192: Conrad of Montferrat, King of Jerusalem, is stabbed to death by Assassins before his coronation.
7. 1256: Alamut fortress falls to the Mongols under the leadership of Hulagu Khan. Before this happened, several other fortresses had been captured, and finally Alamut was weak and with little support.
8. 1257: The Mongol warlord Hulagu attacks and destroys the fortress at Alamut. The Assassin library is fully razed, hence destroying a crucial source of information about the Assassins.
9. Around 1265: The Assassin strongholds in Syria fall to the Mamluk sultan Baybars I.

Military tactics: In pursuit of their religious and political goals, the Ismailis adopted various military strategies popular in the Middle Ages. One such method was that of assassination, the selective elimination of prominent rival figures. The murders of political adversaries were usually carried out in public spaces, creating resounding intimidation for other possible enemies. In the Ismaili context, these assignments were performed by Fida'is (devotees) of the Ismaili mission. They were unique in that civilians were never targeted. The assassinations were against those whose elimination would most greatly reduce aggression against the Ismailis and, in particular, against those who had perpetrated massacres against the community. The first instance of assassination in the effort to establish an Nizari Ismaili state in Persia is widely considered to be the murder of Seljuq vizier, Nizam al-Mulk. While the Seljuqs and Crusaders both employed assassination as a military means of disposing of factional enemies, during the Alamut period almost any murder of political significance in the Islamic lands was attributed to the Ismailis. The military approach of the Nizari Ismaili state was largely a defensive one, with strategically chosen sites that appeared to avoid confrontation wherever possible without the loss of life. But the defining characteristic of the Nizari Ismaili state was that it was scattered geographically throughout Persia and Syria. The notion of the *dar al-Hijra* originates from the time of Muhammad, who migrated with his supporters from intense persecution to safe haven in *Yathrib* (Medina). In this way, the Fatimids found their dar al-Hijra in North Africa. Likewise during the revolt against the Seljuqs, several fortresses served as spaces of refuge for the Ismailis.

Downfall and aftermath: The Assassins were eradicated by the Mongol Empire during the well documented invasion of Khwarizm. They probably dispatched their assassins to kill Mongke Khan. Thus a decree was handed over to the Mongol commander Kitbuqa who began to assault several Hashshashin fortresses in 1253 before Hulagu's advance in 1256. The Mongols besieged Alamut on December 15, 1256. The Assassins recaptured and held Alamut for a few months in 1275, but they were crushed and their political power was lost forever. The last Grand Master of the Assassins at Alamut Imam Rukn al-Din Khurshah (1255–1256) was executed by the Hulagu Khan after a devastating siege. The Syrian branch of the Assassins was taken over by the Mamluk Sultan Baibars in 1273. The Mamluks continued to use the services of the remaining Assassins: Ibn Battutah reported in the 14th century their fixed rate of pay per murder. In exchange, they were allowed to exist. Eventually, they resorted to the act of Taqq'iya (dissimulation), hiding their true identities until their Imams would awaken them.

Legends and folklore: The legends of the Assassins had much to do with the training and instruction of Nizari Fida' is, famed for their public missions during whom they often gave their lives to eliminate adversaries. Misinformation from the Crusader accounts and the works of anti-Ismaili historians have contributed to the tales of Fida'is being fed with hashish as part of their training. In fact, the Saljuqs and Crusaders both employed assassination as a military means of disposing of factional enemies. Yet during the Alamut period almost any murder of political significance in the Islamic lands became attributed to the Ismailis. Thus the Nizari Ismaili community was regarded as a radical and heretical sect known as the Assassins. After being drugged, the Ismaili devotees were said be taken to a paradise-like garden filled with attractive young maidens and beautiful plants in which these Fida'is would awaken. Here, they were told by an "old" man that they were witnessing their place in Paradise and that should they wish to return to this garden permanently, they must serve the Nizari cause. So went the tale of the "Old Man in the Mountain", assembled by Marco Polo. Having destroyed a number of texts of the library's collection, deemed by Juvayni to be heretical, it would be expected that he would pay significant attention to the Nizari gardens, particularly if they were the site of drug use and temptation.

Friedrich Nietzsche: The 19th century philosopher Friedrich Nietzsche gives prominent focus to what he terms "the Brotherhood of Assassins", in section 24 of On the Genealogy of Morality. Nietzsche's signature work is to point to the worthlessness of religion, and to attempt at the transvaluation of values, that is, to transcend the inherited Jewish and Christian politics, psychology and ethics of resentment or guilt. Nietzsche heralds the arrival of the so-called 'free spirits' who no longer believe in truth. Thus, they alone are capable of redeeming the world of the modern ills of comfort, mediocrity, and nihilism. Nietzsche compares the genuine free spirits with the Assassins: "When the Christian crusaders in the Orient came across that invincible order of Assassins –"nothing is true, everything is permitted". Now that was freedom of the spirit, with that, belief in truth itself was renounced."

Assembly of Experts, Iran (1982-): Elections to the eighty two strong Assembly of Experts, each representing about half a million people, were held in December 1982. Only Muslim clerics were allowed to contest. This subcommittee submits its confidential report to the Assembly which meets only twice a year. On the eve of the poll for the Assembly, in October 1998, the Guardians council ruled that a layperson could contest the election provided he was found to be an expert on Islam according to its test. However no non cleric passed the rest.

Assma' ul Husna: "The Most Beautiful Names." A list of the 99 names of God through which Muslims understand what God is like.

Association of Combatant Clergy: Popularly known as James, its nucleus was formed in 1976 when the clerical followers of Ayatollah Ruhollah Khomeini began meeting clandestinely in Tehran to exchange sociopolitical information. It arranged the smuggling of Khomeini's speeches on cassettes from the Iraqi city of Najaf into Iran. This changed totally when its radical members quit to form the society of Combatant Clerics in 1988, leaving it as a distinctly conservative organization. In the subsequent parliamentary polls it formed an alliance with other conservative bodies.

Awami League: a political party I East Pakistan. It was founded in 1952 as the Hinnah Awami Muslim League by H. S. Suhrawardy, although it existed informally before that date. It was renamed the Awami League under pressure from its East Bengal leader, Maulana Abdul Hami Bhashani, who left the part in 1957 to form the National Awami Party. During the 1960s the Awami League grew rapidly under Sheikh Mujibur Rahman, who succeeded Siuhrawardy as leader and in 1970 won a majority, completely dominating East Pakistan, which became Bangladesh in December 1971.

Ayyubids: The dynasty of Salah al Din b. Ayyub (Saladin) ruling between the late 12th and the mid 13th centuries over Egypt. Muslim Syria and Palestine, most of Mesopotamia and the Yemen. Kurdish by origin, Saladin was perhaps the most talented general ever to fight the Frankish Crusaders whom he defeated at Hattin (1187). After his death in 1193 the dynasty concentrated on Egypt and Syria, and Mesopotamia gradually split up into minor states which fell to the Anatolian Seljuks and later to the Mamluks and the Mongols. But at Hama there remained a small principality whose penultimate ruler was the celebrated historian Abu l Fida (1310-1331). Under their patronage madrasahs and khanqahs were founded all over Egypt and Syria.

Azeris: Also called Azeri Turks. These Turkic people speak a language that s akin to modern Turkish. In Iran they are the predominant majority in the provinces of east and west Azerbaijan with a combined population of 6.3 million in 2003.

Ba'athism: An Arab political doctrine that combines elements of Socialist thinking with pan-Arabism. This theory of Arab Nationalism conceives of the 'Arab nation' as a single entity stretching from Morocco to Iraq, which has been artificially divided by Imperialism. Ba'athism originated in Syria, where the first Ba'ath Party was founded in 1953. Ba'athists have held power in Syria since 1963 and Iraq since 1968.

Baath "renaissance" party: Promotes pan-Arabism or Arab world unity, subscribes to socialist ideology, and seeks an independent, assertive Arab world position. Different Baath factions rule in Iraq and Syria, although Saddam and President Assad of Syria are enemies.

Baath Party: see Baath Socialist Party

Baath Socialist Party (North Yemen): The first Baath Socialist Party cells were set up in North Yemen in 1955-56. After the end of the Yemeni Civil War in 1970, North Yemen began to receive a substantial amount of aid from Iraq and this enabled the Iraqi Ba'athists to foster the party in North Yemen. In 1976 the Baath party merged with the Democratic party, consisting of former members of the Arab nationalist Movement to establish the National Democratic front.

Baath Socialist party (Syria): In Syria the Arab Baath Party an urban based group turned militant by absorbing the predominantly peasant membership of the Arab socialist party and becoming the Arab Baath Socialist Party. However, after the founding of the United Arab Republic in 1958, UAR President Gamal Abdul Nasser suppressed the Baath in Syria. A coup by Syrian military officers against the Nasser regime in 1961, resulted in Syria seeding from the UAR. However desirable, Syria's secession ran counter to the Baath party's pan Arabian. In the 1994 general election, the Baath party a member of the National Progressive Front, gained less than half of the 250 parliamentary seats. In the 1998 parliamentary pool, the party won 135 seats. In the election held in 2003 the party maintained its previous strength.

Baath Socialist Party(Lebanon): The Baath Socialist Party in Lebanon, which started as the Arab Baath Party in 1948 was hobbled by the enforcement of a law, passed in 1949, that banned parties linked to extraterritorial organizations. Yet in the tolerant climate created by the speedy end to the 1958 Lebanese Civil War, the party was able to host the fourth national congress of the Baath Socialist Party in Beirut in 1959. In the national unity government, formed in December 1990, Amin was given a post. He continued to lead the pro Syrian group.

Baath Socialist Party(South Yemen): The first Baath socialist party cells were set up in South Yemen in 1955-56. After independence in 1967 the party was free to function openly.

Baath Socialist Party: pan Arab political party officially called the Arab Baath Socialist Party, it emerged in March 1954 in Damascus from the Amalgamation of the Arab Baath Party and the Arab Socialist Party. Until 1966 the National Command was based in Damascus. A split in it that year led to a breakaway group establishing itself first in Beirut and then following the

Ba'athist coup in Iraq in July 1968 in Baghdad. The Baath Socialist Party in Iraq, which started secretly as the Arab Baath Party in 1950, had 208 members in 1954. It held its first regional congress in late 1955, when it decided to cooperate with other nationalist groups. During the Third Gulf War in 2003, the invading Anglo American forces made a point of destroying the party offices. With the fall of Saddam Hussein, the party collapsed.

Baath Socialist Party (Jordan): The Baath Socialist Party in Jordan evolved out of the Arab Baath Party in Jordan, which founded secretly in 1948 received a boost from the incorporation of the West Bank into the Hashemite Kingdom of Jordan in 1950. After the collapse of the UAR, the Syrian Ba'athists following their seizure of power in 1963, lent their support. The loss of the West Bank to Israel in the June 1967 Arab Israeli War resulted in a dramatic weakening of the party in Jordan, from which it failed to recover.

Baath: Renaissance the name of the political party that led the anti colonialist revolution in Saudi Arabia and Iraq, espousing secular, socialist prescriptions and pan Arab ideology

Baathism and Ba'athists: see Baath Socialist Party

Babis: Religious sect. The origin of Babis goes back to 20 May, the day when Ali Muhammad Shirazi (1819-50)- a native of the Iranian city of Shiraz who studied theology at the Shi'a centers of Najaf and Karbala declared himself to be the Báb (gate) to the hidden Imam. During the next few years, the Iranian government suppressed the Babi movement, which later evolved into the Bahá'í movement.

Babism: The doctrines of a messianic Shiite Muslim sect founded in 1844 by the Persian Sayyid Ali Muhammad of Shiraz (1819-50). Known as the Báb ed-Din (the gate or intermediary between man and God), he declared himself to be the long-awaited Mahdi. For inciting insurrection by Báb was arrested in 1848 by the government and executed in 1850, his remains being interred (1909) on Mt. Carmel, Palestine. In 1863 Baha'u'llah and his son

Abdul Baha declared themselves the new leaders, and the religion they founded became known as Baha'ism.

Baha'ism: A religion founded in Iran by Baha'u'llah (Arabic, 'Glory of God') (1817-92) with about 5 million adherents throughout the world. Following the suppression of the Millenarian movement Babism in Iran and the execution of its leader, the Báb, in 1850. Baha'u'llah declared himself in 1863 to be the new prophet heralded by the Báb. Baha'u'llah acknowledged the revelations of earlier prophets such as Jesus and Muhammad, but held that the single identity of God must be re-taught by new prophecy to each generation. Baha'is believe in the spiritual progression of the world or unity and their ideal is an international community with one language. Baha'i temples are open to the faithful of all creeds. Baha'ism holds that God can be made known to man through manifestations that have come at various stages of human progress, in universal education, in world peace, and in the equality of men and women.

The administrative center of the world faith is in Haifa, Israel, the site of Baha Allah's tomb. There are some 5 million Baha'is in the world, with the largest communities in India and Iran. Outside the Middle East, Bahá'í centers exist in the US, Germany, India, Uganda, Australia and Panama. In 2000, there were more than 83,000 Bahá'í centers worldwide. Religion founded by Bar Bahaullah; is established in 235 countries today and has +/- 5 million members (www.bahai.org). Slogan: "The Earth is but one country and mankind its citizens."

Bahmani: A dynasty of sultans of the Deccan plateau in central India (1347 – 1518). The dynasty was founded by Ala-ud-din Bahman Shah, who in 1347 rebelled against his Delhi suzerain. His successors expanded over the west-central Deccan, reaching a peak in the late 15th century under Mahmud Gawan, who successfully held encroaching Hindu and Muslim powers at bay. During the early 16th century the Hindu empire of Vijayanagar to the south expanded at the Bahmanis' expense, and between 1490 and 1518 the sultanate gradually dissolved into five successor Muslim states, Bijapur, Ahmadnagar, Golconda, Berar, and Bidar.

Bahrain Nation Liberation Front: see Popular Bloc (Bahrain).

Baluchis: Nomadic community with a tribal structure Baluchis are to be found in present day Iran, Pakistan and Afghanistan. Their recorded history goes back to the tenth century **AD**. Adherents of Sunnism Islam they are now a settled community in Iran. After the Islamic Revolution in 1979, their demand that the Sunni codes of the Islamic law be recognized on a par with the Shi'a code was accepted by the constitution makers.

Banat al-Lah: (Arabic) the Daughters of God; in the Koran, the phrase refers to the three pagan goddesses al-Uzza and Manat. The cult of the Daughters of God.

Banu Harun: Sons of Aaron

Banu Hasin: A clan of the Quraysh tribe to which Muhammad's father belonged.

Banu Hilal: Arab tribe who migrated to North Africa.

Banu Mustaliq: Arab tribe related to the Quraish tribe; fought the Muslims.

Banu Nadir: Jewish tribe in Medina

Banu Nawakht: The agents of the hidden imam (12th)

Banu Qaynuqa: Jewish tribe in Medina

Banu Quaraiza: Jewish tribe in Medina

Banu Umayyah: Muslim clan in Syria

Banu Zuraiza: A Muslim tribe

Barmakids: Barmakids or Barmecides, Persian-descended religious family from Khorasan. They served as viziers to the Abbasid caliphs in the 8th cent. Khalid ibn Barmak, d. 7827, supported the revolution that brought about Abbasid rule. Later, he was appointed governor of Fars and governor of Tabaristan. Yahya,

d. 805, son of Khalid, became secretary to the caliph's son, Harun al-Rashid. Yahya and Harun were imprisoned by the caliph's successor, Musa al-Hadi, who died soon afterward. Harun became caliph and made Yahya chief administrator. Yahya's sons, Ja'far, d. 803, and al-Fadl, d. 808, also became administrators during the reign of Harun. Ja'far headed various interior departments. However, by 800 the Barmakids' power and status were rapidly declining. Ja'far was executed in 803; Yahya and al-Fadl died in prison.

Bayt Al-Hikma: School of Wisdom, Baghdad

Bayt ul-Ansar: Pakistan, founded by Shaykh Abdullah Azzam—The Service Bureau funded extravagantly by the Saudis.

Baytul Hikmah: "House of Wisdom." A scholarly think tank established by Caliph Ma'mun in 830 in the city of Baghdad. Most of the major translations of Greek texts into Arabic took place here.

Bedouin: Bedoun [Arab.,=desert dwellers], primarily nomad Arab peoples of the Middle East, where they form about 10% of the population. They are of the same Semitic stock as their sedentary neighbors (the fellahin; see Arabs) and share with them a devout belief in Islam and a distrust of any but their own local traditions and way of life. From the Arabia Badawi, one who dwells in the desert badw. A term applied from early times to the pastoral nomads of Arabia and later of other desert areas conquered by the Arabs in the Middle East and North Africa. Pastoral nomads tribally organized, of Arabian stock, mostly now inside Arabia. The most famous of their tribes, from whom Muhammad claimed descent, was the Quraysh at Mecca who in the Mid 7th century were extensively involved in trade. The exploits of the pre Islamic Bedouin, mostly animists by religion are the theme of much early Islamic literature.

Bektashi Dervishes: A Turkish Sufi order, the legendary patron of which, Hajji Bektash, probably lived in Anatolia c. 1240, though the order only gained its definitive form under Salim Sultan in the early 16th century. Its heterodox aspects Shiism with Ismaili tendencies, curious rites suggesting confession and the Eucharist, and the participation of unveiled women-may be later accretions. Some of the earliest Bektashi tekkes were in the Balkans, and Bektashi influence upon the Ottoman Janissaries is perhaps connected with the Balkan origins of the Janissary troops. a Sufi order, Shi'a oriented. Their mentor is the Turkish poet Hajji Bektash Wali, born in 1248, in Iran. The order to which the Janissaries belonged. An "order" which emerged before the Naqshbandis; gained great influence under the Ottomans. They are Shi'a-oriented; their mentor was the Turkish poet Hajj Bektash Wali, an Iranian born in 1248. suppressed by the Wahhabis.

Beluch/Baluch/Baloc: Iranian nomads organized in tribes, now largely confined to Baluchistan (Persia east of Kirman to Sind in Pakistan). Kirman fell to the Arabs in 644 but the Beluch were not subdued till the arrival of the Ghaznavids and then the Great Seljuks whose centralized government made raiding, their principal occupation, unprofitable and encouraged migration eastwards. Their history before 1500 is however extremely obscure.

Berbers: The indigenous peoples of northern and north-western Africa. Traditionally, they speak Berber languages, although most literate Berbers also speak Arabic. The Berbers are Sunni Muslim and their local tribal groups are often led by a hereditary religious leader. The Berber peoples include several distinct groups: settled farmers living in the Atlas mountains, transhumance farmers (who move their livestock seasonally from region to region): and the nomadic Taureg of the Sahara. *History:* The Berbers have occupied the mountains and deserts of northern Africa since prehistoric times. Herodotus recorded that they were found in various tribes. They do not seem commonly to have formed kingdoms, although they co-operated on occasions, for example against Roman rule.

Black Muslim Movement: An Islamic organization in the USA. It was founded in 1930 and led by Elijah Muhammad from 1934 until his death in 1975. The Movement expanded greatly in the 1950s when Malcolm X became one of its spokesmen; by the 1960s, at the height of the Black Power Movement, it probably had over 100,000 members. With the suspension of Malcolm X from the Movement and his assassination in 1965, it lost some of its influence to the Black Panthers. Elijah Muhammad was succeeded in 1975 by his son, Wallace D. Muhammad, who advocated a more moderate form of Islam and racial integration. This led to disagreements within the Movement and in 1976 it split into the American Muslim Mission and the radical Nation of Islam, led by Louis Farrakhan.

Black September Organization: A Palestinian group This Palestinian group, led by Wadi Haddad, was formed by militant members of Fatah soon after the defeat members of Fatah soon after the defeat of the Palestinian commandos by the Jordanian army in Jordan in September 1970, and was named after that month. Following the assassination in November 1971 of Jordanian Premier Wasfi Tal in Cairo the four Palestinians claiming responsibility for it declared that they belonged to the Black September Organization (BSO). In retribution. Israel's three day long air raids on Palestinian refugee camps in Syria and Lebanon killed 200 or 500 people, mostly civilians. Later, Mossad assassinated twelve Palestinians believed to have been involved in the Munich attack. A Palestinian organization founded in 1971 when Jordan drove the Palestinian refugees into Lebanon. It carried out the Munich Olympics atrocities.

Black Sheep: A Turcoman dynasty, the Qaraqoyunlu, which controlled Mesopotamia and much of West Persia between 1375 and 1468, with a subsidiary branch at Baghdad in the 15th century. Their history is a series of pitched battles, advances and retreats and virtually the only Qaraqoyunlu monuments remaining are a few tombs and gravestones, some in the form of sheep, at Ahlat. Khilat on Lake Van in Eastern Turkey.

Bohra or Bohora: a branch of the Ismaili sect, consisting of those who remain faithful to the line of the Fatimid caliphs despite the split after the death of the Caliph al Mustansir in 1035/36 CE and the secession of Nizhar. Bohras are to be found chiefly in western India and in Yemen.

Bugis: Muslim mercenaries and traders of south-east Asia. They were enterprising seamen and traders living in villages in Sulawesi (Celebes). When Macassar fell to the Dutch (1667) they lost their livelihood. Thereafter they sought employment as mercenaries and engaged in piracy in Borneo, Java, Sumatra, and Malaya. They fought for and against the Dutch. They suffered a reverse when their leader Raja Haji was killed while assaulting Malacca (1784), but went on to found states like Selangor and Riao, on the Malay Peninsula. Their Prahus, boats with a triangular sail and a canoe-like outrigger, continued to trade throughout the archipelago.

Burgi (Burji): the name of the Mamluk regiment, from which the sultans of Egypt were drawn, 1382 – 1517, from the name of their barracks in the citadel (burg, Burf) in Cairo.

Buwayhids or Buyids a Shi'i: Dynasty from Daylam (N Persia) who occupied first the Iranian plateau (Isfahan, Fars, Kirman and Azerbaidzhan) and then Baghdad and Abbasid Iraq in the 10th and 11th century. They established their supremacy over the caliphs and their viziers and reinforced the Iqta as a means of paying the army but their most conspicuous influence was in the revival of Persian culture in the very center of Orthodox Islam.

Buyid: Shiite Islamic dynasty of N Persian descent that controlled Iraq and Persia from c.945 to 1060; founded by the sons of Buyeh. In the 930s, Buyeh's sons (Ali, Hasan, and Ahmad) seized such cities as Isfahan, Kerman, Rayy, and Baghdad. With the capture of the Abbasid capital, Baghdad, in 945, the Buyids assumed control of the Abbasid Empire. Under their dynasty the Sunni caliphs were reduced to administrative figureheads, while Ahmed ruled under the title of *Amir al-Umara,* or chief commander. Buyid control peaked during the reign (949-83) of Adud ad-Dawlah, who increased the dynasty's territorial domain, adding Oman, Tabaristan, and Jordan. He also made himself sole ruler, eliminating the temporal functions of the caliph. Discord among later Buyid leaders led to the eventual decline of their power by 1060; they were replaced by other dynasties, who divided Buyid territory. The Seljuks (see Turks), first under Tughril Beg, ruled most of their territory. A Persian family that had taken control of Western Persia, entered Baghdad, and ousted the Abbasids in loss by the Seljuk Turks. Fought bitterly against the Seljuks, winning and losing Baghdad several times (1040-1060). Iranian Shi'a dynasty, which occupied Baghdad in 945.

Byzantine empire: The eastern half of the Roman empire. Emperor Constantine (306-34) had reunited the two halves, divided by Diocletian (284-305), and had refounded the Greek city of Byzantium as his eastern capital, calling it Constantinople (330). At his death in 395 Emperor Theodosius divided the empire between his sons. After the fall of Rome to the Ostrogoths (476) Constantinople was the capital of the empire and was famous for its art, architecture, and wealth. ...Emperor Justinian reconquered North Africa and part of Italy, making Ravenna the western capital, but his success was short-lived. After Muhammad's death (632) Muslim Arab forces swept through Persia and the Middle East, across North Africa, and into Spain. By 750 only the Balkans and Asia Minor remained unconquered. From the 9th century Charlemagne's Frankish empire dominated the West.

Calendar (Islamic): The: Muslims like Christians, created a new calendar with a new era, beginning with the founder of their faith. Unlike the Christians however they did not date it from the birth of the Prophet Muhammad but from his migration from Mecca to Yathrib, later known as Medina. The Arabic name for the migration is Hijra, in English, commonly misspelled Hegira. According to traditional accounts, the Prophet left Medina on the date corresponding to 16 July 622 and arrived in Medina on 22 September of the same year. The Muslim calendar, dating from the beginning of the Arab year in which the Hijra took place, was formally promulgated by the second caliph, Umar, some 17 years later and has been universally used in the Muslim world ever since. The Hijra is seen as an epoch-making event and the dawn of a new era. Unlike Christians, Muslims did not usually reckon backward as well as forward from the beginnings of their era.

There is no accepted Muslim equivalent of the Western system of dating known as BC= Before Christ, or more recently BCE

Before the Common Era. From early times, this calendar posed some problems. The Muslim year is purely lunar, consisting of 12 months, each containing 29 or 30 days. The year is thus approximately 11 days shorter than the solar year. Unlike the Jews and the Christians the Muslims did not adopt the corrective of leap years, with the result that in the course of a century, the individual months and therefore al the feasts and fasts of the calendar, rotate through all the solar seasons. Muslims, like others, accepted the ancient divisions of the day into 24 hours. In traditional Muslims usage, however, the day did not begin at midnight, as in the Western world, but from sunset as in the ancient and still current Jewish traditions.

Muslims have disagreed in the past as to whether the beginning and end of the day should be determined by calculation or by observation. The beginning of the 15th century of the Muslim era, that is the first day of the first month of the year 1400, corresponded to 21 November 1979. The year 1430 of the Hijra begins on 29 December 2008 CE. Since the Muslim lunar year does not correspond to the seasons, and since the government finances for so long depended on such seasonal matters as the harvest, it was found necessary from an early date to use other calendars for fiscal and more generally for bureaucratic purposes. Sometimes these were the pre existing solar calendars, Christian and other, in the countries that embraced Islam, sometimes they were solar adaptations of the Islamic calendar.

The most important of these is the Iranian solar era, introduced in 1925. The numbering is based on the Hijra, but it is calculated in solar years, using an adaptation of the old pre Islamic Iranian month names. This era is now used in Iran for most purposes other than purely religious, for which the Hijra calendar is used and international for which the Common Era is used. The Iranian New Year, the first day of the first month of Farvardin, falls in the third week of March. To convert the Iranian solar year to the Common Era, add 622 to dates from 1 January to 21 March, and 621 to dates from 21 March to 31 December.

Caliphate: Formerly the central ruling office of Islam. the dominion of the chief Muslim ruler, who is regarded as a successor of

Muhammad's. The political embodiment of Islamic rule. The first caliph (Arabic, *Khalifa,* 'deputy of God' or 'successor of his Prophet') after the prophet Muhammad's death in 632 was his father-in-law Abu Bakr, and he was followed by Umar, Uthman, and Ali: these four are called the Rashidun (rightly guided) caliphs. When Ali died in 661 Shiite Muslims recognized his successors, the imams, as rightful possessors of the Prophets authority, the rest of Islam accepting the Umayyad dynasty. They were overthrown in 750 by the Abbasids, but within two centuries they were virtually puppet rulers under Turkish control. Meanwhile and Umayyad refugee had established an independent emirate in Spain in 756 which survived for 250 years, and in North Africa a Shiite caliphate arose under the Fatimids, the imams of the Ismailis (909-1171). After the Mongols sacked Baghdad in 1258 the caliphate, now only a name, passed to the Mamluk rulers of Egypt, and from the Ottoman conquest of Egypt in 1517 the title was assumed by the Turkish sultans, until its abolition in 1924. Those who replaced Muhammad in 632; continued until 1926, ending with the Ottoman Empire.

Central Treaty Organization: multilateral defense pact involving Middle Eastern countries. A western sponsored regional alliance, briefly known as the Baghdad Pact, it started as the middle East Treaty Organization in 1954. Following the Islamic revolution in early 1979 Iran quit Cento, destroying its geographic continuity and military effectiveness and hastening its demise.

Cerrahis: Sufi Order

Chancery (Arabic diqan al insha): the department of state concerned with formulating royal decrees, serving for both interior and foreign affairs. Islamic chanceries attracted the most eminent scribes, and because of the grandeur and importance of their documents are particularly important for the evolution of calligraphic hands.

Chishtiyyah: Sufi order (mysticism).

Circassian (Cherkes): A group of peoples in the northern Caucasus speaking a variety of N Caucasian languages, Sunni Muslims of the Hanafi school who were converted gradually in the 16th to 18th centuries. In Egypt "Circassians" were an important element in the Mamluk state from the time of Wala'in (1279-90) and the dynasty of Circassian Mamluks (1382-1517), the Burjis. Their exact race and language are unknown, confusingly they virtually all have Turkish/Qipchaq names though differing from them in, implausibly, claiming Arab lineage. In 1829 the Ottomans ceded the region to Tsarist Russia. But Circassians resisted Russian domination until 1864. After that, many Corcassian clans fled to Turkey and Greater Syria.

Committee for Advice and Reform (Saudi Arabia): In July 1994 Osama bin Laden signed a document describing the Committee for Advice and Reform as an all encompassing organization that aims at applying the teachings of God to all aspects of life in general and promoting peaceful and constructive reform in the governance of Arabia deliberately committing the qualifying Saudi and establishing its office in London, with Khalid al Fawwaz its director. Farwaz collected all the pertinent media publications, videotapes, and newspaper cuttings available in Britain. He had a full office working on that and supplying bin laden with this information after 9/11 Fawwaz was detained in London.

Committee for the Defense of Legitimate rights (Saudi Arabia): Encouraged by the holding of the first multi party general election in Yemen in April 1993 six Saudi human rights activists, professors, lawyers and civil servants established the Committee for the Defense of Legitimate Rights. The Saudi efforts to get Masari deported from Britain failed. Later, there was a split in the CDLR with al Masaari's erstwhile colleague Saad al Faqih forming the rival Islamic Reform Movement. This and lack of funds left the CDLR weak and ineffective.

Communist Movement in Egypt: In 1921 a breakaway faction of the Socialist Party of Egypt founded the Communist Party of Egypt. On the eve of the group's admission to the Moscow based Communist International in 1923, its program included demands for Egypt's independence from Britain, land reform and the recognition of existing trade unions. Its policy of calling strikes brought it into conflict with the government, leading to a ban in 1924 on the Confederation of the Trade Unions dominated by it. Since the National unity Law of September 1972 specified a heavy penalty for political activity outside the ASU they found themselves in a dilemma. When parliament decided to allow three forums within the ASU the communist allied with leftist Nasserites to form the National Progressive Unionist Alliance in May 1976.

Constitutional Revolution (Iran) : (1907- 11): Yielding to demonstrations in Tehran and Qom for an elected parliament, the Shah of Iran, Muzaffar al Din Qajar issued a decree in August 1906 stating that an Assembly of Delegates be elected by the ulama the Qajar family and nobles, landowners merchants and guilds. To placate the tsar the Iranian regent dismissed the Majlis for having defied the Russian ultimatum. Though the regret did not abrogate the 1906-07 constitution., his dismissal of the Majlis marked the end of the Constitutional Revolution.

Cyrenaica and Egypt: Tulunids at al-Fustat until 905; under 'Abbasids, 905-935; Ikhshidids at al-Fustat, 935-969; Fatimid conquest, 969-972, at Cairo after 972: (5) 975-996, Nizar al-'Aziz (son of no. 4), (6) 996-1021, al-Mansur al-Hakim (son of no. 5) Under 'Abbasids until 868; nominally under 'Abbasids but actually ruled by Tulunids at al-Fustat after 868

Dar al Harb: (Domain of War or House of War), refers to the territory under the hegemony of unbelievers, which is on terms of active or potential belligerency with the Domain of Islam, and presumably hostile to the Muslims living in its domain. In theory, all territory outside the Dar al Islam the Land of Islam, though states might conclude truces with Muslim states against payment of tribute without actual conversion which did not recognize Islam were under threat of a missionary war (jihad), as were territories like 10th and 12th century Syria, which were temporarily recaptured by Non Muslims Byzantines or Crusaders.

Dar al Islam: Realm of Islam, originally those lands under Muslim rule, later applying to lands where Muslim institutions were established. The whole territory in which the law of Islam prevails, recognizing the community of the Faithful (Ummah), the unify of the law (sharia) and the protected status of the People of the Book (ahl al kitab, hence Dhimmi). Literally, "House of Islam". Also known as dar as-salaam, or the abode of peace.

Dar Al-Ilm: House of Learning; founded in early 11th century in Fatimid, Cairo.

Dar as Salam: the house of peace, a Qur'anic epithet for Paradise; a place that participates in the peace of the Divine Presence. Equivalent to dar al-Islam. House of Peace

Democratic Front for the Liberation of Palestine: *Palestinian political organization* A breakaway group of the Popular Front for the Liberation of Palestine (PFLP)(*qv*), the Democratic Front for the Liberation of Palestine (DFLP) was formed in 1969 by Nayif Hawatmeh (*qv*) and Bilal Hassan. It participated in the al Aqsa Intifada (*qv*) launched by the Palestinians in September 2000. About a year later two DFLP members became the first Palestinians to infiltrate an Israeli military outpost in the Gaza Strip and kill three soldiers.

Deputies Committee: The crisis management group that reported to the "Gang of Eight" and provided it with information, analyses, options, and strategies for dealing with problems.

Dervish: From the Persian Darvesh meaning poor indigent. A common term for Sufis of any persuasion, but particularly applied to the wandering Sufis (Qalandariyya) whose failure to belong to the established orders excited reproaches of vagrancy, heresy or vice. This is the term used to denote a member of a religious more specifically Sufi fraternity. There are many such fraternities, each professing a version of Sufi Islam, and each with its own distinctive rites and rituals. The most famous are the Mevlevi, sometimes known as the dancing or whirling dervishes. This order, founded by the great poet Jalal al Din Rumi, played a role of some important in the Ottoman Empire. Some of these orders are now strongly established in the US. They and their version of Islam are totally rejected by the Wahhabis. Islamic devotee dedicated to a life of poverty and chastity, some of whom practice whirling as part of their religious experience.

Druse/Druze: Sect stemming from the Ismailis mostly inhabiting the Lebanon, the Hawran in Syria and parts of Palestine. The sect originated in the reign of the Fatimid caliph al Hakim who became its Messiah, whom the Druse have been passively awaiting ever since. They are Hanafi, though their practices are otherwise scarcely Muslim, and their identifiable beliefs are strongly Gnostic. A closed, tightly knit, relatively small, religious and political sect of Islamic origin with Shiite influences. The main communities are in Syria, Lebanon, and Israel. Founded by Ismail Darazi (d. 1019), from whom they take their name, the Druze maintain an Ismaili notion that God manifests himself to mankind in different ages, the last manifestation being the Shiite Fatimid Caliph Hakim, who took the title *imam*. He is said not to have died, but to have hidden; he will reappear as a new Muslim messianic leader, or *Mahdi* (see Millenarianism).

The Druze are led by a hereditary Rais (chief). After the French mandate was created in Syria (1920) Druze tribes rebelled (1925-27) against French social and administrative reforms. In retaliation the French bombarded Damascus city in 1925 and 1926. In 1944 the Druze of Syria became, theoretically, amalgamated under the country's central government; in reality, many fled. After 1945 in Lebanon, the Druze held high political office and played a significant role in the civil war in Lebanon (1975-91). A Middle Eastern religion characterized by monotheism and a belief in al Hakim as the embodiment of God

Dzajarist: member of the Islamist movement in Algeria, opposed to Salafists; usually well educated with technology background

El Hashasheen: Shiite Muslims who believed killing the enemy was an Islamic command to be martyred; used "hashish"

El Kharij: seventh century Islamic movement calling for return to purity of faith

El-Khazrahg: Jewish clan in Arabia that was forced to convert to Islam.

Eunuch: A castrated human male. Eunuchs were used as guardians of harems in ancient China and in the Persian Empire of the Achaemenids and also at the courts of the Byzantine emperors and the Ottoman Sultans....used to produce male adult sopranos – castrati – in Italy until Pope Leo XIII banned the practice in 1878.

Fajarah: Wicked evil doers, plural of Fajir

Fakir (Faqir): Islamic holy men who vow to live a life of poverty and that rivaled the Abbasid dynasty; poor in spirit.

Fedaiyan e Islam: Persian Self sacrificers of Islam): Iranian religious political group. Formed in 1945 by a young theological student, Nawab Safavi , Fedaiyan e Islam went beyond the customary Islamic call for the application of the Sharia, as provided by the Iranian constitution of 1906-07, and demanded a ban on tobacco, alcohol, cinema, opium, gambling and the wearing of foreign attire. The assassination of Mustafa Shafiq, a nephew of the shah in Paris in December 1979 was widely attributed to Fedaiyan e Islam.

Fedayeen: The plural of an Arabia word meaning one who is ready to sacrifice his life for the cause. It was used by a political religious terrorist group in Iran in the 1940s and 1950s. After an unsuccessful attempt on the life of the Prime Minister in 1955, the movement was suppressed and the leaders were executed. The term was revived by the militant wing of the Palestine Liberation Organization and since the 1960s has been their common self description.

Franjieh clan: The Maronite Franjieh clan is based in the Zghorta region at the northern boundary of the Maronite heartland, which stretches to Jezzine at the southern tip of Mount Lebanon. A presidential candidate in 1952 he withdrew in favor of Camille Chamoun. When he retired five years later due to illness the clan leadership passed to his younger brother, Suleiman.

Franks: The French and European armies forming the Crusaders. A term widely used in the Middle East to denote Western, that is, catholic and Protestant, Europeans. In Muslim usage, the Christians of West Europe.

Freedom Movement of Iran: see Liberation Movement of Iran

Free Officers Committee: Led the Egyptian Revolution in 1952, ending King Faruq's monarchy (July 23).

Fundamentalist Islam: radical legalism. In modern times, a response to the West which holds that Islam holds all the answers.

Futuwwah: a corporate group of young urban men, formed after the twelfth century, with special ceremonies of initiation, rituals and sworn support to a leader that were strongly influenced by Sufi (q.v.) ideals and practices. The Muslim code of battlefield honor that Europeans copies and labeled chivalry. Guild

Gabha Al Aslamia Lilncaz: Islamic salvation front

Gama'a Al-Islamiyya: Egyptian, Islamic movement Islamic association; name given to several Egyptian Islamist movements in the 1970s and 1980s

gamaa/Jamaa: Literally "society or group" al gamaa al Islamiyya is the name adopted by a number of political Islamic groups and movements group, society

Gang of Eight: President Bush and his small group of seven principal advisers who made critical decisions during the Gulf crisis.

General People's Congress (Yemen): Yemeni political party having survived a few coup attempts by military officers since assuming power in October 1977, President Ali Abdullah Salih a lieutenant general, decided to consolidate his authority through a political means. In October 1981 he set up a 1,000 member General People's Congress, partly by appointment and partly by indirect elections. On the eve of unification of North and South Yemen in

May 1990, the GPC was transformed into a licensed political party. In the 1997 general election it secured 187 seats and 25 of the 29 cabinet posts.

Ghassanids: An important Arabian tribe who settled as client kings c. 490 AD in Syria in the eastern sector of the Byzantine empire. Once there they became Monophysite, protected in the Syrian church, established capitals of which Sergiopolis/Rusafa in NE Syria is the best preserved and patronized the great pre Islamic poets of Arabia. Their power was crushed by the Sasanian invasion of 613-14 and then the Muslim conquest.

Ghatafan: The pagan Arabian tribe that, along with the Quraysh, laid siege to Medina in the Battle of the Trench

Ghaznavid Dynasty: Founded by Mahmud of Ghazna, conqueror of North India.

Ghaznavids: Strongly Sunni Turkish dynasty founded by a Samanid governor, Sebuktegan (977-97) with Ghazna as its capital, ruling over east Persia, modern Afghanistan and finally part of the Punjab till 1187. Its most famous ruler was Mahmud I (988-1030) the patron of Firdawsi who dedicated his Shahname to him, and the historian and scientist al Biruni. The most important archaeological remained at Ggazna, Bust and Lashkari Bazaar in Afghanistan are mostly dateable to the reign of Mas'ud III (1099-1115), but new discoveries are coming to light ever year.

Ghurids: Sunni Turkish dynasty ruling first over mountainous Afghanistan with a capital at Firuzkuh and then in India. With the decline of the Ghaznavids and the Great Seljuks in the mid 12th century they made themselves independent, the devastation wrought by the ruler Ala al Din Husayn (1149-61) earned him the nickname of World Burner. The most impressive architectural patron of the dynasty was Ghiyath al Din Muhammad (1163-1203) whose works at heart, Jam, Shah I Mashhad and Chisht all in Afghanistan, have recently been discovered, brick constructions of fascinating virtuosity. The Dynasty collapsed in 1215 just before the Mongol invasions.

Ghuzz: A primitive tribe of horse nomads from central Asia; invaded Persia in 1029, massacred, looted and raped as they went.

GIA: armed Islamic group

Gog and Magog: 2 tribes who will ravage the earth on the Day of Resurrection.

Guardians Council: (Iran) Established by the 1979 constitution of the Islamic Republic of Iran, the task of the twelve-member Council of Guardians is to ensure that all laws and regulations passed by parliament are compatible with the Iranian constitution and Islamic percepts. The Council also vets all candidates for public office at the national level for their loyalty to the constitution and Islam and the results of the elections.

Guardians of the Cedars: *Lebanese political group* Names after the cedar, the national symbol of Lebanon, the Guardians of the Cedars emerged soon after the outbreak of the Lebanese Civil War in April 1975. Led by Etienne Saqr, the Guardians were ultranationalist Maronites. When the civil war ended in favor of their adversaries in October 1990, their influence declined. Their backing of the electoral boycott by the Maronites of the parliamentary poll of 1992 further marginalized them.

Gulf Cooperation Council: *Regional body consisting of Bahrain, Kuwait, Oman, Qatar, Saudi Arabia, and the United Arab Emirates* Official title: Cooperation Council for the Arab Gulf States. (*Arabic: Majlis al Taawun li Dual al Khaleej al Arabiyah*). In 2001 the GCC's secretary-general was Jamil Ibrahim Hejailan.

Gulf States: Though eight countries border the Gulf, the six monarchies that are collectively known as the Gulf states are Bahrain, Kuwait, Oman, Qatar, Saudi Arabia, and the United Arab Emirates. The remaining states with shorelines along the Gulf are Iran and Iraq.

Halif Al-Fudul: The League of the Virtuous.

Hamdanids: The Shi'a Arab rulers of Mosul and Aleppo in the 10th century. The most famous of them all was Sayf al Dawla who controlled Aleppo from 944 to 967 a brilliant general who fully exploited the strength of his Bedouin clients in fighting against the Byzantines and whose court attracted a dazzlingly collection of poets and prose writers. The Mosul branch was absorbed by the Persian Buwayhids and Aleppo early in the 11th century came under the domination of the Fatimids of Egypt.

Hamula: An Arabic term for the extended family usually applied to a group of people descended from a common ancestor. The duration of the Hamula was normally from five to seven generations. In traditional society, the Hamula usually formed a territorial group, cultivating adjoining plots of land, and cooperating economically as a matter of course and otherwise when needed. They were bound together by strong ties of loyalty, reinforced by the common practice of marrying within the Hamula, usually cousins. The Hamula formed a single group with regard to the blood wit. Family honor and social obligation alike required members of the Hamula to help each other when possible and to avenge each other when necessary.

Thus, when a member of a Hamula obtained a position of power or authority, he was expected to use it to help his fellow members of the family. In terms of Western values, this might be described as nepotism. In terms of traditional values, it was the fulfillment of a social and moral obligation. Not favoring relatives but failing to do so would be seen as an offense. The pace of modern life has often weakened and sometimes broken the Hamula but the system and still more its values have by o means disappeared. A group of descendents from a common ancestor, usually from five to seven generations.

Hanafi Code: Sunni Islamic legal school The Hanafi Code is the school. The Hanafi Code is the school of the Sharia founded by Abu Hanifa al Numan AD 699-767 an Iranian merchant scholar based on Kufa. Once they had usurped the Caliphate from the Mamluks and established an Islamic empire (1517-1918), the Hanafi doctrine became the official code. It has continued to enjoy official status even in those former Ottoman territories where the majority of local Muslims follow a different school.

Hanafi: a follower of the school of Abu Hanifa al Muhammad 'man; a school of Islamic jurisprudence which advocates tolerance of other beliefs and is generally moderate on issues like women's rights and religious observance. Referring to the Sunni Legal madhhabs ascribed to Abu Hanifa. School of law founded by Abu Hanifah (d. 767). This school is dominant in many countries that formed part of the Turkish Empire, and in India.

Hanafis: School of law founded by Abu Hanifa (died 767) which was particularly influential in the Mashriq, the Great Seljuks, the Mamluks, the Ottomans and probably the Anatolian Seljuks as well were all solidly Hanafi. The school is normally regarded as the most favorable to the development of Islamic economics commercial partnership, the rules governing permissible investment and the theory of Waqf Ahli a family trust which was also a pious foundation all owe much to Hanafi influence. A school of jurisprudence created by Abu Hanafi, most tolerant of differences and opinions.

Hanbali Code: Sunni Islamic legal school The Hanbali Code is the school of the Sharia founded by Ahmad ibn Hanbal AD 780-855. Opposed to the legal superstructure built upon the Quran and the Sunna. Hanbal argued that a legal decision must be reached by referring directly to the Quran and the Sunna. Tmaya's views were well received by the Mamluk caliphs (1250-1517) in Cairo. During the subsequent Ottoman Empire, Muhammad ibn Abdul Wahhab (1703-87), a Najdi cleric, was inspired by Hanbal and Taymiyyah. In 1745 he formed an alliance with the ruler of Najd, Muhammad ibn Saud who adopted the Wahhabi doctrine. One of the four recognized schools of law in Sunni Islam, established by Ibn Hanbal (d. AD 855); followed, in particular, by Ibn Abdul-Wahhab in the eighteenth century, and therefore dominant in modern Saudi Arabia.

Hanbalis: Followers of the Islamic scholar Ahmad ibn Hanbal

Hanbalis: School of theology: and to Sufi mysticism though many of his followers practiced both. It was particularly important in 11th

century Baghdad under the Great Seljuks and then in 12th century Syria. Its influence later declined though the severity of the celebrated scholar Ibn Taymiyyah (died 1328) in Mamluk Egypt ultimately inspired Wahhabism the present rite of Saudi Arabia. Hanbalism, is chiefly known for its literalism, the doctrine that the dicta of the Koran must be believed and obeyed to the very letter.

Hanbalite: one of the four juridical schools of Sunni Islam, prominent in Saudi Arabia characterized by extreme rigor and a literal interpretation of the holy texts; has had a strong influence on the Islamist movement; one of the four juridical schools of Sunni Islam, prominent in Turkey and India

Hanif: one of the pious believers before Muhammad, not Christians or Jews, who submitted to God's oneness. True believer, a term used to describe those Arabs who were monotheists before the revelation of the Quran. Monotheists.

Harem/Harim: The private parts of a house or palace inhabited by the women of the family hence inaccessible to adult males. A sacred place, sanctuary, forbidden area; the private rooms of a house; the women's quarters. The secluded women's quarters of an old style Turkish or other Muslim house. The harem included wives and concubines, sometimes also female relatives and the servants in former times, slaves, including eunuchs, who attended and guarded them.

Harkat: movement

Hashemite Clan: Muhammad's poor, but respected, arm of the Quraish tribe Muhammad's clan, within Quraish. A clan of the Quraysh tribe, to which Muhammad was born.

Hashemite: a descendent of Hashim the great grandfather of the Prophet. Though not necessarily directly descended from the Prophet, the Hashimites are his kinsmen, and this title was claimed by a number of dynasties, notably the Abbasid caliphs of Baghdad and the former ruling house of the Hijaz and its descendants in Iraq and Jordan is the Hashemite Kingdom of

Jordan

Hausa: the people of north-western Nigeria and southern Niger. The original Hausa states, which include Kano and Zaria, were for many years the vassals of Kanem-Bornu. Muslim missionaries seem to have come in the 14th century, but during the reign of Muhammad Rumfa of Kano (1463-99) the celebrated divine al-Maghili is said to have introduced the Sharia (the Muslim code of law), Sufism, and a body of constitutional theory. The Hausa states were conquered by the Songhay in 1513 and by the Fulani in the early6 19th century.

Hezb-I-Islami: Islamic party

Hezbollah: Hezbollah (Arabic: *Hizbu*-llāh, literally "Party of God") is a Shi'a Muslim militant group and political party based in Lebanon. It receives financial and political support from Iran and Syria, and its paramilitary wing is regarded as a resistance movement throughout much of the Arab and Muslim worlds. The United States, the Netherlands, the United Kingdom, Australia, Canada and Israel classify Hezbollah as a terrorist organization, in whole or in part. Hezbollah first emerged in response to the 1982 Israeli invasion of Lebanon, during the Lebanese civil war Its leaders were inspired by Ayatollah Khomeini, and its forces were trained and organized by a contingent of Iranian Revolutionary Guards. Hezbollah's 1985 manifesto listed its four main goals as "Israel's final departure from Lebanon as a prelude to its final obliteration," ending "any imperialist power in Lebanon," submission of the Phalangists to "just rule" and bringing them to trial for their crimes, and giving the people the chance to choose "with full freedom the system of government they want," while not hiding its commitment to the rule of Islam.

Hezbollah leaders have also made numerous statements calling for the destruction of the state of Israel, which they refer to as the "Zionist entity." Hezbollah, which started with only a small militia, has grown to an organization with seats in the Lebanese government, a radio and a satellite television-station, and programs for social development. Hezbollah maintains strong support among Lebanon's Shi'a population, and is able to mobilize demonstrations of hundreds of thousands. A national unity government was formed in 2008, giving Hezbollah and its opposition allies control of eleven of thirty cabinets seats; effectively veto power. Hezbollah receives military training, weapons, and financial support from Iran, and political support from Syria.

Following the end of the Israeli occupation of Lebanon in 2000, its military strength grew significantly. Despite a June 2008 certification by the United Nations that Israel had withdrawn from all Lebanese territory, in August, Lebanon's new Cabinet unanimously approved a draft policy statement which secures Hezbollah's existence as an armed organization and guarantees its right to "liberate or recover occupied lands." Since 1992, the organization has been headed by Hassan Nasrallah, its Secretary-General.

History 1980s: Ending Israel's occupation of Southern Lebanon, which lasted for 18 years, was the primary focus of Hezbollah's early activities Israel had become militarily involved in Lebanon in combat with the Palestine Liberation Organization, which had been invited into Lebanon after Black September in Jordan. Israel had been attacking the PLO in Southern Lebanon in the lead-up to the 1982 Lebanon War, and Israel had invaded and occupied Southern Lebanon and besieged Beirut. When the Shi'a population of southern Lebanon realized that Israel had no intention of leaving, they rebelled. The Amal Movement ("hope"), the main political group, initiated guerrilla warfare.

Hezbollah waged an asymmetrical guerrilla war against Israel using suicide attacks against the Israel Defense Forces (IDF) and against Israeli targets outside of Lebanon. Hezbollah is reputed to have been among the first Islamic resistance groups to use tactical suicide bombing, assassination, and capturing foreign soldiers in the Middle East. Hezbollah turned into a paramilitary organization and used missiles, Katyusha, and other type of rocket launchers and detonations of explosive charges instead of capturing, murders, and hijackings. At the end of the Lebanese

Civil War in 1990, despite the Taif Agreement asking for the "disbanding of all Lebanese and non-Lebanese militias," Syria, in control of Lebanon at that time, allowed Hezbollah to maintain their arsenal, and control the Shiite areas in Southern Lebanon along the border with Israel.

After 1990: In the 1990s, Hezbollah transformed from a revolutionary group into a political one, in a process which is described as the Lebanonisation of Hezbollah. Unlike its uncompromising revolutionary stance in the 1980s, Hezbollah conveyed a lenient stance towards the Lebanese state. In 1992, Hezbollah decided to participate in elections, and Ali Khamenei, supreme leader of Iran, endorsed it. Former Hezbollah secretary general, Subhi al-Tufayli, contested this decision, which led to a schism in Hezbollah. Hezbollah won all twelve seats which were on its electoral list. At the end of that year, Hezbollah began to engage in dialog with Lebanese Christians. Hezbollah regards cultural, political, and religious freedoms in Lebanon as sanctified, although it does not extend these values to groups who have relations with Israel. In 1997, Hezbollah formed multi-confessional Lebanese Brigades to Fighting the Israeli Occupation, which was an attempt to revive national and secular resistance against Israel, which marks the Lebanonisation of resistance.

Islamic Jihad Organization: Whether the Islamic Jihad Organization (IJO) was a *nom de guerre* used by Hezbollah or a separate organization, is disputed. A 2003 decision by an American court found IJO was the name used by Hezbollah for its attacks in Lebanon, and parts of the Middle East, and Europe. Hezbollah also used another name, Islamic Resistance, or *al-Muqawama al-Islamiyya*, for its attacks against Israel. The names Islamic Jihad Organization, Organization of the Oppressed on Earth and the Revolutionary Justice Organization are considered to be synonymous with Hezbollah by the United States, Israel and Canada.

Ideology: The ideology of Hezbollah has been summarized as Shi'i radicalism. Hezbollah was largely formed with the aid of the Ayatollah Khomeini's followers in the early 1980s in order to spread Islamic revolution and follows a distinct version of Islamic Shi'a ideology (*Valiyat al-faqih* or Guardianship of the Islamic Jurists) developed by Ayatollah Ruhollah Khomeini, leader of the "Islamic Revolution" in Iran. Although Hezbollah originally aimed to transform Lebanon into a formal Faqihi Islamic republic, this goal has been abandoned in favor of a more inclusive approach.

The Hezbollah manifesto: On February 16, 1985, Sheik Ibrahim al-Amin issued Hezbollah's manifesto. Translated excerpts from Hezbollah's original 1985 manifesto read:

"We are the sons of the Ummah (Muslim community) ...
... We are an Ummah linked to the Muslims of the whole world by the solid doctrinal and religious connection of Islam, whose message God wanted to be fulfilled by the Seal of the Prophets, i.e., Prophet Muhammad. ... As for our culture, it is based on the Holy Quran, the Sunna and the legal rulings of the faqih who is our source of imitation..."

Hezbollah follows the Islamic Shi'a theology developed by Iranian revolutionary leader Ayatollah Ruhollah Khomeini.

Attitudes, statements, and actions concerning Israel and Zionism: From the inception of Hezbollah to the present, the elimination of the State of Israel has been one of Hezbollah's primary goals. Some translations of Hezbollah's 1985 Arabic-language manifesto state that "our struggle will end only when this entity [Israel] is obliterated". According to Hezbollah's Deputy-General, Na'îm Qasim, the struggle against Israel is a core belief of Hezbollah and the central rationale of Hezbollah's existence. Hezbollah says that its continued hostilities against Israel are justified as reciprocal to Israeli operations against Lebanon and as retaliation for what they claim is Israel's occupation of Lebanese territory. Finally, Hezbollah consider Israel to be an illegitimate state. For these reasons, they justify their actions as acts of defensive jihad.

Attitudes and actions concerning Jews and Judaism: Hezbollah officials say that the group distinguishes between Judaism and Zionism. However, various anti-Semitic statements have been attributed to them. Hezbollah's hatred of Jews is more religiously motivated than politically motivated. "Like the Hamas propaganda for holy war that of Hezbollah has relied on the endless vilification of Jews as 'enemies of mankind 'conspiratorial, obstinate and conceited' adversaries full of 'satanic plans' to enslave the Arabs. It fuses traditional Islamic anti-Judaism with Western conspiracy myths, Third Worldist anti-Zionism and Iranian Shiite contempt for Jews as 'ritually impure' and corrupt infidels". Conflicting reports say Al-Manar accused either Israel or Jews of deliberately spreading HIV and other diseases to Arabs throughout the Middle East. Hezbollah also used anti-Semitic educational materials designed for 5-year old scouts. The group has been accused by American analysts of engaging to Holocaust denial.

Organization: The supreme decision-making bodies of the Hezbollah were divided between the Majlis al-Shura (Consultative Assembly) which was headed by 12 senior clerical members with responsibility for tactical decisions and supervision of overall Hizbullah activity throughout Lebanon, and the Majlis al-Shura al-Karar (the Deciding Assembly), headed by Sheikh Muhammad Hussein Fadlallah and composed of eleven other clerics with responsibility for all strategic matters. After the death of Iran's first Supreme Leader, Khomeini, Hezbollah's governing bodies developed a more "independent role" and appealed to Iran less often.

Since the Second Lebanon War, however, Iran has restructured Hezbollah to limit the power of Hassan Nasrallah, and invested billions of dollars "rehabilitating" Hezbollah. Structurally, Hezbollah does not distinguish between its political/social activities within Lebanon and its military/*jihad* activities against Israel. "Hezbollah has a single leadership," according to Naim Qassem, Hezbollah's second in command. "All political, social and jihad work is tied to the decisions of this leadership ... The same leadership that directs the parliamentary and government work also leads jihad actions in the struggle against Israel."

Funding: Hezbollah says that the main source of its income comes from donations by Muslims. Hezbollah receives substantial amounts of financial, training, weapons, explosives, political, diplomatic, and organizational aid from Iran and Syria According to reports released in February 2010, Hezbollah received $400 million dollars from Iran. The US estimates that Iran has been giving Hezbollah about US$60–100 million per year in financial assistance. Other estimates are as high as $200-million annually. U.S. law enforcement officials have identified an illegal multimillion-dollar cigarette-smuggling fund raising operation and a drug smuggling operation

Social services: Hezbollah organizes an extensive social development program and runs hospitals, news services, educational facilities, and encouragement of Nikah Mut'ah. One of its established institutions, Jihad Al Binna's Reconstruction Campaign, is responsible for numerous economic and infrastructure development projects in Lebanon. Hezbollah has set up a Martyr's Institute (Al-Shahid Social Association), which guarantees to provide living and education expenses "for the families of fighters who die" in battle. An IRIN news report of the UN Office for the Coordination of Humanitarian Affairs noted: "Hezbollah not only has armed and political wings – it also boasts an extensive social development program".

Hezbollah currently operates at least four hospitals, twelve clinics, twelve schools and two agricultural centers that provide farmers with technical assistance and training. It also has an environmental department and an extensive social assistance program. Medical care is also cheaper than in most of the country's private hospitals and free for Hezbollah members." According to CNN, "Hezbollah did everything that a government should do, from collecting the garbage to running hospitals and repairing schools." In July 2006, during the war with Israel, when there was no running water in Beirut, Hezbollah was arranging supplies around the city.

Political activities: Hezbollah alongside with Amal is one of two major political parties in Lebanon that represent the Shiite Muslims. It holds 14 of the 128 seats in the Parliament of Lebanon and is a member of the Resistance and Development Bloc. Hezbollah, along with the Amal Movement, represents most of Lebanese Shi'a. However, unlike Amal, Hezbollah has not disarmed. Hezbollah participates in the Parliament of Lebanon. On May 7, 2008 Lebanon's 17-month long political crisis spiraled out of control.

The fighting was sparked by a government move to shut down Hezbollah's telecommunication network and remove Beirut Airport's security chief over alleged ties to Hezbollah. Hezbollah-led opposition fighters seized control of several West Beirut neighborhoods from Future Movement militiamen loyal to the backed government, in street battles that left 11 dead and 30 wounded. The opposition-seized areas were then handed over to the Lebanese Army. At the end of the conflicts, National unity government was formed by Fouad Siniora on July 11, 2008 and Hezbollah has one minister and controls eleven of thirty seats in the cabinet.

Media operations: Hezbollah operates a satellite television station, *Al-Manar* TV ("the Lighthouse") and a radio station *al-Nour* ("the Light"). Hezbollah's television station al-Manar airs programming designed to inspire suicide attacks in Gaza, the West Bank and Iraq. The United States lists al-Manar television network as a terrorist organization.

Military activities: Hezbollah has a military branch known as *Al-Muqawama al-Islamiyya* ("The Islamic Resistance") and is the possible sponsor of a number of lesser-known militant groups, some of which may be little more than fronts for Hezbollah itself, including the Organization of the Oppressed, the Revolutionary Justice Organization, the Organization of Right Against Wrong, and Followers of the Prophet Muhammad. United Nations Security Council Resolution 1559 called for the disarmament of militia with the Taif agreement at the end of the

Lebanese civil war. Hezbollah denounced, and protested against, the resolution.

The 2006 military conflict with Israel has increased the controversy. Failure to disarm remains a violation of the resolution and agreement as well as subsequent United Nations Security Council Resolution 1701 The Lebanese cabinet, under president Michel Suleiman and Prime Minister Fouad Siniora, guidelines state that Hezbollah enjoys the right to "liberate occupied lands." In 2009, a Hezbollah commander (speaking on condition of anonymity) said, "[W]e have far more rockets and missiles [now] than we did in 2006."

Suicide attacks and kidnappings: Between 1982 and 1986, there were 36 suicide attacks in Lebanon directed against Americans, French and Israelis forces by 41 individuals with predominantly leftist political beliefs and of both major religions, killing 659. Hezbollah denies involvement in any attack.

2000 Hezbollah cross-border raid: On October 7, 2000, three Israeli soldiers – Adi Avitan, Staff Sgt. Benyamin Avraham, and Staff Sgt. Omar Sawaidwere – were abducted by Hezbollah while patrolling the Israeli side of the Israeli-Lebanese border. The soldiers were killed either during the attack or in its immediate aftermath. Israel Defense Minister Shaul Mofaz has, however, said that Hezbollah abducted the soldiers and then killed them. The bodies of the slain soldiers were exchanged for Lebanese prisoners in 2004.

2006 Lebanon War: The 2006 Lebanon War was a 34-day military conflict in Lebanon and northern Israel. The principal parties were Hezbollah paramilitary forces and the Israeli military. The conflict was precipitated by a cross-border raid by Hezbollah during which they kidnapped and killed Israeli soldiers. The conflict began on July 12, 2006 when Hezbollah militants fired rockets at Israeli border towns as a diversion for an anti-tank missile attack on two armored Humvees patrolling the Israeli side of the border fence, killing three, injuring two, and seizing two Israeli soldiers. Israel responded with airstrikes and artillery fire on targets in Lebanon that damaged Lebanese civilian infrastructure, including Beirut's Rafic Hariri International Airport (which Israel said that Hezbollah used to import weapons and supplies), an air and naval blockade, and a ground invasion of southern Lebanon.

Hezbollah then launched more rockets into northern Israel and engaged the Israel Defense Forces (IDF) in guerrilla warfare from hardened positions. The war continued until August 14, 2006. Hezbollah was responsible for thousands of Katyusha rocket attacks against Israeli civilian towns and cities in northern Israel, which Hezbollah said were in retaliation for Israel's killing of civilians and targeting Lebanese infrastructure. According to *The Guardian*, "In the fighting 1,200 Lebanese and 158 Israelis were killed. Of the dead almost 1,000 Lebanese and 41 Israelis were civilians."

2010 Gas Field Claims: In 2010, Hezbollah claimed that the Dalit and Tamar gas field, discovered by Noble Energy roughly 50 miles (80 km) west of Haifa in Israeli exclusive economic zone, belong to Lebanon, and warned Israel against extracting gas from them. Senior officials from Hezbollah warned that they would not hesitate to use weapons to defend Lebanon's natural resources. Figures in the March 14 Forces stated in response that Hezbollah was simply looking for another excuse to hold on to its arms.

2010 Lebanon Takeover Drills: In 2009, the United Nations special tribunal investigating the murder of former Lebanese Prime Minister Rafiq Al-Hariri reportedly found evidence linking Hezbollah to the murder.

Armed strength: Hezbollah has not revealed its armed strength. It has been estimated by Mustafa Alani, security director at the Dubai-based Gulf Research Centre that Hezbollah's military force is made up of about 1,000 full-time Hezbollah members, along with a further 6,000–10,000 volunteers. Hezbollah possesses the Katyusha-122 rocket, which has a range of 29 km (18 mi) and carries a 15-kg (33-lb) warhead. Hezbollah also possesses about 100 long-range missiles. They include the Iranian-made Fajr-3 and Fajr-5, the latter with a range of 75 km (47 mi), enabling it to strike the Israeli port of Haifa, and the Zelzal-1, with an estimated 150 km (93 mi) range, which can reach Tel Aviv. Fajr-3 missiles have a range of 40 km (25 mi) and a 45-kg (99-lb) warhead, and Fajr-5 missiles, which extend to 72 km (45 mi), also hold 45-kg (99-lb) warheads.

It was reported that Hezbollah is in possession of Scud missiles that were provided to them by Syria. The reports were denied by Syria. According to various reports, Hezbollah is armed with anti-tank guided missiles, namely, the Russian-made AT-3 Sagger, AT-4 Spigot, AT-5 Spandrel, AT-13 Saxhorn-2 'Metis-M', AT-14 Spriggan 'Kornet'; Iranian-made Raad (version of AT-3 Sagger), Towsan (version of AT-5 Spandrel), Toophan (version of BGM-71 TOW); and European-made MILAN missiles. These weapons have been used against IDF soldiers, causing many of the deaths during the 2006 Lebanon War. A small number of Saeghe-2s (Iranian-made version of M47 Dragon) were also used in the war. For air defense, Hezbollah has anti-aircraft weapons that include the ZU-23 artillery and the man-portable, shoulder-fired SA-7 and SA-18 surface-to-air missile (SAM).

One of the most effective weapons deployed by Hezbollah has been the C-802 anti-ship missile. Israeli commander Gui Zur called Hizbullah: "by far the greatest guerrilla group in the world". In April 2010 United States Secretary of Defense Robert Gates claimed that the Hezbollah has far more missiles and rockets than the majority of countries. He said that Syria and Iran are providing weapons to the organization. Israel also claims that Syria is providing the organization with these weapons. Gates added that Hezbollah is possibly armed with chemical or biological weapons, as well as anti-ship missiles with a range of 65 miles (105 km) that could threaten U.S. ships.

Current Estimates: As of 2010, the Israeli government believed Hezbollah had an arsenal of more than 15,000 long-range rockets stationed on its border with Lebanon. Some of these missiles were said to be capable of penetrating cities as far away as Eilat. The Israeli Ambassador to United States Michael Oren expressed deep concern with the revelation.

"The Syrian-Iranian backed Hizbullah poses a very serious threat to Israel...Hizbullah today now has four times as many rockets as it had during the 2006 Lebanon war. These rockets are longer-range. Every city in Israel is within range right now, including Eilat".
The IDF has accused Hezbollah of storing these rockets beneath hospitals, schools, and civilian homes.

Targeting policy: Although Hezbollah has denounced certain attacks on civilians, some people accuse the organization of the bombing of an Argentine synagogue in 1994. Argentine prosecutor Alberto Nisman, Marcelo Martinez Burgos, and their "staff of some 45 people" said that Hezbollah and their contacts in Iran were responsible for the 1994 bombing of a Jewish cultural center in Argentina, in which "eighty-five people were killed and more than 200 others injured." In June 2002, shortly after the Israeli government launched Operation Defensive Shield, Nasrallah gave a speech in which he defended and praised suicide bombings of Israeli targets by members of Palestinian groups for "creating deterrence and equalizing fear."

Nasrallah stated that "in occupied Palestine, there is no difference between a soldier and a civilian, for they are all invaders, occupiers and usurpers of the land." Alleged Involvement in Murder of Rafic Hariri: On June 30, 2011, the Special Tribunal for Lebanon, established to investigate the death of the former prime minister Rafic Hariri, issued arrest warrants against four senior members of Hezbollah. On July 3, Hezbollah leader Hassan Nasrallah rejected the indictment and denounced the tribunal as a plot against the party, vowing that the named persons would not be arrested under any circumstances.

Foreign relations: Hezbollah has close relations with Iran. It also has ties with the leadership in Syria, specifically with President Hafez al-Assad (until his death in 2000) and his son and successor Bashar al-Assad. Although Hezbollah and Hamas are not organizationally linked, Hezbollah provides military training as well as financial and moral support to the Sunni Palestinian group. Furthermore, Hezbollah is a strong supporter of the ongoing Al-Aqsa Intifada.

Public opinion: According to **Michel Samaha**, Lebanon's minister of information, Hezbollah is seen as a legitimate resistance organization that has defended its land against an Israeli occupying force and has consistently stood up to the Israeli army. According to a survey released by the "Beirut Center for Research and Information" on July 26 during the **2006 Lebanon War**, 87 percent of Lebanese support Hezbollah's "retaliatory attacks on northern Israel", a rise of 29 percentage points from a similar poll conducted in February. More striking, however, was the level of support for Hezbollah's resistance from non-Shiite communities. Eighty percent of Christians polled supported Hezbollah, along with 80 percent of **Druze** and 89 percent of **Sunnis**. In 2010, a survey of Muslims in Lebanon showed that 94% of Lebanese Shi'a supported Hezbollah, while 84% of the Sunni Muslims held an unfavorable opinion of the group. Throughout most of the Arab and Muslim worlds, Hezbollah is referred to as a resistance movement, engaged in national defense.

In the Western World: In 1999, Hezbollah was placed on the US State Department list of Foreign Terrorist Organizations. After Hezbollah's condemnation of the September 11, 2001 attacks on the USA, it was removed from the list, but it was later returned to the list. The European Union does not list Hezbollah as a "terrorist organization"; In addition, on March 10, 2005, the European Parliament passed a non-binding resolution recognizing "clear evidence" of "terrorist activities by Hezbollah" and urging the EU Council to brand Hezbollah a terrorist organization and EU governments to place Hezbollah on their terrorist blacklists, as the bloc did with the Palestinian Hamas group in 2003.

In the midst of the 2006 conflict between Hezbollah and Israel, Russia's government declined to include Hezbollah in a newly released list of terrorist organizations. Human rights organizations Amnesty International and Human Rights Watch have accused Hezbollah of committing war crimes against Israeli civilians. Argentine prosecutors hold Hezbollah and their financial supporters in Iran responsible for the 1994 AMIA Bombing of a Jewish cultural center, described by the Associated Press as "the worst terrorist attack on Argentine soil," in which "eighty-five people were killed and more than 200 others injured."

In the Arab and Muslim world: In 2006 Hezbollah was regarded as a legitimate resistance movement most of the Arab and Muslim worlds. Following the 2009 Hezbollah plot in Egypt, Egypt has officially classified Hezbollah as a terrorist group. During the 2011 Bahraini protests, Bahrain foreign minister Khalid ibn Ahmad al Khalifah labeled Hezbollah a terrorist group and accused them of supporting the protesters. During the 2011 Syrian uprising Hezbollah's has voiced support for Syrian President Bashar Assad's government which has prompted criticism from anti-government Syrians. In 2011, a bipartisan group of members of Congress introduced the Hezbollah Anti-Terrorism Act. The act ensures that no American aid to Lebanon will enter the hands of Hezbollah. On the day of the act's introduction, Congressman Darrell Issa said, "Hezbollah is a terrorist group and a cancer on Lebanon. The Hezbollah Anti-Terrorism Act surgically targets this cancer and will strengthen the position of Lebanese who oppose Hezbollah.

Hezbollah

Leader : Hassan Nasrallah

Founded: 1982-1985 (officially)

Ideology: Shi'a Islamism, Anti-Zionism

Religion: Shi'a Islam

Hijri Calendar: The Islamic calendar or Muslim calendar or Hijri calendar is a lunar calendar based on 12 lunar months in a year of 354 or 355 days, used to date events in many Muslim countries [concurrently with the Gregorian calendar], and used by Muslims everywhere to determine the proper day on which to celebrate Islamic holy days and festivals. Its first year was the year during which the Hijra, i.e. the emigration of the Prophet of Islam, Muhammad from Mecca to Medina, occurred. Each numbered year is designated either H for Hijra or AH for the Latin anno Hegirae [in the year of the Hijra]. A limited number of years before Hijra [BH] are used to date events related to Islam, such as the birth of Muhammad in 53 BH. The Islamic calendar is not to be confused with the lunar calendar. The latter is based on a year of 12 months adding up to 354.37 days. Each lunar month begins at the time of the monthly "conjunction", when the Moon is located on a straight line between the Earth and the Sun. The month is defined as the average duration of a rotation of the Moon around the Earth [29.53 days]. By convention, months of 30 days and 29 days succeed each other, adding up over two years successive months to 59 full days.

This leaves only a small monthly variation of 44 man to account for, which adds up to a total of 24 hours [i.e. the equivalent of one full day] in 2.73 years. To settle accounts, it is sufficient to add one day every three years to the lunar calendar, in the same way that one adds one day to the Gregorian calendar, every four years. The technical details of the adjustment are described in Tabular Islamic Calendar. The Islamic calendar, however, is based on a different set of convictions. Each month has either 29 or 30 days, but usually in no discernible order. Traditionally, the first day of each month is the day [beginnings at sunset] of the first sighting of the Hilal [moon] [either because clouds block its view or because the western sky is still too bright when the moon sets...], and then the day that begins at that sunset is the 30th. Such a sighting has to be made by one or more trustworthy men testifying before a committee of Muslim leaders. Determining the most likely day that the Hilal could be observed was a motivation for Muslim interest in astronomy, which put Islam in the forefront of that science for many centuries. Islamic lunar calendar, consists of twelve months of 29 or 30 days each, is about 11 days shorter than its Georgian equivalent.

Hostage Taking and Hostages: American hostages in Iran: Western hostages in Lebanon Hostage taking for political reasons in the West and elsewhere has a long history, dating back at least to Roman Emperor Julius Caesar (102-44 BC), who referring to his crossing of the Rhine River in 55 BC mentioned the conquered Ubii tribe establishing ties of friendship and giving hostages as a guarantee of good behavior in the future.

House of Saud: The ruling dynasty of Saudi Arabia. The House of Saud is named after Saud, a member of the Musalikh clan of the Ruwalla tribe of the Anaiza tribal federation at the turn of the eighteenth century in the Diraiya Riyadh region. The surviving members of the House of Saud, including Abdul Aziz ibn Abdul Rahman al Saud (1879-1953), took refuge in Kuwait. He regained Riyadh in 1902 and began to expand his realm which he named Saudi Arabia in 1932. With this the House of Saud. Aal Saud consisting of Abdul Aziz and his five brothers, became the ruling dynasty of Saudi Arabia. In 2000, the male progeny of these six brothers by wives and concubines totaled about 6,400.

House of Wisdom: In Baghdad; created by the Caliph Ma'mun (813-833).

Hypocrites: Muhammad's opponents

Ibadhis: Islamic sect Ibadhis are named after Abdullah ibn Ibadh a member of the Azd Khariji extremists, who considered that non Khariji Muslims were polytheists whereas he regarded them as mere infidels. In AD 850 the Omani tribes, professing Ibadhism, split from the Abbasid Caliphate, based in Baghdad and set up an independent domain in the plateau of Jebel Akhdar, Green Mountain Today two thirds of Omani Muslims are Ibadhi. The Ibadis or Ibadiyya, a sect within Islam and an offshoot of the Kharijites. Though distinct from both Sunnis and Shi'a they are much closer to the former. They take their name from 7th to 8th century scholar of Basra called Abdullah ibn Ibad but the effective founder of the group was a disciple of his from Oman which remains the main center of Ibadhism to the present day.

Ijma **(Arabic consensus)**: One of the four pillars of Islamic jurisprudence ijma means consensus of the community, Ummah the remaining pillars being the Quran, Prophet Muhammad's Sunna later codified as the Hadith and ijtihad interpretative reasoning. Until Muhammad ibn Idris al Shafii founded the discipline of religious jurisprudence based on these pillars ijma had been construed as consensus of ahl al hall wal aqd. But Shafii enlarged it to include the whole community. In more modern times Muhammad Abdu an Egyptian Islamic thinker, interpreted ijma as public opinion. The consensus of the entire Muslim community upon which a legal decision is then delivered. Such judgments could, some twentieth-century Muslim scholars argue, be soundly based on what was deemed best for the community. Collective consensus.

Ijtihad (Arabic: applying effort to form an opinion): Interpretative reasoning with time it became necessary for Muslims and their rulers to interpret the Quran and the Prophet Muhammad's Sunna together forming the Islamic law) to address unprecedented situations. By the mid ninth century Ad four major schools of Islamic law ranging between the rigid Hanbali school and the liberal Hanafi school had emerged within Sunni Islam. Unlike in Sunnism in Shi'a Islam ijtihad did not remain dormant for long the destruction in 1258 of the Sunni Abbasid caliphate by the Mongol ruler Hulagu Khan (1217-65) created a political ideological vacuum in which the Shi'a doctrine thrived. Jamal al Din ibn Yusuf al Hilli, a Shi'a thinker, rehabilitated the concept and practice of Ihtihad. (Arabic reflection): The means by which the early lawyers arrived at legal decisions from the Koran from Tradition or by deduction.

In principle all such decisions were consistent, but inevitably they led to the multiplication of local idiosyncrasies and the establishment of the main legal schools replaced individual judgment by generally accept rules. (Arabic) independent reasoning. During the early times of Islam the possibility of finding a new solution to a juridical problem. Has not been allowed in conservative Islam since the middle ages. However liberal movements within Islam generally argue that any Muslim can perform ijtihad given that Islam has no generally accepted clerical hierarchy or bureaucratic organization. Independent judgment on religious matters or principles of Islamic jurisprudence that are not specifically outlined in the Quran. The opposite of ijtihad is Taqlid. Arabic for "imitation." The process of personal reflection on the meaning of the Holy Qur'an, allowing individual interpretation of the words and actions of the Prophet Muhammad. Juristic matters.

Ikhwan (Arabic : Brethren or brotherhood): Islamic military movement in Arabia. Abdul Aziz ibn Abdul Rahman al Saud ruler of Najd conceived the idea of settling the nomadic tribes in colonies in order to teach them the tenets of Islam as a step toward replacing their customary law with Islamic law and their traditional tribal bonds with religious ones. Implementing this idea after 1913, he called the settlements Hijra Arabic migration. And the settlers al Ikhwan. By 1920 their colonies had become the primary source of soldiery to Abdul Aziz al Saud. During the next several years the Ikhwan helped him to expand his realm to nearly four fifths of the Arabian Peninsula. This led to conflict between the Ikhwan and al Saud in March 1929 with 8,000 Ikhwan facing 30,000 well armed soldiers of al Saud. The rebel Ikhwan were defeated. Further battles followed and it was not until January 1930 that the last of the defiant Ikhwan chiefs surrendered. 'brethren'; specifically, the former Bedouin, converted to Wahhabi Islam and settled on the land, who formed the shock troops to Abdul-Aziz al Sa'ud in his conquest of Arabia in the early twentieth century.

Ikhwan al Muslimun: Muslim brotherhood, a society founded in 1928 by Hasan al Banna, originally aimed at reestablishing a Muslim policy in Egypt.

Ikhwan al Safa: Brothers of Purity, a group of Ismail influenced thinkers based in Basra in the tenth century.

Ikhwan: The brothers soldiers of Abd al Aziz founder of the Saudi dynasty, and adherents of the Hanbali reformer Abd al Wahhab.

Brethren of Wahhabi Tribesmen Brotherhood; al-Qaida. Founded in 1912, a militia.

Ikraam: honoring, hospitality, generosity-Dhul jalaali wal Ikraam is one of the 99 names of Allah.

Imamat: supreme leadership of Muslims after the Prophet Muhammad Sunnis distinguish between the early caliphate of the Rightly Guided Caliphs, Abu Bakr ibn Abu Qahafa, Omar ibn Khattab, Othman ibn Affan and Ali ibn Abu Talib and the latter Imamat, which was characterized by worldly monarchy. Shi'as do not accept the Imamat of Abu Bakr, Omar, and Othman arguing that the Prophet Muhammad had designated Ali as his successor. The Twelver Shi'a doctrine formulated by Imam he must be free from sin and error and he must be the most exemplary of all Muslims.

Imami: The school of law adopted by the Twelver Shi'a. It rejects jihad which can only be proclaimed by the absent imam on his return, and does not recognize the legal dicta of the Umayyad caliphs, but its general attitude is fairly close to the Sunni Hanafis.

IMU: Islamic Movement of Uzbekistan

Intifada: (Arabic: shivering or shaking off): Palestinian uprising against the Israeli occupation 1987-93. Intifada erupted spontaneously in the Palestinian refugee camp of Jabaliya In the Gaza Strip on 9 December 1987, when thousands marched in protest against the killing of four Palestinians by an Israeli truck near the settlement. *The intifada stemmed from twenty years of collective and individual frustration and humiliation that the Palestinians had endured in their dealings with the Jews and the Israeli authorities, both military and civilian. By early January 1988 the secular PLO had set up the United National Leadership of the Uprising to direct the movement while the Islamic center formed Hamas for the same purpose. The campaign against the Israeli agents intensified in the early 1990s and destroyed Shin Beth's 20,000 strong intelligence network among the Palestinians, making it extremely hard for the occupying Israeli authorities to reimpose full control and restore law and order. By the end of the intifada

1,636 Palestinians including 316 minors had been killed 1,346 by the Israeli security forces and 290 by Jewish civilians.

Iran Hostage Crisis: (4 November 1979-1920 January 1981) A prolonged crisis between Iran and the USA. In the aftermath of Iran's Islamic Revolution, followers of the Ayatollah Khomeini alleged US complicity in military plots to restore the Shah Muhammad Reza Shah Pahlavi, and seized the US Embassy in Teheran, taking 66 US citizens hostage. All efforts of President Carter to free the hostages failed, including economic measures and an abortive rescue bid by US helicopters in April 1980. The crisis dragged on until 20 January 1981, when Algeria successfully mediated, and the hostages were freed. It seriously weakened Carter's bid for presidential re-election in November 1980 and he lost to Ronald Reagan.

Iranis: Shi'ites who believe that only a divinely inspired Imam descended from Ali, son-in-law of the Prophet, could be the true restorer of Islam, and conquer the entire world as Mahdi, and usher in a millennium before the end of all things.

Iraq Kurdistan Front: In May 1987 six Iraqi Kurdish groups formed the Iraqi Kurdistan Front with the aim of intensifying resistance to the repressive policies of Baghdad with regard to Iraqi Kurdistan. After the second Gulf War the IKF negotiated, unsuccessfully with Baghdad.

Iraqi National Congress: Iraq political grouping. The Iraqi National Congress was formed in Vienna at the meeting of 300 Iraqi delegates, funded by the US Central Intelligence Agency which used Ahmad Chalabi as the front man. Led by Chalabi, it committed itself to waging a war of liberation against the regime of Iraqi President Saddam Hussein with the objective of establishing a democratic Iraq. Following the bitter intra Kurdish violence in September 1996, when the CIA withdrew its agents and informers from Iraqi Kurdistan, the INC left the region and moved its head office to London.

IRP: Islamic Republic Party

Islamic Action Front (Jordan): see Muslim Brotherhood (Jordan).

Islamic Amal (Lebanon): Lebanese religious-political organization. The Islamic Amal was established in July 1982 by Hussein Musavi, a member of the command council of Amal after he had left Amal in protest at its leaders passivity toward Israel's occupation of two fifths of Lebanon. Following the end of the Lebanese Civil War in October 1990, the influence of the Islamic Amal declined as the Hezbollah emerged as the main party of radical Shi'as.

Islamic conference organizations (1969): An arson attack on al Aqsa Mosque in Jerusalem, the third holiest shrine of Islam by Michael Rohan, an Australian fundamentalist Christian in August 1969 shocked the Muslim world. Funded primarily by Saudi Arabia, it provided the kingdom with an opportunity to project itself as the leader of the Islamic world. In 1975 it set up al Quds committee to implement ICO resolutions on the status of Jerusalem. The sixth summit in Dakar, Senegal, in December 1991 was boycotted by twelve Arab heads of state in protest at the invitation extended to the Palestine Liberation Organization PLO and Jordan which had sided with Iraq in the Second Gulf War. In 2003 the ICO had fifty seven members, including the PLO which was not a state. Its secretary general was Abdel Ouahed Belkeziz, a Moroccan.

Islamic Consultative Assembly (Iran): see Majlis.

Islamic front of Syria: Syrian political alliance in 1980 the moderate faction of the Muslim Brotherhood combined with the Islamic Liberation Party the Society of Abu Dharr and the Northern Circle to form the Islamic Front of Syria. The Muslim Brotherhood, the IFS's leading constituent wanted the IFS to adopt its pro Iraq policy. In March 1982 Saad al Din led the IFS into an alliance with seventeen other opposition groups to form the National Alliance for the Liberation of Syria under Amin Hafiz in Baghdad.

Islamic fundamentalism: Fundamentalism is the term used for the effort to define the fundamentals of a religion and adhere to them. Whether a Muslim majority state today is fundamentalist or not can be judged by a single criterion: It is legislation derived solely from the Sharia. By this standard Saudi Arabia is the oldest Islamic fundamentalist state in the world. Since its inception in 1932, it has known nothing but the Sharia. The belief that the revitalization of Islamic society can only come about through a return to the fundamental principles and practices of early Islam. Fundamentalist movements have often been a response to political and economic decline, which is ascribed to spiritual and moral decay. These movements shared the belief that religion is integral to both state and society and advocated a return to a life patterned on the 7th century political community of the faithful established by Muhammad at medina, governed by the Shari (Islamic law), and supported if need be by Jihad (holy war). No doubt that the Iranian revolution has been an inspiring example to many Muslims of all persuasions throughout the world.

Islamic fundamentalists: Refers to Muslims who are strict adherents to the Koran, the written word of Allah, as revealed through his prophet, Muhammad. Many of them believe that religion should significantly guide government.

Islamic Iranian Participation Front (Iran): Popularly known as Moshakerat. Formed on the eve of the first local elections in Iran in early 1999, the left of center Islamic Iranian Participation Front was led by Muhammad Reza Khatami, a younger brother of President Muhammad Khatami.

Islamic Jihad (Lebanon): The Islamic Jihad a pro Iranian Shi'a group was formed in Lebanon in the spring of 1982. In April 1983 it truck bombed the US Embassy in West Beirut. Seventeen of the sixty three people killed were American, most of them senior Central Intelligence Agency operative. On 23 October 1983 IJ militants truck bombed the US Marines headquarters at Beirut International Airport, killing 241 troops and the French paratroops in Bir Hassan district, killing fifty nine soldiers. A similar explosion caused by another IJ activist destroyed the Israeli military headquarters in Tyre leaving sixty people dead half of them Israelis.

Islamic Jihad (Palestine): Dissatisfied with the policies of the Muslim Brotherhood in the Occupied Territories its militant members split to form the Islamic jihad in 1981. Its leader, Fathi Abdul Aziz Shikaki was assassinated by Mossad agents in Malta in October 1995. He was succeeded by Ramadan Shallah. It participated actively in the al Aqsa Intifada that erupted in September 2000, and was responsible for a few suicide bombings. Some of its activists became victims of Israel's policy of targeted killings.

Islamic Mandinka: West African Muslims, slaves

Islamic modernism: A movement in Islamic thought that seeds to reinterpret Islam to meet the changing circumstances of contemporary life. By contrast with Islamic Fundamentalism, Islamic modernism is a response to Western imperialism and economic dominance that attempts to reform legal, educational, and social structures. From the 19th century leading Muslim thinkers such as Jamal al-Din al-Arghani and his followers in Egypt, Muhammad Abduh (1849-1905) and Rashid Rida (1865-1935), were concerned at the stagnation they perceived in Muslim intellectual, political, and social life. They advocated the reform of the Sharia by reopening the door of I*jtihad* or reinterpretation, which orthodox Sunni Muslims have regarded as closed since the 9th century.

Islamic movement of Kurdistan: Iraqi political organization their opposition to the draft agreement between representatives of the Iraqi Kurdistan Front and the Baghdad government in June 1991 led the Kurdish Hezbollah, the Kurdish Mujahedin and the Kurdish Ansar e Islam to form the Islamic Movement of Kurdistan under the leadership of Shaikh Osman Abdullah Aziz and Shaikh Ali Abdullah Aziz. In late 1993 it began to expand its base through force in southeast Kurdistan at the expense of the Patriotic Union of Kurdistan.

Islamic Republican Party (Iran): The Islamic Republican Party was established within a month of the February 1979 revolution by Iran's leading clerics, including Ali Akbar Hashemi Rafsanjani and Ali Hussein Khamanei. Following President Muhammad Ali

Rajai's assassination in August, the IRP's secretary general, Ali Khamanei, successfully contested the office in October 1981.

Islamic Revolution (Iran: What started in early 1977 as a demand by Iranian intellectuals to abolish censorship ended up as a revolutionary overthrow of the most powerful pro Western monarchy in the Middle East, the Pahlavi shahs two years later. Khomeini made adroit use of Shi'a history and Iranian nationalism to attract ever increasing support, and he united disparate anti shah forces, both secular and religious by his most radical demand: the deposition of Muhammad Reza Shah Pahlavi. What finally sealed the fate of the Pahlavi state was an indefinite strike by oil workers, orders by Khomeini on 31 October 1978. The ten day Shi'a ritual of Ashura in December enhanced religious feeling in the nation, now paralyzed by a strike of civil servants.

Islamic Revolutionary Komitehs (Iran): see Revolutionary Komitehs.

Islamic Salvation Front: (French, *Front Islamique du Salut,* FIS) Algerian Islamic Fundamentalist political party. The FIS was formed by an alliance of five smaller Muslim parties after the introduction of multiparty politics in Algeria in 1989. Commonly known as FIS from its French name, Front Islamique du Salut. A radical Islamist group in Algeria founded in 1989. In December 1991, it did very well in the first round of elections for the Algerian National Assembly and seemed more than likely to win a clear majority in the second round. In January 1992, amid growing tension, the army canceled the second round and established a military regime. A bitter and bloody struggle followed, and in 1997, Amnesty International assessed the number of victims at 80,000, most of them civilians. It remains a powerful force in Algeria.

Islamic Salvation Front: Algerian political party

Islamic Salvation front: North Africa's first legal Islamic political party, first recognized by Algeria's government in 1988, later split into a moderate group and a more militant wing called the Islamic Salvation Army

Islamism and Islamists: When Islam is used as a political ideology, it is described as Islamism and its adherents are called Islamists. The ideological belief in the requirement to enact the political tenets of Islam as the basis of political life.

Ismaili: A branch of Shiite Islam that recognizes seven rather than 12 *imams* (spiritual leaders). They include Mustalians in India and Yemen, and Nizaris in Afghanistan, East Africa, India, Iran, and Syria. Ismail, the eldest son of the sixth *imam*, Ja'far al-Sadia (d. 765) was disinherited and most Shiites recognized his brother Musa al-Kazim as *imam*. Ismailis regarded Ismail as the seventh and last *imam* and expected that he would soon return as the Mahdi (expected one) to overthrow existing corrupt governments and establish justice on earth. The Fatimid dynasty (909-1171) promoted their beliefs in Egypt and Syria but attempted no mass conversions among the Sunni majority. The Ismailis developed the idea that the religious precepts have a secret inner meaning, passed from Muhammad to Ali and from him to later imams, who could thus instruct the ignorant.

A group of Shi'as recognizing Ismail., the son of the sixth imam Ja'far al Sadiq as their Messiah. In the late 9th century they appear as a missionary movement radiating from Iraq to Khurasan and Transoxania, Bahrain, the Maghrib, Yemen and Sind, though the advent of the Ismaili Fatimids caused internal dissensions which were accentuated by extremists like the Assassins in Persia and Syria, and the different communities tended to draw apart. Communities of Ismailis survived the Mongols, particularly in Transoxania, but the most important group today are the adherents of the Agha Khan. Islamic group Part of Shi'a Islam, Ismailies are distinguished from the other sub sects Zaidis and Imamis or Twelvers by the number of revered figured they regard as Imams. An Ismaili group set up the Fatimid. Muhammad and the wife of Imam Ali, caliphate in Tunis which after conquering Egypt also in AD 969 rivaled the Abbasids, based on Baghdad their rule lasted until 1171.

ISNA: Islamic organization

Israeli Arabs: The term Israeli Arabs applies to those Arabs who did not leave Palestine before or during the 1948 Arab Israeli War and acquired Israeli nationality. According to the Israeli census taken in November 1948, the 156,000 Israeli Arabs represented 18 percent of the total population. Due to natural growth 2000, including 232,000 living in east Jerusalem anointing to 20 percent of the Israeli population. In the 1999 Knesset poll, the number of Israeli Arab members rose to twelve. Israeli Arabs largely back the idea of a Palestinian state on the West Bank and Gaza and have been keen supporters of the Oslo Accords of 1993 and 1995. In the national unity government of Ariel Sharon formed in March 2001, Salah Tarif, a Druze member of the Labor Party, became the first Israeli Arab to become a cabinet minister, albeit without portfolio.

Israeli Socialist Organization: Israeli political party formed by a group of former Jewish members of Maki in 1962, the Israeli Socialist Organization was better known by the name of its journal, Mastzpen (Compass).It opposed the June 1967 Arab Israeli War.

Ithna Ashari: twelve Imam Shiism; resting on the belief in the twelve Imams; dominant in Iran.

Ja'afari: A branch of Sha'ariah, Islamic law, followed mainly by Shi'as

Ja'afari Code: Shi'a Islamic legal school, This Islamic legal code is named after Imam Ja'far al Sadiq (AD 699-765), the sixth Imam of Twelver Shi'as.

Ja'fari: Referring to the sole Shi'ite madhhabs ascribed to the Imam Ja'far al Sadiq

Jahaliya: "Ignorance." Refers to the time before the advent of Islam when superstitious and barbaric customs were a part of Arabian life.

Jalairids: Mongol dynasty which in the breakup of the Il Khanate following the death of Abu Said established itself at Baghdad and controlled part of western Persia and Tabriz. The rise of the Timurids put an end to any hopes for Jalairid domination of Persia and then even Baghdad fell to the Black Sheep in 1410.

Jamaa: association, group, company

Jamaat I Islamic: fundamentalist Islamic organization of Pakistan

Jamaat I-Islami: Pakistani fundamentalist movement.

Jamaat: group or society; congregation.

Jami'ah: Gathering, i.e. a university, a mosque or more generally a community or association.

Jamiat: association

Jamaat-I-Islami: Radical movement founded by Maududi in India

Janissaries: (Turkish, *Yeni Cheri*, 'new troops') An elite corps of slave soldiers, bound to the service of the Ottoman sultans. They were originally raised from prisoners of war, but from the time of Bayezid I (1389-1403) they were largely recruited by means of the *devshirme* ('gathering'), a levy of the fittest youths among the sultan's non-Muslim subjects. Having been converted to Islam, most after intensive training, served as foot soldiers, while the ablest passed into civil administration. Decimation in the great wars against Persia and Austria (1578-1606) lowered the traditionally high quality of the intake and opened the corps to Muslim. They exercised a powerful role in political life until their abolition in 1826. [Turk.,=recruits], elite corps in the service of the Ottoman Empire (Turkey). It was composed of war captives and Christian youths pressed into service; all the recruits were converted to Islam and trained under the strictest discipline. It was originally organized by Sultan Murad I. The Janissaries gained great power in the Ottoman Empire and made and unmade sultans.

By 1600, Muslims had begun to enter the corps, largely through bribery, and in the 17th cent. membership in the corps became largely hereditary, while the drafting of Christians gradually ceased. In 1826, Sultan Mahmud II rid himself of the unruly (and by now inefficient) Janissaries by having them massacred in their barracks by his loyal Spahis. From the Turkish Yeni Cheri new soldiers, the famous Ottoman infantry. These were at first recruited among Christian prisoners of war and then by means of the devshirme, a periodic levy of boys from the Christian subject populations of the empire. This method was abandoned in the 17th century after which the janissaries became a closed and increasingly hereditary corps As such it became a strong and to some degree even an independent power within the Ottoman system. An early 19th century British visitor even called it an Ottoman equivalent of the French chamber of Deputies, though not interestingly of the house of Commons. The corps, seen as an obstacle to reform was abolished by the Sultan in 1826.

Janissaries: "New Troops"; infantry corps; conscription from among Christian boys in the Balkans and raised as Muslims.

Janissaries: Elite corps of the Ottoman army; made up of Christian prisoners of war who embraced Islam and were under the command of the sultan himself. Not allowed to marry; members of the Bektashi Order.

Jahiliah (adjective, jahili): the Age of Ignorance. Originally the term was used to describe the pre-Islamic period in Arabia. Today Muslim fundamentalists often apply it to any society, even a nominally Muslim society, which has, in their view, turned its back upon God and refused to submit to God's sovereignty.

Jews in Arab Middle East: In 1945 there were 870,000 Jews in the Arab Middle East.. Following the founding of Israel and the First Arab Israeli War their number fell to 70,000 with 600,000 migrating to Israel and the rest elsewhere.

Jim'ah **(A):** The traditional gathering for prayers on Friday

Jumblat clan: Also spelled Jumblat. Of Kurdish origin, the Jumblats claim lineage from Salah a Din Ayyubi who defeated the Crusaders in 1187. When power passed from the Maans to the Shehabis at the turn of the eighteenth century, the Jumblats struggled against the Shehabis. Following the end of the Ottoman Empire in Lebanon in 1918, the successor French mandate tried to woo ethnic and religious minorities such as the

Druzes, thus underwriting the continued importance of the Jumblats. After the Assassination of Fuad Jumblat in 1922, power passed to his widow, Nazira. Their son, Kamal became an eminent Lebanese politician. Nasserite head of the Progressive Socialist Party—Lebanon

Jumu'ah: the gathering, the prayer that Muslim men must attend on Friday afternoon

Kafirs: Signifies one who denies or rejects the truth, i.e. who disbelieves in the message of the Prophets. Since the advent of Muhammad (peace be on him), anyone who rejects his Message is a **Kafir**. An Arabic word meaning unbeliever from a verb meaning to disbelieve or deny. The Turkish form is Gavur. It is the term commonly used in Arabic and other Islamic languages to denote non Muslims. Islamic law and practice make an important distinction between two categories of unbelievers: The first form is Gavur. It is the term commonly used in Arabic and other Islamic languages to denote non Muslims. Islamic law and practice make an important distinction between two categories of unbelievers: The first consists of monotheists to whom at some time in the past God sent prophets who brought books of revelation.

In principle, this category consisted of Jews, Christians, and a third group known as the Sabaens or Sabi'a. For many centuries now, it has been limited to Jews and Christians and the books in Question to the Old and New Testaments. These when they come under the authority of the Muslims state, may be accorded the status of Dhimmi. The second category are those who have no book or at least none recognized by Islam as a divine origin and who worship false or plural Gods. These according to the holy law, may not be accorded tolerance, but must be given choice of conversion or death. The latter may, however be commuted to enslavement. Some have suggested that the term Kafir should apply only to the second and not the first category.

Kahins: Traditional shamanistic soothsayer in Arabia at the time of Muhammad.

Kahinun: A priestly tribe in Arabia

Karaite: A fundamentalist movement

Karmathians: or Carmathians, a Muslim sect of the 9th and 10th cent., similar to the Assassin sect. They were part of a movement for social reform that spread widely though Islam from the 9th to the 12th cent. Although heretical, their doctrine had a great influence on Islamic philosophy and remnants of it are today found in the religion of the Druze. The chief importance of the Karmathians came with their establishment of an independent communist community in lower Mesopotamia before 900. They were the source of rebellions in Khorasan and Syria, and after 900 they conquered all of Yemen. In spite of the efforts of the Abbasid caliph at Baghdad, the Karmathians continued their career until (c.930) they created a sensation that rocked Islam by carrying away the Black Stone from the Kaaba at Mecca. Ten years later the Karmathians returned the stone. They were in constant touch with the founders of Fatimid rule in Egypt, alternately at war or peace with them. They ceased to be a political power after 1000.

Kedar and Nebaioth: Sons of Ishmael, who is traditionally known to be the father of the Arabs.

Khalifat Rashidun: four first caliphs, believed by most Muslims to be most righteous rulers in history

Khalji: A Muslim dynasty of Turkish origin which seized power in northern India in 1293. its three kings successively ruled the Delhi sultanate for the next thirty years. Ala ud-Din (1296-1316), the second sultan, was the most successful. His armies held off Mongol threats, subdued large parts of Rajasthan and Gujarat, then carried Islam to Madurai in the extreme south of the subcontinent. Their object was pillage rather than permanent empire, yet Khalji expansion began a new era of Muslim penetration of Hindu southern India. On Ala ud-Din's assassination the dynasty declined, to be replaced in 1320 by the Tughluq dynasty.

Khanqah: Sufi hospice mainly in areas of Persian influence; a building where such Sufi **(q.v.)** activities as dhikr **(q.v.)** take place, where Sufi masters live and instruct their disciples. An endowed foundation governed by a Shaikh with provision for the maintenance of Sufis/ Khanqahs were particularly popular as funerary foundation in 12th and 13th century Syria and 13th to 15th century Egypt. They are in some respects similar to medieval Europeans monasteries except that there was no specific rule to govern the order. Often however they were so richly endowed that their inmate must have found even spiritual poverty difficult to practice.

Khariji: Secessionists. The party refused to recognize Ali's treaty with his opponents after his death at Siffin with the result that in their view any miscreant imam loses his divine authority becoming an infidel and may be removed it necessary by force. (adj. or noun): the branch of Islam that developed in the seventh century from the conviction that the most capable Muslim should become caliph; outsider or succeder

Kharijis (Arabic: Seceder, sing. Of Khawarij): Islamic sect During the battle of Siffin on the banks of the Euphrates in July AD. 657 between Ali ibn Abu Talib and Muawiya ibn Abu Sufyan about the succession to the caliphate, Muawiya proposed that he and Ali should settle their differences by referring them to two arbitrators, who would judge the matter according to the Quran. They denounced Ali's claim to the caliphate, declaring that that any pious Muslim was worthy of becoming caliph and did not have to belong either to the household of the prophet Muhammad or his Quraish tribe. They branded infidel anyone who disagreed with their stance. In July AD 658 Ali attacked the Khawarij in their camp at Nahrawan and defeated them. "The seceders." The faction that rebelled against Caliph Ali. Plural: **Khawarij**.

Kharijism, Kharijites: the first sect to secede from the Islamic community. A group of extreme puritans, who insisted that they alone were the true Muslims, and therefore undertook **jihad** against the mainstream community and its leaders.

Kharijite: polemical name applied to a member of certain extremists Islamist groups that condemn all other Muslims as sinners; early

Muslim sectaries who believed in a wholly elective Caliphate, and rejected the doctrine of justification without works. Succeeders, killers of Ali (661).

Khawaja: In Egyptian dialect, Khawaga. At one time widely used in the Arabic speaking countries as a polite form of address for foreigners, specifically non-Arab, non Muslim foreigners. The word is derived from the Persian Khaja, a term used as a specially respectful form of address to a rich merchant, a senior scholar or teacher, a venerable old man, a lord or master, a vizier or other high dignitary of state. It is also used perhaps ironically to address a eunuch. The Turkish form Hoca pronounced Hodja is used to address or refer to a Muslim man of religion or in a secular context to a teacher. A famous example Is the Hodja Nasreddin Efendi, hero of a rich folklore of humorous anecdotes.

Khawarij: Rebels of Islam. Fundamentalists that emerged from the ranks of Ali's supporters, espoused dictatorship of the seemingly virtuous – they declared both Uthman and Ali as un-Islamic traitors and un-believers. Known for their extreme pietism while preparing rebellion and mass murder. Many of their leaders came from the Banu Tamin, a powerful Najd tribe of which Ibn Abd al-Wahhab, more than 1,000 years later, was a member. Dissenders (order of...)

Khazraj: A tribe in Mecca

Khedive: a division of the Ismailis **(q.v.).**

Khilafat Movement: an Indian Muslim movement that aimed to rouse public opinion against the harsh treatment accorded to the Ottoman Empire after World War I and specifically against the treatment of the Ottoman sultan and caliph (Khalifa). The movement began in 1919 and, under the leadership of the Ali brothers, Muhammad Ali (1878-1931) and Shaukat Ali (1873-1938), assumed a mainly political character.

Khlafa or Rashidah: Rightly Guided Caliphs

Kharijites (Khawarij): Those who refused recognition of the Shi'ah and Sunni caliphs; they believed that the caliphate should be open to any Muslim of sound mind and body; "Those who withdrew"; one assassinated Ali, the 4th caliph, in Kufa, Iraq.

King Crane Commission (1919): US commission on the Middle East, Pursuing the self determination doctrine he had been advocating. US President Woodrow Wilson, at the Paris Peace Conference of the Council of four in March 1919, proposed that an Allied Commission on Mandates in Ottoman. While sympathizing with Zionist aspirations and plans, they concluded that the extreme Zionist program must be greatly modified if the civil and religious rights of the non Jewish inhabitants of Palestine are to be protected in accordance with the terms of the Balfour Declaration. Since the US withdrew from the Peace Conference in December 1919-a preamble to its refusal to join the League of Nations which was formed the following month the report lost its importance. It was not until December 1922 that it was published unofficially.

Knights Templars: A military religious order properly called the Poor Knights of Christ and of the Temple of Solomon, founded in 1118 by Hugh de Payens, a knight of Champagne in France. He and eight companions vowed to protect pilgrims traveling on the public roads of the Holy Land (Palestine). At the Council of Troyes (1128) approval was given to their version of the Benedictine rule. They quickly became very influential, attracting many noble members and growing in wealth, acquiring property throughout Christendom. When Jerusalem fell in 1187 they moved to Acre together with the Knights Hospitallers and great rivalry and hatred developed between the orders.

In 1291 when Acre also fell, the Knights Templar retreated to Cyprus. In Cyprus their great wealth enabled them to act as bankers to the nobility of most of Europe and this affluence attracted much hostility, in particular that of Philip IV of France. In 1307 they were charged with heresy and immorality. Though some of the charges may have teen true, envy of their wealth seems to have been the reason for their persecution. They were condemned, their wealth confiscated, and the order suppressed. The Grand master and many others were burned at the stake.

Komala-e Jian-e Kordestan (Kurdish: Association of Revival of Kurdistan): Kurdish organization in Iran. During the Soviet occupation of northern Iran (1941-46), nationalist Kurds secretly established the Komala-e Jian-e Kordestan, often called Komala, in 1943 in Mahabad. under the leadership of Ja'far Shafii it participated in the 1977-78 revolutionary movement. In its strongholds in the northern Revolutionary Komitehs. In the confrontation between Ayatollah Ruhollah Khomeini and President Abol Hassan Bani Sadr in 1981, it sided with the latter, who lost. It then joined the National Resistance Council. As the Iran Iraq War (1980-88) dragged on, Komala began to cooperate with Iraq. But once the PUK had decided on repairing its stained relations with Iran in September 1996 after suffering a humiliating defeat by the rival Kurdistan Democratic Party, the KOPCI lost its base in Iraq- and with it any importance it had.

Kordestan Democratic Party of Iran: see Kurdistan Democratic Party of Iran.

Kpri: Koprulu, family of humble Albanian origin, several members of which served as grand vizier (chief executive officer) in the Ottoman Empire. The name is also spelled Kuiprili, Koprili, and Kuprili. Mehmed Koprulu, 1583-1661, became grand vizier of Muhammad IV in 1656. He reorganized the Ottoman fleet, conquered (1658) Transylvania, restored internal order (by executing dissidents), reformed the finances, and built forts along the Don and Dnieper rivers. During his vizierate the Ottoman Empire regained some of its former prestige and vitality. He was succeeded as vizier by his son Ahmed Koprulu, 1635-76.

An able statesmen and soldier, he took (1669) the last Venetian stronghold in Crete, but he was severely defeated (1664) by Montecucculi at Szentgotthard in Hungary and suffered reverses in his campaigns against John III of Poland. Ahmed was succeeded as vizier by Kara Mustafa, his brother-in-law. Ahmed's brother, Mustafa Koprulu, 1637-91, became vizier in 1689, at a time when the Austrians and their allies were advancing victoriously into the Ottoman Empire. He drove the Austrians from Serbia but was killed in the battle of Slankamen. His cousin, Huseyin Koprulu, d. 1702, became vizier after the

Turkish defeat at Senta in 1697. Recognizing the exhaustion of Turkey, he negotiated a humiliating peace (Karlow, Treaty of). Mustafa Koprulu's son, Numan Koprulu, d.1719, was vizier in 1710-11. Another son, Abdullah Koprulu, d. 1735, was acting vizier from 1723 until his death.

Kurdish Democratic Party (Iraq): see Kurdistan Democratic Party (Iraq).

Kurdish Revolutionary Party (Iraq): a breakaway group of the Kurdistan Democratic Party. The Kurdish Revolutionary Party (KRP) was formed in 1964 in protest against the authoritarian leadership of Mustafa Barzani. Following the agreement of the Kurdistan Democratic Party with Baghdad in 1970, many KRP members returned to the parent body.

Kurdistan Democratic Party (Iraq): Official Kurdish title: Partiya Demokrata Kurdistan. Between the end of the Kurdish Republic of Mahabad in December 1946 and his crossing into the Soviet Union from Iran in June 1947, Mustafa Barzani set the guidelines for an Iraq based Kurdish Democratic Party (KDP). Inspired by Marxism-Leninism, it would dedicate itself to liberating Iraq from foreign imperialism and domestic reaction and would fight for Kurdish autonomy within Iraq. Following the July 1958 revolution, Barzani was allowed to return home. He backed the new regime under Abdul Karim Qasim who legalized the KDP In March 1969 and the KDP resumed its armed struggle against the central government, now run by the Baath Party.

After March 1974, when the government created the promised Kurdistan Autonomous Region (KAR), the KDP went on the warpath. The KDP leadership passed on to Barzani's sons, Idris and Masud. When they moved into Iran after the 1979 Islamic revolution, Tehran began to provide them with aid. The outbreak of the Iran Iraq War in 1980 compelled Baghdad to reduce its troops in the Kurdish areas. This led to an expansion in the Iraqi border area under KDP control. KDP leaders escaped to Iran or Syria, but during the crisis created by Iraq's occupation of Kuwait in August 1990, which drew most of the Iraqi troops away from the KAR, they returned to the KAR. Barzani's subsequent talks with Baghdad failed. Protected by the air forces of the US, Britain and France, the KDP, along with other Kurdish parties, held legislative Council elections in May 1992.

The KDP commanding 25,000 troops and backed by 30,000 militiamen, shared power equally with the Patriotic Union of Kurdistan (PUK). Yet the traditional rivalry between the two parties continued. In May 1994 intra Kurdish clashes left over 1,000 people dead. It was not until six months later that, assisted by mediators, Barzani worked out a modus Vivendi with Talabani. When after defeating the Taliban regime in Afghanistan in December 2001, the US administration of President George W. Bush turned its attention to ousting Saddam's government by force the importance of Barzani as well as Talabani rose. Following the collapse of the Saddam Hussein regime in the face of an invasion by the Anglo American forces in April 2003, Barzani publicly welcomed the US proconsul Gen. Jay Rayner.

Kurdistan Democratic Party of Iran: Iranian political party. In September 1945, when Iran's Kurdish region was under Soviet occupation, the Kurdish Democratic Soviet occupation, the Kurdish region was under Soviet occupation, the Kurdish Democratic Party (KDP) (Kurdish: Hizb Dimokrat-e Kurd) was established in Mahabad by Qazi Muhammad who had led an autonomous local council since 1941. The republic lasted a year before being overthrown by the forces of Muhammad Reza Shah Pahlavi after the Soviet withdrawal in May 1946. The KDP went underground. After the revolution, when the central government, led by Ayatollah Ruhollah Khomeini, tried to establish control in the Kurdish areas, the KDPI came into conflict with it. The Iraqi invasion of Iran in September 1980 helped Khomeini in that it created a surge of nationalism in which ethnic differences were forgotten, for the time being.

The KDPI backed President Abol Hassan Bani Sadr in his confrontation with Khomeini in June 1981 and lost. As the Iran Iraq War (1980-88) dragged on, the KDPI began to side with Iraq. Its leader, Abdul Rahman Qasimlou, tried to reconcile Baghdad with its Kurdish nationalists and managed to get the central government and Jalal Talabani of the Patriotic Union of Kurdistan to negotiate in 1984-85. Following the establishment of the no fly zones in northern Iraq by America and Britain in late 1991, the Iraqi PUK began providing refuge to the KDPI forces, with their headquarters in the Iraqi border town of Qala Diza. They made a point of killing the personnel of Iran's Revolutionary Guard Corps which in turn hit back. Tension between the KDPI and Iran rose sharply after Washington's adoption of the Dual Containment point in May 1993.

Kurds in Iran: Nationally Kurds make up about 8 percent of the Iranian population. They are predominant in Kurdistan and are a substantial community in the provinces of East Azerbaijan (pop. 3.3 million), West Azerbaijan (Pop 2.5 million), Kerman (Pop, 2.0 million), and Ilam (Pop. 0.5 million).

Kurds in Iraq: Nationally Kurds accounted for about 19 percent of the Iraqi population. Of the 3.6 million Kurds in the country in 1991, nearly two thirds were in the Kurdistan Autonomous Region. By amalgamating (in December 1925) the predominantly Kurdish province of Mosul. During the Second World War, Mustafa Barzani led a failed rebellion. He fled to Iran, and later to the Soviet Union. Following the 1958 coup in Iraq he returned home and backed the new republican regime. In exchange, Baghdad legalized the Kurdistan Democratic party (KDP) and promulgated a constitution that stated: "Arabs and Kurds are associated in this nation." Ignoring the noncooperation of the KDP, the Baghdad government enforced the Kurdish autonomy law in March 1974, including the appointment of a Kurd, Taha Muhyi al Din Maruf, a diplomat, as a vice president of the republic, the formation of the Kurdistan Autonomous Region (KAR), comprising the provinces of Dohak, Irbil, and Suleimaniya, and establishment of the (Largely nominated) Kurdistan Legislative Council. During the 1980-88 Iran-Iraq War, the activities of the Kurdish insurgents, allied with Tehran, compelled Iraq to deploy divisions in the north to the detriment of its war effort elsewhere.

During the crisis created by Iraq's occupation of Kuwait in August 1990, which drew most of the troops away from the

KAR, the KDP leaders returned to Kurdistan. Having fully regained the region, Baghdad signed a truce with the insurgents in Mid April. With 16,000 Western Troops deployed in the 3,600 sq. mile/ 9,325 sq. km security zone created by the US Led anti Iraq coalition in the Iraqi Turkish corner region, Baghdad was forced to withdraw its forces from the KAR by late October. Kurds thus acquired a semi independent administrative political entity. See further Kurdistan Democratic Party and Patriotic Union of Kurdistan.

Kurds in Syria: Nationally Kurds make up about 6 percent of the Syrian population. Apart from a small community in Damascus dating back to the times of Salal al Din (Saladin) Ayyubi (r. 1169-93), himself a Kurd, they are concentrated in the Jazira region in the northeast corner of the country and in the mountainous area north of Aleppo among the border with Turkey. Following the merger of Syria with Egypt to form the United Arab Republic (UAR) in 1958, the new pan Arabist regime repressed the KDP. In late 1971 the government for the first time distributed land reform land to Kurdish peasants in Jazira. In 1976 President Hafiz Assad officially renounced the population transfer plans for Jazira.

Kurds: Kurds are members of an ethnic group that inhabit the Zagros and Taurus Mountains of southeastern Turkey, north western Iran, northern Iraq, and the adjacent areas in Syria and Nakhichevan. It was not until the seventh century AD that they embraced Islam. Like Persians, who also embraced Islam, they retained their languages, but unlike them, they remained predominantly Sunni. The Kurdish general, Salal al Din (Saladin) Ayyubi, overpowered the Shi Fatimid dynasty in Egypt and established the Ayyubid dynasty (1169-1250). Since the Treaty of Sevres (1920) which specified an autonomous Kurdistan, was not ratified, and since the subsequent Treaty of Lausanne (1923) made no mention of it, the aspirations of Kurdish nationalists remained unfulfilled. See also Kurds in Iran, Kurds in Iraq, and Kurds in Syria.

Kurds: Twenty-five ethnically related and distinct people, concentrated mainly on the border areas of Iraq, Syria, Turkey, and Iran, where they want an independent state. Bordering states oppose it, fearing it will destabilize them.

Labor Islamic Alliance (Egypt): Egyptian political party. On the eve of April 1987 parliamentary poll, the semi clandestine Muslims Brotherhood, allied with the opposition Socialist Labor Party and Liberal Socialist Party to form the Labor Islamic Alliance (LSA).

Lakhmids: An Arab dynasty of Yemeni origin established in Iraq by the 5th century and controlling much of Syria from its capital Hira, southeast of modern Najaf. Its rulers were Nestorian Christians, courted simultaneously by the Byzantines and the Sasanians and patronizing famous poets from the Arabian Peninsula.

League of Arab States (est. 1945): Members: Egypt, Syria, Lebanon, Iraq, Transjordan, Saudi Arabia, Yemen.

League of Arab States : see Arab League.

Lebanese National Movement: Lebanese Palestinian political alliance Formed on the eve of the April 1975 October 1990 Lebanese Civil War the Lebanese National Movement was a confederation of various nationalist and progressive Muslim dominated parties. It formed an alliance with the Palestine Liberation Organization PLO in its fight with the Maronite Lebanese Front and the Lebanese Forces. When the LNM-PLO alliance gained the upper hand in the fighting, Syria intervened in June 1976 on the side of the Christians. Its troops expelled LNM-PLO forces from the Christians areas they had captured. Kamal Jumblat's assassination in March 1977 derived the LNM of a charismatic figure. The mantle passed on to his son, Walid who lacked experience and leadership qualities. Israel's siege of Beirut in August 1982 resulted in the departure of both PLO and LNM fighters from West Beirut. This enfeebled the LNM.

Lebanese Syrian Treaty: of Brotherhood cooperation and coordination (1991): The six article Lebanese Syrian Treaty of Brotherhood, Cooperation and Coordination was signed by the presidents of the two countries in Damascus in May 1991. In 2001, Lebanon and Syria created a customs union.

Lebanese-Israeli (Putative) Peace Treaty (1983-84): Under US pressure, President Amin Gemayel soon after assuming office in September 1982, agreed to enter into talks with Israel provided the United states acted as the mediator. In February 1984, Gemayel found himself without his Western guardians. He therefore decided to abrogate the treaty, and at his behest parliament did so almost unanimously on 5 March 1984.

Lebanese-Palestine Liberation Organization Agreement (1969): see Cairo Agreement (Lebanese PLO 1969).

Liberal Socialist Party (Egypt): Egyptian political party. The Liberal Socialist Party was formed in May 1976 by Mustafa Kamel Murad to represent the rightist forum within the Arab Socialist Union. It advocated liberal economic policies and greater freedom for private enterprise. Like its allies in the ISA it boycotted the 1990 election when the government rejected their call to lift the state of emergency and conduct the poll under the supervision of a nongovernmental organization. In the 1995 poll it secured one seat, retaining it in the 2000 election.

Liberation Movement of Iran: Iranian political party. After his release from jail (as a leader of the National Front in 1961, Mahdi Bazargan teamed up with Ayatollah Mahmud Taleani to form the Liberation Movement of Iran. In a parliamentary speech in August, Bazargan, who had opposed the Iranian invasion of Iraq two months earlier, criticized the government for labeling dissidents as heretics. In April 1985 Khomeini dismissed his appeals for a truce with Iraq as demoralizing to the armed forces. Once the Iran Iraq War had ended in 1988 the party lost its strongest card against the government. The death of Bazargan in 1995 caused a decline in the LMI's following.

Lodi: a family of Afghan origin whose rule over northern India (1451 – 1526) marked the last phase of the Delhi sultanate era. Their founder, Bahlul (1451-89), who already had a strong base in the Punjab, took advantage of Sayyid weakness to seize power in Delhi. He and his two successors extended power eastward through Jaunpur to the borders of Bengal and threatened Malwa to the south.

Majlis (Arabic/Persian: Assembly): parliament in Iran; council. Majlis is the popular term that has been used for the Iranian parliament since its inception during the 1906-07 Constitutional Revolution. It is the longest standing elected legislative body in the Middle East. See also Iran: Constitution and Legislature.

Majlis I Shura: Consultative council, parliament

Makhzum: A Meccan clan.

Malawi's: Sufi order, most famous among non-Muslims. they were founded by the poet Rumi (1207-1273), born in Afghanistan. They're known as the "Whirling Dervishes" for their dhikr while turning on one foot.

Maliki code: Sunni Islamic school, the Maliki Code is the canonical school of Sunni Islam founded by Malik ibn Anas Ad 714-96, a jurist resident in Medina. Like other schools it is based on the Quran the Sunna and ijma. The Maliki code's initial dominance of the Arab heartland of Islam gave way to the Shafii Code.

Maliki: The school of law founded by Malik b. Anas in which the principle of compromise was initially extremely important. It was chiefly established in the Maghrib and virtually all Islamic Africa including much of Upper Egypt. Referring to the Sunni Legal madhhabs ascribed to Malik ibn Anasa; school of law founded by Malik ibn Anas (d.795). This school predominates in the Arab West and West Africa.

Marja e Taqlid (Persian: source of Emulation): In Twelver Shiism the idea of a living Mujtahid interpreting the Sharia took hold in the late eighteenth century. Muhammad Baqir Behbehani, a Mujtahid based in Karbala ruled that every believer must choose a Mujtahid to emulate who was given the honorific of marja-e Taqlid. They carried the title of Grand Ayatollah. See also Mujtahid and Titles, Religious (Shi'a Islam).

Maulvi: an honorific Islamic religious title often but not exclusively, given to Muslim religious scholars or Ulema preceding their names. Maulvi generally means any religious cleric or teacher.

Mawali (clients): the name given to the early non-Arab converts to Islam, who had to become nominal clients of one of the tribes when they became Muslims. Clients or associates. Non Arab Muslims. Associates, or clients, status at first given to non Arab converts in Islam. sing. Mawla: clients or associates

Mawali: new-comers to Islam, converts, "clients", to distinguish them from the ruling Arab class.

Mawl'a al-Islam (A): Friends of Islam; master (lord) of Islam

Mevlevi: a Sufi order founded by Mevlana Jalal Ad-Din or Ar-Rumi. Members are sometimes called "whirling dervishes" because of their revolving dance done for spiritual realization. The order of whirling dervishes, followers of Jalal al Din Rumi who spread from Konya through Anatolia and thereafter throughout the Ottoman Empire. The order was pantheistic in tendency and symbolized this in its dances, whirling with the right foot as a pivot to the melancholy music of reed flutes violins and drums or tambourines. The spiritual linage of Mawlana Jalaluddin Rumi; the Sufi order that he founded

Middle East Defense Organization: In an effort to link various Middle Eastern countries in a military alliance against the Soviet Union, London, Backed by Washington, conceived the Middle East Defense Organization as a multilateral defense pact.

Middle East: Early Western geographers divided the East into the Near East the area extending from the Mediterranean Sea to the Persian Gulf, the Middle East (the region extending from the Persian Gulf to southeast Asia); and the Far East (covering the regions facing the Pacific Ocean). But during the Second World War, when the term Middle East was applied to the British military command in Egypt, the traditional definitions underwent a change and the Middle East encompassed the region previously called the Near East. To its south lies Sudan, to its west Arab North Africa, and to its north Turkey and Cyprus. The narrowest definition of the Middle East includes only the core and the wildest the core and its three peripheries.

Middle Eastern Political leaders: Cyrus the Great (600-530bc) Kemal Ataturk (1881-1938), Anwar el Sadat (1918-1981), Mohammed Pahlavi (1919-1980)

Moguls: (or Mughals) A Muslim dynasty of mixed Mongol and Turkish descent that invaded India in 1526, expanded over most of the subcontinent except the extreme south, and ruled in strength until the early 18th century. The first emperor was Babur (1483-1530). He was succeeded by a line of remarkable emperors: Humayun, Akbar, Jahanger, Shah, Jahan, and Aurangzeb. They created a strong administration for the rapidly growing empire, while the official attitude of conciliation towards the majority Hindu population encouraged religious harmony. Culturally, the introduction of the Persian language and Persian artistic styles led to a distinctive indo-Muslim style in miniature painting and architecture, a legacy remaining today in the tombs and palaces of Delhi, Agra, and several other cities of India and Pakistan. In 1857 the last Mogul king was exiled and the title abolished.

Muhammadanism: The name Europeans gave to the religion of Islam in the seventeenth century, thinking that Muslims worshipped Muhammad as god

Monotheists: believers in and worship of only one God; relating to the belief in one Supreme God

Moor: A term commonly used by European authors from the Middle East onwards as a loose synonym for Saracen. The Spanish and Portuguese used it of the Muslim inhabitants of North Africa and of Spain; and then, by extension, applied it to Muslim as distinct from pagans in Africa, and from Hindus in India. However, the term was particularly applied to the Arab conquerors of Spain, who landed first in 710. In 711, under Tariq Ibn Zaid, a Barber army swept the country, and the Visigoth kingdom collapsed. The Moors reached the Pyrenees, and crossed into France. Their defeat near Poitiers in 732 marked the limit of their expansion. The new state of al-Andalus (Andalusia) was consolidated by the Umayyad Amir Abd al-Rahman ibn Mauwiya in 756, and succeeded by a caliphate that lasted from 912 until 1031.

Seville was the first capital, but was superseded by Cordoba in 717. Following the collapse of the caliphate, the state dissolved among the Reyes de Taifas or 'Party Kings' (1031-85), while the Christian kingdoms further north expanded southwards. But in 1090 new North African invaders, the Almoravids, who were primarily fighting men, made themselves supreme. They gave way in 1145 to another Berber group, the Almohads, whose collapse early in the 13th century gave the Christians their opportunity, and by 1235 only the kingdom of Granada remained, covering most of the present Andalusia. Torn by factions, it could not withstand the united monarchy of Ferdinand V (the Catholic) and Isabella who brought an end to Moorish rule in Spain in 1491. The Moorish period in Spain was the zenith of Islamic culture in learning, law, poetry, art, and architecture. The Great mosque of Cordoba and the Alhambra of Granada were among their supreme creations.

Moriscoes: Muslims who sailed with Columbus

Mu'awiya: Son of Abu Sufyan; later became the first Muslim governor of Syria and the first caliph of the Umayyad Dynasty. One of Uthman's relatives; governor of Syria; founder of the Mu'awiyah Dynasty.

Mu'tazilis: Those who stand aloof, theologians belonging to the rationalist school which introduced speculative dogmatism into Islam.

Mu'tazilite: Islamic theological school; started about 2 decades before the coming of the Abbasids; eventually rejected. Moderate withdrawers

Mubaligh: person who recites the Quran

Muezzin: The official on the staff of a pious foundation charged with giving the call to prayer five times a day. Most foundations had two but the mosque madrassa of Sultan Hasan in Cairo had a whole chorus of muezzins.

Mughals: Islamic dynasty in India. King Shah Jahan built the Taj Mahal at Agra (1630-1648) for his wife who died giving birth to their son,

Mumtaz Mahal. The word of "Mongols" in Persian; related to the Turks.

Muhajirin: Those who emigrated from Makka to Medina with Muhammad. See also Hijra. **Muhajirun:** Migrants, those who made the Hijra. The first Muslims that accompanied Muhammad when he traveled to Medina.

Muhamah, The: Islamic Congress; founded by Sheikh Ahmed Yasin in Gaza

Muhammadans: a name often used incorrectly by non-Muslims in referring to followers of Islam (Muslims). The term is unacceptable to Muslims, for it implies that their worship and religion revolve around the man Muhammad.

mujahedeen: combatants in a jihad, name of various militant groups, especially in Iran and Afghanistan and of armed Islamic formations. **Mujahed:** Pl Mujahedin, one who engages in jihad.

Mujahedin-e Islam (Persian: Combatants of Islam): Iranian political party. The Mujahedin e Islam was formed in 1945 by Ayatollah Abol Qasim Kashani a nationalist cleric. His return home in Mid 1950 failed to revive the party, especially as another semi clandestine group, Fedaiyan e Islam had by then struck roots and won Kashani's patronage.

Mujahedin-e Khalq (Persian: The People's Combatants): Iranian political party. Official title: Sazman-e Mujahedin e Khalq e Iran (Iranian People's Combatants' Organization). The Mujahedin ee Khalq was founded secretly in 1965 by young former members of the Liberation Movement who felt that their leaders were too moderate. The party activists started their guerilla actions in August 1971 with a view to disrupting the celebrations of 2,500 years of monarchy in October. In mid 1975 the central committee, dominated by Tehran based leftists, adopted a manifesto that described Islam as "the ideology of the middle classes" and Marxism as "the ideology of the working class," concluding that Marxism was the truly revolutionary creed. Yielding to popular pressure in 1977-78, the government freed most Mujahedin prisoners.

When Mujahedin-e Khalq members refused to surrender their arms to the Islamic government as ordered by Ayatollah Ruhollah Khomeini they came into conflict with the new regime. The party's armed struggle against the Khomeini regime continued with its guerillas led by Musa Khiyabani, targeting revolutionary guards and parliamentarians. With war against Iraq raging along the international border, the Tehran government successfully labeled those creating disorder at home as unpatriotic agents of Baghdad.. After Khomeini's death in June 1989, Iraqi President Saddam Hussein halted all anti Iranian activities including hostile broadcasts of the Mujahedin e Khalq radio in order to improve relations with post Khomeini Iran. In October 1997 Washington declared the Mujahedin e Khalq a terrorist organization, thus barring it from collecting funds in America its chief source of income. During the Gulf War III the Mujahedin military bases were hit but not destroyed by as yet unidentified forces. The US signed a cease fire agreement with it which required it to disarm. With this its future became uncertain. Person who strives in the cause of Allah.

Mujahid: (pl. **mujahidin**): soldier of God. Soldier fighting a holy war or jihad.

Mujahideen: Arabic for "those who strive"; a term used to refer to holy warriors engaged in battles throughout the world to advance their vision of Islam

Mujtahid: (*Arabic: one who strives*) A Mujtahid is one who practices Ijtihad and the term applies to both Sunni and Shi'a clerics. In Twelver Shiism, the idea of a living Mujahid interpreting the Sharia took hold in the late 18th century. In the Shi'a world the honorific "Mujtahid" was replaced by "ayatollah" around the time of the 1907-11 Constitutional Revolution in Iran. In 2000 there were twenty-seven ayatollahs in that country. A jurist who has earned the right to exercise **ijtihad (q.v.),** usually in the Shii world. A person qualified to undertake **ijtihad.** A scholar who uses reason for the purpose of forming an opinion or making a ruling on a religious issue. Plural: Mujtahidun. A Shi'i cleric recognized as competent to deliver independent opinions on matters relating to the *Shari'ah*. Muslim scholars qualified to use their knowledge of the Holy Qur'an as a source for legal decisions.

Mukhabarat: (*Arabic" lit., intelligence; fig., organization collection information*) Mukhabarat is the popular term used in Arab countries for the intelligence apparatus both at home and abroad. In addition, there is *Amn al Askariya (Arabic: Military Security)*. The generic term Mukhabarat covers up to five intelligence agencies.

Multi National Force (In Lebanon, 1982-84): Following a seventy day siege of Beirut during the 1982 Israeli invasion of Lebanon, an agreement was brokered in August by the US between Israel, Syria, and Lebanon that a Multi National Force composed of about 1,200 troops each from the US, France, and Italy would be deployed to ensure the safe withdrawal of Palestine Liberation Organization and Syrian forces from West Beirut. On 13 September president elect Bashir Gemayel was assassinated. Between 16 and 18 Christian Phalangist militiamen killed some 2,000 men, women and children in the Palestinian camps of Sabra and Shatila in Beirut. About a year later the UD and France intervened with warplanes and warships in the Lebanese Civil War on the side of the Maronite dominated Lebanese Army. Washington ordered the withdrawal of its troops from Beirut and London, Rome, and Paris followed suit. The MNF withdrawal was completed by 31 March 1984.

Multinational Force and Observers (1979): To ensure compliance with the provisions of the 1979 Egyptian Israeli Peace Treaty concerning the level of forces of the two neighbors in and near the Sinai Observers of 2,600 troops from eleven countries was posted in the peninsula in August 1981.

Muluk Al-Tawa'f: Party kings

Mu'minin: believers

Munafiqin: Hypocrites

Munazamat: organization Minkar: vicegerent Muqawama: resistance

Murabiteen (Almoravids): Fanatical Berber Muslims from Morocco, crossed to Spain in 1086 and defeated Alfonso VI; the Spaniard's Sagrajas – Christians.

Murabitun: (Arabic: Faithful of the Sermon): Lebanese militia. Formed in the early 1970s by Ibrahim Qulaylat, the Murabitun was the armed wing of the Independent Nasserite Movement. Opposed to the traditional Sunni leadership the Beirut Based INM had its following among poor Sunnis. Following the end of the civil war in October 1990 it was dissolved along with other militias.

Mushrikun: Idol worshippers, pagans.

Muslim Brotherhood (Egypt): Egyptian political religious party. Official title: Ikhwan al Muslimin (Arabic: Brotherhood of Muslims). In 1928 Hassan al ?Banna established the Muslim Brotherhood as a youth club committed to effecting moral and social reform though information and propaganda. During the Second World War the Brotherhood's ranks swelled with student, civil servants, artisan, petty traders and middle income peasants. After the war the Brotherhood participated in an escalating Anti British struggle. In 1946 the party claimed 500,000 members with as many sympathizers, organized among 5,000 branches. Its volunteers fought in the 1948-49 Palestine War. Many Egyptian officers picked up the Brotherhood ideology and the Brethren acquired military training from them.

Blaming Egypt's political establishment for the debacle in the 1948-49 conflict the Brotherhood resorted to terrorist and subversive activities. Supporting the government's abrogation of the Anglo Egyptian Treaty, it declared a campaign against the British occupiers and participated in the January 1952 riots in Cairo. On 23 October a Brotherhood activist Abdul Munim Abdul Rauf, tried unsuccessfully to assassinate President Gamal Abdul Nasser. He and five other Brethren were executed and more than 4,000 party activists were arrested. Several thousand brethren fled to Syria, Saudi Arabia, Jordan, and Lebanon. The humiliating defeat the Israelis inflicted on Egypt in June 1967 created a popular feeling that God had punished Arabs for turning away from their faith and tinkering with alien concepts such as Arab socialism.

Sensing a change in the popular mood, Nasser released 1,000 Brethren in April 1968. Reversing Nasser's policies, President Anwar Sadat promised that the Sharia would be the chief source of legislation and released all Brotherhood prisoners. Most of the nearly 2,000 dissidents arrested in September 1981 were Brethren or other Islamic fundamentalists. On 6 October Sadat was assassinated by four Islamist soldiers. In the 1987 elections the Brotherhood allied with the opposition Socialist Labor Party and the Liberal Socialist Party to form the Labor Islamic Alliance. During the Kuwait crisis and the Gulf War, the Brotherhood, a traditional ally of Saudi Arabia, largely supported Iraqi President Saddam Hussein.

Muslim Brotherhood (Jordan): Jordanian religious body with a political wing, called the Islamic action front. During his visits to Jordan between 1942 and 1945, Hassan al Banna set up Muslim brotherhood branches in many towns. Since King Hussein of Jordan was one of the Arab leaders Nasser tried to overthrow, the Jordanian Brotherhood turned increasingly pro Hussein. During the decade after the June 1967 Arab Israeli War with the star of Saudi Arabia rising in the Arab East, King Hussein grew closer to Riyadh for financial and ideological reasons and began co opting Brotherhood leaders into his regime. It opposed the Jordanian Israeli Peace Treaty signed in October 1994. In the 1997 general election it won eight seats.

Muslim brotherhood (Palestine): Religious political organization in Palestine/the West bank and Gaza. During his visits to Palestine between 1942 and 1945, Hassan al Banna set up Muslim Brotherhood branched in many towns. After the 1948-49 Palestine War, the Gaza Strip came under Egyptian authority and the West Bank was annexed by Jordan. After the June 1967 Arab Israeli War. Israel occupied the West Bank and Gaza. In order to weaken the Palestine Liberation Organization in the Occupied Territories in 1973 Israel issued a license to Shaikh Ahmad Yassin, the brotherhood leader in the Occupied Territories, to set up the Islamic Center as a charity to run social, religious and welfare institutions. With eruption of the intifada in December 1987, Yassin and six other leaders of the Brotherhood decided to join the mass movement against the Israeli occupiers. The result was the founding of Hamas as the activist arm of the Brotherhood.

Muslim Brotherhood (Saudi Arabia): Following the dissolution of the Muslim Brotherhood in Egypt in 1954, hundreds of Brethren took refuge in Saudi Arabia. In their struggle against Nasser and Nasserism, the Saudi monarchs began to fund the Brotherhood in different Arab Countries, a practice that continued after Nasser's death in 1970 until the Second Gulf War in 1991.

Muslim Brotherhood (Syria): The Muslim Brotherhood in Syria emerged in the mid 1930s when Syrian students of theology returning from Egypt began to form branches in different cities under the title Shabah Muhammad (Youths of Muhammad). Following the dissolution of Egypt's Muslim Brotherhood in 1954, many Egyptian activists took refuge in Syria and strengthened and radicalized the local variant. When Syria joined Egypt in 1958 to form the United Arab Republic and the ban on political parties in Egypt was extended to Syria, the Brotherhood was formally dissolved. The Arab defeat in the June 1967 Arab Israeli War split the party into moderates, advising caution and radicals advocating a jihad against the Ba'athists. When Hafiz Assad became president in late 1971 the Brotherhood attacked the regime strongly because Assad was an Alawi. Pro Brotherhood clerics demanded that Islam be declared the state religion.

Antigovernment rioting followed. Assad compromised by directing parliament to specify that the head of state must be Muslim and it complied. He described the October 1973 Arab Israeli War as a jihad against the enemies of Islam and referred to the Syrian troops as the soldiers of Allah. In early 1974 he undertook an Umra to Mecca. Later, Imam Musa al Sadr an eminent Shi'a theologian, issued a religious verdict that Alawis were part of Shi'a Islam. The Brotherhood called strikes in Aleppo and Hama which paralyzed those cities. Assad dispatched elite troops to these cities. They arrested some 5,000 people and summarily executed several hundred. The protest petered out. Another wave of official retribution followed an unsuccessful assassination attempt on Assad on 25 June 1980. In 1998 Hafiz Assad freed some Brotherhood leaders. And soon after succeeding his father, Bashar Assad ordered more releases.

Muslim Brotherhood: a movement founded in Egypt that has as its ultimate goal the restoration of an Islamic caliphate, or political unification of the Muslim **Ummah.**

Muslim brothers: In Arabic, al-Ikhwan al-Muslim in, a militant, radical, Islamist movement. Founded in 1928 by the Egyptian schoolmaster Hasan al Banna, it has become the most powerful opposition group in Arab and other Muslim countries. The Muslim Brothers have been particularly active in opposing secular regimes even anti Western nationalists regimes, seen by them as undermining the faith. In December 1948, they were accused of responsibility for the assassination of the Egyptian Prime Minister, Mahmud Fahmi al Nuqrashi, as well as some other assassinations. Severe measures were taken against them. In 1966, Sayyid Qutb, one of the intellectual leaders of the movement and a major figure in modern Islamist thought, was executed in Egypt on a charge of plotting the assassination of President Nasser. An even more dramatic clash occurred in the Syrian city of Hama in 1982. The troubles began with an uprising headed by the local Muslim Brothers. The Syrian government responded swiftly and violently, first attacking the city with tanks, artillery, and bomber aircraft, and following these with bulldozers to complete the work of destruction.

A large part of the city was reduced to rubble and the number killed was estimated by Amnesty International at somewhere between 10,000 and 25,000. Curiously an significantly at the time this evoked little comment and less protest in the Muslim world or in the wider international community. Since then there has been no comparable massacre, but the party's political activities, such as participation in elections, have been subject to obstruction and harassment. More recently, the leaders of the Muslim Brothers have sought to differentiate themselves from more violent and terrorist Islamic groups, preferring rather to portray themselves as peaceful and even as democratic reformists.

Muslim League: An Indian political party founded in 1905 to represent the interests of Muslims, many of whom felt threatened by the prospect of a Hindu majority in any future democratic system. The radical nationalists' elements in the League forged a pact with the Congress in 1916 on the basis of separate electorates and reserved seats in Muslim minority provinces. In 1940 it put forward the demand for an autonomous Muslim homeland, Pakistan. Its leader, M. A. Jinnah, subsequently demanded that this be a fully independent state during the negotiations to end British rule in India and called for a Direct Action Day in August 196. Mass rioting followed, whereupon the British and the Congress agreed to partition India. The League was virtually wiped out at the first elections in Pakistan.

Muslims: The collectors of an authoritative anthology of Hadith reports. (Muslim): " a person who is surrendering to God and finding peace." A follower of the religion of Islam. (noun): an adherent of Islam; (adj.): pertaining to Muslims. Member of the Ummah, or worldwide community of Muslims.

Mustadafeen: the disinherited

Mutawiyin: Volunteers, enforcers of Wahhabism in Saudi Arabia

Mu'tazilah: (Arabic) the Muslim sect which attempted to explain the Koran in rational terms. **Mu'tazilis:** Rationalists. **Mu'tazilite:** an extreme conservative sect in early Islam.

Muwahhideen (Almohades): A Moroccan Berber sect.

Muwahhidun: (Arabic: Unitarianism): See Wahhabism and Wahhabis.

Nadha Al Islamia: Islamic movement

Nadir: A Jewish tribe of Medina; Muhammad besieged and exiled themselves Nakhla: An Arabian town where the Muslims carried out their first military raid against the Quraysh

Naqshbandi: A Sufi Muslim group that considers it vital to adhere to Prophet Muhammad's example. established by Muhammad Bahaudin Naqshband, born near Bukhara in 1317. **Naqshbandiyyah:** A Sufi order established by Khwajah Naqshband. Sufi order (mysticism).

Nasab: Family, lineage, descent. Pedigree: among the father and a variable list of ancestors, each name being introduced by the word ibn, "son of." This is also written bin and Ben and is often abbreviated to b. The feminine is bint. Writers may quote as many generations as they feel to be necessary, and in extreme cases, will go all the way back to Adam. The usual practice is to give one or two; e.g. Ali b. Muhammad b. Ahmed= Ali son of Muhammad, son of Ahmad. It is not uncommon for an ancestor in the list to be mentioned by a name other than his Ism; e.g. Ali b. Abi Talib= Ali the son of Abu Talib (the father of Talib).

Nasara: The Islamic term for Christian. It comes from the name Nazareth. It is also related to the term for **helper**, which is how Jesus' disciples are viewed in the Qur'an .

Nation of Islam: Islamic movement which asserts superiority of black people; not considered true Islam; founded by Wallace Fark Muhammad in Detroit, succeeded by Elijah Muhammad. Splinter group of the Black Muslim Movement, formed in 1985 by the radical African-American preacher Louis Farrakhan (1933--), who trained as a teacher and was converted to Islam by Malcolm X. the Nation of Islam was the original name of the Black Muslims (disbanded in 1985 by the son of their founder Elijah Muhammad) and was adopted by Farrakhan to proclaim his group's adherence to the ideals of the movement, in particular Black separatism. In 1995, a 'million-man' march on Washington DC was attended by around 400,000 supporters.

National and Progressive Front (Lebanon): In 1969 Kamal Jumblat established the National and Progressive Front, consisting of leftist Lebanese parties and major Palestinian groups based in Lebanon.

National Consultative assembly (Iran): see Majlis

National Cultural club: (Kuwait): In 1953 Ahmad Khatib formed the National Cultural Club (NCC) as a front for the Arab Nationalist Movement. It did well in the local elections held in 1954.

National Democratic Assembly Balad: Israeli Arab political party. Established in 1999 by Azmi Bishara the National Democratic Assembly-Balad aims to change Israel from a Jewish state into a democratic state according equal treatment to all its citizens, Jews and Arabs alike. It advocated Israel's withdrawal from all the Occupied Arab Territories and the establishment of an independent Palestinian state in the Occupied Territories with East Jerusalem as its capital.

National Democratic Front (North Yemen): North Yemeni political party. In 1976 the Revolutionary Democratic party, the Marxist Democratic Party of Popular Unity, and the Ba'athists secretly merged to form the National Democratic Front under the leadership of Sultan Ahmad Omar. The NDP welcomes the unity of the two Yemen's in 1990. In the general election of 1993 it won four seats in a house of 301.

National Democratic Party (Egypt): The National Democratic Party NDP was founded by President Anwar Sadat in August 1978 after the parliament at his behest, had outlawed wide ranging political activities such as preaching Marxism and class struggle, advocating laissez faire capitalism, demanding a religion based state. Following the Camp David Accords in September 1978 Sadat appointed Khalil as premier and became the NDP's president. In the 2000 poll it won 176 places with a further 212 deputies having been elected as independent joining the party later.

National front (Iran): Iranian political party. In 1949 the Iran Party and the Democrat Party combined to form the National Front under the leadership of Muhammad Mussadiq. When the shah fled in mid August 1953 the party split with one section calling for a republic and the other for a constitutional monarchy. In February 1979 Premier Mahdi Bazargan appointed Karim Sanjabi, the NF leader as foreign minister. He resigned after the occupation of the US Embassy in Tehran by militant students in November.

National Front for the Liberation of South Yemen: see National Liberation Front (South Yemen).

National Guard (Saudi Arabia): An armed force drawn from the most loyal of the tribes in Saudi Arabia, the National Guard was the new name given to the White Guard after the dissolution of the Ikhwan. As the kingdom's most reliable armed force, the National Guard deals with anything that remotely threatens the regime be it a strike, a demonstration, a tribal revolt, or disaffection in the military. In 2003 it had 75,000 active troops and 25,000 reserves. Its arms included 730 armored personnel carriers and 70 major artillery pieces.

National Liberal Party (Lebanon): Camille Chamoun established the National Liberal Party soon after stepping down as president in September 1958. During the initial phase of the 1975-90. Lebanese Civil War in the NLP cooperated with the Phalange in building up the infrastructure of a state in the Christian area, with its capital in Jounieh, working for a decentralized unity of Lebanon and strengthening links with Israel. After Chamoun's death in August 1987 the mantle of NLP leadership passed to his son Danny. In August 1990 he backed Gen. Michel Aoun when the latter challenged parliament's power to alter the constitution and pass reform laws. Danny Shaman and his family were murdered in the aftermath of Aoun's defeat in mid October 1990.

National Liberation Front (South Yemen): South Yemeni political party. Official title: National Front for the Liberation of South Yemen. The National Liberation front was set up in Sanaa, North Yemen in early 1963 to achieve independence from Britain through an armed struggle. In October a unification congress decided to weld the NLF, the Ba'athist Vanguard Party and the Marxist Popular Democratic Union into the United Political Organization, National Front to be reconstituted as the Yemen Socialist Party in 1978.

National Liberation Front: Algerian political party

National Pact, 1943 (Lebanon): Constitutional agreement in March 1943, prodded by the British, the Free French, led by Charles de Gaulle-who had retaken Lebanon from the pro German French Government in June 1941 with British assistance-restored Lebanon's 1926 constitution. Gen. Edward Spears, the British representative in Beirut, mediated between feuding Muslims and Christians about the apportioning of parliamentary seats.

National Progressive and Patriotic Front (Iraq): Iraqi political alliance. In July 1973, on the fifth anniversary of the Ba'athist coup, the parties that had signed the National Action Charter formed the National Progressive and Patriotic Front. When parliamentary elections were introduces in 1980, only NPPF constituents were allowed to contest.

National Progressive Front (Syria): Syrian political alliance. The national Progressive Front, formed in March 1972 on the ninth anniversary of the Ba'athist revolution, comprised the Baath party, the Communist Party, the Arab Socialist Union, the Arab Socialist movement and the Organization of Socialist Unionists. (OSU). In the 2003 election the total was the same. 167 divided among the constituents almost as before.

National Progressive Unionist Alliance (Egypt): Egyptian political party. When in May 1976 the government allowed the political role of the Arab Socialist Union to be taken over by three tribunes, the leftist forum was represented by the National Progressive Unionist Alliance. At the next election in 1995 its strength rose to five and then to six in 2000 when the party leadership claimed 160,000 members.

National Reconciliation Charter 1989: (Lebanon): The National Reconciliation Charter is the document adopted by the Lebanese parliamentarians at their session in Taif, Saudi Arabia, In October 1989 to resolve the issues at the core of the Lebanese Civil War. By accepting Syria's continued presence for at least two years after the national unity government had agreed on constitutional reform, Christian deputies provided Syria with legitimacy-something it had lost with the expiration of the 1976 Arab League mandate in mid 1982 and conceded Syria's strategic concerns in Lebanon. Implementation began in August 1990. The civil war ended in October and to implement the next stage of the charter a second national unity government was formed in late December 1990. Its main task was to effect the administration decentralization stipulated by the charter.

National Resistance Council (Iran): Iranian political alliance. Following their escape from Iran to Paris in July 1981, Abol Hassan Bani Sadr and Masud Rajavi, head of the Mujahedin-e Khalq formed the National Resistance Council to oppose violently the Islamic regime of Iran. With the Iran Iraq War dragging on, the NRC concentrated on this issue advocating an immediate cease fire and blaming Ayatollah Ruhollah Khomeini for continuing the conflict in order to divert public attention away from worsening domestic problems. Following the weakening of the Baghdad based Mujahedin-e Khalq due to the Gulf War III the NRC's future became more uncertain.

National Unity Front: (Qatar): Qatari political party. The National Unity Front was formed in 1963 to channel the discontent Qatari citizens felt at the squandering of oil wealth by the ruling al Thani clan coupled with its tight grip over political and economic power.

Neo Wafd Party : Egyptian political party. The Neo Wafd Party was established by Fuad Serag al Din, a veteran of the Wafd Party in early 1978 when he won the loyalty of twenty two parliamentarians thus meeting the legal requirements for new political groups. Serag al Don was one of the opposition leaders to be rounded up by Sadat three years later. President Hosni Mubarak reversed Sadat's policy and the Neo Wafd reemerged in August 1983. On the death of Serag al Din during that year, Numan Jumaah became the party leader.

Niyazi Misri: Sufi Order

Nizam Shahi: Muslim dynasty of Ahmadnagar, based in the north-western Indian Deccan region, that flourished from 1490 to 1637. Its founder was Malik Ahmad who revolted against the Bahmanis and set up an independent kingdom centered on a new capital, Ahmadnagar, which took its founder's name. His main achievement was the conquest of Daulatad (1499). He and his successors then engaged in almost constant warfare. After abandoning an alliance with the Hindu kingdom of Vijayanagar, they participated in the final destruction of that city in 1565. The dynasty presented spirited resistance to subsequent Mogul encroachment into its territories but had lost all independent existence by 1637.

Nizari Islamis: A violent sect that plagued the Abbasid caliphs; an offshoot of the Shi'a, also known as "The Assassins". **Nizari:** The largest and most active group of the Isma'ili sect of Islam. They are named after Nizar, the eldest son of the Fatimid Caliph al Mustansir (died 1094). When Nizar's younger brother succeeded to the Fatimid caliphate in Cairo, they became an opposition group in exile. There were active in the Yemen, then in Iran, Syria and other places. In India and Pakistan, they are known as Khojas. The most celebrated branch was that of the militant medieval group known in the West as the Assassins. At the present time, Nizari communities are found in Central Asia, the Indian subcontinent, the Middle East as well as émigré communities in Africa and North America. A neo-Islami assassin sect, founded by Hasan-i-Sabbah.

Non-fundamentalist: in modern times, a traditionalist, a reformist, or a secularist.

North Yemeni Civil War (1962-70): Following the overthrow of Imam Muhammad al Badr by pan Arabist military officers in September 1962, Egyptian President Gamal Abdul Nasser agreed to help the republican side which commanded only 6,000 troops. Having placed the republican president, Abdullah Sallal under house arrest in Cairo, Nasser King Faisal in Jiddah. Following the Egyptian debacle in the June 1967 Arab Israeli war, Nasser agreed with the Saudi King to pull out his troops from North Yemen by December 1967. By early 1969 Riyadh had ceased to back al Badr militarily. In March 1970 President al Iryani reached an agreement with Riyadh whereby Saudi subsidies to the royalists were stopped. The eight year conflict caused come 200,000 deaths.

North Yemeni Soviet Friendship Treaty (1984): It was signed by President Ali Abdullah Salih and Kostantin Chernenko in Moscow. **Nubians:** A people who live chiefly in Egypt and the Sudan, between the First and Fourth Cataracts of the River Nile, Their recorded history begins with raids by Egyptians c. 2613 BC, when their country was called Kush. Then a Nubian dynasty ruling at Napata from c. 920 BC conquered all Egypt. The Nubian Shabaka ruled as King of Kush and Egypt with Thebes as his capital but Assyrians forced Taharka, his successor, to withdraw (680-669 BC). After several further struggles, the Nubians drew back to Napata, and c. 530 BC their capital moved to Meroe. The dynasty continued until 350 AD, when Aezanas of Axum destroyed it; its 300 pyramids remain. Nubia was converted to Christianity in c. 540 AD. Three Christian kingdoms emerged, but in 652 AD an Egyptian army conquered that at Dongola, granting peace for an annual tribute of slaves and at the end of the 13th century Mamluks took the north. The southern kingdom survived until the 16th century, when the Funj kingdom of Sennar absorbed it.

Oau: Organization of African Unity.

OIC: Organization of the Islamic Conference

OPEC: (Organization of Petroleum Exporting Countries). An international organization seeking to regulate the price of oil. The first moves to establish closer links between oil-producing countries were made by Venezuela, Iran, Iraq, Kuwait, and Saudi Arabia in 1949. In 1960, following a reduction in the oil price by the international oil companies, a conference was held in Baghdad of representative from these countries, when it was decided to set up a permanent organization. This was formed in Caracas, Venezuela, the next year. Other countries later joined: Qatar (1961, Indonesia (1962), Libya (1962), United Arab Emirates (1967), Algeria (1969), Nigeria (1971), Ecuador (1973), and Gabon (1975). Ecuador left OPEC n 1993 and Gabon withdrew in 1996. OPEC's activities extend through all aspects of oil negotiations, including basic oil price, royalty rates, production quotas, and government profits. The Organization of Arab Petroleum Exporting Countries (OAPEC), based in Kuwait, was established in 1968, to co-ordinate the different aspects of the Arab petroleum industry, and safeguard its members' interests.

Orientalist: The term used to describe Western Christian and Jewish scholars who made the study of Islam their vocation in the nineteenth and twentieth century's.

Organization of African Unity: (OAU) An association of African states. It was founded in 1963 to promote unity and solidarity among African states and the elimination of colonialism. All African states have at one time belonged. The leaders of 32 African countries signed its charter at a conference in Addis Ababa in 1963. There is an annual assembly of heads of state and government, a council of ministers, a general secretariat, and a commission or mediation, conciliation, and arbitration. The 1991 Assembly in Abuja, Nigeria, agreed on the creation of an African Economic Community (AEC). In 1994, South Africa was admitted as the 53rd member of the organization.

Organization of Arab Petroleum Exporting Countries: The organization of Arab Petroleum Exporting Countries was formed in Kuwait in January 1968 in the aftermath of the Arab Defeat in the June 1967 Arab Israeli War and consisted of Algeria, Iraq, Kuwait, Libya and Saudi Arabia. During the October 1973 Arab Israeli War, OAPEC members, reacting to US President Richard Nixon's order to airlift weapons to Israel on a massive scale, decided on 17 October to cut output by 5 percent of the September figure and to maintain the same rate of reduction each month until the Israeli forces had withdrawn from all Arab territories occupied during the 1967 war and the Palestinians legitimate rights had been restored. The embargo hurt the United States, reducing its annual gross domestic product by 10-20 billion. Following the Egyptian Israeli Peace Treaty in 1979, Egypt was suspended from OAPEC's membership. It was readmitted ten years later. During the Iraqi occupation of Kuwait in 1990-91, the OAPEC headquarters was moved to Cairo. After the Second Gulf War the headquarters returned to Kuwait.

Organization of Islamic conference: see Islamic conference

Organization.

Organization of Petroleum Exporting Countries: OPEC.

Organization of Petroleum Exporting Countries: The organization of Petroleum Exporting Countries is an international body to coordinate the hydrocarbon policies of its constituents. Following a meeting in Baghdad in September 1960 of the representatives of Iran, Iraq, Kuwait, Saudi Arabia, and Venezuela, it was formally inaugurated to January 1961 in Geneva. Its subsequent members included Watar, Indonesia and Libya, Abu Dhabi, which transferred to the United Arab emirates in 1974, Algeria in 1969, Nigeria in 1971, Ecuador in 1973 and Gabon in 1975. In 1970 Libya's year old republican regime imposed production cuts on oil companies as a pressure tactic to secure higher taxes and royalties.

Organization of the Islamic Conference: Founded in 1969, it is composed of 57 states. Its declared purpose is to strengthen solidarity and cooperation among Islamic state in the political, economic, cultural, scientific and social fields. Under its charter, it also aims to safeguard the Holy Places, support the struggle of the Palestine people, and work to eliminate racial discrimination and all forms of colonialism. A not insignificant number of states were accepted as members on the basis of Muslim minorities; these include two states in the Western hemisphere-Surinam and Guyana-admitted to membership in 1996 and 1998, respectively. One member, Albania, is in Europe; the remainder are in Asia and Africa. The Turkish Cypriot Authority and Bosnia Herzegovina were admitted to observer status in 1979 and 1994, respectively. The Palestine Authority was admitted to full membership from the very beginning of the organization in 1969.

Organization of the Islamic Revolution in the Arabian Peninsula: In the course of rioting in late November 1979 during the Ashura processions by Shi'as in the eastern region of Saudi Arabia, the existence of the Shi'a dominated Organization of the Islamic Revolution in the Arabian Peninsula came to light. Despite the repression suffered by the OIRAP with its leader, Said Saffran, forced into exile in Iran, it continued to operate secretly.

Oriental Jews: The term applied to non Ladino speaking Jews from the Arab countries, Iran, India or Central Asia. In biblical times their ancestors left Palestine for North Africa or the Middle East from where they migrated to Central Asia or the Indian subcontinent. In the late 1960s the 1.5 million Oriental Jews formed about one ninth of the world's Jewry. But due to the influx of 540,000 Jews from the former Soviet Union from 1990-1994. However to describe someone originating in Morocco, Algeria or Tunisia part of the Arab West as Oriental is inexact. The most logical and ethnically correct, term is Arab Jew which parallels European Jew or American Jew.

Ottoman: name of Turkish dynasty descended from Othman, 1281-1924. **Ottoman:** The name of a Muslim dynasty that ruled over the Middle East and part of Europe until 1918. Turkish dynasty originating as a minor principality in western Turkey in the late 13th century. Their first historical ruler, Osman/Uthman extended their dominions to Bursa which long remained their capital. It was transferred to Edirne/Adrianople in the 15th century but in 1453 was moved to Constantinople on its fall to Mehmed II.

Outremer: A Christian kingdom based in Jerusalem, established by the Crusades (1096-1291)

PELP: Popular front of the Liberation of Palestine; directed by Christian George Habash.

PLO: Palestine Liberation Organization: A political and military body formed in 1964 to unite various Palestinian Arab groups in opposition to the Israeli presence in the former territory of Palestine. From 1967 the organization was dominated by al-Fatah, led by Yasser Arafat. The activities of its radical factions caused trouble with its host country, Jordan, and, following a brief internal war in 1970, it moved to Lebanon and Syria. In 1974 the organization was recognized by the Arab nations as the representative of all Palestinians. The Israeli invasion of Lebanon (1982) undermined its military power and organization, and it regrouped in Tunisia. Splinter groups of extremists, such as the 'Popular Front for the Liberation of Palestine' and the 'Black September' terrorists have been responsible for kidnappings, hijackings, and killings both in and beyond the Middle East. In 1988 Arafat persuaded the movement to renounce violence and its governing council recognized the state of Israel. The PLO was then accepted by an increasing number of states as being a government in exile. It took part in the US-sponsored Middle East peace talks in 1992, in spite of East Jerusalem's representative being rejected by Israel. Following secret negotiation, a peace agreement was concluded in 1993 between the PLO and the Israeli government. As part of this accord, the PLO renounced terrorism, but has been accused of supporting other militant groups, such as Hamas.

Pahlavi Dynasty: Following a law passed in the spring of 1925, which required all Iranian citizens to acquire a birth certificate and a surname, Reza Khan, then Iran's prime minister and commander in chief, chose for his family the name Pahlavi, the language of Persians for seven centuries. The Pahlavi rule lasted until January 1979, when Muhammad Reza Shah Pahlavi left the country. He died in exile the following year. **Pahlavi Dynasty:** Iran (1925-1979); founded by Reza Khan; ended by the Islamic Revolution in 1979.

Palestine Liberation Army: The Palestine Liberation Army the military wing of the Palestine Liberation Organization was established in 1964. After the PLO moved to Beirut in 1972 the PLA consisted of 8,000-10,000 troops, organized into three brigades, two of which were integrated into the Syrian army. In the Lebanese Civil War between October 1975 and January 1976 Syrian President Hafiz Assad dispatched two brigades of the Syrian officered PLA from Damascus to Lebanon to help the PLO Lebanese National Movement alliance. After the June 1982 Israeli invasion the Palestinian forces that left Beirut in early September included 3,500 PLA troops. The estimated strength of Palestinian troops stationed in other Arab countries was 8,000. Later most of them returned to the Palestinian areas controlled by the PA.

Palestine Liberation Organization (PLO): a political and military body formed in 1964 to unite various Palestinian Arab groups in opposition to the Israeli presence in the former territory of

Palestine. From 1967 the organization was dominated by al-Fatah, led by Yasser Arafat. The activities of its radical factions caused trouble with its host country, Jordan, and, following a brief internal war in 1970, it moved to Lebanon and Syria. In 1974 the organization was recognized by the Arab nations as the representative of all Palestinians. The Israeli invasion of Lebanon (1982) undermined its military power and organization, and it regrouped in Tunisia. Splinter groups of extremists, such as the 'Popular Front for the Liberation of Palestine' and the 'Black September' terrorists have been responsible for kidnappings, hijackings, and killings both in and beyond the Middle East.

In 1988 Arafat persuaded the movement to renounce violence and its governing council recognized the state of Israel. The PLO was then accepted by an increasing number of states as being a government in exile. It took part in the US-sponsored Middle East peace talks in 1992, in spite of East Jerusalem's representative being rejected by Israel. Following secret negotiation, a peace agreement was concluded in 1993 between the PLO and the Israeli government. As part of this accord, the PLO renounced terrorism, but has been accused of supporting other militant groups, such as Hamas.

Palestine National Charter: Though originally adopted by the Palestine National Council at its inaugural session in East Jerusalem in May-June 1964, the Palestine National Charter became significant in July 1968 when the fourth PNC congress in Cairo inserted the statement Armed struggle is the only way to liberate Palestine. Official title: National Council of the Palestine Liberation Organization. Founded in May 1964 in East Jerusalem with 350 delegates representing the various groups affiliated to the PLO the Palestine National Council was inaugurated by King Hussein of Jordan. Any Palestinian Arab Born in Palestine before 1947 or born of a Palestinian father after that, irrespective of his her birthplace, was entitled to PNC membership. The expulsion of the PLO from Beirut in September 1982, followed by the conflict between Arafat and Syrian President Hafiz Assad had a divisive impact on the PNC. A letter that Yasser Arafat had addressed to US President Bill Clinton in January revoking all those paragraphs of the Charter that clashed with the 1993 Oslo I Accord.

Palestine National Fund: The Palestine National fund was set up by the Palestine Liberation Organization to meet its financial requirements.

Palestine National Liberation Army: See Palestine Liberation Army.

Palestine People's Party: See Communist Party of Palestine.

Palestinian Authority: The Palestinian Authority is the name of the legislative and executive body responsible for exercising all powers and functions devolved by Israel to the autonomous Palestinian areas under the Oslo Accord I in September 1993. According to the law passed by the PLC its tenure is to expire when Israel had implemented all its obligations under the Oslo Accord II originally by September 1998. Within a year the PLC passed a draft constitution which Arafat would sign only in 2002. With the election of Benjamin Netanyahu as Israel's prime minister in 1996, the Oslo Accords suffered a hemorrhage from, which they did not recover during 1999-2001 when Ehud Barak was the chief executive of Israel. Following the outbreak of the Second Intifada backed by all the Palestinian parties in September 2000, Israel hit the PA headquarters in Gaza and the West Bank.

Palestinian National Authority: This is the term used by some Palestinians for the Palestinian authority.

Pan Arabism: Pan Arabism is a doctrine that maintains that no matter where Arabs live they are part of a single community. It first manifested itself in the Arab territory of the Ottoman Empire from 1876-78 when a written constitution, promulgated by Sultan Abdul Hamid II, provided some element of free expression. Following the 1948-49 Palestine War and the establishment of Israel, pan Arabism centered on the Arab struggle for the retrieval of Palestine from the Zionists. With the Free Officers successful coup in Egypt in 1952 the mantle of pan Arab leadership fell on Gamal Abdul Nasser president of the most populous an strategic Arab country. Nasser's first step toward creating a unified Arab state in 1958, the merger of Egypt and Syria into the United Arab Republic failed three years later. Yet on the eve of the June 1967 Arab Israeli war, he was able to lead a joint military command of Egypt Syria and Jordan. The military alliance of Egypt and Syria in October 1973 backed by the military and oil muscle of the rest of the Arab world, was the next manifestation of pan Arabism. In 1991 the military regime in Algeria struck a blow against pan Islamism by aborting the imminent electoral victory of the Front for Islamic Salvation.

Pan-Africanist Congress: South African political movement. A militant off-shoot of the African National Congress (ANC), it was formed in 1995 by Robert Sobukwe. He advocated forceful methods of political pressure and in 1960 sponsored the demonstration at Sharpeville, in which 67 Black Africans were killed and 180 wounded by police. The South African government outlawed both the PAC and the ANC and imprisoned Sobukwe and other leaders.

Pan-Arabism: a movement seeking to unite the Arab nations of the Middle East and North Africa.

Pan-Islam: the drive to unify Muslims; in modern times, to foster cooperation between them.

Parsi: (Parsee) the name given to the Indian followers of the ancient Persian religion of Zoroastrianism. The Parsis emigrated to India from Iran in about the 8th-10th centuries, to avoid persecution by Muslims. Their belief and worship are based on the *Avesta*, the scripture attributed to Zoroaster (628-c.551 BC; also known as Zaratjistra). Parisi are monotheists, believing in only on God, but they subscribe to the dualist belief that the earth is a battleground for the forces of good (*Ahura Mazda*) and evil (*Angra Mainyu*). Religious practice includes the fire temple, where a sacred flame is kept alight, and the tower of silence, upon which the dead are left exposed. Parsis in India live chiefly in Bombay and surrounding areas.

Partisans of Ali: Shiah

Pasdaran: guardians of the Islamic Revolution

Pashtun: Afghani tribe and language.

Pathan: A Pashto-speaking people of Pakistan and Afghanistan, more especially the tribesmen of the mountainous regions along the North-West Frontier of Pakistan. After 1849, when control of the region passed from the Sikhs to the British, a series of frontier uprisings took place. In 1893 an international frontier, the Durand Line, was established, with probably about two-thirds of the Pathans in British Indian and one-third in Afghanistan. A Pathan rebellion against this frontier occurred in 1899-98, necessitating an extensive British military occupation, but the frontier was inherited by Pakistan in 1947 when the Pathans of the British North-West Frontier Province voted to join the newly independent Pakistan. The Pathans consist of 60 tribes and over 5 million people. Each tribe traces its origins to one ancestor and is divided into Clans and sub-clans.

Patriarch: the title in the Christian hierarchy above Archbishop of the principal historic patriarchates of Rome, Jerusalem, Antioch, Alexandria and Constantinople, and, as an honor to certain other sees.

Patriotic Union of Kurdistan: Iraqi Kurdish party. The Patriotic Union of Kurdistan was formed in mid 1976 by the merger of the Kurdish Workers League and the Social Democratic Movement under the leadership of Jalal Talabani. Both PUK constituents had emerged from the Kurdistan Democratic Party after its leader, Mustafa Barzani fled to Iran in the wake of the March 1975 Algiers Accord. With the outbreak of the Iran Iraq War in September 1980 the chances of Kurdish guerrilla activity improved sharply, with the PUK concentrating its operation in its stronghold area. Both the PUK and the KDP set up liberated areas along Iraq's borders with Iran and Turkey. The Crisis created by the Iraqi invasion of Kuwait in August 1990 revived the PUK and other IKF members.

In March 1991, soon after the end of the Second Gulf War the PUK and the KDP revolted against the central government and within a few weeks they had taken over three quarters of the KAR. Following the general election in the KAR in May 1992 held under the protection of Western air forces, the PUK shared power equally with the KDP. Following the passage of the Iraq Liberation Act by US Congress in October 1998, which authorized the White House to designate Iraqi opposition groups eligible for military aid by Washington, the PUK found itself included on the list of six such factions. On the ground very little changed with Kurdistan divided administratively into two sectors with the PUK's territory ruled from Suleimaniya. It was not until September 2002 when Washington's plans to invade Iraq went into higher gear, that the PUK decided to bury its hatchet with the KDP.

People of the book: Jews and Christians so named in the Quran

People's Democratic Republic of Yemen, 1970-90: See South Yemen.

People's Republic of South Yemen, 1967-70: See South Yemen.

Phalange and Phalangists: (Lebanon) *Lebanese political party and militia* Official title: Lebanese Kataeb Social Democratic arty. The Phalange is a derivative of *phalanx* (or battalion) the literal translation of the Arabic work *Kataeb*. It was established in November 1936 by Pierre E. Gemayel, who had been inspired by the Nazi Youth Movement rallies he had seen during his visit to the Berlin Olympics in the summer. Its pro-Western stance and opposition to pan-Arabism led it to back President Camille Chamoun in the 1958 Lebanese Civil War. Its leaders began to highlight the presence of Palestinians, whose numbers had been boosted by the June 1967 Arab-Israeli War and the 1970-71 Jordanian Civil War. On the eve of the Lebanese Civil War of 1975-90 the party, now 20,000 strong, had a militia under the command of Bashir Gemayel, who later became commander of a coalition of Maronite militias, the Lebanese Forces (LF). Politically it was part of an umbrella organization called the Lebanese Front, led by Chamoun.

Intent on eliminating any serious rivals to his dominance in the Christian camp, in the summer of 1980 Bashir Gemayel used the

Phalange militia to wipe out the militia of Chamoun's National Liberal Party, and largely succeeded. In early 1982 he began to liaise with Israel in its plans to attack Lebanon. The invasion occurred in June, and by September the Phalange had been catapulted into the leading position, with Bashir Gemayer elected to the presidency. In early 1985 Samir Geagea, a leading member of the LF Command council, declared the LF independent of the Phalange in security, policing, and finance, thus depriving it of much of its influence. Due to its decision to boycott the 1992 general election, the Phalange's influence waned. Its headquarters was blown up in December. founded in 1936, Lebanon

PIEDAD: Islamic organization

PLO: Palestine Liberation Organization

Popular Bloc: (Bahrain): *Bahraini political party* After the Bahraini constitution had been promulgated in June 1973 the Bahrain National Liberation Front allied with the Bahrain Nationalist Movement to form the Popular Bloc, with a nationalist-leftist program, under the leadership of Hussein Musa.

Popular Democratic party: (Saudi Arabia): *Saudi political party* In 1970, former members of the Arab Nationalist Movement, remnants of the local Baath party, and the Marxists outside the National Liberation Front combined to form the Popular Democratic Party (PDP).

Popular Front for the Liberation of Oman and Arab Gulf: (1971-74): In 1971 the third congress of the Popular Front for the Liberation of the Occupied Arab Gulf lowered its sights from effecting a socialist revolution to effecting a national democratic revolution. Once the British had departed from Bahrain in mi-1971 and the ruler , Shaikh Isa al Khalifa, had made desultory moves to share power with his ministers, the PFLOAG's Bahraini section began to flex its muscles.

Popular Front for the Liberation of Oman: (1974-82): Faced with a vigorous onslaught by its enemy, the congress of the Popular

Front for the Liberation of Oman and the Arab Gulf (PFLOAG), meeting in July 1974, decided to narrow its field of action to Oman and renamed its organization the Popular Front for the Liberation of Oman (PFLO).

Popular Front for the Liberation of Palestine: *Palestinian political party* The Popular Front for the Liberation of Palestine (PFLP) was formed in December 1967 by a merger between the Palestinian section of the Arab Nationalist Movement and the Syria-based Palestine Liberation Front, under the leadership of George Habash. The PFLP's campaign inside the Occupied Territories involved 220 armed operations in 1970. Between 7 and 9 September 170 its members hijacked three airliners, took them to an abandoned airfield near Amman, emptied them of passengers, and blew them up. when in 1974 the Palestine National Council (PNC) accepted the idea of a Palestinian state on the West Bank and Gaza as an intermediate step toward the liberation of all of mandate Palestine, the PFLP boycotted the PLO executive committee and the central council.

After the expulsion of the PLO from Beirut in September 1982 the PFLP moved its headquarters to Damascus, but did not join the Syrian-instigated fight against Yasser Arafat and Fatah. However, after Arafat's agreement with king Hussein of Jordan to pursue a joint negotiating strategy in early 1985, the PFLP joined with the pro-Syrian Palestinian factions to form the Palestine national Salvation Front. During the crisis created by Iraq's invasion of Kuwait in August 1990, the PFLP backed President Saddam Hussein, especially when the latter tried to link Iraq's evacuation of Kuwait to Israel's withdrawal from the Occupied Arab Territories. Following the assassination of Israeli tourism minister Gen. Zeevi Rechavam in retribution for Mustafa's killing, in October by PFLP activists, Sadat was arrested by the Palestinian Authority under pressure by Israel.

Popular Front for the Liberation of the occupied Arab Gulf: (1968-71): At its second congress in September 1968 in south Yemen, a Marxist state, the Dhofari Liberation Front (DFL) decided to extend its revolutionary activities to the rest of Oman and other Gulf states and changed its name to the Popular Front for the

Liberation of the Occupied Arab Gulf (PFLOAG). this alarmed the British, the dominate political power in the country, and led to a London-engineered coup that replaced Sultan Said ibn Taimur with his son, Qaboos.

Popular Front for the Liberation of the Palestine-General Command: *Palestinian political party:* Having merged his Palestine Liberation Front with the Palestinian section of the Arab Nationalist Movement to for the Popular Front for the Liberation of Palestine (PFLP) in the late 1967, Ahmad Jibril led his supporters out of the PFLP about a year later to form the Popular Front for the Liberation of Palestine-General Command (PFLP-GC) It then affiliated to the Palestine Liberation Organization (PLO). After the 1982 Israeli invasion of Lebanon, when the PL's constituents were forced to vacate Beirut, the PFLP-GC moved its headquarters to Damascus. In 1983 it joined an anti-Yasser Arafat rebellion masterminded by Syrian President Hafiz Assad.

After the blowing up of a Pan-Am airliner near the Scottish town of Lockerbie in December 1988 (causing the death of 278 people, in probable retaliation for the US Navy shooting down an Iranian civilian airliner in July 1988, killing 290 people). US intelligence sources alleged that the PGLP-GC was responsible for the act (later the blame was shifted to the agents of Libya). It rejected the Israeli-PLO Accord of September 1993, because it failed to concede Palestinians' right to self-determination and the right of refugees to return home. With Jibril moving closer to Iran, the PFLP-GC split in 1999.

Popular Islamic Conferences: (Iraq): During the 1980-88 Iran-Iraq War, in order to parallel Tehran in the religious arena, Iraqi President Saddam Hussein sponsored the First Popular Islamic Conference in Baghdad in April 1983. the Second Popular Islamic Conference was held in Baghdad in April 1985 and was attended by 300 Iraqi and foreign clerics and pious laymen. the third conference, meeting on 11 January 1991 in Baghdad, called for a jihad if Iraq was attacked by the US-led coalition that had been formed to expel Iraq from Kuwait, which it had occupied since August 1990

Progressive Socialist Party: (Lebanon): the Progressive Socialist party (PSP) was formed in 1949 by Kamal Jumblat. Predominantly Druze, it had some Sunni, Shi'a, and Christian members. the PSP was a leading actor at the reconciliation conference held in Switzerland in March 1984. But in December 1985 Jumblat, along with the commanders of Amal and the Lebanese Forces (breakaway faction), failed in his attempt to end the conflict on the basis of the 'National Agreement to Solve the Lebanese Crisis.' Following the end of the civil war in October 1990 some 2,800 fighters from the PSP militia, which at its peak had 15,500 armed men, were taken into the regular Lebanese army. President Lahoud naming Hariri as the new prime minister, and the PSP winning sixteen seats, including seven allocate to Druzes, Jumblat's nominee, Marwan Hamadeh, became minister of displaced persons.

Prophets: there are two classes: **Rasool** (messenger or envoy), who brings a new religion or major revelation, and **Nabi** (prophet), whose mission lies within the framework of an existing religion. A messenger appointed by Allah to invite a community to believe in Him; one who speaks on God's behalf.

Qadiri: A Sufi order

Qadiriyyah: A group of Muslim scholars

Qadiriyyah: Sufi order (mysticism)

Qajar: A Turkic tribe in north-east Iran that produced the Qajar dynasty, which ruled Persia (Iran) from 1794 t 1925. The dynasty was established by Agha Muhammad (1742-97), a eunuch who made Tehran his capital and was crowned Shah in 1796. He was succeeded by his nephew Fath Ali Shah (1797-1834), during whose reign Iran was forced to cede the Trans-Caucasian lands to Russia. The constitutional revolution of 1906 established a parliament. Muhammad Ali (1907-09) was deposed for attacking the constitution and after a lengthy regency, Muhammad Ali's son Ahmad Shah (1914-25), became the last Qajar ruler, being deposed by an army officer, Reza Shah Pahlavi, in 1925.

Qalandariyya: Wandering dervishes without fixed abode strangely shaven and beringed whose coarse garments and unconventional behavior provoked astonishment in Damascus in 1213 and subsequently much disapproval. They practiced physical mortification but were slack in their observances and were held to be immoral both by the orthodox ulama and by other orders of Sufis.

Qawm: people or nation; tribe

Qaynuqah (Banu): A Jewish tribe in Medina, allied with the Meccans

Qipchaq: Turkish tribes now spread out from the Dniepr to Siberia but in the 13th to 15th centuries mostly concentrated in the Volga Don steppes. Speaking a characteristic dialect and mostly pagan, they were imported en masse into Mamluk Egypt and formed the core of the Mamluk elite.

Quraysh: (A) externally, it is a ritual method for the slaughter of animals, to purify them and make them permissible, or **Halal**, to eat. Inwardly, it is to sacrifice one's life to the devotion and service of God and to cut away the beastly qualities within the heart of man that cause him to want to slaughter animals. Powerful governing tribe of Mecca at the time of Muhammad's birth; Muhammad's father a trader named Abdullah was a member of this tribe. The pagan Arabs of Mecca, Muhammad belonged to this tribe, but they rejected his prophetic message; the tribe that controlled Mecca during Muhammad's lifetime. The Quraysh persecuted Muhammad and his followers, seeing them as a threat to their control of trade in Mecca.

Qurayzah: A Jewish tribe of Medina; Muhammad supervised their massacre after they betrayed an alliance with the Muslims Jewish tribe, enemy of Muhammad

Rashidun: Sunnis consider the first four caliphs as the orthodox or rightly guided caliphs. They were Abu Bakr, Umar, Uthman and Ali. the four "rightly guided" caliphs, who were the companions and the immediate successors of the Prophet Muhammad: Abu Bakr, Umar ibn Al-Khattab, Uthman ibn Affan and Ali ibn Abi

Talib. The Rightly-Guided. The first four caliphs: Abu Bakr, Omar, Uthman, and Ali; "The Rightly Guided".

Rastakhiz Party: (Iran) (*Persian: Resurgence*): *Iranian political party.* The Rastakhiz Party was established by Muhammad Reza Shah Pahlavi in March 1975 as the sole governing party after he had dissolved the ruling New Iran Party, founded by him in 1963, and the Mardom Party, the official opposition. With the revolutionary movement gathering pace during the summer of 1978, the shah dissolved the party in September.

Reconquista: Reconquest; Christian group who fought the Muslims and retook Spain in 1085, led by Alfonso VI. **Reconquista:** Sp., the recovery of Spanish territory, finally in 1491, by stages, following the Islamic conquest of 711.

Reformist Islam: the view that Muslims can respond successfully to modern life only by withdrawing Islam from public affairs.

Revolutionary Komitehs (Iran): Following Ayatollah Ruhollah Khomeini's taped messages in August 1978 from the Iraqi city of Najaf, his senior clerical followers formed *Komitehs* (derivate of *Comite, [French; Committee]*) in mosques to guide those struggling against the regime of Muhammad Rhea Pahlavi. Following the outbreak of war with Iraq in September 1980, the government charged the Komitehs with rationing essential goods. They thus became part of the civilian administration.

Rightly Guided Caliphs: the first four Caliphs – Abu Bakr, Umar, Uthman, and 'Ali – who led the Islamic community before the Shi'a-Sunni split.

Sa'ad: A tribe which raised Muhammad in childhood.

Saadi-Jibawis: Sufi Order in Palestine

Sabaeans, Sabi'a: In mandating tolerance for monotheists who have received a previous divine revelation, the Koran mentions three such groups, the Jews, the Christians and the Sabaeans. The names Jews and Christians are clear and unequivocal, but the

Sabaeans, thrice named in the Koran, are somewhat more enigmatic. The name originally seems to have been applied to a Judeo-Christian sect in Mesopotamia, also known as the Mandaeans. The name was later claimed and used by another religious group, probably pagan, in the town of Harran, in a successful attempt to claim the same measure of tolerance as was accorded to the Jews and Christians. After the great Islamic conquests in Asia and Africa, the name was sometimes used to accord the same measure of tolerance to other, previously unknown religions.

Sabra: *(Arabic: cactus):* Sabra is the popular term for native-born Israeli Jews who, like the local cactus plant, are thought to be prickly on the outside but soft and sweet on the inside. In 1996 only 21% of Israeli Jews were Sabra. Palestinian refugee camp in Lebanon

Sadaqa: Voluntary alms given by Muslims.

Safavid Dynasty: Ruled Persia from 1500 to 1722; its name is derived from the Safawiyya Order, founded in the 14th century by Shaykh Safi Al-Din. Ismail I: Safavid, Iranian dynasty (1499-1736), that established Shiite Islam in Iran as an official state religion. The Safavid state provided both the territorial and societal foundations of modern Iran. Founded by Shah Ismail, this Turkic-speaking dynasty claimed descent from a Shiite Sufi order. Shiite views, propagated with the help of clerics recruited from Jabal Amil (today in Lebanon) and Iraq, endowed Iran with an identity distinct from its Sunni neighbors. The consolidation of Safavid rule was completed during the reign of Shah Abbas I. Recognizing his military inferiority vis-a-vis the Ottoman Sultanate, Abbas accepted the Ottoman occupation of the western parts of his domain and was thus able to concentrate his efforts on creating a standing army and halting Uzbek incursions from the east. He established Isfahan as his capital and transformed it into an architectural showcase. The strategic location of Iran and Safavid animosity toward the Ottomans, who were a continuing threat to European powers, generated European interest.

Shah Abbas received numerous European legations and, with the help of English warships, conquered Hormoz, the Portuguese colony at the entrance of the Persian Gulf. His project to create a major competing maritime trade center at Bandar-i Abbas failed. Benefiting from a change in the balance of power, he expanded into Ottoman territory, annexing the holy Shiite cities of Karbala and Najaf. A period of upheaval followed his death, during which Ottoman pressure from the west and Mughal attacks from the east led to substantial territorial losses. Shah Abbas II (1642-66) attempted to eliminate bureaucratic corruption, and gained a peace, largely due to the military exhaustion of Iran's neighbors. Shah Husayn (1694-1722) devoted his energy to reconquering the island of Bahrayn, ignoring the opposition centered in Afghanistan. In 1722, Afghan forces entered Isfahan and forced Husayn to abdicate, putting an effective end to Safavid rule. The final blow came in 1736 when the Afshar Nadir, regent of young Abbas III, deposed him, becoming shah himself (see Nadir Shah)

Safawids: The descendents of Shaykh Safi al Din of Ardebil, the founder of the Safawiyya order of dervishes. This was originally puritan and Sunni but under Shaykh Junayd the order assumed its militantly Shi'a character which enabled Ismaili who seized power in Persia in 1502 to proclaim Shiism as the state religion.

Saffarids: East Persian dynasty founded by a coppersmith Yaqub b Layth who controlled al Seistan by 867 then expanded into Kirman and Khurasan. His brothers descendants maintained themselves in Seistan till 1163 but the beginning of the Saffarids are the most interesting since they were the first Person Islamic dynasty to base their authority on their Persian lineage.

Sahaba: Companions of the Prophet. The people who accepted Islam and saw or heard him directly. Companions of Muhammad's Sahih: Sound in Isnad, a technical attribute applied to the Isnad of a Hadith.

Saiqa: (*Arabic: Thunderbolt*) *Palestinian commando force* Saiqa is the military wing of the Vanguards of the Popular War of Liberation, sponsored by the Syrian Bath Party after the June 1967 Arab-Israeli War. Following Assad's seizure of power in November, he purged Saiqa of its leftist elements, appointed his protégé, Zuhair Mohsen, as secretary-general, and brought it under the control of the Syrian defense ministry. For most of the 1970s Mohsen headed the PLO's military department. After it had been expelled from Beirut in 1982 and had based itself in Damascus, Saiqa joined the pro-Syrian Palestine National Salvation Front against PLO Chairman Yasser Arafat. During the Kuwait crisis of 1990-91, taking its cue from Syria it opposed Arafat's backing of Iraqi President Saddam Hussein. In September 1993 it rejected Oslo Accord I. In 2000 its leader was Issam Qadi.

Salaf: ancestors; the Muslims of the first generation(s). Predecessors appellation of the first generation of Muslims, Salafi: term describing the 20th century reform movement inspired by them. Early Muslims. Literally, the *predecessors*, whose acts and beliefs provided a model for later generations of Muslims. Later Muslims, inspired by the interpretative insights of these early Muslims, attempted to follow their example and developed a movement known as the Salafiyya school of thought. the forerunners, early successors to Muhammad

Salafi: a conservative school of Islamic law, or jurisprudence, which advocates a return to adherence to what it sees as fundamental principles of Islam. Forerunners the original, pious successors of Muhammad.

Salafism: A term derived from the Arabic word for predecessors or early generations, Salafism is an austere Islamic movement that claims to be returning to the pure Islam practiced by Prophet Muhammad and the first generation of Muslims

Salafist: follower of the pious ancestors or of original Islam, characterized by extreme rigor. **Salafiyya movements and Salafin:** (*Arabic: pl. of* Salafi, *follower of ancestors*): *A Sunni Islamic reformist movement* A derivative of *Salaf al Salihin* (the pious ancestors), the Salafiyya movement was influenced by Jamal al-Din Afghani (1838 – 97), an Islamic thinker who noted the militancy of the *Salaf (*ancestors) of the early Islam. One of his disciples, Muhammad Abdu (1849-1905), stressed the impact that the Salaf had had on the shaping of the Sharia. Some

Kuwaiti Salafin participated in the armed uprising against the Saudi royal family at the Grand Mosque of Mecca in November 1979. As a quasi-political organization, the Salafin won four seats in the Kuwaiti general election of 1992. They performed better in the subsequent polls, securing seven seats in 1999. **Salafiyya:** ideology of following the precedents of the first generation of Muslims

Samaritans: *quasi-Jewish community:* This ancient Hebrew-speaking sect claims descent from the Kingdom of Israel when, following King Solomon's death in 920 BC, the Samaritans formed the Kingdom of Israel and the Jews formed the Kingdom of Judah. In 1917 there were only 146 Samaritans in the world. Sixty years later, they numbered 583, divided between settlement of Kiryat Luza on Mount Gerizim and Holon, south of Tel Aviv.

Sammaniyyah: A Sufi order

Sanusi: Popular name for the *Sanusiyyah*, a Muslim brotherhood that acquired considerable political importance in Libya and North Africa. It was founded in Mecca in 1837 as a Sufi religious order by an Algerian, Sidi Muhammad al-Sanusi al-Idrisi, but in about 1843 he retired to the desert in Cyrenaica. The movement spread in Libya under the son and grandson of al-Sanusi; by 1884 there were 100 *Sawiyas* or daughter houses, scattered through North Africa and further afield. It became more militant in the 20th century, attacking the British occupation of Egypt in both World Wars and opposing the Italians in Libya. When Libya became independent in 1951, the leader of the order at that time, Idris I, became the country's first king.

Sanusiayyah: A movement

Saracens: A word of disputed etymology, used in late Greek and Latin and subsequently in the languages of Christian Europe to designate first the nomadic peoples of the desert adjoining Syria and Iraq, later the Arabs and eventually the Muslim peoples of the Mediterranean countries in general. The term is now obsolete. Originally nomads belonging to tribes of the Syrian or Arabian deserts but at the time of the Crusades the name used by

Christians for all Muslims. In a surge of conquest Muslim Arabs swept into the Holy Land (western Palestine), north into the Byzantine territory of Asia minor, and westward through North-Africa during the 7th and 8th centuries. Spain was conquered (Moors), together with most of the islands in the Mediterranean; they held Sicily from the 9th to the 11th century. Their expansion was halted by the Carolingians in France only with great difficulty. The Crusades against them, through initially effective, did not prove decisive in the long term, and they were not finally expelled from Spain until the 15th century.

Sarekat Islam: An Indonesian Islamic political organization. Formed in 1911 as an association of Javanese batik traders to protect themselves Chinese competition, it had developed, by the time of its first party congress in 1913 into a mass organization dedicated to self-government through constitutional means. Its leader H.Q.S. Cokroaminoto (1882-1934), was viewed by many as a latter-day Messiah, but the organization was weakened from within by the political challenge posed by the emergent PKI in the early 1920s; thereafter it gradually faded away as more radical nationalist parties, most prominently Sukarno's PNI were formed.

Sasanians: (Sasanids) Persian dynasty 224-637 AD The principle eastern enemies of the Romans, then the Byzantines, ruling over Persia, Iraq and much of the Caucasus and Central Asia.

Sassanid: Sasanid, or Sassanian, last dynasty of native rulers to reign in Persia before the Arab conquest. The period of their dominion extended from c.A.D.224, when the Parthians were overthrown and the capital, Ctesiphon, was taken, until c.640, when the country fell under the power of the Arabs. The last Sassanian king died a fugitive in 651, but he had been forced to yield Ctesiphon to the Arabs in 626. Under the Sassanids, who revived Achaemenid tradition, Zoroastrianism was reestablished as the state religion. The name of the dynasty was derived from Sassan, an ancestor of the founder of the dynasty, Ardashir I, who took and ruled Ctesiphon (224-40). During his reign and many that followed, war with the Romans occupied much attention. Sassanian persecution of Christians led to wars with Byzantium.

Syria and Armenia suffered particularly from invading armies. Ardashir I was succeeded by his son Shapur I, who was victorious over Roman Emperor Valerian and ruled until 272. The next reign of importance was that of Shapur II (309-79), a period of particular significance and glory. Bahram V, ruling 420-38, was defeated by the Emperor Theodosius but succeeded against the White Huns. The Armenians were overwhelmed by Yazdagird II in 451, and their land was overrun by Sassanians under Khosrow I, who reigned 531-79 and who also invaded Syria. Both countries were again overrun by Khosrow II (ruled 590-628), whose conquest of Egypt was the final victorious achievement of the dynasty. The last representative of the family on the throne was Yazdagird III, who began his reign in 632. His struggle against the Arabs ended in the fall of the Sassanid dynasty. Persia and Byzantium.

Saud: the ruling family of Saudi Arabia. Originally established at Dariyya in Wadi Hanifa. Nejd, in the 15th century, its fortunes grew after 1745 when Muhammad ibn Saud allied himself with the Islamic revivalist Abd al-Wahhab (Wahhabism), who later became the spiritual guide of the family. The first wave of Saudi expansion ended with defeat by Egypt in 1818, but Saudi fortunes revived under Abd al-Aziz ibn Saud (c. 1889-1953), who captured Riyadh (1902), al-Hasa (1913), Asir (1920-26), Hail (1921), and the Hejaz (1924-25), thus assembling the territories that formed the kingdom of Saudi Arabia in 1932. He imposed a settled way of life onto many of the nomadic tribes, but reduced tribal conflicts and crime, especially crimes against pilgrims traveling to Mecca. He granted drilling rights to US oil companies to exploit Saudi oil, much of the revenue from which was spent by the royal family Abd al-Aziz was succeeded by his sons Saud 1953-64), whose lack of administrative control and extravagant lifestyle almost bankrupted the country Faisal Ibn Abd Al-Aziz (1964-75, Khalid (1975-82), and Fahd (1982-   ), Fahd briefly handed power over to Crown Prince Abdullah in late 1995, after suffering a stroke, but resumed control of the country in February 1996.

Sayyids: descendants of the Prophet; also called Sharif and Shah

Sayyid dynasty: Muslim rulers of the Delhi sultanate in northern India (1414-51). They seized power from the Tughluqs, but never equaled their predecessors' imperial pretensions. Rival neighbors soon threatened their claims even in the north, and in 1448 their last sultan abandoned Delhi, to be replaced three years later by the Afghan Lodis. The name 'Sayyid' reflected the family's claim to be direct descendants of the Prophet Muhammad. : (Lit) lord or prince; (fig) a hereditary title applied to a male descendants of Prophet Muhammad A title of honor, roughly equivalent to lord or master. In the past, it was usually though not invariably restricted to the descendants of the Prophet. In modern times, it has come to be used much more widely and at the present day is no more than the equivalent of mister. Ar., a title, in wide usage, from Prince to Mr.; esp. also for descendants of Husayn, grandson of the Prophet by his daughter Fatima. Descendant of Ali sons Husain. Sidi Is applied to members of saintly lineages; lit, lord or prince, fig. A hereditary title applied to a male descendants of Prophet Muhammad's Shaab: people; master or descendant of a relative of Muhammad's.

Sayyids: descendants of the Prophet Muhammad

Sazman-e Cherikha-ye Khalq-Iran: *(Persian: Organization of People's Self-sacrificing Guerrillas): see* Fedai Khalq.

Sazman-e Mujahedin-e Khalq: *(Persian: Organization of People's Holy Warriors): see* Mujahedin-e Khalq.

Schools (Islamic):
1. Madhahib (Muhammad ibn Hanbal),
2. Malikiyya (Malik ibn Anas)
3. Hanifiyya (Abu Hanifa),
4. Shaf'iyya (Al shafi'i)

Seljuks: a Turkish dynasty that achieved its greatest power in the late 11th century. Its early members rose to prominence as mercenaries, raising Turkish nomad troops to serve and ultimately to challenge the troops to serve and ultimately to challenge the Ghaznavids. By 1055, under the leadership of Tughrul Beg, they had entered Baghdad and subjected the eastern lands of the Muslim empire to their control, while maintaining the fiction of an Abbasid caliphate and using the existing administrative system and such talented officials as the vizier Nizam alo-Mulk.

Reaching their apogee under Alp Arslan (1063-72) and Malik Shah (1072-92), they disturbed the existing regional balance of power, crushing the Byzantines at Manzikert, and, by interrupting the Pilgrimage to Jerusalem, indirectly provoking the First Crusade. They were ultimately undermined by the turbulence of their own nomad troops among a settled populating and by the rivalries of ambitious subordinates. Their decline in the early 12th century was, however, soon followed by the emergence in Asia Minor of the Seljuk sultanate of Rum, centered on Konya, under Kilij Arslan II (1155-92). Under Kayobad I (1220-37) this regime achieved great splendor, but it suffered a crushing defeat at Mongol hands at Kosedagh in 1243 and became a dependency of the Mongol Il-Khans of Persia until its extinction in 1308.

Semites: The term Semite/Shemite is based on *Genesis* (10:1): "These are the descendants of Noah's sons: Shem, Ham and Japheth." Initially those believed to be the descendants of Shem were called Semite. a group of peoples of the Middle East, including the Jewish People and the Arabs. According to the Bible they were descended from Shem, the son of Noah. The original Semites were farmers in Arabia who spread north and west to create some of the major empires of antiquity. The inhabitants of Akkad who overthrew the Sumerians were Semites, as were the Assyrians, the Aramaeans, The Canaanites the Phoenicians, and the Hebrews. The earliest known alphabetic writing systems were developed by Semites in about 2000 BC. Modern Semitic languages include Hebrew, Arabic, and Maltese.

Sepoy: From the Persian Sipahi a "horseman," hence a cavalryman, sometimes more loosely used of soldiers in general. From Persian, the word moved via Urdu to India and via Turkish to North Africa. In both places it was used by the imperial powers-by the British in India in the form Sepoy, by the French in Algeria in the form Spahi-to designate the native troops in their service. The terms Askari and lascar are sometimes used in the same sense. Both of these derive from the Arabic Askar or with the definite article, al Askar, an Arabic word meaning army itself probably derived from the Latin word for army-exercitus. Since the passing of the European empires, these terms have become in effect obsolete. The Indian mutiny of 1857 to 1859, among Indian troops in the British army, is known as the "Sepoy Mutiny" because it was started by Sepoys. According to a story current at the time, they were provoked to revolt by a report, probably untrue, that their cartridges were greased with pig fat.

Sha'irs: Poets

Shadhiliyyah: Sufi order (mysticism)

Shafa'i: Islamic school, Sunni. **Shafeite:** one of four juridical schools of Sunni Islam, prominent in Southwest Asia and East Africa

Shafi'd: school of law founded by Muhammad ibn Idris Ash-Shafi'd (d. 820). This school is dominant in Indonesia, Malaysia, and the Philippines. Along with the Hanafi and Maliki schools, it is also observed in Egypt, and is followed in Central Asia and the Caucasus.

Shafi'i: The legal school founded by the Imam al Shafi'l who died in Egypt in 820. Originally most influential in Baghdad and Cairo, it was adopted at Mecca and Medina and in much of Persia and Central Asia. With the triumph of Saladin in Egypt and Syria it achieved preeminence in the central lands of Islam but was displace by the Ottoman conquests in favor of the Hanafi school.

Shafi'i: The name of the Sunni school of theology and law founded by Abu Abdallah Muhammad al Shafi'i (767-820 CE)

Shafi'i's: Followers of the Islamic scholar Muhammad ibn al-Shafi'i.

Shafii Code: *Sunni Islamic school* The Sunni [*qv*] Islamic school was named after Muhammad ibn Idris al Shafii (A.D. 767-820) The Shafii school, founded by Shafi's disciples and originating in Egypt, reached southern Arabia and from there spread along the monsoon route to East Africa and Southeast Asia through Arab traders. Today it is particularly strong in Yemen.

Shahids: Usually translated martyrs, from an Arabic verb meaning to bear witness or to testify. At the present time, it is used commonly to denote the new phenomenon of the suicide bomber. Shahid is the linguistic equivalent of the Greek word martyrs, "witness," from which our word martyr is derived. The Muslim conception of martyrdom is however, somewhat different from that of either the Jews or the Christians. The words of the Oxford English Dictionary, a martyr is one who voluntarily undergoes the penalty of death for refusing to renounce the Christian faith, one who undergoes death on behalf of any belief or cause, or through devotion to some object. In the Muslim perception, a Shahid is one who gives his life fighting for the faith, in other words, in a holy war. The Shahid enjoys special rewards in heaven. A word from the same root, Shahada in the sense of testifying to the true faith is one of the five pillars of Islam

Shahname: (The book of Kings): A collection of Persian legends from the creation of the world. Including the heroic exploits of heroes like Rustam a version of the Alexander Romance and the more or less historical exploits of the Sasanian kings. This was written down by several authors but in particular by Firdawsi whose compilation has become the Persian national epic.

Sheikhs: Elders, head of the tribe or Sufi masters; elder teachers Sufi masters; lit. old man, fig. Sacred law of Islam in Arab Iraq, either an Arab tribal chieftain or a religious scholar; in Kurdish Iraq, a man of saintly descent, usually head of the religious order

Sharifian: The name given to two Moroccan dynasties whose rulers claimed the title of *Sharif* (noble) by reason of their descent from al-Hasan son of Muhammad's daughter Fatima. The *Sharifs* of Mecca, and others, claim similar descent. The Sadian dynasty of *Sharifs* originated in Sus in 1509, and speedily conquered all Morocco. Sharif Muhammad traded with Spain and England, a policy followed by his successors. In 1664, after a period of great confusion, a cadet branch of *Sharifs* known as Filali supplanted them, and remain the ruling dynasty of Morocco.

Shazalis: Sufi Order in North Africa

Sheikh or Shaykh: An Arabic word meaning "old man." This term is frequently mispronounced. To achieve an approximately correct pronunciation, one should pronounce the first part rather like the English word "shake" and the final consonant like the ch in the Scottish Loch. At a time and in a place when older men were presumed to have greater wisdom and were, therefore, entrusted with greater power, the word also acquired the connotations of leadership, dignity, and authority. Among the Bedouin Arabs, a sheikh has been since remote antiquity, and still is today, the head of the tribe. In some of the principalities of modern Arabia, it has been used as a hereditary title of rulers. Such territories are sometimes called sheikhdoms. After the advent of Islam, sheikh also came to be used as the title of a religious dignitary, especially a graduate of a theological seminary. It was also applied to the heads of religious orders and fraternities and sometimes also of craft guilds, often associated of such fraternities.

The title "Sheikh al Islam" literally the old man of Islam was in medieval times conferred by consensus on eminent theologians. Under the Ottomans, it was the official title of the Chief Mufti of Istanbul, the head of the entire religious establishment of the Empire. A similar but not identical semantic development in the usage of words connoting, old age maybe also be observed in English. From the Anglo Saxon "old," we get elders and aldermen; from the Latin Senex an old man, came senior, senator and senile. 'old man' – a title indicating respect. Most commonly used for learned teachers, but in Arabia also for political rulers, or simply people of importance; a tribal leader or elder, the leader of a Sufi community; term of reverence for an ordained religious leader in Islam

Sheikhdom: literally, the domain ruled by a sheikh; here used as a shorthand for the oil exporters with the smallest populations and the largest per capita incomes.

Shi'ati Ali: Supporters of Ali; Shiites.

Shi'a *(Arabic: Partisan): Islamic sect* Shi'a or Shi'at means Shi'a/Shi'at Ali, Partisans of Ali, cousin and son-in-law of the Prophet Muhammad (A.D. 570-632). They were an important part of the coalition that engineered the Abbasid revolution in A.D. 751 against the Umayyad caliphs (A.D. 661-750) The consequences were the subjugation of the Sunni caliph in Baghdad [*qv*] by a Shi'a king, Muizz al Dawla al Buyid, in A.D. 932, and the emergence of an Ismaili [*qv*] Shi'a caliphate, the Fatimids, in Cairo [*qv*] in A.D. 969. By then three branches of Shiism had crystallized: Zaidis [*qv*], Ismailis, and Imamis [*qv*]. During the Buyid hegemony in Baghdad (A.D. 932-1055) two collections of Shi'a Hadith [*qv*] were codified. The Shi'a credo consists of five basic principles and ten duties. While sharing three principles with Sunnis–monotheism, i.e., there is only one God; prophethood, which is a means of communication between God and humankind; and resurrection, i.e., the souls of dead human beings will be raised by God on their Day of Judgment and their deeds on earth judged–Shi'as have two more: *Imamat* [*qv*] and *Aadl* (justice), the just nature of Allah.

Shi'as believe that only those in the lineage of the Prophet Muhammad–and thus of his daughter, Fatima, and her husband, Ali–can govern Muslims on behalf of Allah, and that the imams, being divinely inspired, are infallible. (In contrast, Sunnis view Islamic history essentially as a drift away from the ideal community that existed under the rule of the first four Rightly Guided caliphs: Abu Bakr, Omar, Othman and Ali). Shi'a emotionalism finds outlets in mourning Imams Ali (assassinated), Hassan (poisoned), and Hussein (killed in battle), and in the heartrending entreaties offered at their shrines. Unlike in the Sunni religious establishment, Shi'a clerics are ranked from *thiqatalislam* (trust of Islam) to *Hojatalislam* (proof of Islam) to *ayatollah* (sign of Allah) to *ayatollah-ozma* (grand ayatollah). partisans or followers. Literally, "party" or "sect," specifically referring to the "party of Ali"; a Muslim who follows Ali (the cousin and fourth successor of Muhammad), who was deposed as leader of Muhammad's followers.

Shiah I-Ali: The partisans of Ali

Shi'at Ali: *(Arabic: Partisan of Ali):* **Shi'at Ali:** The Party of Ali (The Partisans of Ali); Ali's followers and army; established the Shi'a sect within Islam (1570).

Shii Muslims: they belong to the Shiah i-Ali, the Partisans of Ali; they believe that Ali ibn Abi Talib, the Prophet's closest male relative, should have ruled in place of the Rashidun **(q.v.),** and revere a number of imams **(q.v.)** who are the direct male descendants of Ali and his wife Fatimah, the Prophet's daughter. Their difference from the Sunni majority is purely political.

Shiism: the party of Ali, the doctrine and movement claiming descent from the family of the prophet, through the line of imams beginning with Ali., the prophets son in law, includes about 15% of the world's Muslims, chiefly in Iran and Iraq and in India, Pakistan, Lebanon and Bahrain

Shiite: Shi'a Muslims, the minority in Islam (+/- 15%). Their largest group is known as the "Twelver Shi'ah"; reside mostly in Iran, Iraq, Kuwait, Lebanon, and India.

Shiites or Shi'a: In contrast to the "orthodox" majority of Sunni Muslims, Shiites follow Caliph Ali and his successors and hold different views on the nature and conduct of Islam. They are the majority in Iran, Iraq, and Bahrain, although in Iraq and Bahrain the political leadership is Sunni.

Shiites: (from Arabic, 'sectarians'; originally known as Shi'at Ali) The minority division within Islam, which consists of about one-fifth of all Muslims. Shiites are in the majority in Iran (where Shi'a Islam is the state religion), southern Iraq, and parts of Yemen, and are also found in Syria, Lebanon, East Africa, northern India, and Pakistan. They originated as the Shi'at Ali, the 'party of Ali', who was the cousin and son-in-law of Muhammad. Ali and his descendants are regarded by Shiites as the only true heirs to Muhammad as leader of the faithful. Shiites now differ from Sunni Muslims in a number of ways but primarily in the importance they attach to the continuing authority of the *imams,* who are the authentic interpreters of the *Sunna* (customs), the code of conduct based on the Koran and *Hadith.*

The suffering of the House of the Prophet, chiefly of Husain and his martyrdom in Karbala, and the Millenarian expectation of a future *imam* or Mahdi who is currently hidden from the world, permeate much Shiite thinking, providing a set of beliefs in which oppression and injustice figure largely. The tenth day of Muharram marks the martyrdom of Ali and his sons. Shiites also believe in an inner hidden meaning of the Koran. There are hundreds of different Shiite sects: the main ones are the Zaydis, Ismailis, and Ithna Ashariya (or Twelvers, who await the return of the hidden twelfth *imam*). Followers of Ali. The dispute over leadership of the new Islamic world after the prophet's death in the seventh century led to the biggest schism ever within Islam. Shiites believe in Ali as the successor of Muhammad. Compare to Sunni.

Sicily: Kalbid governors for Fatimids until 1060 (invaded by Normans in 1025, by Byzantines and Normans, 1038-1042); disputed among Fatimids, Sicilian Muslims, and Normans, 1060-1091 (Palermo [Balarm] taken by Normans in 1070); held by Normans after 1091 Under Aghlabids until 909 (Taormina taken 902); under Fatimids after 909 (in revolt under Ahmad ibn-Qurhub 912-916; Kalbid governors partially independent after 948; Taormina lost to Byzantine invasion repulsed after 909). Under Byzantines until 827; gradually conquered by Aghlabids, 827-902, with only Taormina (Taurominium) in Byzantine hands in 900

Silsilah: "Chain of inherited sanctity or kinship connecting the leaders of Sufi orders to their founders. Chain of tradition handed down by Sufi Shaykhs to their pupils comprising the individual teachings of a particular order of dervishes.

Slave trade, Arab: A form of commerce in slaves that existed from earliest times in the Arabian Peninsula. The Prophet Muhammad forbade his followers to enslave Muslims, but did not free slave converts. His legislation insisted on humane treatment and gave slaves rights against oppressive masters. In early Islam slaves were recruited from prisoners of war (including women and children) and were acquired by raiding and by purchase in Eastern and Southern Europe, Central Asia, and Central, East, and West Africa. Under the caliphs the trade was brisk. Saves served a variety of purposes: agricultural, mining, domestic, and clerical, and for military service. Many slave women employed as concubines were given the rights of wives. Men and children often received vocational training after capture. Through international pressure, the trade was largely abolished during the 19th century.

Socialist Labor Party: (Egypt): *Egyptian political party* After President Anwar Sadat had drained the Arab Socialist Party of Egypt of almost all its parliamentary deputies by forming his own National Democratic Party in August 1978. In 2000 the state-controlled Political Parties Committee suspended it and its weekly paper *Al Shaab* (The People), which had been preeminent in exposing corruption in high places, for "exceeding its political mandate."

Socialist National Front: (Lebanon): *Lebanese political party* Composed of opposition groups, the Socialist National Front (SNF) was formed in 1952. It was led by Camille Chamoun, Kamal Jumblat, and other concerned mainly with domestic reform. The conflict ended in a compromise, with Chamoun stepping down at the end of his term after dropping his plans for a constitutional amendment that would let him seek reelection. He was succeeded by General Fuad Chehab. During Chehab's presidency the SNF became dormant.

Society of Combatant Clerics: (Iran): (Official title, *Persian: Majma-e Ruhaniyoun-e Mobraz)* Popularly known as Majma, it was formed on 21 March 1988 with the tacit backing of Ayatollah Ruhollah Khomeini after the dissolution of the ruling Islamic Republican Party. Karrubi was elected Speaker by 186 votes to none, with the parliament dominated by leftist and left-of-center deputies, with thirty of them belonging to the Majma.

South Lebanon Army: *Lebanese militia* Formed by Israel during its occupation of southern Lebanon from March to June 1978, the South Lebanon Army (SLA), consisting mainly of Christian militiamen, was put under the command of Saad Haddad, a former (Christian) Lebanese army major. Upon its final withdrawal from Lebanon in June 1985, Israel handed over its positions in the self-declared security zone to the 3,000-strong SLA and left behind 1,000 Israeli troops as a back-up force. During the Second Gulf War (January-February 1991) there were armed exchanges between pro-Iraqi Palestinian commandos and the IDF-SLA alliance. Following the signing of the Lebanese-Syrian Treaty of Brotherhood, Cooperation, and Coordination in May 1991, which was condemned by Israel, the IDF-SLA alliance hardened its position. On the eve of Israel's unconditional withdrawal from south Lebanon in May 2000, more than 6,000 present and past SLA troops escaped to Israel.

South Yemini-Soviet Friendship Treaty (1979): After several years of hesitation, often induced by the prospect of unity with North Yemen, South Yemen signed a twenty-year friendship and cooperation treaty with the Soviet Union in October 1979 during a visit by its president, Abdul Fattah Ismail, to Moscow.

Spahis: Spahis or Sipahis, Ottoman cavalry. The Spahis were organized in the 14th cent. on a feudal basis. The officers held fiefs (*Timars*) granted to them by the sultan and commanded the personal loyalty of the peasants who worked the land. The Spahis were entitled to all income from the fief in return for military service to the sultan. Until the mid-16th cent. they provided the bulk of the Ottoman army. Committed to the tradition of light cavalry, they were slow to adopt firearms, whose development made the cavalry less important. They remained politically important until Mahmud II revoked their fiefs in 1828, two years after he crushed the Janissaries with modern artillery in his effort to build a modern army. In the French army certain Algerian and Senegalese cavalry units were also called Spahis. The term is sometimes spelled Sepahis

Spanish Inquisition: a council authorized by Pope Sixtus IV in 1478 and organized under the Catholic monarchs Ferdinand II and Isabella I of Spain to combat heresy. Its main targets were converted Jews and Muslims, but it was also used against Witchcraft and against political enemies. The first Grand Inquisitor was Torquemada. Its methods included the use of torture, confiscation, and burning at *autos-de-fé*. It ordered the expulsion of Jews from Spain in 1492, the attack on the Moriscos (Muslims living in Spain who were baptized Christians but retained Islamic practices) in 1502, and, after the Reformation, attacked all forms of Protestantism. In the 16th century there were 14 Spanish branches and its jurisdiction was extended to the colonies of the New World, including Mexico and Peru, and to the Netherlands and Sicily. Its activities were enlarged in the reign of Philip II, who favored it as a Counter-Reformation weapon. It was suppressed and finally abolished in the 19th century.

Steadfastness Front: *Front of radical Arab states* Formed in Tripoli, Libya, in December 1977, in the wake of a visit to Jerusalem by Egyptian President Anwar Sadat, the Steadfastness Front consisted of Algeria, Libya, the Palestine Liberation Organization (PLO), Syria, and South Yemen. At its meeting in Damascus in September 1978, the Front opposed the July 1978 Arab League resolution against South Yemen and supported the Omani people's struggle for liberation. Under the leadership of President Chadli Ben-Jedid (president from 1979-91), Algeria began gradually to dissociate itself from the Front, a trend accelerated by its economic decline following the collapse of oil prices in the spring of 1986.

Sufi: (adj. or noun): the Islamic form of mysticism; devotees organized into orders which carried great political weight by the eighteenth century. (Arabic "Woolen") Mystical or ascetic orders in Islam united under the authority of Shaykh who draws his teachings from a chain of his predecessors. Sufism becomes apparent in Islam as early as the 8th century, but contrary either Shi'a or Heterdox Sufis are often referred to as the poor. Sufi, Sufism: the mystics and mystical spirituality of Islam. The term may derive from the fact that the early Sufis and ascetics preferred to wear the coarse garments made of wool (Arabic, SWF) favored by Muhammad and his companions. member of an Islamic mystical (*Sufi*) order wool (suf) coarse woolen garment.

Sufism *(Arabic: Sufi, derivative of* suf, *wool; hence man of wool, ascetic): mystical philosophy in Islam* Subscribing to the general theory of mysticism that direct knowledge of God is attainable through intuition or insight, Sufism is based on the doctrines and methods derived from the Quran. Hassan al Basri (d. A.D. 728) was the first known Sufi personality. In time, two types of Sufis emerged: ecstatic and sober. Among the latter, Abu Hamid Muhammad al Ghazali (1058-1111) was the most prominent. His work became the living document for the Sufi orders/brotherhoods that sprang up soon after his death. The first Sufi order was Qadiriyyah. Founded by Baghdad-based Abdul Qadir al Gailani (1077-1166), it stressed piety and humanitarianism.

Sufism grew rapidly between 1250 and 1500, when the caliphate was based in Cairo under Mamluk sultans (1250-1517), and when Islam penetrated central and western Africa and southern India and Southeast Asia along the land and sea routes used by Arab traders. Today Sufi brotherhoods exist, overtly or covertly, in most Muslim communities. A mystical tradition that emphasizes the inner aspect of spirituality through meditation and remembrance of God. The Islamic mystic movement, whose practices center on devotion to earlier Muslims renowned for their piety and, in some cases, their supernatural powers, called *Baraka* in Arabic. the guardians of tradition and spiritual Islam.

Sultanate: A territory subject to sovereign independent Muslim rule. The word 'sultan' is used in the Koran and the traditions of the Prophet Muhammad to mean 'authority'. Mahmud of Ghazna was the first Muslim ruler to be addressed as sultan by his contemporaries. The term thereafter became a general title for the effective holders of power, such as the Seljuk or Mamluk dynasties, though it was also used as a mark of respect under the Ottomans for princes and princesses of the imperial house The term 'sultanate' was also used of a number of virtually independent centers of Muslim power, such as the sultanate of Dekhi (1206-1526), the predecessor of the Mogul empire in India, and the Sulu sultanate, a trading empire in the southern Philippines, which flourished between the 16th and 19th centuries.

Sunna: *(Arabic: custom, path):* In the pre-Islamic society of Arabia the term *Sunna* applied to social practices based on ancestral precedents. After the rise of Islam under the Prophet Muhammad

(A.D. 570-632), early converts took their cue either from the behavior of the Prophet's companions or the residents of Medina, the capital of the Islamic realm. Though the Prophet Muhammad was an exemplar for Muslims, it was not until the eminent jurist Muhammad ibn Idris al Shafii (A.D. 767-820) had ruled that all legal decisions not stemming directly from the Quran must be based on a tradition going back to the Prophet Muhammad himself that a serious effort was made to compile the Prophet's sayings and doings. The *Sunna* was then employed in the exposition of the Quran and in *Fiqh* (Islamic jurisprudence). Literally the path following the example of Muhammad set out in the Quran and Hadith, refers to the majority Muslims denomination. The pattern of God in ordering the Creation and function of the material world; the exemplary conduct of the Prophet Muhammad, conveyed in reports of his deeds, dicta and endorsements (Hadith); the necessary companion and complement to the Qur'an for many Muslims.

Sunnis: *(Persian: derivative of Ahl al Sunna; Arabic; People of the path [of the Prophet Muhammad]): Islamic sect* The majority of the elites and people in the Muslim world; the major "orthodox" division of Islam. Sunnis are the leading sect within Islam. They regard the first four caliphs–Abu Bakr, Omar, Othman, and Ali (r. A.D. 656-61)–"Rightly Guided." They belong to one of the four schools of jurisprudence–Hanafi, Maliki, Shafii, and Hanbali-and accept the six "authentic books" of al Hadith, the first of which was compiled by Muhammad al Bukhari (d. A.D. 870). Sunnis and Shi'as also differ on the organization of religion and religious activities. Sunnis regard religious activities as the exclusive domain of the (Muslim) state. The Sunni ethos, too, is different from the Shi'a.

There is no emotional outlet for mourning the martyrdom of early Islamic leaders, as in the Ashura celebrations of Shi'as. Sunni clerics are not given the religious titles of their Shi'a counterparts. Those Muslims who believe that succession after Muhammad was to be decided by the community of believers and not by divine authority or prophetic appointment; they accept the history of the first Hijri century and the authority it conferred on the Righteous Caliphs; they acknowledge Ali as the Fourth

Caliph but not as the First Imam. Their successors are the Umayyad, then the Abbasid Caliphs.

Supreme Assembly of Islamic Revolution in Iraq: *Iraqi political organization (Arabic: Majlis al Aala lil Thawra al Islamiya fi al Iraq)* The Supreme Assembly of Islamic Revolution in Iraq (SAIRI) was formed in Tehran in November 1982 by three Iraqi Islamic organizations: al Daawa al Islamiya, the Mujahedin Movement, and the Islamic Action Organization. Led by Ayatollah Muhammad Baqir al Hakim, a Shi'a cleric with a history of resistance to the Iraqi Baath regime, SAIRI aimed to found an Islamic state in Iraq. In late 1986 it participated in the Conference on Solidarity with the Iraqi People, held in Tehran and attended by the delegates of various Kurdish autonomist groups. When Washington's Iraq Liberation Act, 1998, authorized the president to name Iraqi groups entitled to receiving military aid to topple the regime of Saddam Hussein, President Bill Clinton name SAIRI as one such faction along with five others. But SAIRI, maintaining an army of 8,000 to 12,000 exiled Iraqis, rejected the entitlement, arguing that the American move made the Iraqi opposition appear as U.S. agents. Following the overthrow of the Ṣaddam Hussein regime by the Anglo-American forces in April 2003, the soldiers and activists of SAIRI returned to Iraq and took control of some Iraqi villages and towns along the Iranian border. SAIRI partisans also entered Najaf as Karbala.

Supreme Council of Islamic Revolution in Iraq: *see* Supreme Assembly of Islamic Revolution in Iraq.

Syrian Social Nationalist Party: (Lebanon): *Lebanese political party* The Syrian Social Nationalist Party (SSNP) emerged in 1947 out of the Syrian Nationalist Party, founded in 1932 by Antun Saada with the aim of creating a Greater Syria that could accommodate all the people forming the Syrian nation, which Saada described as an ethnic fusion of Canaanites. The outbreak of the Second World War found Saade in Latin America on a mission to forge links with the Syrian settlers there. In June 1949 there was fighting in Beirut between the SSNP and the Phalange Party, which, the SSNP alleged, had been provoked by the government of Riyadh Solh. Led by Inam Raad, the SSNP remained bitterly opposed to the Phalange. When the Lebanese Civil War broke out in April 1975, it allied with the Movement of the Disinherited, led by Musa al Sadr, to form the pro-Syrian Nationalist Front. Later the party's leadership passed to Jibran Araiji.

Tabiun: successors are those who benefited and derived their knowledge from the Companions of the Prophet.

Tahirids: short lived east Persian dynasty founded by Tahir b al Husayn (755-822) with a capital at Nishapur they were celebrated for their patronage of Arabic culture but were displaced gradually by the Saffarids.

Taif Accord (Lebanese): *see* National Reconciliation Charter 1989 (Lebanon).

Taliban: "Students." The name of a Muslim militant group that arose in Afghanistan in the late 1990s. An Islamic Fundamentalist political and military grouping that seized control of most of Afghanistan, including the capital Kabul, during 1994-96. Taliban means 'seekers' in the Pasto language and the Taliban militia was formed by Islamic theological students in the south of the country in 1994 with the intention of unifying Afghanistan. Rival Mujaheddin factions had been fighting since the withdrawal of Soviet forces in 1989. After initial reverses, the Taliban captured the city of heart in September 1995 and advanced to take Kabul in August 1996. A strict Islamic code of law was immediately imposed, which debarred women from paid work and education and proscribed television. The Taliban regime is intensely hostile to both Communism and Western interests. Opposition to Taliban rules is concentrated in the north-east of Afghanistan under an alliance of forces known as the United Islamic Front for the Salvation of Afghanistan (UIFSA). Fierce fighting between the Taliban and UIFSA has continued despite attempts by the international community to broker a peace deal. Islamic fundamentalist group of Afghanistan. Came to Afghanistan in 1994.

Tanzimat reforms: (1839-71) A series of reforms in the Ottoman Empire. They were promulgated under sultans Abdulmecid I (1839-61) and Abdulaziz (1861-76) in response to western pressure Under Mustafa Resid Pasha (1800-58) a program of reform was steadily developed. The army was reorganized, on the Prussian model and the slave trade was abolished. **Tanzimat:** Administrative decrees, reforms instituted by the nineteenth century Ottoman sultans; reorganization; the reforms undertaken in the Ottoman Empire during the mid-nineteenth century, under West European influence.

Tariq/Tariqa: road; (Arabic) an order of **Sufi** mystics **(q.v.).** (plural al **Alim**): a particular Sufi 'path' to knowledge of God; hence, an order or brotherhood following a particular **Shikh.** A Sufi lodge. Literally, a way, road; the rule of a dervish fraternity. Path of mystical and spiritual guidance, a term which also came to be applied to the organization through which a Tariqa extends itself in Muslim society. Order, the way, direction. **Tariqa:** Path, way; the path we need to walk in our personal and social lives in order to live in conformity with reality. **Tariqahs:** Sufi; "ways", paths Islamic mystical order (Sufi)

Tartars: (or Tatars) A number of Central Asian peoples who, over the centuries, were a threat to civilized people in Asia and Europe. More specific names, for example Mongol, Turk, Kipchak, emerge for some of these peoples who were constantly moving, often over great distances, and who spoke a variety of related Turkic and Mongol languages. The name "Tartars" is applied specifically to tribesmen living south of the Amur who were defeated by the Ming emperor Yongle in the early 15th century. Papal envoys (c. 1250) to the Mongols consistently called them Tartars, probably by association with Tartarus, the place of punishment in the underworld of Greek mythology. The name was also applied to the Golden Horde. Some of the Cossacks (originally Kahsaks, 'free men') on the River Dnieper were Tartars. Later nay people of Turkish stock in Russia were called Tartars. In the 16th century the khanates of the Volga Tartars came under Russian rule. The khanate of the Crimean Tartars, formed in the 15th century, paid tribute to the Ottoman Turks until annexed by Russia in 1783.

Tashnak Party (Lebanon) *(Armenian: Federation): Lebanese political party* The Tashnak, the leading party of Armenian Orthodox Christians in Lebanon, is center-right in its policies. During the 1975-90 Lebanese Civil War, while being close to the Phalange Party, it insisted on maintaining "positive" neutrality.

Tatar: Originally a Mongol tribe which mainly settled in the Lands of the Golden Horde after the Mongol invasion, on the steppes between the Volga and the Dnepr where they became the ancestors of the modern Tatars. By the mid 13th century if not earlier it was Turkish speaking. However the close association with the Mongols remained since their Muslim and their Western cotemporaries both refer to Mongols as Tatars.

Teheran Conference: (28 November -1 December 1943) a meeting between Churchill, Roosevelt, and Stalin in the Iranian capital. Here Stalin, invited for the first time to an inter-Allied conference, was told of the impending opening of a Second Front to coincide with a Soviet offensive against Germany. The three leaders discussed the establishment of the United Nations after the war and Stalin pressed for a future Soviet sphere of influence in the Baltic States and Eastern Europe, while guaranteeing the independence of Iran. Tehran Conference, Nov. 28-Dec. 1, 1943, meeting of President Franklin Delano Roosevelt, Prime Minister Winston Churchill, and Premier Joseph Stalin at Tehran, Iran.

The conference was held to strengthen the cooperation of the United States, Great Britain, and the USSR in World War II. It followed the Cairo Conference with Chiang Kai-Shek and was the first three-power war conference attended by Stalin. Agreement was reached on the scope and timing of operations against Germany, including plans for the Allied invasion of France. Stalin reaffirmed his pledge to commit Soviet forces against Japan after the defeat of Germany. The final communiqué also stressed the need for cooperation through the United Nations in meeting the problems of peace. A separate protocol pledged the three powers to maintain the independence of Iran

Teutonic Knights: a German division of the Knights Templar.

The Asma al-Husna: are the ninety-nine beautiful names of His duties. They were revealed to Prophet Muhammad in the Qur'an, and the explained them to his followers. This is a vast **Hahr al-Dawlah,** a very deep ocean of His grace and His limitless, infinite, and undiminishing wealth. If we go on cutting one of these ninety-nine **wilayat** over and over again, taking one piece at a time, we will see ninety-nine particles revolving one around the other without touching. This applies to each one of the ninety-nine **wilayat**. This is the **Asma al-Husna**. As we go on cutting, we lose ourselves in that. We die within that. How can we ever hope to reach and end of the ninety-nine? If we receive only one drop of that, it will be more than sufficient for us. The person who has touched the smallest, tiniest drop becomes a good one. These are merely His powers. If you go on cutting just one of His powers, it is so powerful that it will draw you in. That power will swallow you up, and you become the power [**wilayah**]. Then you come to the stage at which you can lose yourself within Allah; you can disappear within Allah.

Tijaniyya: A Sufi order. A dervish fraternity of worldwide membership, **Tijaniyya** dervishes – a strict **Tariqa (q.v.)** principally in Ghana, Guinea and Senegal.

Timurids: Timurids, dynasty founded by Timur (or Tamerlane). After the death of Timur (1405) there was a struggle for power over his empire, which then extended from the Euphrates River to the Jaxartes (Syr Darya) and Indus rivers. The western empire, which included Tabriz and Baghdad, lasted only a few years because of internal wars. The so-called Black Sheep Turkmen horde brought it to an end when they took (1410) Baghdad. Shah Rukh, Timur's son, ruled (1409-46) the eastern empire, including Khorasan and Transoxiana (region E of the Amu Darya, or Oxus, River). He fought the Black Sheep and succeeded in recapturing Tabriz and much of W Persia. His domain was the focal point of trade between the East and the West, and it attained a spectacular prosperity.

Because all the Persian cities were desolated by previous wars, the seat of Persian culture was now in Samarkand and Herat; these cities became the center of the Timurid renaissance. This cultural rebirth had a double character; on one hand, there was a renewal of Persian civilization and art (distinguished by extensive adaptations from the Chinese), and on the other, an original national literature in the Turk-Jagatai language, which borrowed from Persian sources. Shah Rukh was succeeded by his son, Ulugh Beg (ruled 1447-49). He had earlier been (1409-47) viceroy of Transoxiana. He constructed many public buildings and was a patron of Persian art and literature; he made Samarkand a center of Muslim civilization. After his succession (ruled 1447-49) to the throne the Timurid empire fell into anarchy; the Turkmen horde known as the White Sheep conquered much territory, while the Uzbeks looted Samarkand. Petty princes took over the rule, and local dynasties sprang up. One of the princes, and the last of the Timurids, was Babur

Trucial States: Seven Arab emirates on the Persian Gulf, known as the Trucial States from the early 1820s until 1971 when they were established as the United Arab Emirates. The name was derived from the annual 'truce' obtained by the British in the 1820s by which the local rulers undertook to abstain from maritime warfare. Other treaties with Britain extended the ban to the arms and slave traders and the Exclusion Agreements of 1892 provided for British control of the external affairs of the states. The Trucial States in the Lower Gulf included the principalities of Abu Dhabi, Ajman, Dubai, Fujaira, Ras al Khaima, Sharjah, and Umm al Qaiwan. With oil revenues beginning to rise in the was named the United Arab Emirates.

Tudeh Party of Iran: *(Persian: masses):* Official name: Tudeh Party of Iran: Party of Iranian Working Class. The Tudeh Party, formed in January 1942, evolved out of the Communist Party of Iran (established in June 1920), which had helped to found the Soviet Republic of Gilan along the Caspian Sea. In 1937, fifty-eight members of the Marxist Circle were convicted in Tehran. Following the occupation of Iran by Soviet and British troops in August 1941, and the deposition of Reza Shah Pahlavi, all political prisoners were released. In November 1946, Premier Ahmad Qavam Saltane arrested hundreds of Tudeh activists to forestall a threatened strike in Tehran.

In February 1949, claiming that his would-be assassin, an Islamist journalist, was a card-carrying member of a union affiliated to the pro-Tudeh labor federation, Muhammad Reza Shah Pahlavi suppressed the party. Kianouri and his aides returned from abroad to revive the party openly. In March the central committee met in Tehran, its first such meeting for a quarter of a century. Despite its backing for the government in its defense of Iranian territory when attacked by Iraq in September 1980, the authorities raided its office in Tehran and suspended its newspaper. When the Tudeh advised against marching into Iraq in June 1982 during the Iran-Iraq War, it drew the ire of the authorities, who accelerated the purge of Tudeh members from official institutions. In February 1984 there were further convictions, and ten Tudeh leaders were executed. Committed to the secularization and democratization of Iran, it continued to publish a journal, *Nameh Mardom (Persian: People's Journal)*, in Persian from Berlin.

Turcoman: Used in the medieval sources for the Oghuz/Ghuzz tribes of the Turks who were forced westwards by Seljuk and then Mongol expansion. In the 12th century they formed principalities in Azerbaidzhan and Anatolia but were not fully absorbed by the Seljuks of Rum. On the disintegration of the Seljuk state they established new emirates of whom the Ottoman became the most famous but most of the Turcomans never settled and remained as they are today, nomads.

Turkmen: Also spelled Turcoman or Turkoman. The term Turkmen applies to those who speak Turkmen, a member of the south Turkic language group.

Turks: A central Asian people who were originally nomads from Turkistan. During the 6th century AD the Turks controlled an empire stretching from Mongolia to the Caspian Sea. With the conquest of western Turkistan in the 7th century by the Abbasids, many were converted to Islam and moved westwards, retaining their distinctive language and culture. In the 11th century, under the Seljuks they replaced the Arabs as rulers of the Levant and

Mesopotamia, then expanded north-west at the expense of Byzantium (Constantinople's). The Rival house of Osman continued this trend, founding the Ottoman Empire, which endured for 600 years and embraced most of the Middle East, North Africa, and the Balkans.

Twelver Shi'as: The predominant category among Shi'as, Twelvers or Twelver Shi'as are so called because they believe in twelve *imams*: Ali, Hassan, Hussein, Zain al Abidin, Muhammad al Baqir, Ja'far al Sadiq, Musa al Kazem, Ali al Rida/Reza, Muhammad al Taqi Javad, Ali al Naqi, Hassan al Askari, and Muhammad al Qasim. They believe that Muhammas al Qasim, the infant son of the eleventh imam, went into occultation in Samarra, Iraq, in A.D. 873, leaving behind four special assistants. As the last of them failed to name a successor, the line of divinely inspired imams became extinct in A.D. 940. **Twelvers:** Twelver Shi'as. The largest branch of Shiite Islam. They believe that the twelfth imam, (successor to 'Ali in Shi'a belief) was taken by Allah and will return as a messiah figure to lead Shiite Muslims at Judgment Day.

Ulama/Ulema: *(Arabic: pl. of Alim, possessor of* Ilm, *knowledge):* Ulama is the term used collectively for religious-legal scholars of Islam. Since *Ilm* in Islam means knowledge of the Quran and the *Sunna*, the ulama are theologians and canonists. They are the ultimate authority on the issues of law and theology, personifying the right of Muslims to govern themselves. The custodians of Ilm or knowledge who transmit it from generation to generation as teachers and jurists within the Ummah. (plural of Alim): learned men, Islamic scholars. Ar., literally, 'the knowledgeable persons', scholars of Islamic religious subjects. Essentially scholars who had to traditional madrassa education in the Koran and its exegesis, tradition, and canon law. Such scholars were appointed to the judiciary or other posts in the administration and came to form a class of urban notables, the ahl al Qalam. those learned in Islamic law. The leaders of Islamic society, including teachers, Imams, and judges. The custodians of 'Ilm, or knowledge, who transmit it from generation to generation as teachers and jurists within the Ummah. The established body of religious scholars. Their thoughts and writings are often closely tied to the requirements of incumbent political authorities in need of religious sanction for political acts.

Ulus: The kingdoms of the successors of Genghis Khan. The Great Khan remained first at Qaraqrum in Mongolia and later under Qubilay at Peking. Khan Baligh. The lulus of Jochi the Lands of the Golden Horde, stretched roughly from Dnepr to the Oxus, its eastern frontier that of Chaghatay occupied Transozania.

Umayyad: Umayyad, the first Islamic dynasty (661-750). Their reign witnessed the return to leadership roles of the pre-Islamic Arab elite, and the rejuvenation of tribal loyalties. The Banu Umayya constituted the higher stratum of the pre-Islamic Meccan elite. Having entered into an agreement with Muhammad in 630, they succeeded into the political power structure. The assassination of Uthman, the third caliph, and a member of the Umayya, presented the dynamic Umayyad figure of Muawiya the opportunity to challenge the otherwise troubled rulership of Ali. With the death of Ali, Muawiya succeeded in establishing himself as the caliph, making Damascus the capital of the Islamic empire. His efforts concentrated on strengthening his rule by entering into a truce with the Byzantines, renewing tribal alliances and securing the succession of his son Yazid. With the death of Muawiya in 680, Yazid faced the opposition of Husayn, the son of Ali.

The resistance and subsequent martyrdom of Husayn at Karbala in a battle where the Umayyad forces outnumbered him and his partisans is the focus of the central yearly Shiite observance of *Ashura*. Yazid also faced further resistance in the Hijaz (today Saudi Arabia), led by Abdallah ibn az-Zubayr. With his death, the caliphate was transferred to the Marwanid branch of the Banu Umayya. Abd al-Malik succeeded in consolidating Umayyad rule, and proceeded with a series of administrative reforms including the conversion of the bureaucracy from Greek to Arabic, and the minting of new currency. This consolidation set the stage for the renewal of territorial expansion in Asia and Africa under Walid I (705-15), and the increasing military pressure against Byzantium under Sulayman (715-17).

Sulayman's successor, Umar II (717-20) unsuccessfully attempted to reverse the course of tribal-based politics in an effort to restore the Islamic political ideal of transcending partisanships.

His successors, Yazid II (720-24), Hisham (724-43), and Walid (743-44) pursued the tribal-based territorial conquests. The expansion of the Islamic empire led to the emergence of a substantial class of non-tribal Muslims (*Mawali*), who became the base from which anti-Umayyad movements drew their supporters. The most notable of these movements was the Abbasid, which eventually succeeded in toppling the last Umayyad caliph, Marwan II, in 750. A branch of the Umayyad family, led by Abd Ar-Rahman ad-Dakhil, was able to reach Cordoba and to reestablish Umayyad rule (780-1031) in Muslim Spain. Ruled the Muslim world from Damascus for 90 years until 750 ACE.

Ummah: A derivative of either the Arabic umm, meaning mother or source; or a loan-word from Hebrew *Ummah* or Aramaic *Ummtha; Ummah* appears many times in the Quran, always alluding to ethnic, linguistic, or religious groups who were part of Allah's plan of salvation. In modern times the *Ummah*, now meaning the worldwide Islamic community On the other hand, the annual hajj is a dramatic illustration of the existence of Ummah. An Arabic word usually denoting a religious community. In modern usage, it is also used to translate the term nation, as for example in the Arabic name of the United Nations. When one speaks of "the Ummah" without specific qualification or designation, it is usually understood to mean the global Muslim community as a whole. The global community of Muslims, which transcends nationality and nation-states and links all Muslims into a single community.

Union of the Peoples of Arabian Peninsula (Saudi Arabia): An organization of Nasserite persuasion, established in the late 1950s and led by Nasser Said, the Union of the People of Arabian Peninsula (UPAP) aimed to rid Saudi Arabia of the monarchy. Following the takeover of the Grand Mosque in Mecca in November 1979 by Islamic militants, it briefly became active before going into hibernation again.

United Arab Republic: (1958-61): in February 1958 Egypt and Syria merged to form the United Arab Republic (UAR). The creation of a unified military company, in which Syrian officers were relegated to secondary positions, created discontent in the officer corps. These factors created widespread disaffection in Syria and prepared the ground for its secession from the UAR, which came in September 1961 amid much rancor. The union of Syria and Egypt (1958), which was dissolved in 1961 following an army coup in Syria. The United Arab Republic was open to other Arab states to join, but only Yemen entered a loose association (1958), which lasted until 1966. Egypt retained the name United Arab Republic until 1971, when it adopted the name Arab Republic of Egypt.

United Malays National Organization: (UMNO) Malaysian political party. Formed by Dato Onn bin Ja'far, then Prime Minister of Johore, in 1946 in response to British attempts to form the Union of Malaya, UMNO's aim was to fight for national independence and protect the interests of the indigenous population. Since independence in 1957 UMNO has been the dominant party in Malaysia, forming the cornerstone of successive electoral alliances, notably the Alliance party of the 1960s and its successor, the National Front. In 1995, UMNO won its biggest victory since independence. During the south-east Asian financial crisis of 1997-98 its President, Mahathir bin Mohamed blamed foreign speculators for the collapse of the Malaysian economy.

United National Leadership of the Uprising (West Bank and Gaza): following the spontaneous outbreak of the intifada in the Gaza Strip, leaders of the groups affiliated to the outlawed Palestine Liberation Organization and based in the Occupied West Bank and Gaza Strip combined to form the United National Leadership of the Uprising (UNLU).

United Nations (U.N.; established: 1945):

United Nations Disengagement Observer Force (1974-   ): following the disengagement agreement between the Syrian and Israeli forces on the Golan Heights on 31 May 1974, a United Nations Disengagement Observer Force (UNDOF)...

United Nations Emergency Force: (1957-67): during the Suez War, the United Nations General Assembly decided on 4 November 1956 to create a United Nations Emergency Force (UNEF)—composed of troops from countries not involved in the conflict—to supervise the cease-fire. On the insistence of Israel, which had completed its evacuation of Egypt by 8 March 1957, UNEF was stationed only on the Egyptian side of the Canal and in Egyptian-administered Gaza. It was required to safeguard Israeli shipping through the Gulf of Aqaba. on 18 May Nasser asked the UN secretary-general to withdraw UNEF from Egypt, which he was entitled to do since U. N. forces are deployed in a country only so long as its government wishes. The secretary-general complied with Nasser's request. With the UNEF units gone from Sharm al Shaikh at the mouth of the Gulf of Aqaba, Nasser closed the waterway to Israeli shipping.

United Nations General Assembly Resolution 3236: (November 1974): at the end of a long debate on the "Question of Palestine," on 22 November 1974 the United Nations General Assembly reaffirmed the Palestinian people's right to self-determination, independence, and sovereignty and their right to return to their homes and properties.

United Nations Interim Force in Lebanon: (1978--): following the Israeli invasion of southern Lebanon on 14 March 1978, United Nations Security Council Resolution 425 of 19 March called on Israel to cease fire, and authorized the formation of the United Nations Interim Force in Lebanon (Unifil) to confirm the Israeli evacuation and assist the Lebanese government to assume effective control in the area. with the second and larger Israeli invasion of Lebanon in June 1982, resulting in the occupation of southern Lebanon by Israel, Unifil's objective of assisting the Beirut government to assume effective control of southern Lebanon became more distant. So Israel insisted on Unifil continuing its mission.

United Nations Iran-Iraq Military Observer Group: (1988--): following acceptance of his implementation details for U.N. Security Council Resolution 598 on 8 August 1988, the U. N. secretary-general announced the formation of the United Nations Iran-Iraq Military Observer Group (UNIIMOG), consisting of 350 troops and officers drawn from twenty-five countries to supervise the cease-fire that was to come into effect on 20 August 1988.

United Nations Iraq-Kuwait Observer Mission: (1991--) in line with U.N. Security Council Resolution 687 of 3 April 1991, concerning the cease-fire in the Second Gulf War between Iraq and the U.S.-led coalition, the U.N. secretary-general selected a United Nations Iraq-Kuwait Military Observer Group (UNIKOM),composed of 320 military personnel from thirty-five countries. Following a fresh demarcation of the international frontier by a U.N committee at the expense of Iraq in 1993, and its acceptance by Baghdad in November 1994, UNIKOM began to function within the new boundaries.

United Nations Monitoring, Verification and Inspection Commission: (1999): according to the terms of paragraphs 1, 2, and 3 of U. N. Security Council Resolution 1284 (1999) on Iraq, adopted on 17 December 1999, the secretary-general appointed the United Nations Monitoring, Verification, and Inspection Commission (Unmovic) to replace the United Nations Special Commission of 1991. It was not until late November 2002 that, following Iraq's acceptance of U. N. Security Council Resolution 1441, the UNMOVIC staff began performing their tasks.

United Nations Relief and Work Agency for Palestinian Refugees in the Near East: (1949-   ): following a resolution in December 1949 by the United Nations General Assembly to car for those Palestinians who had lost their homes and means of livelihood during the 1948-49 Palestine War, the United Nations Relief and Work Agency for Palestinian Refugees in the Near East (UNRWA) was created at the U.S.'s office in Vienna, Austria. Following Israel's seizure of the West Bank and the Gaza Strip during the June 1967 Arab-Israeli War, there were a further 335,000 displaced Palestinians, of whom 193,600 were eligible for UNRWA support. In 1980, 1,844,300 Palestinian refugees registered with UNRWA.

United Nations Special Commission on Iraq: (1991): according to the terms of paragraph 9 of United Nations Security Council Resolution 687 (1991), adopted on 3 April 1991.

United Nations Special Commission on Palestine: (1947): On 15 May 1947 a special session of the United Nations General Assembly appointed as eleven-member Special Commission on Palestine, consisting of Australia, Canada, Czechoslovakia, Guatemala, India, Iran, the Netherlands, Peru, Sweden, Uruguay and Yugoslavia.

United Nations Truce Supervision Organization: (1948-): to assist the United Nations Mediator and the Truce Commission in supervising the cease-fire in the 1948-48 Arab-Israeli War, the United Nations Truce Supervision Organizations (UNTSO) was created in June 1948.

United States Middle East Force: the United States Middle East Force based itself in Bahrain according to a secret agreement signed by Washington and the emirate on the event of Britain's withdrawal from there in 1971. Because of the proximity to the oil fields of Saudi Arabia, Qatar, and the United Arab Emirates, Bahrain was ideal for naval reconnaissance missions in the Gulf. During the October 1973 Arab-Israeli War, angered at the United States' support for Israel, the Bahraini ruler stated that he had abrogated the agreement with Washington. The Bahraini-U.S. link was confirmed in April 1980, following their unsuccessful attempt to free American hostages in Tehran, U.S. military planes refueled in Bahrain before taking off for Turkey.

Wafd: in modern Egyptian history, a political party. It arose out of the delegation [Arabic *Wafd*=delegation] headed by Zaghlul Pasha that was to have visited Great Britain in 1918 to urge Egypt's independence. Zaghlul formed the party in 1919. In addition to espousing independence, the Wafdists called for extensive social and economic reforms. In the first parliament elected (1924) under the constitution of 1923, the Wafd won a large majority,

King Faud I, who bitterly opposed the party, dissolved parliament and would not call a new election until 1926. Again the Wafd won, and in 1928 its new leader, Nahas Pasha, became prime minister. That year the government introduced a measure forbidding the king to rule without parliament. Faud, asserting that this would give the Wafd absolute control of the country, refused his assent and suspended the constitution.

Nevertheless, in 1930 the Wafd was again victorious. Faud soon dismissed the new cabinet and appointed a conservative prime minister, who made the party illegal. When the constitution of 1923 was restored in 1935, the Wafd returned to power. They formed the cabinet in 1936-37. Relations with the new king, Farouk, were scarcely more cordial than those with his father. In World War II the party, which was anti-Axis, was installed in office from 1942 to 1944 at the insistence of Great Britain, which feared pro-Axis elements. In the elections of 1950 the Wafd triumphed again, and Nahas Pasha returned as prime minister. The party lost much of its popularity because of corruption and the support it had given the British during the war. On Jan. 26, 1952, King Farouk took advantage of riots in Cairo to dismiss the Wafd from power. When the Egyptian revolution took place in July, 1952, Wafd politicians were discredited, and the party was forced to disband. The New Wafd party, established in 1978, had parliamentary representation in the 1980s

Wahhabism & Arabia: The apocalyptic, militaristic, and totalitarian cult called Wahhabism would shed the blood of many fellow Muslims before eventually hurling a murderous challenge to the Judeo-Christian world. Muhammad Ibn Abd al-Wahhab, founder of Wahhabism, was born in 1703, the son of a judge in Uyaynah, a village in the central Arabian region of Najad. Najad means plateau. Until about 500 years ago it was mainly uninhabited. It's only commerce at the time of Ibn Abd al-Wahhab's birth was with Kuwait and the island of Bahrein to the east. Some Christians and Jews remained in Arabia until the final Triumph of Wahhabism in the 1920's. Establishment there of Riyadh, the future capital of Saudi Arabia, by follower of Wahhabism.

He had shown extremist religious tendencies in his youth. Both his father and his brother Suleyman, who were Islamic scholars, warned others against him, and Suleyman even wrote a book in opposition to him, with the piquant title Divine Thunderbolts. Traveled widely to Basra, Baghdad, Damascus, through Kurdistan, Iran and India. Ibn Abd al-Wahhab returned to Najd with a group of African Slaves as a bodyguard. In 1737-40, he publicly announced his call to his version of religion and was joined by some of his younger relatives. He therefore advocated rebellion against the Ottoman caliphate. His chief written work was titled *The Book of Monotheism*. His main inspiration was Ibn Taymiyyah. The Turks had ruled Arabia a little more than 200 years at the time of Ibn Abd al-Wahhab's birth. Wahhabism in Saudi Arabia claims to be returning to the original faith, practiced by the Prophet.

After 1973 the Wahhabi-Saudi institutions began a new and immensely ambitious global campaign for the Wahhabization of the Ummah: Madrasas. Free copies of Qur'an with Wahhabi commentaries, training of imams, dissemination of hate literature, and similar works. The Wahhabis appropriated the term Salafis referring to the original, pious successors of Muhammad. Who remained protected as People of the Book. All others were to be liquidated, beginning with the Shi'a and Sufis. Thus they split the planet between the "house of war" and the "house of peace" or "house of Islam". The Madrasahs (schools) were the basis for the proliferation of Wahhabi influence. Newspaper Jang reported in January 2002 that the number of madresas into that country had risen from 2,861 in 1988 to 6,761 in 2000.

At the end of that period 1,947 belonged to the Wahhabized. The convergence of interests between the Wahhabis and Iraq became more obvious at the conclusion of the 2001-02 Afghan war when the Saudis lobbied Washington against serious Western action to remove Saddam. Bin Laden jeered at the United States for fleeing Lebanon, Somalia, and Yemen. Blaming American and the Saudis for allegedly killing more than half a million Iraqi children. Based on the same foundation that Ibn Taymiyyah established, Muhammad Ibn Abd al-Wahhab Ab al Wahhab (1703-1792) led the Wahhabi movement in Arabia. This movement resisted, fought and overturned the Turkish government. Abd Al Wahhab established a new 100 percent Islamic nation, which eventually became Saudi Arabia. At the same time, the Saudi government is also facing an El Kharij movement, those who would like to go back to the original principles.

Osama bin laden is an example of that group. For Ibn Taymiyyah, the political state and the religious scholars were to function as a single entity. This view was later echoed in the rise of Wahhabism in Saudi Arabia. Taymiyyah declared total war on Sufism and Shi'ism, declaring that the creator had a physical body. As in Judaism, this position is firmly rejected by Muslims, who hold that the divine form is limitless and unknowable. The essence of Ibn Abd al-Wahhab preaching came down to three points. First, ritual is superior to intentions. Second, no reverence of the dead is permitted. Third, there can be no intercessory prayer, addressed to God by means of the Prophet of saints. This latter precept was borrowed directly from Ibn Taymiyyah. Defying centuries of Islamic theology, Ibn Abd al-Wahhab's followers ascribed a human form to God, as Ibn Taymiyyah had also done.

An anthropomorphic view of God had hitherto been considered scandalously heretical in Islam. Ibn Abd al-Wahhab also condemned the habit of those making hajj in Mecca to visit the Prophets tomb in Medina. He particularly hated celebrations of the Prophet's birthday or mawlid an-Nabi. He would not even permit the name of the Prophet Muhammad to be inscribed in mosques which he ordered should be free of all decoration. Demanded that Muslims not shave or trim their beards. Ibn Abd al-Wahhab doctrines explicitly downgraded the status of Muhammad. It seems clear that Ibn Abd al-Wahhab saw himself as an equal of the Prophet, a view that is also thoroughly heretical in Islam. His brother Suleyman accused him of trying to add a "sixth pillar" to Islam: the infallibility of Ibn Abd al-Wahhab.

All other faiths were to be humiliated or destroyed. With his terrible doctrine, the basis had been laid for two and a half centuries of Islamic Fundamentalism, and ultimately terrorism, in response to global change. Soon Ibn Abd al-Wahhab ordered that graves of Muslim saints be dug up and scattered, or turned into latrines. He also burned many books, arguing that Qur'an alone would suffice for humanity's needs. Ibn Abd al-Wahhab and his followers despised music. The Wahhab-Sa'ud alliance first conquered a few local settlements and imposed Ibn Abd al-Wahhab doctrines on them. The first of his political partners, Muhammad ibn Sa'ud, died in 1765 and was succeeded by his son Abd al-Aziz ibn Sa'ud. By 1788, the Wahhab-Sa'ud alliance controlled most of the Arabian Peninsula. In 1792, Ibn Abd al-Wahhab died, and Abd al-Aziz took over. The Wahhabis had an extraordinary hatred of Shi'ism.

Today the Saudi school systems, following Wahhabi tenets, teach their children and other Muslims throughout the Ummah that Shi'a Islam was invented by an imaginary Jewish convert, the Shi'a theologians are liars, that their legal traditions are false and that they are not Muslims at all. In 1801, the Wahhabis attacked the Shi'a holy city of Karbala in Iraq, between Baghdad and the Arabian frontier. They slaughtered thousands of its citizens. They also wrecked and looted the tomb of Husayn, grandson of the Prophet. The Saudi chief Abd al-Aziz was murdered in 1803, possibly by a Shi'a avenger. His son Sa'ud bin Abd al-Aziz succeeded him. The citizens of Ta'if petitioned for an honorable surrender, based on guarantees for the security of their lives and the chastity of their women.

In the taking of Ta'is, it is said that the Wahhabis "killed every woman, man and child they saw, slashing with their swords even babies in cradles. The streets were flooded with blood". The Wahhabis, under the third Saudi ruler, Sa'ud bin Abd al-Aziz, had established a prototype for a modern "Islamic" terrorist regime. The next year Ibn Abd al-Wahhab declared himself leader of the world-wide Ummah backed with a fatwa in which Ibn Abd al-Wahhab ordered Jihad against the Ottomans. In 1788, when Abd al-Aziz ibn Sa'ud was joined by British forces in occupying Kuwait. The hammer of empire and caliphate against the Wahhabis was Muhammad Ali Pasha, the governor of Egypt, and an Albanian born in the heart of the Balkans.

Muhammad Ali Pasha was the ideal man to fight Sa'ud bin Abd al-Aziz, the defiler of the Holy Places, and he acquitted himself gloriously in liberating Mecca and Medina from Wahhabi dictatorship. Two of the worst Wahhabi terrorists, Uthman ul-Mudayiqi (The tormentor of Ta'if) and Mubarak ibn Maghyan, were sent to Istanbul where they were paraded through the streets before being executed, their severed heads posted in the imperial precincts. Next Muhammad Ali Pasha sent troops under his second son Ibrahim Pasha, to cleanse Syria, Iraq, and Kuwait of the Wahhabis. In 1818, the Wahhabi capital, Dariyah, was subjugated and destroyed by the Ottomans, but some of the Al Sa'ud received British protection in Jeddah.

Sa'ud bin Abd al-Aziz had died of fever in 1814. Britain encouraged the Wahhabis, with an eye to the eventual Turkish collapse and division of its possessions. In Bengal in 1831, a peasant named Titu Mir (born in 1782) led a Wahhabi uprising in his view; Bengal was part of the "House of War". Traditional Islam had come to define Hindus as People of the Book, finding a monotheistic essence in the religion of Brahma. Their ultimate goal was political power, as in Arabia. They made forced conversion their weapon. Between 1865 and 1891 the Saudi Wahhabi were lead by Sa'ud Ibn Faysal, who moved his headquarters to Riyadh. "Sons of Asir" were key participants in the September 11, 2001 atrocities, 15 of them were Saudis.

In 1891 Sa'ud and his Wahhabi followers were expelled by the Rashid Dynasty (Kuwait). In 1901 when Abdul-Aziz Ibn Abdur-Rahman Ibn Muhammad Al Sa'ud, then aged 21, departed Kuwait for a new try at subduing the Two Holy Places. He went first to Riyadh, murdering the city's ruler, and took control of it, thereby laying the foundation of what would become Saudi Arabia, a global power of the 20th century. In 1924, the Wahhabis reconquered Mecca, thereby acquiring the right to the collection of taxes and fees from pilgrims in hajj. The seizure of the city of the Ka'abah came at the end of a 23-year campaign by Ibn Sa'ud, accompanied by the usual mass murder: Nearly half a million people had been killed or injured by Wahhabi zealots. A million people had fled the areas they had seized.

The new regime emerged from the confusion of the First World War, the collapse of the Turkish Empire, and the end of the Ottoman caliphate as the religious authority for the Sunni world's Muslims. The following year saw the extension of Wahhabi authority to the port of Jeddah and to Medina. Soon Ibn Sa'ud ordered the destruction of the most sacred toms, graveyards and Mosques. All these tombs and gravestones were wrecked by Ibn Sa'ud's minions, who then, like their Wahhabi predecessors in the 19th century, looted the treasure at the Prophet's Shrine. Arabs, Wahhabism introduced into the Arab world the essence of totalitarianism. The Ikhwan represented the ideal of Wahhabi separatism-from other Muslims, from non-Muslims, from the world. Between 1916 and 1928, 26 insurrections by the Bedouin Wahhabi-Saudi authority were suppressed by the Ikhwan with great bloodshed, including the murder of women and children.

As early as 1910 Ibn Sa'ud had begun sending out Wahhabi preachers (Majutawiyah or "volunteers") to the desert tribes "to kindle in them a zeal for holy war." The Sharif of Mecca saw the Unionists sacrificing thousands of Muslim youth to their horror, and in 1916 he issued two calls to Arab revolt. Ibn Sa'ud had agreed to a treaty with Britain in 1915, making his domain a protectorate. He promised in return for cash and arms, to fight Al Rashid. Having taken Hasa, Ibn Sa'ud was confirmed by the Turkish authorities as Emir of Riyadh. Arabia: Sharif Husayn of Mecca was now styled King of Hejaz and Ibn Sa'ud. Saw their leaders as candidates to succeed the Ottoman sultan as caliph of Islam worldwide.

The emir of Kuwait, who had provided Al Sa'ud shelter, would be the first Arabs to be granted British knighthoods. Ibn Sa'ud envisioned control of the Two Holy Places as the basis for Wahhabization of global Islam. Had Britain defended the

Hashemites in the Two Holy Places, Wahhabism would have remained an obscure, deviant cult, and the Peninsula would very likely have developed modern political institutions.

Saudi Ikhwan: The Ikhwan went on to completely demolish the cemetery in Mecca that included the graves of the mother and grandfather of Muhammad and of his wife Khadijah including Muhammad's own house. Of the graves, only that of the Prophet remained intact. But in 1926 Ibn Sa'ud called a global Islamic conference to ratify his control over the Two Holy Places. Ibn Sa'ud had first concentrated on destroying the remaining power of Al Rashid, a rival dynasty from Najd. Ruled Riyadh until Ibn Sa'ud's recapture of the city in 1902.

In 1924 Husayn recognized the Soviet Union, thus aggravating the deterioration of his relations with Britain. Ibn Sa'ud then summoned the *Ikhwan* anew to the conquest of Mecca and Medina. Wahhabism had created a totalitarian system—a dictatorship resting on an ideological militia, the Ikhwan. When the Ikhwan was founded in 1912: The Ikhwan was young sons of the desert who had emerged from a hopeless nothingness of petty rivalries and banditry. They would teach the world about the emptiness in their hearts, which reproduced the voice of their social existence. Death in Jihad was attainment of paradise. The Wahhabis established a system of governance based on a monopoly of wealth by the elite, backed by extreme repression and a taste for bloodshed.

The Ikhwan, who reproduced the mentality of the Khawarij, also anticipated the terrorism of the Saudi-backed Hamas in Israel, which became infamous for their suicide bombing attacks on civilians. The League for the Encouragement of Virtue and Prevention of Vice Public Morals Committees to act as its eyes and ears among the masses. (They are known in Arabic as the Mutawiyin, or "volunteers"). The Soviet Union was the first government to recognize Ibn Sa'ud as King of Hejaz, in 1927. An Ikhwan faction commenced provocative raids into Iraq, ruled by King Faisal, the Hashemite son of Sharif Husayn of Mecca. The Ikhwan incursions were met by British air raids. Thus by

1932, all power had been concentrated in Ibn Sa'ud's hands and the kingdom of Saudi Arabia was proclaimed, the only country in the world named for a living person, non-Wahhabi Sunnis have proven impossible to remove completely from the country.

The Wahhabis worked to spread their rigid variant of Hanbali jurisprudence to the whole country. With the discovery of oil in Arabia, the Wahhabi-Saudi state would soon pass irrevocably from the British to the U. S. Sphere of influence. Hydrocarbons turned the Wahhabis and Al Sa'ud, already the most extreme totalitarians on the planet, into the world's richest and most powerful ruling elite. Social did not find oil in Saudi territory until 1938. In 1936, Socal and the Texas Oil Company had created a partnership, which would come to be named Aramco— the Arabian-American Oil Company. Ibn Sa'ud again revealed his family's penchant for duplicity by giving asylum to Rashid Ali, leader of the Iraqi coup. Social convinced the administration of Franklin Roosevelt that support for Ibn Sa'ud would results in the United States permanently excluding Britain from the exploitation of Arabian oil.

The Saudi monarchy was granted millions of dollars in lend-lease aide. The Saudi monarchy entered another new phase in 1945 when Roosevelt met with Ibn Sa'ud aboard the USS Quincy in Egypt's Great Bitter Lake. The American president tried unsuccessfully to gain Saudi approval for increased Jewish settlement in Palestine. The new arrangement was predicated on Saudi Arabia declaring war on the Axis, which it did within a month of the Roosevelt-Ibn Sa'ud encounter. The United States had clearly adopted a "hands off" policy toward Saudi internal and ideological matters. Ten years later, in 1948, Aramco discovered Ghawar which remains the largest oil field on the planet.

Saudi Arabia was surrounded by war fronts. The Germans, who lacked energy resources, were aggressively interested in Arab oil (Rommel in North Africa). After the war was over, displaced Palestinians were barred from entering the Saudi Kingdom. King Faisal, a son of Ibn Sa'ud and a female member of the family of

Ibn Abd al-Wahhab, reigned from 1964 until he was murdered by a nephew in 1975. Meanwhile the voracious demand of Ibn Sa'ud and his cohort for women produced armies of wives and concubines, as well as an enormous dynasty of princes. By the end of the 20th century the ranks of the main princely lines were estimated at 4,000. The Saudi aristocracy would become known as "airport Wahhabis". Their tastes led to taverns, casinos, brothels, and similar establishments. They bought fleets of automobiles, private jets, and yachts the size of warships. They spent as they wished, become patrons of international sexual enslavement and the exploitation of children. They bought influence everywhere.

The evil of Saudi Arabia: Glorified by the Saudi regime as a pillar of Islamic wisdom, a blind Wahhabi Imam, Abdul-Aziz bin Baz issued a fatwa in 1969 stating that the earth is a flat disk around which the sun revolves and that any belief otherwise was heresy, to be severely punished. He corrected himself after Prince Sultan, a grandson of Ibn Sa'ud, took a ride in an American space shuttle in 1985 and told bin Baz that he had personally witnessed the roundness of the earth. Bin Baz also authored a notorious fatwa against women driving. Al Sa'ud, controlled the world's largest single source of petroleum. Ibn Sa'ud aided the more radical Mufti of Jerusalem, Haj Amin al-Husayni, who became a German agent during the Great War. After 1945, the British sought al-Husayni for trial, but Ibn Sa'ud provided secret shelter to the Mufti, as he had previously welcomed Rashid Ali, the Nazi agent from Iraq. Ibn Sa'ud publicly supported the war on Israel (1948) but did not send troops to the front. The Wahhabi-Saudi power drew many of these groups into its orbit. By 1978, Islamic radicalism had been in great part Wahhabized. Muslim World League was established by the Saudis.

Saudi lobby & political organizations: Academic endowments have been provided for major universities, including U.C. Berkeley, Harvard, the University of London, and Moscow University. Islamic Saudi Academy in Washington D.C. Fairfax, Virginia is host to the Institute for Islamic and Arabia Sciences in

America, also sub sized by the kingdom. On September 17, 2001, President George W. Bush stood in the Islamic Center of Washington, the capital's most important mosque. "The face of terror is not the true face of Islam," he said. "Acts of violence against innocents violate the fundamental tenets of the Islamic faith and it's important for my fellow Americans to understand that".

Mid 1980s, Hamas, the Wahhabi organization fighting Israel, decided to open a political front in U.S. territory: a "Wahhabi Lobby". Muslim Public Affairs Council (MPAC). Typically defends extremist violence and the aim of destroying Israel and undermining American power. The leadership of MPAC included Maher Hathout, a gynecologist. After the bombing of American embassies in Kenya and Tanzania, as "illegal, immoral, inhuman, unacceptable, stupid and un-American." When a bomber blew up a pizzeria in Israel on August 9,2001, MPAC declared that Israel itself was "responsible for this pattern of violence." The council on American-Islamic Relations (CAIR) is dedicated to pressuring government and media to accept its definition of Islamic issues and sensitivity thereto; while the America Muslim Council (AMC) is an advocacy group aimed at the wider American public through political, community, and "interfaith" activism.

CAIR's nation director, Nihad Awad, an inexhaustible agitator for Hamas. AMC president Yahya Basha and representatives of MPAC were also to be found. American Muslim Alliance (AMA). Distributes Holocaust denial literature. Islamic Society of North America (ISNA). The country's 1,200 officially recognized mosques (out of possible 4,000). ISNA president Muzzammil Siddiqi, described by many of his critics as a power hungry fanatic. Islamic Circle of North America (ICNA). Islamic Association for Palestine (IAP), the American Muslims for Jerusalem, and the Holy Land Foundation for Relief Development (HLF).

These groups appear independent of one another, but nearly all of them draw from the common financial and technical pool at

HLF. Muslim Student Association (MSA). Predecessor of ISNA. The MSA was created in 1963 in close coordinating with the Muslim World League. Letter issued in 1996 endorsing the AMC, sign by American Friends Service Committee. Alleged unfair media scrutiny of AMC's activities. Endorsed AMC as "the premier, mainstream Muslim group in Washington." Both the Wahhabi lobby in American Islam and the Saudi influence in U.S. foreign policy benefited from a "blank check." The Wahhabis and Saudis were repeatedly granted a privileged position without public discussion. Abdurrahman Alamoudi, the godfather of AMC and a man with a well-known history of extremist incitements, including the statement: "O Allah, destroy America!"

1998 CAIR & AMC cosponsored a rally at Brooklyn College, which included an anti-Jewish diatribe by Wagdi Ghunaim, an Egyptian extremist. Ghunaim led 500 people in singing a ditty with the chorus: "No to the Jews descendants of the apes". The gullibility and ignorance of ordinary Americans, the generally pro-Palestinian bias of our academia. The lobby supported terror against Israel, assisted the funders and organizers of terror to operate in the US and promoted the ideology of terror in American mosques. CAIR nation spokesman, Nihad Awad, declared in 1996 "I am in support of the Hamas movement." "We are ALL supporters of Hamas!" In November 1999, CAIR board chairman, Ammar Ahmad, told an audience in Chicago, "Fighting for freedom, fighting for Islam-that is not suicide. They kill themselves for Islam."

At a meeting of the Islamic Association for Palestine (IAP), a Muslim cleric from Kuwait, Tariq Suweidan, preached, "Nothing can be achieved without sacrificing blood." Prosecution-proof. Ludicrous mistakes were made because Americans were concerned to protect the freedom of the enemies of freedom. Sayyid Nosair, assassin in 1990 of Jewish extremist Meir Kahane, was only found guilty on a firearms charge. The FBI impeded the investigation of Zacharias Moussaoui, who was arrested before September 11 and later charged as a member of the conspiracy. America's capacity to defend itself spiritually and intellectually had been deeply harmed. Wahhabi influence in the American prison system. With the growth of Islam among African Americans, the faith was viewed as a major source of personal reform and redemption for those who found themselves in conflict with the law.

Mahdi Bray, head of the National Islamic Prison Foundation, is also national political director of MPAC and an AMC advisory board member. According to Kabbani and other dissenters, 80 percent of American mosques are run by Wahhabi imams directly subsidized by Saudi Arabia. Kalid Duran: " no more than 20 percent of American Muslim congregants support Wahhabism". The Wahhabis are particularly known for the free distribution and dumping on the book market of their literature, including tendentious translations of the Qur'an' that support their doctrinal claims. A Wahhabi bigot, Hamd ibn "Abd al-Muhsin, who demanded that women who drive automobiles in Saudi Arabia be charged as prostitutes and punished by flogging.

In 1999, the Saudi embassy in Washington announced a grant by the Islamic Development Bank of $250,000 to CAIR for the purchase of land in Washington, to be used in the construction of "an education and research center." In 2000 the Muslim World League (a provider of funds to Osama bin Laden) hosted 100 prominent American Islamic personalities on hajj. They were accompanied by a delegation of 60 Latin American "academics and specialists." All expenses for the latter were paid by Prince Bandar, Saudi ambassador to the United States. In 1999, the Saudis paid for 100 influential American Muslims to make the hajj to Mecca. Qatar-based Wahhabi cleric Yusuf Al-Qarahawi.

Qaradhawi is best known for his fatwa legitimating terrorists attacks in Israel; in April 2001, he defines suicide bombings as "martyrdom, not suicide," suicide being forbidden by Islam. Many Wahhabi functionaries in the US maintained an attitude of truculence toward American society, even after September 11, encouraging the more backward elements that blamed the events on Israel or repeated the paranoid claims that 3,000 American Jews had been warned to stay away from the World Trade Center the day the terrorists struck. HLF is the central node of the Hamas front in the US headquartered in Texas. Established in 1989. Musa Abu Marzook, the external director of Hamas, who lived in the US until he was deported in 1997. Marzook, brother-in-law, Ghassan Elashi, chairman of HLF, finances six terrorist attacks in Israel from his home in Falls Church, Virginia.

In 1995 the US authorities asked for the arrest and deportation of Marzook to Israel. The US deported Marzook to Jordan. In addition to defending suicide bombers, the foundation paid annuities to the children of Palestinian "martyrs". The keystone of the Saudi-sponsored Northern Virginia network was the Saar Foundation, created by Suleiman Abdul Al-Aziz al-Rajhi, a scion of one of the richest Saudi families. The Saar Foundation is connected to Al-Taqwa. Notorious neo-Nazi and Islamist, Ahmed Huber. Saar has also been linked to Khalid bin Mahfouz. Ex-head of the Nation Commercial Bank of Saudi Arabia. Mahfouz has been named by French intelligence as a backer of Osama bin Laden; Mahfouz endowed the Muwaffaq Foundation. Muwaffaq's former chief Yasin al-Qadi.

Men like al-Rajhi, Mahfouz, and al-Qadi are big players in the financing of Islamic Extremism. Saar received 1.7 billion in donations in 1998, although this was left out of the foundations tax filings until 2000. Joining the world-wide Wahhabi "jihad" is not a matter of filling out a form. One does not have to go to a recruiting office to sign up. Mosques in Western countries are permeated with Wahhabi "jihad" rhetoric, encountered the minute one walks in the door. Some imams preach "jihad". The murder of Wall Street Journal reported Daniel Pearl in Pakistan. With the recovery of Perl's corpse, in May 2002, the Pakistani Wahhabi terror group Kashkar-i-Janghvi was identified as the journalist's portable killers. Saudi airlines were asked to provide advance passenger lists for flights to the US. 15 out of the 19 terrorists involved in the attacks on New York and Washington were Saudi citizenship-most of bin Laden's funds also came from the kingdom.

In both cases the Saudis refused compliance. The Saudi Embassy's official website in Washington turned out to have advertized the outlay of hundreds of millions of dollars for the families of "martyrs" in Israel. A Saudi telethon collected $109 million more for the "martyrs" in April 2002. The Wahhabi cleric who hosted the telethon, Shaykh Saad al-Buraik, preached in a mosque in Riyadh, calling for an enslavement of the Jewish women of Israel, once Palestinian victory was achieved. Referring to Jews as "monkeys" "Muslim brothers in Palestine, do not have mercy or compassion toward the Jews, their blood, their money, or their flesh." Verses were published by the Saudi ambassador to Britain, Ghazi Alghosaibi, praising a suicide terror bombing by a teenaged Palestinian girl. Despite official Saudi denials, documents seized by Israeli troops in the West Bank revealed the final destination of the funds from the Saudi state budget-their payment to the families of terrorists.

The Saudis had never committed to a full and transparent investigation of the Khobar Towers bombing in 1996. Nineteen Americans had been killed and 372 injured. The Saudis blamed this atrocity on Iranian sympathizers. The special relationship between US and Saudi Arabia had become an obstacle to American security interests. In the Saudi kingdom there is no separation of powers. Al Sa'ud, the royal family is the state: The royal family is the owner of the energy resources; Abd al-Wahhab, are indistinguishable from the institutions of religion, justice, and education. Najdis are the sole holders of power in Saudi Arabia, occupying all administrative and decision-making posts.

Although no more than 40 percent of the Saudi population are Wahhabi, the cult holds a monopoly on religious life in the kingdom. There are no judges representing Hanafi, Maliki, Shafi'i, or Shi'a jurisprudence. Until very recently no defendants had the right to representation by lawyers. Prince Nayif is one of the "Sudairi Seven"-sons of Ibn Sa'ud and full brothers of King Fahd. The group is named for their mother, the favorite wife of Ibn Sa'ud, Hussah bin Ahmad Sudair, a member of a powerful Najdi family that rose to prominence in the 19th century (Ibn

Sa'ud had 17 wives and hundreds of concubines, and his male offspring totaled 36).

Prince Bandar, who was born in 1950 and Prince Turki, a son of King Faisal, born in 1945, who was chief of foreign intelligence until his abrupt departure from that post of August 31, 2001. Prince Turki is said to have been close to bin Laden. Prince Sultan's business deals with American arms manufacturers. Crown Prince Abdullah was seen as a pious Muslim with strong anti-American tendencies. The Sudairi seven are considered to cleave to the US, not from friendship, but as an expression of the historical Wahhabi strategy of dependence on the Christian powers.

Pan-Arab nationalist favoring a pluralistic vision of Islam in the interest of Arab unity. Virginia based Saudi Institute on torture in the kingdom points out that the Qur'an' prescribes flogging as an Islamic punishment for only two crimes: adultery-which requires four creditable eyewitnesses and libel against the honor of a woman. For adultery, no more that 100 lashes, and for libel only 80 are mandated. In addition, Islamic law calls for 40 to 80 lashes for drinking alcohol. Saudi kingdom has routinely delivered sentences totaling thousands of lashes; at the beginning of 2002 a man in Judah was whipped 4,750 times for sexual relations with his sister-in-law. Flogging is carried out in the kingdom using wooden rods and metal cables, which causes extraordinary suffering.

No other Islamic society in the world imposes such punishments. Shi'a Islam is described in the Wahhabi-Saudi curriculum as a Jewish conspiracy, in addition, the inevitability of war against the Jews is taught to all students. Grand Mufti Shaykh Abd Al-Aziz al-Alshaikh issued a fatwa authorizing a "cyber jihad" that encouraged Wahhabi fanatics to hack into and disable Shi'a and non-Wahhabi websites. On the other hand, the regime encourages the establishment of websites promoting hatred of non-Wahhabi Islam. Cheney is famous, or infamous, for his comment that "The good Lord didn't see fit to put oil and gas only where there are democratically elected regimes friendly to the US." His former employer, Halliburton, an oilfield technology firm, gained a $140 million contract from the Saudis; Halliburton subsidiary Kellogg Brown & Root formed a consortium with two Japanese firms to build a $40 million ethylene plant in the kingdom.

In 1990 the defense secretary Cheney went to the kingdom to convince the Saudi rulers of the wisdom of letting their country be used as a base against Saddam Husayn. A useful relationship became a permanent one and then a lucrative one. Cheney is viewed as the most active in diverting the president from any actions detrimental to Saudi interests. Cheney argues against pressing the Saudis on their involvement in September 11. He insists that they are our firmest allies, and seems to believe they must not be challenged on any ground. Crown Prince Abdullah went straight from Crawford to a friendlier dinner with Bush Sr. whose associates at Carlyle include former defense secretary James Baker, former CIA head Frank Carlucci, former budget chief Richard Darman, former CIA head Robert Gates, and former US ambassador to Japan Michael Arm.

While Cheney directly and aggressively advocated for the Saudis, Powell assumes his "I love everybody" role. For Powell, the Saudis have problems, but they are still our friends. Rumsfeld was something of a cipher in all this: he was reluctant to go after the Saudis, viewing them as a major military ally. One Shi'a divine, Shaykh Mahdi Theab al-Mahaan was released from jail in January 2002, he had been imprisoned for 3 years and had received 3000 lashes, a common punishment for religious nonconformity. Shaykh Ahmed Turki al-Sa'ad who was quoted in the Wall Street Journal on the difficulties facing Shi'a Muslims in the Saudi Kingdom, was arrested on January 15, 2002 six days after his comments appeared, he was sentenced to seven years in prison and 1,200 lashes.

The divisions between the "Sudairi seven" Crown Prince Abdullah, and the younger generation of princes make a serious, and even a bloody, conflict possible. Both Prince Sultan and Crown Prince Abdullah have control over bodies of armed men.

Sultan as defense minister, remain head of the army. Crown Prince Abdullah on the other hand controls the National Guard a domestic sectary body. Certain Turkish Islamists have begun arguing that Mecca should not be subject to the sovereignty of any single country but rather should become an international city-state comparable to the Vatican. The contradictions between Wahhabism and the life-style of the 4,000 princes.

These problems are further increased by the continuing Iranian challenge. Many Westerners remain haunted by the Iranian example and fear the rise of a new and more fearsome fundamentalism in Saudi Arabia. President Bush, Cheney, Powell, and Rumsfeld repeatedly assured the public that the Saudi monarchy was a firm ally of the West in the anti-terror effort. They offered continuous objections to a resolution of the problem of Saddam Husayn, who after all, had served as their weapon against Iran during the 1980s. It is clear that Wahhabism-Saudism is part of the "axis of evil" and possibly the most dangerous part. The fall of Wahhabism could help foster new relations between Jews, Christians, and Muslims, all believers in the monotheism of Abraham. Currently the world views the Israel-Palestinian conflict as a religious one, and therefore despairs of a solution.

The moment must come when the children of Abraham at last recognize their common birthright. Saudi Arabia: Ibn Sa'ud (also known as 'Abd-al-Aziz') united Saudi Arabia into a single kingdom in 1932 and ruled it until his death in 1953. It produces 6.8 million barrels a day. More than eighty active oil and gas fields. More than a thousand working wells. 12.5 percent of all the known oil in the world. Ghawar, the world's largest onshore reserves. Oil fields; and Safaniya, the largest offshore field in existence. Saudi oil moves through roughly seventeen thousand kilometers of pipe. A typical Saudi oil well produces five thousand barrels a day. Iraq-Saudi pipeline, shut down in 1990 following the Iraqi invasion of Kuwait. Capable of transferring 2.5 million barrels of oil and other fuel per day to tankers. On an average day, about 4.3 million barrels of oil leave Saudi Arabia via the Ju'aymah terminal.

One of the most dangerous navigable sites on earth. 4.5 million barrels of sustainable daily export. An attack would be more economically damaging than a dirty nuclear bomb set off in midtown Manhattan. Saudi Arabia sits on 25 percent of the world's proven reserves, maybe barrel per barrel the cheapest oil in the world to extract. The Saudis own half the world's surplus production capacity-two to three million barrels a day. No matter what country you buy your oil from, Saudi Arabia determines the world price. It was Saudi Arabia that broke the back of the 1973 OPEC embargo (though not before it enriched itself by tens of billions of dollars). Without its surplus capacity, the price of a barrel of oil likely would have soared over a hundred dollars.

In 1974, in the wake of the OPEC embargo, when inflation soared to 11 percent; and in 1979-81, when inflation topped out at 13.5 percent. By 1981, the price of a barrel of crude had hit $53.39. The sheikhdoms collectively own 60 percent of the world's oil reserves. 1985 was the first time the U.S. government budget topped the $1.5 trillion mark. Saudi Arabia was America's anchor in the Arab Middle East. It banked our oil under its sand. Losing it would be like losing the Federal Reserve. The Saudi ambassador's wife in Washington had been sending money to the hijackers. Saudi Arabia transferred half a billion dollars to al Qaeda in the ten years beginning 1992. Five extended, dysfunctional families own about 60 percent of the world's oil reserves.

The mosques of Saudi Arabia preach a hatred of the West and the non-Islamic world that is as vitriolic as anything heard in Iran at the height of the ayatollahs. Never forget that it is the Al Sa'ud who ultimately sign the checks for these mosque schools. Khalid Sheikh Muhammad, the purported mastermind of September 11, was finally grabbed in Pakistan in early March 2003. The conviction that all the oil money has corrupted the ruling family beyond redemption. The Al Sa'uds are reviled for failing to protect fellow Muslims in Palestine and Iraq and for standing by helplessly as Islam is humiliated. Saudi Arabia is no abstraction. It's a powder keg waiting to explode. Does Washington have the capacity to see the Saudi kingdom for what it is? Or does it have its hand so deep in the Saudi wallet that it won't see and won't act? Money helps disguise a lot of unpleasant truth.

Arms dealers don't go into the business because they're patriots. The Saudi government probably spends more per capita than any other country in the world on arms. In fact, the Al Sa'ud's militia hasn't fought a war since the 1930s. Personal protection of the royal family. Dubai is where most of the money for the September 11 attacks was banked. The kingdom's 4,431 kilometer land border and 2,640 kilometer shoreline are indefensible. Contributing to charities like the International Islamic Relief Organization (IIRO), which funneled money to bin Laden and other militant Saudis.

In 1996 the Saudi government simply declined Sudan's offer to turn over Osama bin Laden. Since September 11, not a single indictment or even a useful lead has come out of Saudi Arabia. Long after September 11, Saudi Arabia refused to provide advance manifests for flights coming into the U.S., a basic and potentially fatal breach of security. With few exceptions, American journalists are not issued visas to visit the kingdom. In the fall of 2002, when Saudi Arabia started to lead the Arab campaign against a war in Iraq. In 2002 America found itself begging Qatar to provide a communications base for our invading forces. Saudi Arabia tops the world in public beheadings. No one in the kingdom, national or visitor, can practice any religion but Islam.

July 2002, Na'if bin Sultan bin Fawwaz al'Shaalan was indicted by a Florida grand jury on charges that he used his personal plane to transport two tons of cocaine from Caracas to Paris in 1999. When King Fahd's family visits the palace at Marbella, they spend on average $5 million a day in the local stores. Al Sa'uds are obsessed with sex, everything from prostitutes to little boys. The Saudis are probably the most sexually repressed people in the world. Only 5 percent of women work. A woman cannot drive. Adultery, she's stoned to death, along with her lover. Filipina and Indonesian servants in the kingdom live in constant fear of rape. No one has any idea how much rape goes on in the country.

It's common for seventy-year-old Saudi men to marry girls in their early teens. London's Red-light districts and call-girl services cater largely to Saudis and other Gulf Arabs. All fifteen Saudis who took part in the 9/11 attacks should have been turned down for visas. With male unemployment in the kingdom hovering around 30 percent. Right through September 11, 2001, Saudis were not even required to appear at the U.S. embassy in Riyadh or the consulate in Jeddah for a visa interview. That year Na'if released from prison two clerics who had issued fatwas to kill Americans. One of them, Safar al-Hawali, inspired bin Laden. Beginning in the mid-1970s, Saudi Arabia poured over $1 billion into Pakistan to help it develop an "Islamic" nuclear bomb to counter the "Hindu" nuclear threat from neighboring India.

Hypocrisy and corruption: CIA directors had picked up long ago that the door to the Oval Office was always open to Saudi ambassador Bandar bin Sultan and not to them. Woolsey was one of the few CIA directors to come out and tell the truth about the kingdom. Ibn Sa'ud. Founded the modern Saudi kingdom in 1932, Khashoggi was serving the mid-1970s as middleman on an estimated 80 percent of all arms deals between the United States and Saudi Arabia. Given Khashoggi $450,000 to bribe Saudi generals into buying the company's wares. (Having served as basically a pimp for the Shah of Iran in the 1970s). Richard Nixon. "Forgot" his briefcase, which happened to be stuffed with $1 million in hundreds. Washington was for sale. Nixon's first visitor in the White House was Fahd.

The idea was to get the Saudis to underwrite the U.S. budget deficit. Depositing over $1 billion in a U.S. Treasury account. The cookie jar was bottomless. There's hardly a living former assistant secretary of state for the Near East; CIA director; White House staffer; or member of Congress who hasn't ended up on the Saudi payroll in one way or another. This includes two living presidents. Russia has plans in place to build pipelines across

Siberia, which one day might cause Saudi Arabia to lose its Asian market. In 1997, Saudi Aramco set up a joint venture with Texaco, Inc., later joined by Shell Oil, to refine roughly eight hundred thousand barrels of Saudi crude a day.

In 1998 the same three companies joined to form Motiva Enterprises. The U.S. would buy the House of Sa'ud's oil and provide protection and security, and the Saudis would buy their weapons, construction services, communications systems, and drilling rigs from the U.S. Washington's franchise players head straight for the Carlyle employment office as soon as they're out of the government. James Baker. Frank Carlucci. Arthur Levitt. William Kennard. Afsaneh Beschloss. Michael Beschloss. Richard Darman. Former British prime minister John Major serves as chairman of Carlyle Europe. Frank Carlucci. Deputy director of the CIA from 1978 to 1980. Donald Rumsfeld. Caspar Weinberger. Colin Powell. Fred Malek found Bush a slot on the board of a Carlyle subsidiary: Caterair. Governor of Texas, the state teachers' pension fund invest $100 million with the Carlyle Group.

Carlyle's most famous advisor is George Herbert Walker Bush. Compensated for his time. $80,000 to $100,000 range for each speech. Carlyle and the bin Ladens parted company in October 2001, some five weeks after the World Trade Center and Pentagon attacks. Cheney also helped put together a 1993 deal between Kazakhstan and Chevron as he was serving on the Kazakhstan Oil Advisory Board. Kissinger's take for a mere five months on the board was $876,000 after expenses. Rumsfeld $1.09 million, while Powell pocketed $1.49 million. The Saudis have a trillion dollars on deposit in U.S. banks. The Saudis hold another trillion dollars or so in the U.S. stock market. For good measure, Bandar also contributed an even $1 million to the construction of the Bush Presidential Library in College Station, Texas.

At Bandar's suggestion, King Fahd sent another $1 million to Barbara Bush's campaign against illiteracy just as he had donated $1 million to Nancy Reagan's "Just Say No" campaign against drugs. King Fahd to donate $23 million to the University of Arkansas's new Center for Middle Eastern Studies. Richard Perle: " Saudi Arabia "central to the self-destruction of the Arab world and the chief vector of the Arab crisis and its outwardly directed aggression. The Saudis are active at every level of the terror chain, from planners to financiers, from cadre to foot-soldier, from ideologist to cheerleader." In early March 2001 Princess Haifa hosted a lunch at her McLean digs for eighty of Washington's most prominent women. It wasn't until February 14, 1945, that King Sa'ud, then in his mid-sixties, met his first Western head of state: Franklin Delano Roosevelt. America would have access to Saudi ports. It could construct the military air bases on Saudi soil, albeit with a lease limited to five years. Trans-Arabian pipeline to the Mediterranean. Would consult equally with Jews and Arabs over any change in U.S. policy toward Palestine. He also vowed that America would not seek to occupy Saudi soil. Oil production: from 21.3 million barrels extracted in 1945 to 142.9 million in 1948 and over 300 million by 1952.

In 1801 a Wahhabi raiding party sacked Karbala, the site of the tomb of the prophet's grandson Husayn, and one of Shi'a Islam's most holy shrines. In the course of eight hours, the Wahhabis massacred some five thousand Shi'a and destroyed Husayn's tomb, a horror and an insult the Shi'a have never forgiven. Ibn Sa'ud unified the conquests, named the vast bulk of Arabia after himself and his family, established Wahhabism as the state religions. The formation of OPEC in 1960 handed the House of Sa'ud a lever by which it could begin prying itself loose from its corporate masters in America.

The United States, not Saudi Arabia, held the global surplus oil balance. President Dwight Eisenhower imposed mandatory quotas on foreign oil imports in 1959. Fourteen years later, Richard Nixon removed the import quotas. Ibn Sa'ud was succeeded upon his death in 1953 by his free-spending son Crown Prince Sa'ud. Forced his abdication in 1964 in favor of his half brother Faysal, but the pattern of royal excess wouldn't disappear. Nor would the Wahhabis' insistence that Islam be purified. In 1979 Sunni fundamentalists took over the Mecca's mosque. The Saudi army refused to take orders. Since Christians supported the Crusaders, the thinking went, they deserved death. It was also the obligation of a good Muslim to die for the cause. Ibn Taymiyyah has been the mainstay of Wahhabi Islam.

In November 1978 Iran had unofficially declared war on the United States when partisans of Ayatollah Khomeini occupied our embassy in Tehran. On October 23, 1983, it killed 241 Marines in Lebanon. September 11 was almost a class reunion for the Syrian Muslim Brothers. Arafat was forced to leave Egypt because of his association with the Brotherhood, the Kuwaitis happily took him and the other Palestinian Brothers. "God is our purpose, the Prophet our leader, the Qur'an' our constitution, jihad our way, and dying for God's cause our supreme objective." He sold the Brothers on the idea that all Christians and Jews were infidels who deserved to be killed. Egypt executed Sayyid Qutb in 1966.

The first serious Islamic uprising against the Soviets in Central Asia occurred in 1918. A famine soon followed that would kill as many as a million Central Asians. Afghanistan was the main corridor of East-West trade. In March 1979 Muslim fundamentalists seized control of the 17th Division of the Afghan army, headquartered in Herat. The Red Army invaded. The first troops crossed the border on Christmas Eve 1979. Mistake of biblical proportions. Russia: An estimated 260 billion barrels of oil reserves, and with greater gas reserves than all of North America. Soviet Union collapsed in 1991. The capital expenses for lifting Caspian Sea oil was roughly six dollars a barrel, while lifting a Saudi barrel cost only one to two.

International Islamic Relief Organization, the richest and most active Islamic charity in the world, the same one that was raided after September 11. Founded in 1978. Chechen separatists who declared their independence in 1991. On June 22, 1998, forty Chechens were quietly brought to a secret military camp located seventy-five miles southeast of Riyadh. Secretary of State Henry Kissinger set up the arms-for-oil mechanism in the early 1970s.

For years upon years, the Saudis have been the world's number-one consumer of American armament and weapon systems. For every deal, there's a commission; and for every commission, there's a Saudi royal waiting behind the door to take his cut. In the summer of 1992, George H.W. Bush approved the sale of up to seventy-two F-15s to Saudi Arabia, at a total cost of $9 billion. Israelis have more reason than most states to worry about the massive sales of sophisticated weaponry to a government that sits atop a powder keg of Wahhabi-inspired Islamic extremism.

As history has proved time and again, arms sales to unstable nations have a way of circling back and biting the seller in the ass. Saudi Arabia operates the world's most advanced welfare state, a kind of anti-Marxist non-workers' paradise. Saudis travel first class; about a quarter of Saudi Arabia's population. Of all those aged fifteen to sixty-four, are foreign nationals. Refineries. Seven in ten of all jobs in Saudi Arabia- and closer to 90 percent of all private-sector jobs- are filled by foreign laborers. Every dollar decline in the price of a barrel of oil translates to about a $3 billion loss to the Saudi treasury. A prince will have multiple wives and sire forty to seventy children during a lifetime of healthy copulation. Incapacitated King Fahd turned seventy-nine in 2002; Crown Prince 'Abdallah was seventy-eight. The House of Sa'ud stood at thirty thousand members.

In 1979, 127 Saudi troops and 117 Saudi insurgents died in a pitched two-week battle after Wahhabi fanatics seized the Grand Mosque at Mecca. Wealthy Saudis channel hundreds of millions of dollars to radical groups in hopes of buying protection. November 29, 1995, King Fahd suffered his near-fatal stroke. Crown Prince 'Abdallah drifted into chaos. The $4.1 billion AT&T contract, Azouzi landed a staggering $900 million commission. 'Abdallah had more immediate concern with the radicals. In September 1996 the newly appointed air force chief commissioned five followers of bin Laden. They could no longer count on the loyalty of junior military and intelligence officers. The spread of Islamic radicals inside the military only encouraged Azouzi to give more to radical causes. In September 1997 he coordinated a $100 million aid package to the Taliban.

Salam was in charge of the charities whose money found its way into the pockets of bin Laden and the Muslin Brothers.

Bandars and the Boeings, the Carlyle Groups and the Exxons ran Washington. A couple of hundred thousand dollars bought you instant access to the president. Until we start demanding the truth from Saudi Arabia; and telling ourselves the truth, too, there will be more September 11s and more tragedies like Danny Pearl's murder. Even when the Al Sa'uds were offered Osama bin Laden's head on a platter by the Sudanese, they said no, thank you. Adnan Khashoggi. Conveniently left behind the briefcase stuffed with $1 million during his visit to Richard Nixon at San Clemente.

In the entire history of America's dependence on foreign oil, there has never been a single honest, sustained effort to reduce long-term U.S. petroleum consumption. Like it or not, the U.S. and Saudi Arabia are joined at the hip. Its future is our future. It is this mostly shallow coastal strip less than 400 miles in length that provides 40 percent of present OPEC production and that has by far the world's largest proven reserves (over 50 percent of total OPEC reserves and 40 percent of the world's reserves). The vast majority of peaceful Muslims show no signs of resisting or condemning the global Islamic jihad that is being fought in their name. Many have viewed the U.S. efforts to democratize the world- especially nations in the Middle East- as an imposition or invasion on their sovereign rights.

Waynuqah: A Jewish tribe in Medina

Western hostages in Lebanon: During the first twelve years of the 1975-90 Lebanese Civil War some 14,000 people were kidnapped of whom about 10,000 were killed. A further addition to the list came in January 1987; Terry Waite, an envoy of the British Archbishop of Canterbury, who has been engaged in an effort to secure the release of earlier captives. The release of the last three American captives and 450 Lebanese and Palestinian prisoners occurred about four months late, thus bringing to an end a decade long saga.

White Revolution: (Iran): In early January 1963 Muhammad Reza Shah Pahlavi launched a six-point socioeconomic reform package called the White Revolution. Opposition to the White Revolution, emanating primarily from hostility to the monarchial regime, came from both the secularist national Front and militant Muslim clerics. The Shah celebrated the tenth anniversary of the White Revolution in January 1973 by announcing that the National Iranian Oil Company would take over the ownership and operation of the Western oil consortium that had been running the petroleum industry since 1954.

White Sheep: A confederation of Sunni Turcoman tribes which first appeared in the Diyarbekir area SE Turkey c 1350 and which for 150 years was important in NW Persia. The most famous White Sheep ruler was Uzun Hasan with his capital at Tabriz though he restored inter alia the Great Mosque at Istafan.

World Islamic Front for Jihad against Crusaders and Jews: Official title: *Al Jabah al Islamiya al Islamiyyah li Qital al Yahud wa al Salibiyin* At their base in Afghanistan, Osama bin Laden of Al Qaida, Ayman al Zawahiri of Al Hi al Islami, Abu Yasser Rifia Ahmad Taha of al Gamaat al Islamiya, Mir Hamza of Jamiar al Ulama (Pakistan), and Fazl ul Rahman of Harkat Al Jihad , (Bangladesh), announced the formation of the World Islamic Front for Jihad against Crusaders and Jews—or the World Islamic Front for Jihad (WIFF) for short—in February 1998. Having caused the death of one million Iraqis through economic sanctions, Washington was intent on fragmenting and destroying Iraq. Committing such crimes and sins by the Americans was tantamount to a declaration of war on Allah, Prophet Muhammad, and Muslims. Therefore, the communiqué added, "The ruling to kill the Americans and their allies—civilians and military—is an individual duty for every Muslim who can do it in any country in which it is possible to do it, in order to liberate the al Aqsa Mosque [in Jerusalem] and the Holy Mosque [in Mecca] from their grip, and for their armies to leave all the lands of Islam, defeated, and unable to threaten any Muslim."

World Muslim League: (Official title: *Arabic: Rabitat al Alam al Mussalmeen):* Propaganda issued by Egypt under President

Gamal Abdul Nasser against the Saudi royal family led Crown Prince Faisal ibn Abdul Aziz to establish the World Muslim League (WML) in Geneva in 1962. After the founding of the Islamic Conference Organization (ICO) in 1969, headquartered in Jiddah, the WML was moved to Mecca. It remained tied to the House of Saud and reflected the official policies of Saudi Arabia.

Ya Sabur: one of the ninety-nine names of Allah. God, who in a state of limitless patience is always forgiving the faults of His created beings and continuing to protect them.

Ya Shakur: one of the ninety-nine beautiful names of Allah. To have **Shukr** with the help of the One who is **Ya Shakur** is true **Shukr**.

Yasaviyya: the first Sufi order to be fully acclimatized among the Turks

Yasawi's: a Sufi order named for the 12th century saint of Turkestan, Ahmad Yasawi, the first major Sufi to appear in the central Asian heartland

Yazidis: *A religious group* the origin of the Yazidi doctrine—an amalgam of pagan, Sabaen, Shamanistic, Manichean, Zoroastrian, Jewish, Christian, and Islamic elements—is unknown. Though Yazidis do not believe in evil, sin, or the devil, they are often described as devil worshipers.

Yemeni Islah Group *Yemeni political party* Official title: *Al Tajami al Yemeni lil Islah* (the Yemeni Group for Reform). Following the legislation of political parties after the Yemeni unification in May 1990, the Islamic and Zaidi tribal forces combined to form the Yemeni Islah Group (YIG), led by Shaikh Abdullah Hussein al Ahmar and Shaikh Abdul Wahhab al Anisi.

The Young Turks: In 1876, Sultan Abdul Hamid II had granted his subjects the first written constitution in the Islamic world. Almost immediately, he suspended it. Over the following decades, the Sultan built railways, telegraph lines, and increased the strength of his army. Abdul Hamid used secret police and brutality against opponents, and ordered the brutal massacre of

Armenians in eastern Turkey in 1894-1896. In these same years, young educated members of the Turkish elite became inspired by nationalist ideas. Known as the Young Turks, they demanded reform. In 1908, part of the Ottoman army rebelled. The Sultan gave in to their demands, including freedom of the press and the right to form political parties. In the following year, the Sultan was replaced. Turkey soon lost Tripoli (in the Middle East) and its remaining territories in the Balkans.

Zaidi: A branch of the Shi'a usually designated as moderate that is the closest to the Sunnis in doctrine and law. Zaidism has for long been the dominant form of Islam in Yemen. Islamic sub sect of Shi'a. **Zaidis:** *Shi'a Muslim sect* Zaidis share the first four Imams of Twelver Shi'a—Ali, Hussein, Hassan, and Zain al Abidin, a grandson of Imam Ali, a son-in-law of the Prophet Muhammad (AD 570-632)—but follow a different line with Zaid, son of Muhammad ibn al Hanafiyyah and half-brother of Imam Hussein ibn Ali. The Zaidi state of Yemen, established by Imam Yahya ibn Hussein al Rassi in (North) Yemen in AD 898 continued, with some interruptions, until 1962.

Zaydi: Supporters of the revolt of Zayd ibn Ali who were prepared to support any descendent of Ali and Fatima who rose up as Imam against the illegitimate rulers of Sunni Islam; moral offenses invalidated the imamate and a candidate of greater virtue then had in the Area south of the Caspian and in the Yemen in the 8th and 9th centuries and persisted in the latter.

Zindiqs: Non-Muslims concealing their unbelief, falsely pretending that they are members of the Ummah; mostly Zoroastrians and Manicheans.

Zirids: A Berber dynasty ruling in N Africa with a branch in Spain having Granada as its capital. The former first enjoyed Fatimid favor and its capitals at Qayrawan and Sabre Mansuriyya grew prosperous. But its attempt to cast of Fatimid over lordship brought savage retaliation: the ruler fled to Mahdiyya where his successors established a powerful naval base but the rest of his kingdom disintegrated into petty principalities. The last of the African Zirids died in 1167.

Caliphs and Caliphates (Section #1)

The Rashidun (The Rightly-Guided Caliphs):
The period of the Rashidun was the Golden Age of early Islam. The first three Rashidun should have allowed Ali to take the leadership. They saw Ali as an incarnation of the divine (like Jesus). He would return to inaugurate a utopian realm of justice and peace in the Last Days. The converts to Islam objected to their second class status. The Prophet of Islam left no clear successor. He had daughters, but no sons, so, therefore, the first 4 caliphs who replaced Muhammad were: The Rashidun (Rightly-Guided Caliphs):

1- Abu Bakr (Sunni) 623-624
2- Umar ibn Al Khattab (Sunni) 634-644
3- Uthman ibn Affan (Sunni) 644-656
4- Ali ibn Abu Talib (Shi'a) 656-661

(Muhammad's cousin and son-in-law, the husband of his daughter Fatima)

The Caliphate:
The caliphate (or imamate, as the theorists usually called it) possessed three elements: that of legitimate succession to the Prophet, that of directing the affairs of the world and that of watching over the faith. The Rightly-Guided Caliphs and Companions of the Prophet, Abu Bakr, Umar ibn al-Khattab, Uthman ibn Affan and Ali ibn Abu Talib, were so named because they governed in complete accordance with Muhammad's principles. The Muslim community expanded from its base at Mecca. The caliphate was lead by the caliph or successor to Muhammad. They presided over the first 30 years of the great Islamic expansion into the world.

The caliphate lasted from Muhammad's death in 632 until 1923. To that year, the leader of the Turkish Republic, Ataturk, overthrew the Ottoman emperor, the heir to the Turkish Islamic warriors, who had attained possession of the leadership of Islam for some 500+ years.

Abu Bakr:

The greatest rift in Islam began after the death of the Prophet in 632 ACE. It was Muhammad's old friend, father-in-law and fourth convert to Islam (outside of Muhammad's own family), Abu Bakr who made the announcement: "Oh Muslims! If any of you have been worshipping Muhammad, then I will tell you that Muhammad is dead, But, if it is God that you worship, let me tell you that god is living and will never die."

Abu Bakr, a political and religious leader of the faith, was named caliphate Rasulillah ('Successor to God's Prophet, Messenger of Allah'). Upon replacing Muhammad as the leader of the Islamic Ummah, he told the Muslims that it was their duty to depose him if he failed to rule correctly: "If I do right help me. If I do wrong correct me." Abu Bakr had to fight his own son. The husband of one of Muhammad's daughters fought with the Quraysh against the army of the Prophet. He sent an army of 8,000 men in 633 ACE to engage and convert the Persians in battle.

In central Arabia, his forces put down several real uprisings in the Ridda wars (from Arabic for "Wars of Apostasy", and so-called because a number of rebel leaders declared themselves
prophets to rival Muhammad). Moreover, under Abu Bakr's leadership, Bedouin tribesmen won the first of many astounding victories for the new faith against the Persian Sasanian empire and the Byzantine empire in what is now Iraq and Syria.

According to some traditions, Muhammad appointed Abu Bakr as his successor. Aisha
named him as the one Muhammad would have chosen. Muhammad ordered that Abu Bakr take his place in leading the Muslims in prayer and, indeed, after Muhammad's death became the first caliph. He ruled for two years and died; some say from old age, while others say he was poisoned.

Umar ibn Al-Khattab:
In August 634, Abu Bakr fell seriously ill and before he died appointed Umar ibn Al-Khattab to succeed him as the second caliph. Umar established the Islamic calendar, dating from Muhammad's emigration

to Medina, "God has for the time being made me your ruler. But I am one of you. No special privileges belong to the rulers." He proved to be a tremendously effective leader: directing operations from Madinah, during his ten-year rule (634-644) oversaw major Islamic military expansion as his armies continued the assault against the Byzantine and Sasanian empire.

In 637 they seized Ctesiphon, the Persian capital, forcing the Sasanian King Yazdegerd III to
flee and vanquished the Persian army at the Battle of Nahavand in 642; in 651 Yazdegerd was killed at Merv and the Sasanian dynasty was at an end.

The conquest of Syria led Umar to compose one of the most significant canons of Islamic Law. This was a pact with the large local Christian populace. The agreement, known as the dhimma, would govern Muslim relations with both Christians and the Jews for centuries. The contract mandates protection of those who received God's revelations before Muhammad.

The provisions of the dhimma are restrictive in some ways. They include a bar on construction of new religious structures, whether monasteries, convents, churches, or synagogues. Non-Muslims could not be buried in close proximity to the Muslim dead. The contract also required Jews and Christians to show respect for Muslims by standing in their presence and to refrain from dressing or parting their hair in the manner of Muslims. They could not ride horses, carry arms or lift their hands to threaten Muslims.

They could not build houses higher than those of Muslims. Nor could they employ Muslims as servants. Islamic law, or Shariah, was considered to apply only to Muslims. Because the protected communities were defined religiously, their clergy had the right to tax them for their collective needs. In return for the protection of the Muslim order and exemption from military service, the People of the Book paid a poll tax, also collected by the priests and rabbis. It imposed second-class citizenship on Jews and Christians. These critics seldom note that until the 18th century, Jews had no citizenship in Christendom.

Umar also decreed the expulsion of non-Muslims from the vicinity of the Holy Places in the Arabian Peninsula. After ten years as caliph, in 644 Umar was stabbed in the mosque in Madinah by a Persian slave named Pirouz Nahavandi (or Abu-luluah); he died two days later.

Uthman ibn Affan:
Upon Umar's death, the caliphate chose Uthman ibn Affan, a pious and lenient Muslim elder, who initiated the compilation and codification of an authoritative text of Qur'an. Under his leadership, Islam spread to Cyprus, Libya, Afghanistan and western India. He ruled for 12 years and was murdered by soldiers dissatisfied with his policy of favoring his own family, the Umayyads...(Nepotism). The immediate cause of his undoing, however, was his appointment of many of his relatives and friends to office.

Uthman was reading the Koran when the murderers broke in and spilled his blood over the book he had served so well. The caliph had been murdered by his own fellow Muslims, a deed that was to split Islam and bring civil war and further bloodshed. Some Muslims were unhappy with Uthman as third caliph and dissent burst into the open after Uthman was murdered in 656.

Ali ibn Abi Talib:
The ahl al-bait, who wanted Fatimah and Ali and their descendants to lead the Muslim world, would become the Shiah. Those who wanted to appoint a successor split immediately into rival camps. Most of the immigrants supported the claim of Abu Bakr, who had been Muhammad's closest friend from the very beginning. According to the Shi'a Muslims, leadership of the community should have stayed within the Prophet Muhammad's own family from the very beginning and the appointment of Ali as Caliph was long overdue.

The Prophet's immediate family believed that he would have wanted Ali to succeed him. Ali ibn Abi Talib, Muhammad's cousin and son-in-law, assumed the position of 4th Caliph in 656. He was one of the most respected of all Muslims and one of the very first to accept Muhammad's revelations; he was admired by Arabs for his generosity, eloquence and, more importantly, his ability as a soldier. He moved the capital of the Islamic community from Medina to Kufah (now in Iraq) and met opposition from a leading member of the Umayyad clan named Mu'awiyah, who refused to accept his authority.

Whatever the reason for Aisha's dislike of Ali, she joined forces with the two aspirants to the
caliphate; they gathered around them a group of followers who staged a rebellion, accusing Ali of not bringing Uthman's murders to trial. Seeking support, the rebels went to the military town of Basra in Iraq, near the northern end of the Persian Gulf, where one of the rebel leaders had a following; there they won over the garrison and ousted the governor who had remained loyal to Ali.

Having no army with which to put down this uprising, Ali gathered a few followers in Medina and headed toward Kura, another military town some 200 miles northwest of Basra. The two towns were rivals and Ali capitalized on that fact to win Kufah's support, raising troops there and setting out to suppress the rebels.

The two Muslim armies met at Basra and their encounter became famous in Islamic history as the Battle of the Camel because Aisha urged it on from a litter on a camel's back. The clash ended in victory for Ali. Aisha was escorted back to the city, where she lived out her life in retirement.

Ali was killed in 661and in lieu of his assassination, all Muslims agree that the era of holiness was over, within but a generation after the death of the Prophet, the rule of the enlightened is finished. Muhammad's grandson, Husayn, refused to accept the Umayyad Caliphate and was killed with his small band of companions at the Battle of Karbalah, Iraq, by the Syrian Caliph Yazid.

A faction of the Muslims maintained that Muhammad had actually appointed Ali as his successor. One tradition was Muhammad asking Ali "Aren't you satisfied with being unto me what Aaron was unto Moses?" This suggests succession, for in the Qur'an' Moses says to Aaron, "Take my place among the people."

The Shi'at Ali or Party of Ali known popularly as the Shi'a. Sunnis (so called of their self-proclaimed adherence to the Sunnah or traditions of Muhammad.) Shi'a Muslims make up only about 15 percent of the worldwide Muslim community. The Shi'a concentrate on the sense of immediate loss of the vision betrayed within a day of the Prophet's death. They argue that only Ali was qualified to uphold the spiritual values that underpinned the whole future direction of Islam.

Muhammad Awiya (Syrian) upon going to battle with Ali ordered his soldiers to hang pages of the Qur'an on the ends of their spears... to instill terror in the enemy. Both sides agreed to step down from leadership, but Ali was double-crossed by their men. The Kharijites decided to kill both Muhammad Awiya and Ali and then find them a new Caliph. They were able to sneak up on Ali and stab him. In 661, Ali's son Hassan declared himself next caliph-Mu'awiyah objected and died in 680. Umayyads rule lasted to 750 ACE.

20 years after Ali's death, his son (and Muhammad's grandson) Hussayn, the Third Imam of Shi'ism, was slain by the Umayyads forces in Karbala (Iraq) on the 10th day of the month of Muharram. He was killed with his infant son in his arms. Their heads were displayed in public by the Umayyad commander Ubayd Allah Ibn-Ziyad.

"O people, you have killed the son of Fatima; may God destroy those who consent to humiliation and shame " The murder of Ali and the Battle of Karbala were among the most traumatic events in the history of Islam. Karbala became a major shrine and place of pilgrimage for the Shi'ah. The Shi'ah calendar of observance begins with the first 10 days of Muharram.

Events at Karbala:
Hussain ibn Ali, brother of Hassan and grandson of Muhammad, claimed the caliphate. He marched from Makkah to Kufa in Iraq, the base of his father Ali's support. At Karbala on 10 October 680, he was intercepted by a 40,000-strong army sent by Yazid and commanded by Umar ibn Said. Hussain was vastly outnumbered, with only 72 men in his travelling party. The only survivor was Hussain's son Ali ibn Hussain, who was too sick to fight and was carried off to Damascus and kept as a prisoner of Caliph Yazid. However, many years later he was freed and in time he became the fourth Shiah imam.

The Battle of Karbala was a key cause of the centuries-long split between Sunni and Shiah Muslims. Sunnis (so called because they claim to follow Muhammad's sunnah or 'example') celebrate Abu Bakr, Umar, Uthman, Muawiyah and the Umayyads, in addition to Ali as the rightful successor of Muhammad.

THE UMAYYADS
Mu'awiya ibn Abi Sufyan I, 661-680
Yazid I, 680-683
Mu'awiya II, 683-684
Marwan I, 684-685
'Abd al-Malik, 685-705
al-Walid I, 705-715
Sulayman, 715-717
'Umar ibn 'Abd al-'Aziz, 717-720
Yazid II, 720-724
Hisham, 724-743
al Walid II, 743-744
Yazid III, 744
Ibrahim, 744
Marwan II, 744-750
Abu'l-'Abbas al-Saffah, 749-754
al-Mansur, 754-775
al-Mahdi, 775-785
al-Hadi, 783-786
Harun al-Rashid, 786-809
al-Amin, 809-813
al-Ma'mun, 813-833
al-Mu'tasim, 833-842
al-Wathiq, 842-847
al-Mutawakkil, 847-861
al-Muntasir, 861-862
al-Musta'in, 862-866
al-Mu'tazz, 866-869
al-Muhtadi, 869-870
al-Mu'tamid, 870-892
al-Mu'tadid, 892-902
al-Muktafi, 902-908

al-Muqtadir, 908-932
al-Qahir, 932-934
al-Radi, 934-940
al-Muttaqi, 940-944
al-Mustakfi, 944-946
al-Muti', 946-974
al-Ta'i', 974-991
al-Qadir, 991-1031
al-Qa'im, 1031-1075
al-Muqtadi, 1075-1091
al-Mustazhir, 1094-1118
al-Mustarshid, 1118-1135
al-Rashid, 1135-1136
al-Muqtafi, 1136-1160
al-Mustanjid, 1160-1170
al-Mustadi, 1170-1180
al-Nasir, 1180-1225
al-Zahir, 1225-1226
al-Mustansir, 1226-1242
al-Musta'sim, 1242-1258

Mu'awiyah, the governor of Syria and relative of the third caliph, Uthman, established the Umayyad dynasty (661—750), an era of Arab-Islamic conquest and prosperity. Muslims who accepted Umayya rule as legitimate – the vast majority – came to be called Sunni Muslims. The partisans of 'Ali, on the other hand, became a despised minority in the larger Islamic world. The Umayyads remained in power, but were challenged by supporters of Ali ibn Abi Talib.

Umayyad-ruled Syria was under the governorship of Mu'awiyah. Umayyad caliph, having overcome the Shi'as, ruled during the great wave of Arab conquests, lasting until the middle of the 8th century. The Umayyad capital, Damascus, became a great world city. In Jerusalem, the Dome of the Rock was completed in 691, under the Umayyad caliph Abd al-Malik.

Civil War:
The civil war was sparked by the clash between Ali and Mu'awiyah continued into the next generation and led to the infamous murder of

Ali's son Hussain by Mu'awiyah's son Yazid in 680. Not long after assuming power as caliph, Ali ibn Abu Talib dismissed the regional governors appointed by his predecessors. Mu'awiyah refused to obey and proved a formidable opponent. A leading member of the Umayyad clan, Mu'awiyah had a significant independent power base and had won major military victories, including the conquests of Cyprus in 649 and Rhodes in 654.

In response to this show of defiance, Ali led his army into Syria and fought Mu'awiyah in the three-day Battle of Siffin in July 657; the battle was inconclusive and the two men agreed to a six-month armistice followed by arbitration of the dispute. On the 19th day of Ramadan in 661, both Ali and Mu'awiyah were stabbed with poisoned swords while at prayers. Mu'awiyah recovered, but Ali died from his wounds two days later.

Mu'awiyah gains power:
Ali's supporters named his son Hassan caliph and Mu'awiyah marched against them with a vast army. Hassan agreed to withdraw his claim to the caliphate. Mu'awiyah was at last the undisputed caliph. According to Shiah account, Mu'awiyah agreed that the caliphate would pass to Hassan's brother Hussain ibn Ali.

Mu'awiyah ruled as caliph with no further challenges until his death in 680. When he died, however, the terms of his agreement with Ali were ignored in his desire to find a dynasty; the caliphate was passed to his son Yazid.

The revolt that finally toppled the Umayyad dynasty was lead by the Prophet's Uncle Abbas and his son Abdallah, one of the most eminent of the early Qur'an reciters. They began to muster support in the Iranian provinces in 743, occupied Kufah in August 749 and defeated the last Umayyad caliph, Mansur II, in Iraq. In 750, the Umayyad dynasty itself was violently overthrown by the son of a slave, Abu-Abbas. This event marked the beginning of the Abbasid dynasty (750-1258), a long period of relative wealth and peace in the Muslim world.

The Abbasid caliphs would inaugurate a very different kind of society. The Abbasids: The High Caliph Period (750-935). They were determined to make the caliphate an absolute monarchy in the traditional agrarian way. Abu al-Abbas al-Suffah (750-54), the first Abbasid caliph, massacred all the Umayyads. Caliph Abu Ja'far al Mansur murdered all the Shii leaders whom he considered a danger to his rule.

They moved their capital from Damascus to Iraq, settling first in Kufah and then in Baghdad. The centre of Baghdad was the famous "round city," which housed the administration, the court and the royal family. Baghdad was built in a convenient location, beside the Tigris, close to the Sawad, the agricultural base of Iraq and near to the capital of the Persian Sassanids, Ctesiphon.

Ali al-Rida, the eighth imam:
Al-Rida conveniently died, possibly by foul play. Caliph al Mu'tasim attempted to strengthen the monarchy by making the army into his own personal corps. These troops were Turkish Slaves, who had been captured from beyond the River Oxus and converted to Islam.

The caliph moved his capital to Samarra, some sixty miles to the south. During the late ninth and early tenth centuries, there were armed revolts by those militant Shiis who were still committed to political activism.

*

List of Caliphs:

This is a list of Caliphs. All years are according to the Common Era.

Rashidun Caliphs (632-661)

Umayyads Caliphs (661–750/1031):

Caliphs of Damascus (661–750):
- Muawiyah I - 661–680 (Founder of the Umayyad dynasty).
- Yazid I - 680–683

- Muawiyah II - 683–684
- Marwan I - 684–685
- Abd al-Malik - 685–705
- Al-Walid I - 705–715
- Sulayman - 715–717
- Umar II - 717–720 (considered as the fifth of the *Rashidun*).
- Yazid II - 720–724
- Hisham - 724–743
- Al-Walid II - 743–744
- Yazid III - 744
- Ibrahim- 744
- Marwan II - 744–750

Emirs of Córdoba (756–929):
- Abd ar-Rahman I - 756–788
- Hisham I - 788–796
- al-Hakam I - 796–822
- Abd ar-Rahman II - 822–852
- Muhammad I - 852–886
- al-Mundhir - 886–888
- Abdallah ibn Muhammad - 888–912
- Abd-ar-Rahman III - 912–929 (Declared himself Caliph)

Caliphs of Córdoba (929–1031):

(actual authority confined to Spain and parts of Morocco)
- Abd-ar-Rahman III - 929–961
- Al-Hakam II - 961–976
- Hisham II al-Hakam - 976–1009
- Muhammad II - 1009
- Sulayman ibn al-Hakam - 1009–1010
- Hisham II al-Hakam, restored - 1010–1013
- Sulayman ibn al-Hakam, restored - 1013–1016
- Abd ar-Rahman IV - 1021–1022
- Abd ar-Rahman V - 1022–1023
- Muhammad III - 1023–1024

- Hisham III - 1027–1031

Abbasid Caliphs (750–1258/1517):

Caliphs of Baghdad (750–1258):

(Not accepted by the Muslim dominions in the Iberian Peninsula and parts of North Africa).
- As-Saffah - 750–754 (Founder of the Abbasid dynasty).
- Al-Mansur - 754–775
- Al-Mahdi - 775–785
- Al-Hadi - 785–786
- Harun al-Rashid - 786–809
- Al-Amin - 809–813
- Al-Ma'mun - 813–833
- Al-Mu'tasim - 833–842
- Al-Wathiq - 842–847
- Al-Mutawakkil - 847–861
- Al-Muntasir - 861–862
- Al-Musta'in - 862–866
- Al-Mu'tazz - 866–869
- Al-Muhtadi - 869–870
- Al-Mu'tamid - 870–892
- Al-Mu'tadid - 892–902
- Al-Muktafi - 902–908
- Al-Muqtadir - 908–932
- Al-Qahir - 932–934
- Ar-Radi - 934–940
- Al-Muttaqi - 940–944
- Al-Mustakfi - 944–946
- Al-Muti - 946–974
- At-Ta'i - 974–991
- Al-Qadir - 991–1031
- Al-Qa'im - 1031–1075
- Al-Muqtadi - 1075–1094
- Al-Mustazhir - 1094–1118
- Al-Mustarshid - 1118–1135

- Ar-Rashid - 1135–1136
- Al-Muqtafi - 1136–1160
- Al-Mustanjid - 1160–1170
- Al-Mustadi - 1170–1180
- An-Nasir - 1180–1225
- Az-Zahir - 1225–1226
- Al-Mustansir - 1226–1242
- Al-Musta'sim - 1242–1258 (last Abbasid Caliph at Baghdad)

Caliphs of Cairo (1261–1517):

(The Cairo Abbasids were largely ceremonial Caliphs under the patronage of the Mamluk Sultanate):

- Al-Mustansir II - 1261–1262
- Al-Hakim I - 1262–1302
- Al-Mustakfi I - 1302–1340
- Al-Hakim II - 1341–1352
- Al-Mu'tadid I - 1352–1362
- Al-Mutawakkil I - 1362–1383
- Al-Wathiq II - 1383–1386
- Al-Mu'tasim - 1386–1389
- Al-Mutawakkil I (restored) - 1389–1406
- Al-Musta'in - 1406–1414
- Al-Mu'tadid II - 1414–1441
- Al-Mustakfi II - 1441–1451
- Al-Qa'im - 1451–1455
- Al-Mustanjid - 1455–1479
- Al-Mutawakkil II - 1479–1497
- Al-Mustamsik - 1497–1508
- Al-Mutawakkil III - 1508–1517 (surrendered the title to Selim I)

Other Caliphates (910–1269):

Fatimid Caliphs (910–1171):

(The Fatimids belonged to the Ismaili branch of Shi'a Islam and hence are not recognized by the majority of Sunnis, whether subjects in their dominions or from neighboring states).

- Ubayd Allah al-Mahdi Billah - 910–934 (Founder of the Fatimid dynasty).
- Muhammad al-Qa'im Bi-Amrillah - 934–946
- Ismail al-Mansur - 946–953
- Al-Muizz Lideenillah - 953–975 (Egypt is conquered during his reign).
- Abu Mansoor Nizar al-Aziz Billah - 975–996
- Al-Hakim bi-Amr Allah - 996–1021
- Ali az-Zahir - 1021–1036
- Ma'ad al-Mustansir Billah - 1036–1094
- Al-Musta'li - 1094–1101 (Quarrels over his succession led to the Nizari split).
- Al-Amir - 1101–1130 (The Fatimid rulers of Egypt after him are not
 recognized as Imams by Mustaali Taiyabi Ismailis).
- al-Hafiz - 1130–1149
- al-Zafir - 1149–1154
- Al-Faiz - 1154–1160
- Al-Azid - 1160–1171

Almohad Caliphs (1145–1269):

(Not widely accepted, actual dominions were parts of North Africa and Iberia)
- Abd al-Mu'min - 1145–1163
- Abu Yaqub Yusuf I - 1163–1184
- Yaqub al-Mansur - 1184–1199
- Muhammad an-Nasir - 1199–1213
- Abu Ya'qub Yusuf II - 1213–1224
- Abd al-Wahid I - 1224
- Abdallah al-Adil 1224–1227
- Yahya - 1227–1235
- Idris I - 1227–1232
- Abdul-Wahid II - 1232–1242

- Ali - 1242–1248
- Umar - 1248–1266
- Idris II - 1266–1269

Caliphs under the Ottoman Empire (1451–1922):

Originally the secular, conquering dynasty was just entitled Sultan, soon it started accumulating titles assumed from subjected peoples.
- Mehmed (Muhammad) II (the Conqueror of Constantinople) - 1451–1481 (actively used numerous titles such as of Caliph and Caesar)
- Bayezid II - 1481–1512
- Selim I - 1512–1520 (induced al-Mutawakkil III to formally surrender the Caliphate after defeating the Mamluk Sultanate in 1517; actively used the title)
- Suleiman the Magnificent - 1520–1566
- Selim II - 1566–1574
- Murad III - 1574–1595
- Mehmed (Muhammad) III - 1595–1603
- Ahmed I - 1603–1617
- Mustafa I - 1617–1618
- Osman II - 1618–1622
- Mustafa I, restored - 1622–1623
- Murad IV - 1623–1640
- Ibrahim I - 1640–1648
- Mehmed (Muhammad) IV - 1648–1687
- Suleiman II - 1687–1691
- Ahmed II - 1691–1695
- Mustafa II - 1695–1703
- Ahmed III - 1703–1730
- Mahmud I - 1730–1754
- Osman III - 1754–1757
- Mustafa III - 1757–1774
- Abdul Hamid I - 1774–1789
- Selim III - 1789–1807
- Mustafa IV - 1807–1808

- Mahmud II - 1808–1839
- Abdulmecid I - 1839–1861
- Abdulaziz - 1861–1876
- Murad V - 1876
- Abdul Hamid II - 1876–1909 (actively used title of Caliph)

From 1908 onwards the Ottoman Sultan was considered the equivalent of a constitutional monarch without executive powers, with the Parliament consisting of chosen representatives.

- Mehmed (Muhammad) V - 1909–1918
- Mehmed (Muhammad) VI - 1918–1922

Caliph under the Republic of Turkey (1922–1924)
- Abdulmecid II - 1922–1924 (ceremonial Caliph under the patronage of
  the Republic of Turkey and its President Gazi Mustafa Kemal Pasha (Ataturk))

The Office of the Caliphate was transferred to the Grand National Assembly of Turkey which dissolved the office on March 3, 1924, in keeping with the policies of secularism that were adopted in the early years of the Republic of Turkey. The current pretender to the Imperial House of Osman is Bayezid Osman.

After the dissolution of the Office of the Caliphate, the Grand National Assembly of Turkey founded the Presidency of Religious Affairs as the new highest Islamic religious authority in the country.

Al-Saud States (1744 - Present):
The Arabs community believes that the Al-Saud Caliphate is the continuation of the Islamic Caliphate, first being the Rashidun (rightly guided) Caliphate (of Righteous Caliphs). The Al-Saud had three sections/portions to their state.

Rulers of the first Saudi state:
- Muhammad ibn Saud 1726–1744 (Prince of Diriyah), 1744–1765 (Prince of Saudi State)
- Abdul Aziz ibn Muhammad ibn Saud 1765–1803 (1179–1218 H)

- Saud ibn Abdul Aziz ibn Muhammad ibn Saud (Saud Al Kabeer) 1803–1814 (1218–1233 H)
- Abdullah bin Saud 1814–1818
- Founding (1744) = The First Imam I :- Muhammad ibn Saud (d. 1765), also known as Ibn Saud, the founder of Al-Saud state

The rulers of the second state (1819-1891):
- Turki ibn Abdallah ibn Muhammad (first time) 1819–1820
- Turki ibn Abdallah ibn Muhammad (second time) 1824–1834
- Mushari ibn Abd al-Rahman ibn Mushari 1834–1834
- Faisal ibn Turki ibn Abdallah (first time) 1834–1838
- Khalid ibn Saud ibn Abd al-Aziz 1838–1841
- Abdallah ibn Thunayyan ibn Ibrahim 1841–1843
- Faisal ibn Turki (second time) 1843–1865
- Abdallah ibn Faisal ibn Turki (first time) 1865–1871
- Saud ibn Faisal ibn Turki 1871–1871 (first time)
- Abdallah ibn Faisal ibn Turki (second time) 1871–1873
- Saud ibn Faisal ibn Turki (second time) 1873–1875
- Abd al-Rahman ibn Faisal ibn Turki (first time) 1875–1876
- Abdallah ibn Faisal ibn Turki (third time) 1876–1889
- Abd al-Rahman ibn Faisal ibn Turki (second time) 1889–1891

Third Saudi State/Kingdom of Saudi Arabia:
- Abdul-Aziz ibn Abdul-Rahman Al Saud
- Saud ibn Abdul-Aziz
- The Late Malik Hazrat Sheikh Shah Faisal ibn Abdul-Aziz Aal Ash Shaheed (Rehmatullahi - Alaiyh)
- Khalid ibn Abdul-Aziz
- Fahd ibn Abdul-Aziz
- Abdullah ibn Abdul-Aziz

Sharifian Caliphate (1924):

Main article: Sharifian Caliphate
A last attempt at restoring the caliphal office and style with ecumenical recognition was made by al-Husayn ibn `Ali al-Hashimi, King of Hejaz and Sharif of Mecca, who assumed both on 11 March 1924 and held them until 3 October 1924, when he passed the kingship to his son `Ali

ibn al-Husayn al-Hashimi, who did not adopt the caliphal office and style.

Caliph of the Faithful
(Ottoman Empire (1299-1923))

Style	His Imperial Majesty Protector of Islam Commander of the Faithful
Residence	Medina (first)
Term length	Eternal
Inaugural holder	Abu Bakr
Formation	89 June 632
Succession	Electoral during Rashidun Caliphate, later Malik (Succession to Muhammad)

*

'Abd al-Malik ibn Marwan (Arabic: *'Abd al-Malik ibn Marwan*; 646–705) was the 5th Umayyad Caliph. He was born in Mecca and grew up in Madinah (both are cities in modern day Saudi Arabia).

In his reign, all important records were translated into Arabic, and for the first time a special currency for the Muslim world was minted, which led to war with the Byzantine Empire under Justinian II. The Byzantines were led by Leontios at the Battle of Sebastopolis in 692 in Asia Minor and were decisively defeated by the Caliph after the defection of a large contingent of Slavs. The Islamic currency was then made the only currency exchange in the Muslim world. 'Abd al-Malik consolidated

Muslim rule and extended it, made Arabic the state language, and organized a regular postal service.

Campaigns in Iraq and Hejaz:
'Abd al-Malik became caliph after the death of his father Marwan I in 685. Within a few years, he dispatched armies on a campaign to reassert Umayyad control over the Islamic empire. He first defeated the governor of Basra Mosaab Ibn al-Zubair. 'Adb al-Malik then appointed one of his most able generals and administrators who would later change in the face of the Umayyad Empire, al-Hajjaj bin Yousef to march against 'Abd-Allah ibn al-Zubayr, the governor of Hejaz. He besieged Makkah in 692 C.E. with almost 12,000 Syrian troops. The bombardment continued during the month of the Pilgrimage or Hajj. Abd al Malik served first as a messenger to his father Abd al Haija.

After the siege had lasted for seven months and 10,000 men, among them two of Abdullah Ibn al-Zubair's sons, had gone over to al-Hajjaj, Abd-Allah ibn al-Zubayr with a few loyal followers, including his youngest son, were killed in the fighting around the Kaaba (Jumadah I 73 / October 692).

Hajjaj's success led Abd al-Malik to assign him the role of governor of Iraq and give him free rein in the territories he controlled. Hajjaj arrived when there were many deserters in Basra and Kufa.

Under Hajjaj, Arab armies put down the revolt of Abd al-Rahman ibn Muhammad ibn al-Ash'ath in Iraq from 699 to 701 CE, and also took most of Turestan. Abd al-Rahman rebelled following Hajjaj's repeated orders to push further into the lands of Zundil. After his defeat in Iraq, against achieved through Abd al-Malik's dispatch of Syrian reinforcements to Hajjaj, Abd ar Rahman returned east. There one city closed its gates to him and in another he was seized. However, Zundil's army arrived and secured his release. Later, Abd ar Rahman died and Zundil sent his head to Hajjaj who sent it to Abd al-Malik. These victories paved the way for greater expansions under Abd al-Malik's son Al-Marwan.

Campaigns in North Africa:

Caliph Abd al-Malik was effective in increasing the size of the empire. In Maghreb (western North Africa) in 686 CE a force led by Zuhayr ibn Qais won the Battle of Mamma over Byzantines and Berbers led by Kusaila, on the Qayrawan plain, and re-took Ifriqiya and its capital Kairouan.

In 695 Hasan ibn al-Nu'man captured Carthage and advanced into the Atlas Mountains. A Byzantine fleet arrived, retook Carthage but in 698 Hasan ibn al-Nu'man returned and defeated Tiberios III at the Battle of Carthage. The Byzantines withdrew from all of Africa except Ceuta.

He then developed the village of Tunis ten miles from the destroyed Carthage. Around 705 Musa ibn Nusayr replaced Hasan. He pacified much of North Africa, though he failed to take Ceuta.

Reforms:
Abd al-Malik instituted many reforms such as: making Arabic the official language of government across the entire empire, instituting a mint that produced a uniform set of aniconic currency, expansion and reorganization of postal service, repairing the damaged Kaaba and beginning the tradition of weaving a silk cover for the Kaaba in Damascus.

Art and architecture:
He also built the Dome of the Rock in Jerusalem, but parts of that city were also destroyed when Abd al-Malik's armies put down an uprising there.

When Abd al-Malik intended to construct the Dome of the Rock, he came from Damascus to Jerusalem. He wrote, "Abd al-Malik intends to build a dome (Qubbah) over the Rock to house the Muslims from cold and heat, and to construct the Masjid. ...He then gathered craftsmen from all his dominions and asked them to provide him with the description and form of the planned dome before he engaged in its construction. ...He then appointed Raja' ibn Hayweh and Yazid ibn Salam to supervise the construction and ordered them to spend generously on its construction. He then returned to Damascus. ...Abd al-Malik ordered the gold coins to be melted and cast on the Dome's exterior, which at the time had such a strong glitter that no eye could look straight at it.

Al-Muqaddasi reported that seven times the revenue of Egypt was used to build the Dome.

> He sought to build for the Muslims a mosque that should be unique and a wonder to the world.

Death:
The last years of his reign were generally peaceful. Abd al-Malik wanted his son al-Walid I to succeed him, ignoring his father's decree that Abd al-Malik should be succeeded by his brother, Abd al-Aziz. Abd al-Malik is known as the "Father of Kings": his four sons succeeded him as the caliph one after another. Abd al-Malik died at al-Sinnabra in 705.

*

Abd al-Rahman I:

Abd al-Rahman I, or, his full name by patronymic record, **Abd al-Rahman ibn Mu'awiya ibn Hisham ibn Abd al-Malik ibn Marwan** (731-788) was the founder of the Umayyad Emirate of Córdoba (755), a Muslim dynasty that ruled the greater part of Iberia for nearly three centuries (including the succeeding Caliphate of Córdoba). The Muslims called the regions of Iberia under their dominion al-Andalus. Abd al-Rahman's establishment of a government in al-Andalus represented a branching from the rest of the Islamic Empire, which had been brought under the Abbasid following the overthrow of the Umayyads from Damascus in 750.

He was also known by appellations *al-Dakhil* ("the Immigrant"), *Saqr Quraish* ("the Falcon of the Quraysh") and the "Falcon of Andalus". Variations of the spelling of his name include **Abd ar-Rahman I**, **Abdul Rahman I** and **Abderraman I**.

Flight from Damascus:
Born near Damascus in Syria, Abd al-Rahman, grandson of Hisham ibn Abd al-Malik, was the son of the Umayyad prince Mu'awiyah ibn Hisham and a Berber concubine. He was twenty when his family, the ruling Umayyads, were overthrown by a popular revolt known as the Abbasid Revolution, occurring in the year 750. Abd al-Rahman and a small selection of his family fled Damascus, where the center of Umayyad power had been; people moving with him include his brother Yahiya, his four-year old son Sulayman, and some of his sisters, as well as his former Greek slave (a freedman), Bedr. The family fled from Damascus to the River Euphrates. All along the way the path was filled with danger, as the Abbasids had dispatched horsemen across the region to try to find the Umayyad prince and kill him. The Abbasids were merciless with all Umayyads that they found. Abbasid agents closed in on Abd al-Rahman and his family while they were hiding in a small village. He left his young son with his sisters and fled with Yahiya.

Abd al-Rahman, Yahiya and Bedr quit the village narrowly escaping the Abbasid assassins. Later, on the way south, Abbasid horsemen again caught up with the trio: Abd al-Rahman and his companions then threw themselves into the River Euphrates. While trying to swim across the dangerous Euphrates, Abd al-Rahman is said to have become separated from his brother Yahiya, who began swimming back towards the horsemen, possibly from fear of drowning. The horsemen beseeched the escapees to return, and that no harm would come to them. Yahiya returned to the near shore, and was quickly dispatched by the horsemen. They cut the head off their prize, leaving Yahiya's body to rot. Al-Maqqari quotes prior Muslim historians as having recorded that Abd al-Rahman said he was so overcome with fear at that moment, that once he made the far shore he ran until exhaustion overcame him. Only he and Bedr were left to face the unknown.

Exile years:
After barely escaping with their lives, Abd al-Rahman and Bedr continued south through Palestine, the Sinai, and then into Egypt. Abd al-Rahman had to keep a low profile as he traveled. It may be assumed that he intended to go at least as far as northwestern Africa (Maghreb), the land of his mother, which had been partly conquered by his Umayyad predecessors. The journey across Egypt would prove perilous.

At the time, Abd al-Rahman ibn Habib al-Fihri was the semi-autonomous governor of Ifriqiya (roughly, modern Tunisia) and a former Umayyad client. The ambitious Ibn Habib, a member of the illustrious Fihrid family, had long sought to carve out Ifriqiya as a private dominion for himself. Ibn Habib broke openly with the Abbasids and invited the remnants of the Umayyad dynasty to take refuge in his dominions. Abd al-Rahman was only one of several surviving Umayyad family members to make their way to Ifriqiya at this time.

But Ibn Habib soon changed his mind. He feared the presence of prominent Umayyad exiles in Ifriqiya, a family more illustrious than his own, might become a focal point for intrigue among local nobles against his own usurped powers. Around 755, believing he had discovered plots involving some of the more prominent Umayyad exiles in Kairouan, Ibn Habib turned against them. At the time, Abd al-Rahman and Bedr were keeping a low profile, staying in Kabylia, at the camp of a Nafza Berber chieftain friendly to their plight. Ibn Habib dispatched spies to look for the wayward Umayyad prince. When Ibn Habib's soldiers entered the camp, the Berber chieftain's wife Tekfah hid Abd al-Rahman under her personal belongings to help him go unnoticed. Once they were gone, Abd a-Rahman and Bedr immediately set off westwards.

In 755, Abd al-Rahman and Bedr reached modern day Morocco near Ceuta. Their next step would be to cross the sea to al-Andalus, where Abd al-Rahman could not have been sure whether or not he would be welcomed. Following the Berber Revolt of the 740s, the province was in a state of confusion, with the Muslim community torn by tribal dissensions among the Arabs and racial tensions between the Arabs and Berbers. At that moment, the nominal ruler of al-Andalus, emir Yusuf ibn 'Abd al-Rahman al-Fihri (another member of the Fihrid family, and a favorite of the old Arab settlers (*Baladiyun*), mostly of south Arabian or 'Yemenite' tribal stock) was locked in a contest with his vizier (and son-in-law) al-Sumayl ibn Hatim al-Qilabi, the head of the new settlers (*Shamiyum*, the Syrian *Junds* or military regiments, mostly of north Arabian Qaysid tribes, which had arrived only in 742).

Among the Syrian Junds were contingents of old Umayyad clients, numbering perhaps 500, and Abd al-Rahman believed he might tug on old loyalties and get them to receive him. Bedr was dispatched across the straits to make contact. Bedr managed to line up three Syrian commanders – Obeid Allah ibn Uthman and Abd Allah ibn Khalid, both originally of Damascus, and Yusuf ibn Bukht of Qinnasrin The trio approached the Syrian arch-commander al-Sumayl (then in Zaragoza) to get his consent, but al-Sumayl refused, fearing Abd al-Rahman would try to make himself emir. As a result, Bedr and the Umayyad clients sent out feelers to their rivals, the Yemenite commanders. Although the Yemenites were not natural allies (the Umayyads are a Qaysid tribe), their interest was piqued.

The emir Yusuf al-Fihri, had proven himself unable to keep the powerful al-Sumayl in check and several Yemenite chieftains felt their future prospects were poor, whether in a Fihrid or Syrian-dominated Spain, that they had a better chance of advancement if they hitched themselves to the glitter of the Umayyad name. Although the Umayyads did not have a historical presence in the region (no member of the Umayyad family was known to have ever set foot in al-Andalus before) and there were grave concerns about young Abd al-Rahman's inexperience, several of the lower-ranking Yemenite commanders felt they had little to lose and much to gain, and agreed to support the prince.

Bedr returned to Africa to tell Abd al-Rahman of the invitation of the Umayyad clients in al-Andulus. Abd al-Rahman landed at Almunecar in al-Andalus, to the east of Malaga in September 755; however, his landing site was unconfirmed.

Fight for power:
Upon landing in al-Andalus, Abd al-Rahman was greeted by clients Abu Uthman and Ibn Khalid and an escort of 300 cavalry. During his brief time in Málaga, he was able to amass local support quickly. Waves of people made their way to Málaga to pay respect to the prince they thought was dead, including many of the aforementioned Syrians. One famous story which persisted through history related to a gift Abd al-Rahman was given while in Málaga. The gift was a beautiful young slave girl, but Abd al-Rahman humbly returned her to her previous master.

News of the prince's arrival spread like wildfire throughout the peninsula. During this time, emir al-Fihri and the Syrian commander al-Sumayl, pondered what to do about the new threat to their shaky hold on power. They decided to try to marry Abd al-Rahman into their family. If that did not work, then Abd al-Rahman would have to be killed. Abd al-Rahman was apparently sagacious enough to expect such a plot. In order to help speed his ascension to power, he was prepared to take advantage of the feuds and dissensions. However, before anything could be done, trouble broke out in northern al-Andalus. Zaragoza, an important trade city on the Upper March of al-Andalus, made a bid for autonomy. Al-Fihri and al-Sumayl rode north to squash the rebellion. This might have been fortunate timing for Abd al-Rahman, since he was still getting a solid foothold in al-Andalus. By March 756, Abd al-Rahman and his growing following of Umayyad clients and Yemenite Junds, were able to take Sevilla without violence. After settling his bloody business in Zaragoza, al-Fihri turned his army back south to face the "pretender". The fight for the right to rule al-Andalus was about to begin. The two contingents met on opposite sides of the River Guadalquivir, just outside the capital of Córdoba on the plains of Musarah.

The river was, for the first time in years, overflowing its banks, heralding the end of a long drought. Nevertheless, food was still scarce, and Abd al-Rahman's army suffered from hunger. In an attempt to demoralize Abd al-Rahman's troops, al-Fihri ensured that his troops not only were well fed, but also ate gluttonous amounts of food in full view of the Umayyad lines. An attempt at negotiations soon followed in which it is likely that Abd al-Rahman was offered the hand of al-Fihri's daughter in marriage and great wealth. Abd ar-Rahman, however, would settle for nothing less than control of the emirate, and an impasse was reached. Even before the fight began, dissension spread through some of Abd al-Rahman's lines. Specifically, the Yemeni Arabs were unhappy that the prince was mounted on a fine Spanish steed. And the prince's mettle was untried in battle, after all! The Yemenis observed significantly that such a fine horse would provide an excellent mount to escape from battle.

Being the ever-wary politician, Abd al-Rahman acted quickly to regain Yemeni support, and rode to a Yemeni chief who was mounted on a mule named "Lightning". Abd al-Rahman averred that his horse proved difficult to ride and was wont to buck him out of the saddle. He offered to exchange his horse for the mule, a deal to which the surprised chief readily agreed. The swap quelled the simmering Yemeni rebellion. Soon both armies were in their lines on the same bank of the Guadalquivir. Abd al-Rahman had no banner, and so one was improvised by unwinding a green turban and binding it round the head of a spear. Subsequently the turban and the spear became the banner and symbol of the Andalusian Umayyads. Abd al-Rahman led the charge toward al-Fihri's army. Al-Sumayl in turn advanced his cavalry out to meet the Umayyad threat.

After a long and difficult fight "Abd ar-Rahman obtained a most complete victory, and the field was strewn with the bodies of the enemy". Both al-Fihri and al-Sumayl managed to escape the field (probably) with parts of the army too. Abd al-Rahman triumphantly marched into the capital, Córdoba. Danger was not far behind, as al-Fihri planned a counterattack. He reorganized his forces and set out for the capital Abd al-Rahman had usurped from him. Again Abd al-Rahman met al-Fihri with his army; this time negotiations were successful, although the terms were somewhat changed. In exchange for al-Fihri's life and wealth, he would be a prisoner and not allowed to leave the city limits of Córdoba. Al-Fihri would have to report once a day to Abd al-Rahman, as well as turn over some of his sons and daughters as hostages. For a while al-Fihri met the obligations of the one-sided truce, but he still had many people loyal to him; people who would have liked to see him back in power.

Al-Fihri eventually did make another bid for power. He quit Córdoba and quickly started gathering supporters. While at large, al-Fihri managed to gather an army allegedly numbering to 20,000. It is doubtful, however, that his troops were "regular" soldiers, but rather a hodge-podge of men from various parts of al-Andalus. Abd ar-Rahman's appointed governor in Sevilla took up the chase, and after a series of small fights, managed to defeat al-Fihri's army. Al-Fihri himself managed to escape to the former Visigoth capital of Toledo in central al-Andalus; once there, he was promptly killed. Al-Fihri's head was sent to Córdoba, where Abd al-Rahman had it nailed to a bridge. With this act, Abd ar-Rahman proclaimed himself the emir of al-Andalus. One final act had to be performed, however: al-Fihri's general, al-Sumayl, had to be dealt with, and he was garroted in Córdoba's jail.

Rule:
Indeed, Abd al-Rahman only proclaimed himself as emir, and not as caliph. This was likely because al-Andalus was a land besieged by many different loyalties, and the proclamation of caliph would have likely caused much unrest. Abd al-Rahman's progeny would, however, take up the title of caliph. In the meantime, a call went out through the Muslim world that al-Andalus was a safe haven for friends of the house of Umayyah, if not for Abd al-Rahman's scattered family that managed to evade the Abbasids. Abd al-Rahman probably was quite happy to see his call answered by waves of Umayyad faithful and family. He was finally reacquainted with his son Sulayman, whom he last saw weeping on the banks of the Euphrates with his sisters. Abd ar-Rahman's sisters were unable to make the long voyage to al-Andalus. Abd al-Rahman placed his family members in high offices across the land, as he felt he could trust them more than non-family. The Umayyad family would again grow large and prosperous over successive generations. However, by 763 Abd ar-Rahman had to get back to the business of war. Al-Andalus had been invaded by an Abbasid army.

Far away in Baghdad, the current Abbasid caliph, al-Mansur, had long been planning to depose the Umayyad who dared to call himself emir of al-Andalus. Al-Mansur installed al-Ala ibn-Mugith (also known as al-Ala) as governor of Africa (whose title gave him dominion over the province of al-Andalus). It was al-Ala who headed the Abbasid army that landed in al-Andalus, possibly near Beja (in modern day Portugal). Much of the surrounding area of Beja capitulated to al-Ala, and in fact rallied under the Abbasid banners against Abd al-Rahman. Abd al-Rahman had to act quickly. The Abbasid contingent was vastly superior in size, said to have numbered 7,000 men. The emir quickly made for the redoubt of Carmona with his army. The Abbasid army was fast on his heels, and laid siege to Carmona for approximately two months. Abd al-Rahman must have sensed that time was against him as food and water became scarce, and his troops morale likely came into question.

Finally Abd al-Rahman gathered his men as he was "resolved on an audacious sally". Abd al-Rahman hand-picked 700 fighters from his army and led them to Carmona's main gate. There, he started a great fire and threw his scabbard into the flames. Abd al-Rahman told his men that time had come to go down fighting than die of hunger. The gate lifted and Abd al-Rahman's men fell upon the unsuspecting Abbasids, thoroughly routing them. Most of the Abbasid army was killed. The heads of the main Abbasid leaders were cut off. Their heads were preserved in salt, and identifying tags pinned to their ears. The heads were bundled together in a gruesome package and sent to the Abbasid caliph who was on pilgrimage at Mecca. Upon receiving the evidence of al-Ala's defeat in al-Andalus, al-Mansur is said to have gasped, "God be praised for placing a sea between us"! Al-Mansur hated, and yet apparently respected Abd al-Rahman to such a degree that he dubbed him the "Hawk of Quraysh" (The Umayyads were from a branch of the Quraysh tribe).

Despite such a tremendous victory, Abd al-Rahman had to continuously put down rebellions in al-Andalus. Various Arab and Berber tribes fought each other for varying degrees of power, some cities tried to break away and form their own state, and even members of Abd al-Rahman's family tried to wrest power from him. During a large revolt, dissidents marched on Córdoba itself; However, Abd al-Rahman always managed to stay one step ahead, and crushed all opposition; as he always dealt severely with dissidence in al-Andalus. Despite all this turmoil in al-Andalus, Abd al-Rahman wanted to take the fight back east to Baghdad. Revenge for the massacre of his family at the hands of the Abbasids must surely have been the driving factor in Abd al-Rahman's war plans. However his war against Baghdad was put on hold by more internal problems. The seditious city of Zaragoza on the Upper March revolted in a bid for autonomy. Little could Abd al-Rahman have known that as he set off to settle matters in that northern city, his hopes of warring against Baghdad would be indefinitely put on hold.

Problems in the Upper March:
Zaragoza proved to be a most difficult city to reign over for not only Abd ar-Rahman, but his predecessors as well. In the year 777–778, several notable men including Sulayman ibn Yokdan al-Arabi al-Kelbi, the self-appointed governor of Zaragoza, met with delegates of the

leader of the Franks, Charlemagne. "(Charlemagne's) army was enlisted to help the Muslim governors of Barcelona and Zaragoza against the Umayyad (emir) in Cordoba..." Essentially Charlemagne was being hired as a mercenary, even though he likely had other plans of acquiring the area for his own empire. After Charlemagne's columns arrived at the gates of Zaragoza, Sulayman got cold feet and refused to let the Franks into the city. It is possible that he realized that Charlemagne would want to usurp power from him. Charlemagne's force eventually headed back to France via a narrow pass in the Pyrenees, where his rearguard was wiped out by Basque and Gascon rebels (this disaster inspired the epic Chanson de Roland).

Now Abd al-Rahman could deal with Sulayman and the city of Zaragoza without having to fight a massive Christian army. In 779 Abd ar-Rahman offered the job of Zaragoza's governorship to one of Sulayman's allies, a man named al-Husayn ibn Yahiya. The temptation was too much for al-Husayn, who murdered his colleague Sulayman. As promised, al-Husayn was awarded Zaragoza with the expectation that he would always be a subordinate of Córdoba. Within two years, however, al-Husayn broke off relations with Abd al-Rahman and announced that Zaragoza would be an independent city-state. Once again Abd al-Rahman had to be concerned with developments in the Upper March. He was intent on keeping his important northern border city within the Umayyad fold. By 783 Abd al-Rahman's army advanced on Zaragoza. It appeared as though Abd al-Rahman wanted to make clear to this troublesome city that independence was out of the question. Included in the arsenal of Abd al-Rahman's army were thirty-six siege engines. Zaragoza's famous white granite defensive walls were breached under a torrent of ordnance from the Umayyad lines. Abd al-Rahman's warriors spilled into the city's streets, quickly thwarting al-Husayn's desires for independence.

Military and social reforms:
After the aforementioned period of conflict, Abd al-Rahman continued in his improvement of al-Andalus' infrastructure. He ensured roadways were begun, aqueducts were constructed or improved, and that a new mosque was well funded in his capital at Córdoba. Construction on what

would in time become the world famous Great Mosque of Córdoba was started circa the year 786. Abd al-Rahman knew that one of his sons would one day inherit the rule of al-Andalus, but that it was a land torn by strife. In order to successfully rule in such a situation, Abd al-Rahman needed to create a reliable civil service and organize a standing army. He felt that he could not always rely on the local populace in providing a loyal army; and therefore bought a massive standing army consisting mainly of Berbers from North Africa as well as slaves from other areas.

The total number of army-men under his command were nearly 40,000. As was common during the years of Islamic expansion from Arabia, religious tolerance was practiced. Abd al-Rahman continued to allow Jews and Christians and other monotheistic religions to retain and practice their faiths. They did, however, have to pay a tribute tax for this privilege. Abd al-Rahman's policy of taxing non-Muslims, which was often carried out by later rulers, changed the religious dynamic of al-Andalus. Possibly because of excessive tribute taxes "the bulk of the country's population must have become Muslim". However, other scholars have argued that though 80% of al-Andalus converted to Islam, it did not truly occur until near the 10th century.

Christians more often converted to Islam than Jews although there were converted Jews among the new followers of Islam. There was a great deal of freedom of interaction between the groups: for example, Sarah, the granddaughter of the Visigoth king Wittiza, married a Muslim man and bore two sons who were later counted among the ranks of the highest Arab nobility.

Conclusion:
The date of Abd al-Rahman's death is disputed, but is generally accepted to be sometime around 785 through 788. Abd al-Rahman died in his adopted city of Cordoba and was supposedly buried under the site of the Mezquita. Abd al-Rahman's alleged favorite son was his choice for successor and would later be known as Hisham I. Abd ar-Rahman's progeny would continue to rule al-Andalus in the name of the house of Umayyah for several generations, with the zenith of their power coming during the reign of Abd al-Rahman III.

Legends:
In his lifetime, Abd al-Rahman was known as *al Dakhil* ("the immigrant"). But he was also known as *Saqr Quraish* ("The Falcon of the Quraish"), bestowed on him by one of his great enemies, the Abbasid caliph al-Mansur.

*

Abd al-Rahman: "The Falcon of the Quraysh"

At one epic slaughter a Persian general name Abdullah invited 80 of the remaining members of the Umayyad clan to a banquet. At the height of the festivities he had all of them murdered. (only one of the Umayyads escaped, it is said; he was Abd al-Rahman, known as "the Falcon of the Quraysh," who managed to flee to Spain, where he founded a dynasty that flourished for 300 years).

The Shi'ites soon learned that they had been betrayed; the Abbasids not only failed to help their cause, but persecuted them as well. In their thoroughness, the new rulers also ruthlessly executed the men who had helped them gain office, so that the power of these allies could never be used against them.

*

Abd al-Rahman I (Umayyad 729-788):

Founded by Muawiyah ibn Abi Sufyan in 661, the Umayyad dynasty was one of the most powerful empires to have ruled the Muslim world. Of the fourteen Umayyad sovereigns who ruled between 661 and 750, the reigns of Muawiyah, Abd al-Malik ibn Marwan, Umar ibn Abd al-Aziz, al-Walid I and Hisham were the most successful. The demise of the Umayyad dynasty, and the rise of the Abbasids during the middles of the eighth century, represented a momentous change in Islamic history; one influential political dynasty gave way to another, which went on to rule the Muslim world for more than five hundred years.

Abd al-Rahman ibn Muawiyah ibn Hisham, also known as sahib al-Andalus (or 'the Lord of Muslim Spain'), was born in Damascus during the reign of his illustrious grandfather, Caliph Hisham, who ruled the Muslim world for nearly two decades and thereby consolidated Umayyad power. Abd al-Rahman had a privileged upbringing, surrounded by great riches and luxury. When Prince Abd al-Rahman was around fourteen, his grandfather Caliph Hisham died in 743. The death of Hisham marked the beginning of the end for the Umayyads as a protracted succession battle ensued, which severely undermined the Umayyad grip on power. Seeing the Umayyads in utter disarray, the Abbasids swiftly galvanized their forces in Khurasan and launched a series of daring raids against the incumbent Umayyad governors in Rayy and Isfahan. As the Abbasids marched towards Damascus, the last Umayyad ruler fled to Egypt, thus clearing the way for Abbasid victory.

Abul Abbas, who was also known as 'al-Saffah' (or 'the bloodshedder'), was the leader of the Abbasids at the time and went on to become the first Abbasid ruler. Immediately after being sworn in as Abbasid Caliph, he organized a lavish feast in Damascus for all the Umayyad princes and had nearly all of them systematically butchered so that there could never be an Umayyad uprising against the Abbasid. As fate would have it, only Prince Abd al-Rahman, who was twenty at the time, and his younger brother, escaped the ensuing massacre. But, unable to outrun his pursuers, his thirteen-year-old brother was captured and beheaded as young Abd al-Rahman watched in the distance.

From the banks of the Euphrates, he went to Palestine and Egypt, travelling by day and night to avoid being captured and put to the sword by the Abbasid henchmen. After living in hiding for several years, Abd al-Rahman set out for North Africa. Finally arriving in Morocco, he was offered refuge by the North African tribe of Banu Nafisa. Here he soon established himself as an inspirational leader and military strategist. With the Abbasids now firmly in control of the Islamic East, Abd al-Rahman knew that a return to Damascus was no longer a viable option; instead, he decided to carve out a bright future for himself in the Islamic West.

It was a time when the Muslims of al-Andalus (Islamic Spain) became bitterly divided along ethnic lines. Abd al-Rahman skillfully exploited the situation to his advantage in order to install himself as the ruler of Islamic Spain. Since the Spanish Arabs were very sympathetic towards the Umayyads, they assured Badr, Abd al-Rahman's aide, that should Abd al-Rahman decide to come, they would help him to reunite the country under his leadership. Abd al-Rahman reached the shores of al-Andalus in 755 at the age of twenty-five. Thus a new chapter began in the history of Islamic Spain, under the wise and able stewardship of Prince Abd al-Rahman.

After recruiting a sizeable military force, Abd al-Rahman annexed Archidona and Seville and marched toward Cordova, the capital of Islamic Spain, and challenged the authority of the reigning Abbasid governor, Yusuf al-Fihri. Abd al-Rahman's twenty thousand troops met the forces of the governor in 756 as Masara, east of Cordova, and inflicted a crushing defeat on them, forcing al-Fihri to flee to Toledo. This represented a decisive victory for Abd al-Rahman who now became the undisputed ruler of Islamic Spain. His biggest test, though, came in 763 when the great Abbasid Caliph Abu Ja'far al-Mansur dispatched a powerful army under the command of Ala ibn Mughis, in order to drive Abd al-Rahman out of Spain. Abd al-Rahman, however, organized his armed forces with such skill and efficiency that his forces repelled the advancing Abbasid army with great success. Indeed, in the battle, Abd al-Rahman killed Ala ibn Mughis with his own hands and sent his remains – wrapped in an Abbasid flag – to Caliph al-Mansur in Baghdad.

It was not until almost a decade later that the Abbasid Caliph al-Mahdi sent an envoy to Emperor Charlemagne of France to urge him to attack Muslim Spain in order to overthrow Abd al-Rahman. Later, Charlemagne signed a peace treaty with Abd al-Rahman and promised not to attack Islamic Spain again.

After restoring peace and stability across the land, Abd al-Rahman began to construct schools, colleges, hospitals, mosques, fountains and public baths across Spain, and he encouraged the locals to use these state-funded facilities and to do so free of charge.

Having spent his early years in the beautiful gardens of the royal palace in Damascus, Abd al-Rahman was keen to re-create the same ambience in and around his beloved Cordova. At a time when the rest of Europe was emerging from the Dark Ages, Abd al-Rahman transformed Islamic Spain into one of medieval Europe's most prosperous and advanced centers of culture and civilization. The great mosque of Cordova, which Abd al-Rahman built during his long reign of thirty-two years still stands to this day.

Abd al-Rahman died at the age of fifty-nine and was buried in the great Palace of Cordova. The Umayyad rule of Islamic Spain, initiated by Abd al-Rahman, persisted for nearly three hundred years.

*

Abd al-Rahman III (890-961):

The Umayyads ruled the Muslim world from 661 to 750, but when the Abbasids came to power they put most of the Umayyad princes to the sword. Only a handful of the Umayyad princes escaped the ensuing massacre. Abd al-Rahman, the grandson of Umayyad ruler Hisham ibn Abd al-Malik, was one of them. He fled Damascus and travelled on foot and by ship for many years before he finally reached North Africa, where he received a warm welcome from the Berber tribe of Banu Nafisa (in present-day Morocco). In 756, he led an army into battle and defeated the governor's forces before proceeding to Cordova, the capital of al-Andalus, and in so doing inaugurated Umayyad rule in Spain. Abd al-Rahman and his descendants went on to rule Muslim Spain for nearly three centuries. During this period Muslim Spain produced a number of influential rulers, but the most outstanding of them all was Caliph Abd al-Rahman III.

Abd al-Rahman ibn Muhammad, better known as Abd al-Rahman III, was born in Cordova during the reign of his grandfather, Amir Abdullah. Young Abd al-Rahman grew up under the care of his Frankish mother, Muzna, and his grandfather, Amir Abdullah. His mother, Muzna, and grandmother, Iniga, were of European origin. Young Abd al-Rahman was aware of the difficult challenges which confronted his country and contributed as much as he could to alleviating the problems until Amir Abdullah died in 912.

Abd al-Rahman succeeded his grandfather at the age of twenty-two and became the new ruler of Islamic Spain. Immediately after becoming Caliph, his main priority was to restore political stability and civil order across al-Andalus. The Abbasid Caliph in Baghdad, he reminded his people, would not come to their aid should the neighboring Christian powers decide to attack al-Andalus. His message to his people was very loud and clear: unite or you will be consigned to the dustbin of history.

After establishing political and civil order across Cordova and its immediate surroundings, Abd al-Rahman turned his attention to other major cities like Seville and Toledo. But when these self-appointed rulers rejected his conciliatory measures, he launched military actions against them. Since Ordono II, the Christian ruler of Leon, was the chief instigator of these raids, Abd al-Rahman sent an expedition and inflicted a crushing defeat on his forces in 923. After successfully subduing these cities, Abd al-Rahman finally restored peace, order and security across much of al-Andalus. In 929, at the age of thirty-nine, he became the undisputed master of Islamic Spain and adopted the title of al-Khalifah al-Nasir li-din Allah ('the Caliph, the Defender of the Religion of God').

Indeed, under Abd al-Rahman's stewardship, Spain became a beacon of light for the rest of Europe. When there was hardly a college or library worth its name in Europe, al-Andalus boasted some of the finest, and also largest, libraries and educational institutions in the Western world. He transformed the Academy in Cordova into one of the world's most dazzling centers of higher education and research. The thriving and tolerant civil society, known as the Convivencia, fostered by Caliph Abd al-Rahman enabled everyone including Muslims, Jews and Christians to live and work together in peace and tranquility. Renowned Jewish thinkers such as Ibn Gabirol and Judah Halevi also lived and thrived in Islamic Spain.

Then, in 936, Caliph Abd al-Rahman ordered the construction of a new palace city which became known as Madinat al-Zahra (or 'the dazzling city'). This mammoth project took more than forty years to complete. It was in fact Caliph al-Hakam, his son and successor, who finally achieved this in 976.

For nearly eight centuries, under her Mohammedan rulers, Spain set to all Europe a shining example of a civilized and enlightened State. Mathematics, astronomy and botany, history, philosophy and jurisprudence were to be mastered in Spain, and Spain alone.

His reign of forty-nine years was therefore a truly remarkable period in the history of Islamic Spain and Europe as a whole. Caliph Abd al-Rahman III died in Cordova at the age of seventy-one. Al-Andalus began to decline after his death and the Umayyads of Spain were eventually ousted from power in 1031.

*

Al-Mansur, founder of Baghdad as capital:

(Golden Age of Islam):
By the middle of the Tenth Century the mighty Abbasid caliphs had faded to little more than shadowy puppets whose strings were manipulated by their own Turkish Bodyguards. At the beginning of their rule, the Abbasid moved their capital from Damascus to the East.

Abbas, the founder of the dynasty, made his headquarters in Hashimiya, near Kufa. when he died in 754, cut down by smallpox after only four years in office, he was succeeded by his brother, Mansur. At the same time he was looking for a site for a new capital.

Mansur had another motive for establishing a new capital: he wanted it to be a magnificent symbol of Abbasid power. He chose an ancient village named Baghdad, approximately 20 miles northwest of the former Persian capital of Ctesiphon. From the start Baghdad proved an ideal choice. It lay on the west bank of the Tigris, in the midst of a fertile plain, beside a canal linking the Tigris with the Euphrates; the two rivers bent briefly toward each other at this point so that they were only 20 miles distant.

Because of the two rivers that flanked it, and the irrigation canals that crisscrossed it, the land was rich. Equally important, as a capital city it could be easily defended, since enemies could approach only by ship or bridge. To Mansur, the new city that would rise in this "island" between the Tigris and the Euphrates would be a "market place for the world."

Besides being struck by Baghdad's agricultural, commercial and military advantages, the Caliph was said to have been impressed by reports that the region enjoyed two other asset: cool nights and freedom from mosquitoes. Mansur named his new capital Madinat al-Salam ("The City of Peace"), but the people continued to call it Baghdad. (Mansur is said to have been the first caliph who kept an astrologer at court.) to help build the new capital, every city in the empire was bidden to send its most skilled craftsmen. Some 100,000 workers were assembled from every corner of Islam. Syria, Egypt, Mesopotamia, Persia, and they worked four years to complete the extraordinary city.

A great citadel of sun-baked bricks, Baghdad was built in the form of a circle nearly two miles across. It was referred to as "the round city". It was fortified with lookout towers, and, like the other walls, was pierced at opposite points by four large gates that were guarded by soldiers.

The ordinary people of Baghdad lived in houses outside the walls. At the very hub of the round city was the caliph's palace, a magnificent edifice built of marble and stone said to have been carried from the old Persian capital of Ctesiphon. Next to it was the mosque. Mansur had picked this position for his royal residence, declaring that the caliph should live at the very center of his empire. The round city was divided into four pie-shaped quadrants by two highways that cut across it at right angles to one another, linking the gates and running out through them.

But suburbs soon grew around Baghdad's walls, and quickly spread to the east bank of the Tigris. In the Tenth Century the capital had an estimated population of one and a half million. In many ways Baghdad reflected the changes taking place all over the Islamic empire.

The brilliant cultural heritage of Persia gradually percolated into Iraq, and from there it filtered out to affect practically every facet of Muslim life. Under Abbasid rule, the state took on an international character it had never known before. With the end of the wars of conquest, the Arab aristocracy had lost its monopoly of high office. The one-privileged

Arab warriors, to their chagrin, found themselves replaced by Persian soldiers and consequently had their pensions withdrawn.

Persian and other non-Arab influences also entered Islam through intermarriage within the Abbasid family itself; although the family was originally Arabian, of the 37 caliphs in the dynasty, only a few had Arab mothers. Finally, the Abbasid caliphs had absolute power, in the manner of the Persian kings. For centuries, Persian monarchs had reigned not merely as sovereigns, but as semi-divine beings invested with total authority over their subjects.

*

Al-Mu'tasim (Abu Ishaq Abbas 794-842):

Abu Ishaq 'Abbas al-Mu'tasim ibn Harun (Arabic: ’Abu ’Isḥāq al-Mu'tasim ibn Harun) (794 – January 5, 842) was an Abbasid caliph (833-842). He succeeded his half-brother al-Ma'mun. In Arabian communities, al-Mu'tasim is an example of the magnanimity because of the famous incident "Wa Mu'tasimah".

Early life:
Abu Ishaq was born to a Turkic slave mother. His father was then caliph Harun al-Rashid, Abu Ishaq led the pilgrimage in A.H. 200 (815-816) and in 201. Abu Ishaq defeated these Kharijites

In A.H. 214 (829-830) Abu Ishaq subdued Egypt and executed some leading rebels. He returned in 215 to join al-Ma'mun in a campaign against the Byzantines. Abu Ishaq commanded forces that captured thirty Byzantine strongholds.

Caliphate:
Al-Tabari records that al-Mu'tasim was hailed caliph on August 9, 833. He promptly ordered the dismantling of al-Ma'mun's military base at Tyana. He sent Ishaq ibn Ibrahim ibn Mu'sab against a Khurramite

revolt centered near Hamadhan. Ishaq soundly defeated the rebels. Their survivors, under Nasr, fled to the Byzantines.

One of the most difficult problems facing this Caliph, as faced his predecessor, was the uprising of Babak Khorramdin. Babak first rebelled in A.H. 201 (816-817) and overcame a number of caliphate forces sent against him. Finally, al-Mu'tasim provided clear instructions to his general al-Afshin Khaydhar ibn Kawus. Following these al-Afshin patiently overcame the rebel, securing a significant victory of this reign. Babak was brought to Samarra in A.H. 223 (837-838). He entered the city spectacularly riding on a splendid elephant. He was executed by his own executioner and his head sent to Khurasan. His brother was executed in Baghdad.

In that same year of Babak's death, the Byzantine emperor Theophilus launched an attack against a number of Abbasid fortresses, Al-Mu'tasim launched a well planned response. Al-Afshin met and defeated Theophilus on July 21, 838, known as Battle of Anzen. Ankara fell to the Muslim army of 50,000 men (with 50,000 camels and 20,000 mules) and from there they advanced on the stronghold of Amorium. A captive escaped and informed the caliph that one section of Amorium's wall was only a frontal façade. By concentrating bombardment here, al-Mu'tasim captured the city.

On his return home, he became aware of a serious conspiracy centered on al-Abbas ibn al-Ma'mun. A number of senior military commanders were involved. Al-Abbas was executed, as were, among others, al-Shah ibn Sahl, Amr al-Farghana, 'Ujayf ibn 'Anbasa and Akhmad ibn al-Khalil.

The ghilman (sing, ghulam) were introduced to the Caliphate during al-Mu'tasim's reign. The *ghilman* were slave-soldiers taken as prisoners of war from conquered regions, in anticipation of the Mamluk system and made into caliphal guard. The *ghilman*, personally responsible only to the Caliph, were to revolt several times during the 860's, killed 4 caliphs and be replaced by the Mamluk system, based on captured Turkish children, trained and molded within the Islamic lands.

The *ghilman*, along with the *Shakiriya* which had been introduced in the reign of al-Ma'mun, had irritated the Arab regular soldiers of the Caliph's army. The Turkic and Armenian *ghilman* agitated the citizens of Baghdad, provoking riots in 836. The capital was moved to the new city of Samarra later that year, where it would remain until 892 when it was returned to Baghdad by al-Mu'tamid.

The Tahirid dynasty, which had come to prominence during al-Ma'mun's reign after the military province of Khurasan was granted to Tahir bin Husain, continued to grow in power. They received the governorships of Samarqand, Farghana and Herat. Unlike most provinces in the Abbasid Caliphate, which were closely governed by Baghdad and Samarra, the provinces under the control of the Tahirids were exempted from many tributes and oversight functions. The independence of the Tahirids contributed greatly to the decline of Abbasid supremacy in the east.

In A.H. 224 (838-839) Mazyar ibn Qarin who detested the Tahirids rebelled against them. Previously he had insisted on paying the taxes of his Caspian region directly to al-Mu'tasim's agent instead of to Abdallah ibn Tahir's. Al-Afshin, desiring to replace Abdallah as Khurasan's governor, intrigued with Mazyar. Mazyar imprisoned people from Sariya, demolished Amul's walls and fortified Tamis, causing apprehension in Jurjan.

Abdallah and al-Mu'tasim dispatched forces to quell the uprising. Abdallah's commander Hayyan ibn Jabalah convinced Mazyar's Qarin ibn Shahriyar to betray Mazyar. Qarin sent Hayyan Mazyar's brother and other commanders Qarin had taken by surprise. The people of Sariyah rose against Mazyar. Al-Quhyar ibn Qarin betrayed Mazyar. He was brought, along with his correspondence, some implicating al-Afshin, to al-Mu'tasim. Mazyar's commander al-Durri was defeated, captured and executed.

When Mazyar entered Samarra on a mule, al-Afshin was arrested and killed in May or June 841. The Khurramiyyah were never fully suppressed, although they slowly vanished during the reigns of succeeding Caliphs. Near the end of al-Mu'tasim's life there was an uprising in Palestine. Al-Mu'tasim sent Raja ibn Ayyub al-Hidari to restore order. Al-Hidari defeated the rebels and captured their leader Abu Harb al-Mubarqa.

The great Arab mathematician al-Kindi was employed by al-Mu'tasim and tutored the Caliph's son, al-Kindi had served at the *Bayt al-Hikma*, or *House of Wisdom*. He continued his studies in Greek geometry and algebra under the caliph's patronage.

Ideologically, al-Mu'tasim followed the footstep of his half-brother al-Ma'mun. He continued his predecessors support for heretical (agreed upon by the majority of scholars) Islamic sect of Mu'tazilah, applying his brutal military methods for torturing Imam Ahmad ibn Hanbal.

Death:
Al-Tabari states that al-Mu'tasim fell ill on October 21, 841. His regular doctor had died the previous year and the new physician did not follow the normal treatment and this was the cause of the caliph's illness. Al-Mu'tasim died on January 5, 842 (p. 207). This caliph is described by al-Tabari as having a relatively easy going nature, being kind, agreeable and charitable. He was succeeded by his son, al-Wathiq.

Mu'tasim and Samarra:

It was during the reign of Mu'tasim, a son of Harun, who ruled from 833 to 842, that the Abbasid Caliphate began to lose control. Friction grew between the Turks and the local population. The situation became so acute that in 836 the Caliph moved his capital 60 miles up the Tigris, where he built the new city of Samarra. This remained the administrative headquarters of the empire for the next half century, during the reign of seven caliphs.

Located on the east bank of the Tigris, Samarra was renowned for its palaces and parks. On the west bank of the river Mu'tasim laid out a special pleasure ground, which was connected with the capital by a bridge of boats; there he planted lush gardens with palms from Basra and exotic plants from distant regions of the empire. Samarra's Friday Mosque was the largest ever built, covering some 45,500 square yards (nearly three times the ground area of St. Peter's Church, Rome), and was celebrated for its magnificence. The spiral ramped minaret, some 175 feet tall, could be seen for miles.

While in Samarra, the Abbasid caliphs became increasingly dependent on their Turkish guards, until they actually were their pawns. One of Mu'tasim's sons, Mutawakkil, was, in fact, placed on the throne by the guards and was virtually their prisoner. Ultimately Mutawakkil was murdered by the Turks at the instigation of his son, who sought to be the caliph himself.

*

Al-Mutawakkil (821-8610:

Al-Mutawakkil 'Alā Allāh Ja'far ibn al-Mu'tasim (March 821 – December 861) was an Abbasid caliph who reigned in Samarra from 847 until 861. He succeeded his brother al-Wathiq and is known for putting an end to the Mihna "ordeal", the Inquisition-like attempt by his predecessors to impose a single Mu'tazili version of Islam.

Life:
While al-Wathiq was caliph, the vizier, ibn Abd al-Malik, had poorly treated al-Mutawakkil. On September 22, 847, al-Mutawakkil had him arrested. The former vizier's property was plundered and he was tortured in his own iron maiden. He finally died on November 2. The caliph had others who had mistreated him in the previous reign punished.

In A.H. 235 (849) al-Mutawakkil had the prominent military commander Itakh al-Khazari seized in Baghdad. Itakh was imprisoned and died of thirst on December 21. One Mahmud ibn al-Faraj al-Nayshapuri arose claiming to be a prophet. He and some followers were arrested in Baghdad. He was imprisoned, beaten and on June 18, 850 he died.

In A.H. 237 (851-852) Armenians rebelled and defeated and killed the Abbasid governor. Al-Mutawakkil sent his general Bugha al-Kabir to handle this. Bugha scored successes this year and the following year he attacked and burned Tiblis, capturing Ishaq ibn Isma'il. The rebel leader was executed. That year (A.H. 238) the Byzantines attacked Damietta.

In A.H. 240 (854-855) the police chief in Homs killed a prominent person stirring an uprising. He was driven out. Al-Mutawakkil offered another police chief. When the next year saw a revolt against this new police chief, al-Mutawakkil had this firmly suppressed. As Christians had joined in the second round of disturbances, the caliph had Christians expelled from Homs.

Also in 241 occurred the firm response to the revolt by the Bujah, people of African descent just beyond Upper Egypt. They had been paying a tax on their gold mines. They ceased paying this, drove out Muslims working in the mines and terrified people in Upper Egypt. Al-Mutawakkil sent al-Qummi to restore order. Al-Qummi sent seven ships with supplies that enabled him to persevere despite the very harsh terrain of this distant territory. He retook the mines, pressed on to the Bujah royal stronghold and defeated the king in battle. The Bujah resumed payment of the tax.

On February 23, 856, there was an exchange of captives with the Byzantines. A second such exchange took place some four years later. Al-Mutawakkil's reign is remembered for its many reforms and viewed as a golden age of the Abbasids. He would be the last great Abbasid caliph; after his death the dynasty would fall into a decline.

Al-Mutawakkil continued to rely on Turkish statesmen and slave soldiers to put down rebellions and lead battles against foreign empires, notably the Byzantines, from who Sicily was captured. His vizier, Al-Fath bin Khaqan, who was Turkish, was a famous figure of Al-Mutawakkil's era.

His reliance on Turkish soldiers would come back to haunt him. Al-Mutawakkil would have his Turkish commander-in-chief killed. This, coupled with his extreme attitudes towards the Shi'a, made his popularity decline rapidly.

Al-Mutawakkil was murdered by a Turkish soldier on December 11, 861 CE. Some have speculated that his murder was part of a plot hatched by his son, al-Muntasir, who had grown estranged from his father. Al-Muntasir feared his father was about to move against him and struck first.

Accomplishments:
Al-Mutawakkil was unlike his brother and father in that he was not known for having a thirst for knowledge, but he had an eye for magnificence and a hunger to build. The Great Mosque of Samarra was at its time, the largest mosque in the world; its minaret is a vast spiraling cone 55 m high with a spiral ramp. The mosque had 17 aisles and its wall were paneled with mosaics of dark blue glass.

The Great Mosque was just part of an extension of Samarra eastwards that built upon part of the walled royal hunting park. Al-Mutawakkil built as many as 20 palaces (the numbers vary in documents). Samarra became one of the largest cities of the ancient world; even the archaeological site of its ruins is one of the world's most extensive. The Caliph's building schemes extended in A.H. 245 (859-860) to a new city, *al-Ja'fariyya*, which al-Mutawakkil built on the Tigris some eighteen kilometers from Samarra. More water, and al-Mutawakkil ordered a canal to be built to divert water from the Tigris, entrusting the project to two courtiers, who ignored the talents of a local engineer of repute and entrusted the work to al-Farghani, the great astronomer and writer. Al-Farghani, who was not a specialist in public works, made a miscalculation and it appeared that the opening of the canal was too deep so that water from the river would only flow at near full flood.

News leaked to the infuriated caliph might have meant the heads of all concerned save for the gracious actions of the engineer, Sind ibn 'Ali, who vouched for the eventual success of the project, thus risking his own life. Al-Mutawakkil was assassinated shortly before the error became public.

Al-Mutawakkil was keen to involve himself in many religious debates, something that would show in his actions against different minorities. His father had tolerated the Shi'a Imam who taught and preached at Medina, and for the first years of his reign al-Mutawakkil continued the policy. Imam 'Ali al-Hadi's growing reputation inspired a letter from the Governor of Medina, 'Abdu I-Lah ibn Muhammad, suggesting that a coup was being plotted, and al-Mutawakkil extended an invitation to Samarra to the Imam, an offer he could not refuse. In Samarra, the Imam was kept under virtual house arrest and spied upon. However, no excuse to take action against him ever appeared. After al-Mutawakkil's death, his successor had the Imam poisoned: al-Hadī is buried at Samarra. The general Shi'a population faced repression and this was embodied in the destruction of the shrine of Hussayn ibn 'Alī, an action that was carried out ostensibly in order to stop pilgrimages to that site and the flogging and incarceration of the Alid Yahya ibn Umar.

Also during his reign, Al-Mutawakkil met the famous Byzantine theologian Constantine the Philosopher, who was sent to tighten the diplomatic relations between the Empire and the Caliphate in a state mission by the Emperor Michael III.

Of his sons, al-Muntasir succeeded him and ruled until his death in 862, al-Mu'tazz ruled from 866 to his overthrow in 869, al-Mu'eiyyad was murdered by Mu'tazz in 866, al-Mu'tamid reigned as Caliph in 870–892, and al-Muwaffaq was effective regent of the realm until his death in 891.

Caliph Al-Mutawakkil (821-861):

In that year (835-850), al-Mutawakkil ordered that the Christians and all the rest of the Ahl Al Dhimma be made to wear honey colored taylasans and the Zunnar belts. He further commanded that their slaves be made to wear the Zunnar and be forbidden to wear the Mintaqa. He gave orders that any of their houses of worship built after the advent of Islam were to be destroyed and that one tenth of their homes be confiscated.

A document of protection attributed by the Jews to Muhammad. "This is the writ of protection which was extended to the Children of Israel to the Prophet Muhammad's. Long ago, the heathens revolted against the Prophet Muhammad, peace be upon him. But Allah granted him victory over them".

*

Harun al-Rashid (763-809:

Harun al-Rashid (Arabic: properly pronounced **Harun ar-Rashīd**; English: Aaron the Upright, *Aaron the Just*, or *Aaron the Rightly Guided*) (17 March 763 or February 766 – 24 March 809) was the fifth Arab Abbasid Caliph that encompassed modern Iraq. His birth date remains a point of discussion, though, as various sources give the dates from 763 to 766).

He ruled from 786 to 809, and his time was marked by scientific, cultural and religious prosperity. Art and music Hamd o Na'at also flourished significantly during his reign. He established the legendary library Bayt al-Hikma ("House of Wisdom").

Since Harun was intellectually, politically and militarily resourceful, his life and the court over which he held sway have been the subject of many tales: some are factual but most are believed to be fictitious. Among what is known to be fictional is *The Book of One Thousand and One Nights*, which contains many stories that are fantasized by Harun's magnificent court and even Harun al-Rashid himself.

The family of Barmakids which played a deciding role in establishing the Abbasid Caliphate declined gradually during his rule.

Life:
Harun was born in Rey. He was the son of al-Mahdi, the third Abbasid caliph (ruled 775–785), and al-Khayzuran, a former slave girl from Yemen and a woman of strong personality who greatly influenced affairs of state in the reigns of her husband and sons.

Harun was strongly influenced by the will of his mother in the governance of the empire until her death in 789. His vizier (chief minister) Yahya the Barmakid, Yahya's sons (especially Ja'far ibn Yahya), and other Barmakids generally controlled the administration.

The Barmakids were a Persian-Tajik family which dated back to the Barmak of Magi, who had become very powerful under al-Mahdi. Yahya had aided Harun in obtaining the caliphate, and he and his sons were in high favor until 798, when the caliph threw them in prison and confiscated their land.

Harun became caliph when he was in his early twenties. Before that, in 780 and again in 782, he had already nominally led campaigns against the Caliphate's traditional enemy, the Byzantine Empire. The latter expedition was a huge undertaking, and even reached the Asian suburbs of Constantinople. On the day of accession, his son al-Ma'mun was born, and al-Amin some little time later: the latter was the son of Zubaida, a granddaughter of al-Mansur (founder of the city of Baghdad); so he took precedence over the former, whose mother was a Persian slave-girl. He began his reign by appointing very able ministers, who carried on the work of the government so well that they greatly improved the condition of the people.

It was under Harun ar-Rashīd that Baghdad flourished into the most splendid city of its period. Tribute was paid by many rulers to the caliph, and these funds were used on architecture, the arts and a luxurious life at court.

In 796, Harun decided to move his court and the government to Ar Raqqah at the middle Euphrates. Here he spent 12 years, most of his reign. Only once he returned to Baghdad for a short visit. It was close to the Byzantine border. The communication lines via the Euphrates to Baghdad and via the Balikh River to the north and via Palmyra to Damascus were excellent. And from Raqqa any rebellion in Syria and the middle Euphrates area could be controlled. In ar-Raqqah the Barmakids managed the fate of the empire, and their heirs, al-Amin and al-Ma'mun grew up.

Due to the *Thousand-and-One Nights* tales, Harun al-Rashid turned into a legendary figure obscuring his true historic personality. In fact, his reign initiated the political disintegration of the Abbasid caliphate.[1] Syria was inhabited by tribes with Umayyad sympathies and remained the bitter enemy of the Abbasids while Egypt witnessed uprisings against Abbasids due to maladministration and arbitrary taxation. The Umayyads had been established in Spain in 755, the Idrisids in Morocco in 788, and the Aghlabids in Ifriqiya (modern Tunisia) in 800. Besides, unrest flared up in Yemen, and the Kharijites rose in rebellion in

Daylam, Kerman, Fars and Sistan. Revolts also broke out in Khorasan, and al-Rashid waged many campaigns against the Byzantines.

A major revolt led by Rafeh bin Layth was started in Samarqand which forced Harun al-Rashid to move to Khorasan. He first removed and arrested Ali bin Isa bin Mahan but the revolt continued unchecked. Harun al-Rashid died very soon when he reached Sanabad village in Toos and was buried in the summer palace of Humaid bin Qahtabah, the former Abbasid governor in Khorasan, situated near the Sanabad village in the Toos region.

Al-Rashid virtually dismembered the empire by apportioning it between his two sons al-Amin and al-Ma'mun (with his third son, al-Qasim, being belatedly added after them). Very soon it became clear that by dividing the empire, Rashid had actually helped to set the opposing parties against one another, and had provided them with sufficient resources to become independent of each other.[1] After the death of Harun al-Rashid, civil war broke out in the empire between his two sons, al-Amin and al-Ma'mun.

In 802 Harun sent Charlemagne a present consisting of silks, brass candelabra, perfume, balsam, ivory chessmen, a colossal tent with many-colored curtains, an elephant named Abul-Abbas, and a water clock that marked the hours by dropping bronze balls into a bowl, as mechanical knights—one for each hour—emerged from little doors which shut behind them. The presents were unprecedented in Western Europe and may have influenced Carolingian art.

When the Byzantine empress Irene was deposed, Nikephoros I became emperor and refused to pay tribute to Harun, saying that Irene should have been receiving the tribute the whole time. News of this angered Harun. After campaigns in Asia Minor, Nikephoros was forced to conclude a treaty, with humiliating terms.

Harun made the pilgrimage to Mecca several times, e.g., 793, 795, 797, 802 and last in 803. Tabari concludes his account of Harun's reign with these words: "It has been said that when Harun al-Rashid died, there were nine hundred million odd (Dirhams) in the state treasury."

Al-Rashid sent embassies to the Chinese Tang dynasty and established good relations with them. He was called "A-lun" in the Chinese T'ang Annals.

In 808, Harun went to settle the insurrection of Rafi ibn Leith in Transoxania, became ill, and died. He was buried under the palace of Hamid ibn Qahtabi, the governor of Greater Khorasan, Iran. The location later became known as Mashhad ("The Place of Martyrdom") because of the martyrdom of Imam ar-Ridha in 818.

Anecdotes:
Many anecdotes attached themselves to the person of Harun al-Rashid in the centuries following his rule. Al-Masudi relates a number of interesting anecdotes in The Meadows of Gold illuminating the character of this caliph.

Harun, like a number of caliphs, is given an anecdote connecting a poem with his death. Shortly before he died, he is said to have been reading some lines by Abu al-Atahiya about the transitory nature of the power and pleasures of this world.

Muawiya ibn Abi Sufyan (605-680):

The reign of the first four Caliphs of Islam became known as the period of the 'rightly-guided Caliphs' (al-khulafa al-Rashidun) because they ruled in accordance with the teachings of the Qur'an and the Prophetic sunnah (norms and practices). After the death of Uthman, the third rightly-guided Caliph in 656, the Muslim world was plunged into serious political and social turmoil. The death of Caliph Uthman shattered the political unity of Islam. Although Ali, the cousin and son-in-law of the Prophet, succeeded Uthman as the fourth Caliph, he was not able to put an end to the political rivalry and tribal infighting. Amidst the prevailing chaos and disorder, Muawiyah ibn Abi Sufyan emerged to establish the Umayyad dynasty, which subsequently became one of the most powerful dynasties to rule the Muslim world.

Muawiyah ibn Abi Sufyan ibn Harb was born into the powerful Makkan clan of Banu Umayyah. His father, Abu Sufyan, was a wealthy and powerful Makkan chieftain. Muawiyah grew up to be an intelligent, wise and pleasant young man. The Prophet's message of unity, brotherhood, justice and equality clearly threatened Abu Sufyan and his like.

During the next thirteen years, Abu Sufyan – actively encouraged by his wife Hind bint Utba – opposed the Prophet and his small band of followers with great determination. After the Prophet migrated (Hijrah) to the nearby oasis of Madinah, Abu Sufuyan spearheaded a series of military expeditions against the nascent Muslim community but on each and every occasion he failed to breach the strong defense put up by the Muslims. Eventually, in 630, the Prophet, accompanied by his companions, returned to Makkah unopposed and it was then that Abu Sufyan embraced Islam but Muawiyah had already become a Muslim a year earlier. Umm Habibah, the daughter of Abu Sufyan, had embraced Islam much earlier, and she was married to the Prophet. Muawiyah was around twenty-five when he embraced Islam. He volunteered to be one of the Prophet's secretaries (Kuttab al-Wahy).

After the Prophet's death in 632, Muawiyah played an active part in the affairs of the early Islamic State. His services to the Prophet and early Muslim community prompted Umar, the second Caliph, to appoint Muawiyah governor of Syria in 639, following the death of Abu Ubaida ibn al-Jarrah. Muawiyah appointed some of his most trusted and loyal lieutenants to key positions in Government. Syria became one of the most politically stable and economically prosperous provinces of the Islamic State. Following Umar's assassination in 644, Uthman became Caliph and he ruled for twelve years before he, too, was assassinated by a group of insurgents in 656. By the time Ali became Caliph, Muawiyah was already considered the undisputed ruler of Syria in all but name.

Ali, the new Caliph, found himself in an extremely difficult position. Unable, in the circumstances, to hunt down Uthman's assassins or restore peace and security across the Islamic State, the new Caliph was now fighting a losing battle. To make matters worse, a group of Uthman's close relatives, led by his widow Nailah bint Farafisah, then proceeded to Syria and provocatively paraded the bloodstained robes of Uthman before Muawiyah and the people of Syria. Since Muawiyah and Uthman belonged to the same Umayyah clan, Caliph Ali now found himself in conflict with yet another group of Uthman's supporters in Syria who openly refused to pledge allegiance (Bay'ah) to him.

Muawiyah then sent a letter to Caliph Ali with simply the words bismillah al-Rahman al-Rahim (In the name of God, Most Gracious, Most Merciful) inscribed on it. To Ali, this represented an open refusal to acknowledge his Caliphate. The Caliph, on the other hand, demanded an unconditional pledge of loyalty, but Muawiyah refused this. Not willing to tolerate open rebellion, Ali marched to Syria with a fifty thousand strong force and camped at Siffin. Muawiyah came out with his forces to meet the Caliph's army. When the two Muslim armies were about to clash, the Caliph decided to give peace another chance. When the deadlock could not be broken, the two armies clashed on the field of battle at Siffin. As the Caliph's army was about to inflict a crushing defeat on Muawiyah's forces, the latter called for arbitration (Tahkim). Ali stopped the fight and agreed to resolve their differences through arbitration. The decision to engage in arbitration proved fatal for Ali because it led to considerable political tension and dissension within his camp. Ali's reign came to abrupt end in 661, when he was fatally stabbed by a member of the extremist khawarij sect.

Following Ali's assassination his oldest son, Hasan, was elected Caliph but he subsequently abdicated. But after Muawiyah became the ruler of the Muslim world in 661, he rewarded Hasan with a generous State pension for stepping out of his way. After being crowned Caliph, Muawiyah swiftly restored Islamic political unity and actively promoted peace and prosperity across the Islamic dominion. Having lived and worked under the supervision of the Prophet and the first three "rightly-guided Caliphs" of Islam, he developed a thorough understanding of Islamic principles and practices. The brother of Umm Habibah, the Prophet's widow, Muawiyah simply made a mistake in his exercise of juristic discretion (Ijtihad) in his dispute with Caliph Ali.

Muawiyah's well-known motto was, 'I do not use my sword where my stick is sufficient, and I do not use my stick where my words are sufficient; and if there is only a hair (of understanding) between me and the people, I will not allow it to be cut.' After transferring the capital of the Islamic world from Kufah to Damascus, he transformed the city into a prominent center of Islamic learning, culture and civilization. During his reign, the Islamic dominion also expanded rapidly both in the East and the West. Under the command of Uqba ibn Nafi, the Muslim forces not only reasserted their authority in North Africa, but also mounted naval expeditions to Sicily and laid unsuccessful siege to Constantinople. Likewise, in the East, Muslims successfully captured Kabul, Khurasan, Bukhara and Samarqand, thanks to Muawiyah's outstanding and inspirational leadership.

Muawiyah served as a governor for twenty years, and as a Caliph for almost another two decades. After nearly four decades of continuous service to his people, he surprised everyone with his nomination of Yazid as his successor, even though the latter was not fit for the post of Caliphate. Muawiyah died at the age of about seventy-five and was buried in Damascus. But, by nominating his son as his successor, Muawiyah became the founder of the first, and one of the Muslim world's most powerful, political dynasties. The Umayyads ruled the Muslim world for nearly a century before the Abbasids overthrew them in 750.

The governor of Syria who opposed the selection of Ali as caliph after the murder of Uthman Muawiya: founder of the Umayyad dynasty, brilliant political and army commander. The Caesar of the Arabs. The second son of Abu Sufyan and Hind, he may have briefly served Muhammad as a secretary after his submission to Islam in the last two years of the Prophet's life. He rose to prominence when he assisted his elder brother Yazid in the conquest of the Holy Land, and would take over his command after Yazid's death from plague. His outstanding military and organizational talents were recognized by Omar and Uthman who both left him in command of Syria. Ali's refusal to renew Muawiya's command was one of the key motivations behind the civil war that would conclude with Muawiya's triumph. Muawiya, d. 680, 1st Umayyad caliph (661-80), one of the greatest Muslim statesmen; son of Abu Sufyan, a Koreish tribesman of Mecca.

He submitted to Islam the year of the surrender of Mecca and became Muhammad's secretary. Under Umar he became the very able governor of Syria. He struggled with Ali over the government of the empire and led in the deposition of Hasan. As caliph he made Islam an autocracy, retaining the old forms of self-government. His policies ended the ancient hostility that long had separated the North and South Arabian tribes, thus making the Muslim empire the remarkable unified force that it was. Muawiya's administration was always tolerant, and he displayed an enlightened point of view in all his dealings. His name is also spelled Moawiyah.

Muawiyah I: Muawiyah ibn Abu Sufyan, who ruled under the name Muawiyah I, succeeded Ali and was the first leader of Islam after the four righteously guided caliphs. Muawiyah was born in Mecca circa 602 A.D. His father strongly disagreed with Muhammad's teachings and when Muawiyah became a Muslim, he had to hide his faith from his own family. After Muhammad conquered Mecca and eliminated idolatry, Muawiyah became a scribe. Eventually, as the Islamic empire expanded, Muhammad sent Muawiyah and his brother to Syria, where they lead the Islamic army against the Byzantines. Under Caliph Umar, Muawiyah was named the governor of Syria.

As governor, he raised a Syrian army that was strong enough to hold off Byzantine advances, and also to capture Cyprus and Rhodes. Muawiyah's goals changed drastically when Ali, the fourth and final righteously guided caliph, was installed. All chose not to punish the murderers of Uthman, the third caliph, and Muawiyah saw this as a sign that Ali was involved with the murder himself. Muawiyah began to raise an anti-Ali following in Syria. In order to stop this uprising, Ali led his armies against Muawiyah in the Battle of Siffin. Although Muawiyah was losing the battle, he convinced Ali's soldiers to stop fighting and hold a religious arbitration to decide the victor. During this arbitration, Muawiyah convinced many of Ali's soldiers to turn against their leader. This distraction allowed Muawiyah time to send a large number of his followers to Egypt.

When Ali died, Muawiyah, holding both Syria and Egypt, was the most powerful Muslim and the logical choice to replace him. He ruled from 661-680 A.D. Unlike his predecessors, Muawiyah appointed his son, Yazid I, to replace him. In order to both establish the dynasty and continue the old traditions, Muawiyah installed a group of loyalist nobles who would vote for the next caliph. However, these nobles were in the caliph's pocket, rubber-stamping his heir. So began a series of hereditary dynasties, the first of which was the Umayyad, which ruled from 661-750 A.D. The first of the Umayyad caliphs, who ruled from

661 and 680 and brought strong, effective government to the Muslim community after the turmoil of the first Fitna.

Muawiyyah, Caliph (661-680): Son of Muhammad's old enemy, Abu Sufyan, governor of Syria.

*

Yazid II (687-724):

Yazid bin Abd al-Malik or **Yazid II** (687 – 724) was an Umayyad caliph who ruled from 720 until his death in 724.

According to the medieval Persian historian Muhammad ibn Jarir al-Tabari, Yazid came to power on the death of Umar II on February 10, 720. His forces engaged in battle the Kharijites with whom Umar had been negotiating. After initial setbacks, Yazid's troops prevailed and the Kharijite leader Shawdhab was killed. Yazid ibn al-Muhallab had escaped confinement on the death of Umar. He made his way to Iraq. There he was much supported. He refused to acknowledge Yazid II as caliph and led a very serious uprising. Initially successful, he was defeated and killed by the forces of Maslamah ibn Abd al-Malik.

Numerous civil wars began to break out in different parts of the empire such as in the Al Andalus (the Iberian Peninsula), North Africa and in the east. In A.H. 102 (720-721) in Ifriqiyah, the harsh governor Yazid ibn Muslim was overthrown and Muhammad ibn Yazid, the former governor, restored to power. The caliph accepted this and confirmed Muhammad ibn Yazid as governor of Ifriqiyah.

Al-Djarrah ibn Abdullah, Yazid's governor in Armenia and Azerbaijan, pushed into the Caucasus, taking Balanjar in A.H. 104 (722-723). That same year Yazid's governor in Medina, Abd al-Rahman ibn al-Dahhak, incurred the caliph's displeasure because the governor was exerting undue pressure trying to force a woman to marry him. She appealed to Yazid who replaced Abd al-Rahman with Abd al-Walid ibn Abdallah.

Anti-Umayyad groups began to gain power among the disaffected. Al-Tabari records that Abbasids were promoting their cause in A.H. 102 (720-721). They were already building a power base that they would later use to topple the Umayyads in CE 750.

An anecdote told of Yazid is that his wife Sudah learning he was pining for an expensive slave girl, purchased this slave girl and presented her to Yazid as a gift. This woman's name was Hababah and she predeceased Yazid. Yazid II died in 724 of tuberculosis. He was succeeded by his brother Hisham.

***

Muslim Empires & Dynasties (Section #2)

The following is a **list of Muslim empires and dynasties**. It includes states, empires and dynasties with an Islamic foundation or other Muslim majority states ever to exist.

History
In the centuries after the life of Muhammad, Muslim armies poured out into all surrounding Areas, bringing the lands from Persia to Spain under their control. With this huge amount of land under their control, the Umayyad (and latter, the Abbasid) Caliphates allowed merchants and scholars to travel easily through western Eurasia, bringing goods and knowledge which the Muslims greatly expanded upon through the Caliphate and outward to less advanced regions, such as Western Europe. In 751, papermaking from China made its way to the West through Muslims. Trade introduced Islam to the Africans. In the Middle East, the success of Islam meant that culture would be changed forever. Even after the decline of the Abbasid Caliphate, Islam would remain as one of the base institutions of the region. Future states of the region, such as the Safavid, Seljuk, and Ottoman and Mughal Empires, were all "Islamic Empires".

Caliphates
- The Rashidun Caliphate (632–661)
- The Umayyad Caliphate (661–750) - Successor of the Rashidun Caliphate
    - The Umayyad Caliphate of Cordoba in Islamic Spain (756-929-1031)
- The Abbasid Caliphate (750–1258) - Successor of the Umayyad Caliphate
- The Fatimid Caliphate (910–1171)
- The Mamluk Caliphate (Bahri dynasty then preceded by Burji dynasty) (1250–1517)
- The Ottoman Caliphate (1299–1923)

Regional empires
Arabia
- Umayyad Caliphate (661–750 CE)

- Abbasid Caliphate (750–1258)
- Mahra Sultanate (774–present)
- Hamdanid dynasty (890–1004)
- Bani Assad (961–1163)
- Numayrids (990–1081 AD) (Western Iraq)
- Marwanid (990–1085)
- Uqaylid Dynasty (992–1169)
- Artuqids (11th–12th century)
- Burid dynasty (1104–1154)
- Mirdasids (1024–1080)
- Banu 'Ammar (1071–1109) Tripoli, Lebanon
- Zengid dynasty (1127–1250)
- Ayyubid dynasty (1171-1341)
- Baban (1649–1850)
- Alawite State (1920–1936)
- Hashemite Dynasty of Iraq (1921–1958)
- Hashemite Dynasty of Jordan (1921–present)
- Rashidun Caliphate (632–661 CE)
- Ziyadid dynasty (819–1018)
- Sharif of Mecca (864–1496)
- Banu Ukhaidhir (865–1066)
- Rassids (893–1970 AD)
- Sharif of Mecca (967–1925)
- Sulaihid State (1047–1138)
- Banu ZARIE (Makarama) (1083–1200)
- Banu Hatem Alhmdanyen (1098–1174)
- Banu Masud (Makarama) (1093–1150) from Yemen
- Ayyubid dynasty (1174-1341)
- Rasulid (1229–1454)
- Kathiri (1395–1967)
- Jabrids (15th–16th century)
- Tahiride (1454–1526)
- Sultanate of Oman (751–present)
- Qawasim Dynasty (1727–present)
- Qarmatians (900–1073)
- Uyunid dynasty (1076–1239)
- Usfurids (1253–1320 century)
- Jarwanid dynasty (1305–1487)
- Sultanate of Lahej (1728–1744/1839)

- Mahra Sultanate (18th century-1967)
- Emirate of Diriyah (1744-1818)
- House of Saud (1744–present)
- House of Al-Sabah (1752–present)
- Al Nahyan family (1761–present)
- Ajman (18th Century–present)
- Qawasim Dynasty (18th century-present)
- Umm al-Quwain (1775–present)
- Al Khalifa family (1783–present)
- Emirate of Nejd (1818-1891)
- Sultanate of Muscat and Oman (1820-1979)
- Sultanate of Zanzibar
- House of Thani (1825–present)
- Al Maktoum (1833–present)
- Emirate of Jabal Shammar (1836–1921)
- Upper Yafa (19th century–1967)
- Aden Protectorate (1869-1969)
- Sharqi Dynasty (1876–present)
- Qu'aiti (1902–1967)
- Emirate of Beihan (1903–1967)
- Kingdom of Hejaz (1916-1925)
- Mutawakkilite Kingdom of Yemen (1918-1962)
- Mandatory Iraq (1920-1932)
- Sultanate of Nejd (1921-1926)
- Emirate of Transjordan (1921-1946)
- Kingdom of Nejd and Hejaz (1926-1932)
- Syrian Republic (1930-1958)
- Kingdom of Iraq (1932-1958)
- Hashemite Kingdom of Jordan (1946-present)
- All-Palestine Government (1948-1959)
- Arab Federation (1958)
- Republic of Iraq under Qasim (1958-1968)
- United Arab Republic (1958-1971)
- Federation of Arab Emirates of the South (1959-1962)
- Federation of South Arabia (1962-1967)
- Yemen Arab Republic (1962-1990)
- Protectorate of South Arabia (1963-1967)
- People's Democratic Republic of Yemen (1967-1990)
- Federation of Arab Republics (1972-1977)

- Democratic Republic of Yemen (1994)

Persia
- Shirvanshah (799–1579 CE)
- Dulafid dynasty (early 9th century–897)
- Samanid dynasty (819–999)
- Tahirid dynasty (821–873)
- Saffarid dynasty (861–1003)
- Alavids (864–929)
- Sajids (889–929)
- Ziyarid dynasty (928–1043)
- Farighunid (late 9th–early 11th centuries)
- Ma'danids (late 9th–11th centuries)
- Ormus (10th–17th centuries)
- Buyid dynasty (934–1062)
- Sallarid (942–979)
- Shaddadid (951–1199)
- Rawadid (955–1071)
- Hasanwayhid (959–1015)
- Ghaznavids (963–1187)
- Marwanid (990–1085)
- Annazid (990–1116)
- Hadhabani (11th century)
- Seljuq dynasty (11th–14th centuries)
- Ismaili State of Alamut(Iran) (1090–1256)
- Ghurids (1148–1215)
- Hazaraspids (1148–1424)
- Khorshidi dynasty (1155–1597)
- Mihrabanids (1236–1537)
- Ilkhanate (1256–1335)
- Sarbadars (1332–1386)
- Jalayirids (1335–1432)
- Chupanids (1335–1357)
- Injuids (1335–1357)
- Muzaffarids of Iran (1335–1393)
- Timurid dynasty (1370–1526)
- Kara Koyunlu (1375–1468)
- Ak Koyunlu (1378–1508)
- Musha'sha'iyyah (1436–1729)

- Safavid dynasty (1501–1736)
- Khanate of Erevan (1604–1828)
- Quba Khanate (1680–1816)
- Hotaki dynasty (1709–1738)
- Talysh Khanate (1747–1826)
- Baku Khanate
- Afsharid dynasty (1736–1796)
- Shaki Khanate (1743–1819)
- Ganja khanate (1747–1804)
- Karabakh Khanate (1747–1822)
- Khanate of Nakhichevan (1747–1828)
- Shirvan Khanate (1748–1820)
- Zand dynasty (1750–1794)
- Qajar dynasty (1794–1925)
- Pahlavi dynasty (1925–1979)
- Islamic Republic of Iran (1979-present)

Central Asia and China
. Kara-Khanid Kahanate (840-1212 CE)
. Al Muhtaj (10th-early 11th centuries)
. Khwarazm-Shah dynasty (1077-1231)
. Karids (1231-1389)
. Timurid dynasty (1370-1526)
. Kazakh Kahanate (1456-1731)
. Mughal Empire (1526-1857)
. Kahanate of Khiva (1511-1920)
. Kahanate of Kokand (1709-1876)
. Jahangiri (Gabari) Dynasty (1200-1531)
. First East Turkistan Republic (Breakaway Republic) (1933-1934)
. Second East Turkistan Republic (Soviet Satellite) (1944-1955)

South Asia
- Soomra Dynasty, Soomra (1026–1351 CE)
- House of Theemuge (1166–1388)
- Jahangiri(Gabari) Dynasty (1200–1531)
- Mamluk Sultanate (Delhi) (1206–1290)
- Khilji dynasty (1290–1320)

- Tughlaq Dynasty (1321–1398)
- Samma Dynasty (1335–1520)
- Sayyid Dynasty (1339–1561)
- Ilyas Shahi dynasty (1342–1487)
- Bahmani Sultanate (1347–1527)
- Faruqi dynasty (1382–1601)
- Hilaalee dynasty (1388–1558)
- Muzaffarid dynasty of Gujarat (1391–1734)
- Sharqi Dynasty (1394–1479)
- Kingdom of Mysore (1399-1947)
- Bahmani (1400–1600)
- Malwa Sultanate (1401–1561)
- Sayyid dynasty (1414–1451)
- Lodi Dynasty (1451–1526)
- Bidar Sultanate (1489–1619)
- Berar Sultanate (1490–1572)
- Hussain Shahi dynasty (1494–1538)
- Arghun Dynasty (late 15th–16th centuries)
- Mughal Empire (1526–1857)
- Adil Shahi dynasty (1527–1686)
- Suri Dynasty (1540–1556)
- Arakkal (1545–18th century)
- Utheemu dynasty (1632–1692)
- Khan of Kalat (1666–1958)
- Nawab of the Carnatic (1690–1801)
- Isdhoo dynasty (1692–1704)
- Dhiyamigili dynasty (1704–1759)
- Hotaki Dynasty (1709–1738)
- Nawab of Bhopal (1723–1947)
- Nawab of Rampur (1719–1947)
- Nawab of Awadh (1722–1858)
- Hyderabad State (1724–1948)
- Babi dynasty (1735–1947)
- Durrani Empire (1747–1826)
- Nawab of Bengal (1717–1880)
- Huraa dynasty (1759–1968)
- Tonk (princely state) (1798–1947)
- Barakzai Dynasty (1826–1973)
- Dominion of Pakistan (1947-1956)

- Islamic Republic of Pakistan (1956-present)
- Republic of Maldives (1965-present)
- Peoples Republic of Bangladesh (1971-present)
- Khairpur (princely state)
- Nagar (princely state)
- Hunza (princely state)
- Bahawalpur (princely state)
- Mirpur (princely state)
- Kalat (princely state)
- Las Bela (princely state)
- Makran (princely state)
- Kharan (princely state)
- Amb (princely state)
- Chitral (princely state)
- Dir (princely state)
- Hunza (princely state)
- Jandol (princely state)
- Nagar (princely state)
- Phulra (princely state)
- Swat (princely state)
- Yasin (princely state)
- Gilgit (princely state)

South-East Asia
- Daya Pasai (1128–1285 CE)
- Bandar Kalibah.
- Moira Malaya.
- Kanto Kambar.
- Robaromun.
- Kedah Sultanate (1136–present)
- Pasai (1267–15th century)
- Brunei (14th century–present)
- Sultanate of Malacca (1402–1511)
- Pahang Sultanate (mid-15th century–present)
- Sultanate of Sulu (1450–1936)
- Sultanate of Ternate (1465–present)
- Sultanate of Demak (1475–1518)
- Aceh Sultanate (1496–1903)
- Kingdom of Maynila (1500's–1571)

- Mataram Sultanate (1500's – 1700's)
- Pattani Kingdom (1516–1771)
- Sultanate of Maguindanao (1520–c. 1800)
- Sultanate of Banten (1526–1813)
- Perak Sultanate (1528–present)
- Johor Sultanate (1528–present)
- Kingdom of Pajang (1568–1586)
- Sultanate of Terengganu (1725–present)
- Selangor Sultanate (mid-18th century–present)
- Surakarta Sunanate (1745–present)
- Yogyakarta Sultanate (1755–present)
- Kingdom of Aman (1485–1832)
- Palembang (1550–1823)

Turkey
- Danishmends (1071–1178 CE)
- Mengujekids (1071–1277)
- Saltukids (1072–1202)
- Sultanate of Rum (1077–1307)
- Ahlatshahs (1100–1207)
- Ayyubid dynasty (1174–1341)
- Chobanids (1227–1309)
- Karamanids (c. 1250–1487)
- Pervâneoğlu (1261–1322)
- Menteşe (c. 1261–1424)
- Ahis (c. 1380–1362)
- Hamidids (c. 1280–1374)
- Ottoman Empire (1299–1923)
- Ladik (c. 1300–1368)
- Isfendiyarids (c. 1300–1461)
- Teke (1301–1423)
- Sarukhanids (1302–1410)
- Karasids (1303–1360)
- Aydinids (1307–1425)
- Eretnids (1328–1381)
- Dulkadirids (1348–c. 1525)
- Ramadanids (1352–1516)
- Hatay Devleti (1938–1939)

North Africa
- Muhallabids (771–793 CE)
- Rustamid (776–909)
- Idrisid dynasty (780–985)
- Ifranid dynasty (790–1066)
- Aghlabids (800–909)
- Tulunids (868–905)
- Fatimid Empire (909–1171)
- Ikhshidid dynasty (935–969)
- Zirid dynasty (973–1152)
- Banu Kanz (1004–1412)
- Hammadid (1008–1152)
- Almoravid dynasty (1040–1147)
- Almohad dynasty (1130–1269)
- Ayyubid dynasty (1171–1341)
- Hafsid dynasty (1229–1574)
- Nasrid dynasty (1232–1492)
- Ziyyanid dynasty (1235–1556)
- Marinid dynasty (1244–1465)
- Bahri dynasty (1250–1382)
- Mamluk Sultanate of Egypt (1250-1517)
- Burji dynasty (1382–1517)
- Wattasid dynasty (1472–1554)
- Saadi Dynasty (1509–1659)
- Sultanate of Darfur (1603-1874)
- Alaouite Dynasty (1666–present)
- Husainid Dynasty (1705–1957)
- Karamanli dynasty (1711–1835)
- Muhammad Ali Dynasty (1805–1952)
- Khedivate of Egypt (1867-1914)
- Sultanate of Egypt (1914-1922)
- Kingdom of Egypt (1922-1953)
- Republic of Egypt (1953-1958)
- United Arab Republic (1958-1971)

Horn of Africa
- Sultanate of Mogadishu (10th–16th centuries)
- Ifat Sultanate (1285–1415)
- Warsangali Sultanate (1298–present)

- Adal Sultanate (c. 1415–1555)
- Walashma Dynasty (14th–16th centuries)
- Ajuuraan State (14th–17th centuries)
- Aussa Sultanate (16th century–present)
- Emirs of Harar (1647–1887)
- Gobroon Dynasty (18th–19th centuries)
- Majeerteen Sultanate (mid-18th century–early 20th century)
- Kingdom of Gomma (early 19th century–1886)
- Kingdom of Jimma (1830–1932)
- Kingdom of Gumma (1840–1902)
- Sultanate of Hobyo (19th century–1925)
- Dervish State (1896–1920)

East Africa
- Kilwa Sultanate (957–1513 CE)
- Pate Sultanate (1203–1870)
- Sennar (sultanate) (1523–1821)
- Sultans on the Comoros
- Mudaito dynasty (1734–present)
- Sultanate of Zanzibar (1856–1964)
- Wituland (1858–1923)

Central & West Africa
- Kingdom of Nekor (710–1019 CE)
- Za Dynasty in Gao (11th century–1275)
- Sayfawa dynasty (1075–1846)
- Songhai Empire (c. 1340–1591)
- Bornu Empire (1396–1893)
- Kingdom of Baguirmi (1522–1897)
- Dendi Kingdom (1591–1901)
- Sultanate of Damagaram (1731–1851)
- Kingdom of Fouta Tooro (1776–1861)
- Sokoto Caliphate (1804–1903)
- Toucouleur Empire (1836–1890)

Sicily
- Aghlabid Sicily (827–909) CE

- Kalbids (948–1053)

Spain and Portugal
- Caliphate of Córdoba (756–1017 CE, 1023–1031)
- Taifa of Alpuente (1009–1106)
- Taifa of Badajoz (1009–1151)
- Taifa of Morón (1010–1066)
- Taifa of Toledo (1010–1085)
- Taifa of Tortosa (1010–1099)
- Taifa of Arcos (1011–1145)
- Taifa of Almería (1010–1147)
- Taifa of Denia (1010–1227)
- Taifa of Valencia (1010–1238)
- Taifa of Murcia (1011–1266)
- Taifa of Albarracín (1012–1104)
- Taifa of Zaragoza (1013–1110)
- Taifa of Granada (1013–1145)
- Taifa of Carmona (1013–1150)
- Hammudid dynasty (1016–1073)
- Taifa of Santa María de Algarve (1018–1051)
- Taifa of Mallorca (1018–1203)
- Taifa of Lisbon (1022–1093)
- Taifa of Seville (1023–1091)
- Taifa of Niebla (1023–1262)
- Taifa of Córdoba (1031–1091)
- Taifa of Mértola (1033–1151)
- Taifa of Algeciras (1035–1058)
- Taifa of Ronda (1039–1065)
- Taifa of Silves (1040–1151)
- Taifa of Málaga (1073–1239)
- Taifa of Molina (c. 1080's–1100)
- Taifa of Lorca (1228–1250)
- Taifa of Menorca (1228–1287)
- Emirate of Granada (1228–1492)

Eastern Europe & Russia
- Volga Bulgaria (7th century–1240s CE)
- Emirate of Crete (820s–961)
- Avar Khanate (early 13th–19th century)

- Khanate of Kazan (1438–1552)
- Crimean Khanate (1441–1783)
- Nogai Horde (1440s–1634)
- Qasim Khanate (1452–1681)
- Astrakhan Khanate (1466–1556)
- Khanate of Sibir (1490–1598)
- Pashalik of Scutari (1757–1831)
- House of Zogu (1928–1939)

Important Islamic Dynasties

'Abbasids, 749-1258. Caliphs, claiming universal authority; main capital Baghdad.
Aghlabids, 800-909. Tunisia, eastern Algerian, Sicily.
Afsharid Dynasty
Alaouite Dynasty
'Alawis, 1631-today. Morocco.
Almohads (al-Muwahhidun), 1130-1269. Maghrib, Spain.
Almoravids (al-Murabitun), 1056-1147. Maghrib, Spain.
Ayyubids, 1169-1260. Egypt, Syria, part of western Arabia.
Buyids (Buwayhids), 932-1062. Iran, Iraq.
Fatimids, 909-1171. Maghrib, Egypt, Syria. Claimed to be Caliphs.
Hafsids, 1228-1574. Tunisia, eastern Algeria.
Hashimites of Iraq, 1921-58. Iraq.
Hashimites of Jordan, 1923-today. Transjordan, part of Palestine.
Idrisids, 789-926. Morocco.
Ilkhanids, 1256-1336. Iran, Iraq.
Mamluks, 1250-1517. Egypt, Syria.
Marinids, 1196-1464. Morocco.
Mughals, 1526-1858. India.
Muhammad 'Ali and successors, 1805-1953. Egypt.
Muluk al-tawa'if ('party kings'), eleventh century. Spain.
Nasrids, 1230-1492. Southern Spain.
Omayyad Dynasty
Ottomans, 1281-1922. Turkey, Syria, Iraq, Egypt, Cyprus, Tunisia, Algeria, western Arabia.
Rassids, ninth-thirteenth century, end of sixteenth century-1962. Zaydi Imams of Yemen.
Rasulids, 1229-1454. Yemen.

Rustamids, 779-909. Western Algeria.
Sa'dids, 1511-1628. Morocco.
Safavids, 1501-1732. Iran.
Saffarids, 867-end of fifteenth century. Eastern Iran.
Samanids, 819-1005. North-eastern Iran, central Asia.
Sa'udis, 1746-today. Central, then western Arabia.
Tahirid Dynasty
Saljuqs, 1038-1194. Iran, Iraq.
Saljuqs of Rum, 1077-1307. Central and eastern Turkey.
Timurids, 1370-1506. Central Asia, Iran.
Tulunids, 868-905. Egypt, Syria.
Umayyads, 661-750. Caliphs, claiming universal authority; capital Damascus.
Umayyads of Spain, 756-1031. Claimed to be caliphs.
Wattasid Dynasty
Zengid Dynasty
Ziyarid Dynasty

***

Islamic divisions (Section #3)

Muslims are advised to hold together and not divide themselves in matters of faith.

Sunni and Shi'a Muslims:
The very first division in Islam, between Sunni and Shi'a. The issue centered on the question of who was to lead the Muslim community following Muhammad's death. When Muhammad was suffering from his final illness, he appointed his closest companion Abu Bakr to lead the community in prayer. The Companions consulted among themselves and selected Abu Bakr to succeed Muhammad.

Those who agreed with Abu Bakr's appointment became known as Sunni (followers of the tradition of Muhammad). Other members of the community felt that leadership of the Muslim state should stay within the bloodline of Muhammad, within his own family. This concept also became known as "Ahl al Bayt", or people of the house (of Muhammad). Particularly, they felt that Muhammad's son-in-law, Ali, should have been appointed the next leader of the community, and so this group became known as the "Shi'ati Ali" (supporters of Ali), Shi'a or Shi'ite Muslims. Muhammad's bloodline died in the ninth century. In modern times, Imam Khomeini, the ayatollah of Iran from 1978 to 1989, is the most well known Shi'a leader.

Due to political loyalties and deepening mutual distrust, Shi'a Muslims rejected or altered some practices of Islam. Sunni Muslims shun formal clergy status, recognizing only jurists and scholars who offer nonbinding opinions. In contrast, Shi'a Muslim leaders have pope like authority. He is perfect and sinless. His opinions are binding. Shi'a Muslims also tend more on the virtues of martyrdom, with particular attention to the deaths of Ali and his son Hussein.

On one occasion of Ashura, a day in the Islamic calendar honoring Hussein's death at the hands of an opposing army. Shi'a Muslims observe mourning, gathering in the streets and publicly wailing and beating their chests.

Sunni and Shi'a Today:
Today the Shi'a Muslims make up approximately 10-15 percent of the Muslim world. They are mostly found in Iran, with large communities in Kuwait, Lebanon, Iraq, and Bahrain.

Sufism, a mystical faith:
In the early centuries after Muhammad's death some Muslims became disenchanted with the Islamic community's growing interest in worldly affairs and the rigid application of rules within the faith. They strived to purify the soul and develop a connection with Allah. The path of the Sufis is often called the mystic or spiritual trend within Islam. The word Sufi comes from Arabic word for wool (suf). Followers of this trend would often traditionally wear wool because of its simplicity and low cost.

Sufis focus on cleansing of the heart. Overtime Sufis began organizing into various orders, each of which is called a Tariqa or path. A Sufi master, called a "Shaykh" serves as the leader and guide to his followers. Sufis have maintained that they are merely continuing the simple religious lifestyle of Muhammad. Others follow intense devotional practices such as prolonged fasting or prayer. The Quran discourages sectarianism.
Quran 6:159

Rumi & his poetry:
Among Sufis, poetry and music take on religious significance. They are seen as a way to express intense love of God (whom they often call the Beloved). One of the most famous Sufi writers, and indeed one of the most famous poets of all time, was Mevlana Jalaluddin Rumi. Born in Persia and raised in Turkey in the 13th century.

Rumi is also known for founding the Mevlevi Order of Sufism, which is now associated with the whirling dervishes. Their movements are intended to be relaxing and hypnotic, so that the person can become open to receiving God's energy.

The Qadiani Movement:
The Qadiani or Ahmadiyyah, movement began in the late nineteenth century in the Punjab region of India, where a Muslim reformer named

Mirza Ghulam Ahmed first claimed that he was the promised Messiah and later that he was a prophet of Allah who received divine revelation. The Ahmadiyyah are also called Qadiani because their founder was from the city of Wadian in the Punjab province of India. Muslims consider Ghulam Ahmed a false prophet, and all Muslims scholars consider Qadianis to be outside the fold of Islam.

Numerology of the Khalifites:
This relatively new group believes that the Quran is the only source of guidance in Islam, and that the traditions of Muhammad and other prophets are irrelevant. They reject the entire Sunnah (words and acts of Muhammad). The Khalifites claim that there is an intricate mathematical code in the Quran, proving that it is indeed the word of God and could not possibly have been written by any man. This mathematical "miracle" is based on the number nineteen, to multiples of nineteen. The first verse of the Quran has nineteen letters. The first chapter ever revealed consists of nineteen words. The Quran consists of 114 chapters, a number that is divisible by 19 (114/19=6).

The statistics were determined to be false. The theory became questionable at first, and later was determined to be fraudulent. At the center of this controversy was a person named Rashah Khalifa. Mr. Khalifa was an Egyptian who immigrated to the United States and took up residence in Tucson Arizona. Mr. Khalifa determined that there were prophetic references to himself in the Quran and claimed to be a Messenger of the Covenant. In time, Khalifa's fraudulent teachings were exposed and his claims rejected, Rashad Khalifa killed by an unknown assailant in 1990.

The Baha'i Faith:
The Baha'i faith arose from Islam, and has now grown to be a worldwide religion. The Baha'i believe in the unity of God, and in the essential message that has been revealed through the prophets over time. They recognize Muhammad as a prophet, but also believe that Krishna, Buddha, and others were "Great manifestations of God," culminating in the teachings of the founder of their faith, Bahaullah.

The Baha'i faith has its origins in Muslims Persia, when a young man called the Bab ("the gate") announced the imminent arrival of a messenger of God. The Bab was executed as a heretic in 1850. The Baha'i are established in 235 countries and number five million people worldwide. www.bahai.org. The main slogan of the Baha'i is "The earth is but one country and mankind its citizens."

In 1863, a man named Bahaullah (Meaning "the Glory of God" in Arabic) announced that he was the fulfillment of the Bab's promise. Bahaullah began writing a series of letters and documents outlining his views of universal peace and a united world civilization. He died in 1892, with his writings and teachings in relative obscurity.

The Baha'i creeds:
The Baha'i believe in the unity of the world's great religions, that they all came from the same spiritual source. Followers of this faith are heavily involved in issues of world peace, world government, freedom and equality. Islam rejects the notion that any messenger or prophet would ever follow Muhammad.

The Nation of Islam:
In North America, one of the most well known offshoot groups is the Nation of Islam. This movement reached its peak during the mid twentieth century, it is associated with the black pride and civil rights movements of 1960s. In reality their beliefs and practices have very little to do with the faith of Islam.

The nation of Islam preaches the superiority of black people. According to their doctrine, black people were the original inhabitants of the earth, the mothers and fathers of civilization, and that even God himself appeared on earth as a black man. The nation of Islam encourages discipline, the value of family, responsibility and pride.

During the Great Depression, a mysterious figure appeared in Detroit. Calling himself Wallace Fard Muhammad, he claimed to be a mystic and a prophet from Mecca, Saudi Arabia. Many believe he was actually a con. One of his first followers and students was Elijah Poole, who later became known as Elijah Muhammad. When Fard disappeared in 1934, Elijah took over leadership of the growing Nation. Elijah Muhammad came to be known as the Divine Representative, or prophet of this god.

One of the most famous leaders of the nation was Malcolm X. Malcolm credited the Nation with saving his life. Malcolm X discovered orthodox Islam during a pilgrimage to Saudi Arabia, and began to write and preach against the racist beliefs of the Nation.

Malcolm X's pilgrimage to Mecca was a turning point in his life. He was thence known as El Hajj Malik Shabaaz

After Elijah Muhammad's death, his son Imam W. Deen Mohammed also took the path of orthodox Islam. In 1992, he established the Muslim American Society. Elijah Muhammad's teachings have stayed alive, most recently through the leadership of
Minister Louis Farrakhan.

Nearly half of all Muslims in the United States are African American. Muslims reject the most fundamental beliefs of the Nation, and have called upon them to abandon the belief that God could appear as a man on earth or that Elijah Muhammad was a prophet. In February 2000, Farrakhan formally reconciled with his longtime enemy, Imam W. Deen Mohammed, Elijah Muhammad's son.

***

Muslim population by country (Section #4)

Islam is the world's second largest religion after Christianity. According to a 2010 study, Islam has 1.62 billion adherents, making up over 23% of the world population.

Islam is the predominant religion in the Middle East, in the Horn of Africa, in northern Africa, and in some parts of Asia. Large communities of Muslims are also found in China, the Balkans, and Russia. Other parts of the world host large Muslim immigrant communities; in Western Europe, for instance, Islam is the second largest religion after Christianity, where it represents 6% of the total population.

According to the Pew Research Center in 2010 there were 49 Muslim-majority countries. Around 62% of the world's Muslims live in the Asia-Pacific region, with over 1 billion adherents. The largest Muslim country is Indonesia home to 12.7% of the world's Muslims followed by Pakistan (11.0%), India (10.9%), and Bangladesh (9.2%). About 20% of Muslims live in Arab countries. In the Middle East, the non-Arab countries of Turkey and Iran are the largest Muslim-majority countries; in Africa, Egypt and Nigeria have the most populous Muslim communities.

A study conducted by the Pew Research Center in 2010 and released January 2011 found that there are 1.62 billion Muslims around the world, accounting for roughly 1 in 4 people. The study found more Muslims in Germany than in Lebanon and more in China than in Syria.

Country/Region	Muslim population 2010 PEW Repots	Muslim percentage (%) of total population 2010 PEW Report	Percentage (%) of World Muslim population 2010 PEW Report
Afghanistan	29,047,000	99.8	1.8
Albania	2,601,000	82.1	0.2
Algeria *	34,780,000	98.2	2.1
American Samoa	< 1,000	< 0.1	< 0.1

Andorra	1,000	1.1	< 0.1
Angola *	195,000	1.0	< 0.1
Anguilla	< 1,000	0.3	< 0.1
Antigua and Barbuda	< 1,000	0.6	< 0.1
Argentina	1,000,000	2.5	0.1
Armenia	1,000	< 0.1	< 0.1
Aruba	< 1,000	0.4	< 0.1
Australia	399,000	1.9	< 0.1
Austria	475,000	5.7	< 0.1
Azerbaijan	8,795,000	98.4	0.5
Bahamas	< 1,000	0.1	< 0.1
Bahrain *	655,000	81.2	< 0.1
Bangladesh	148,607,000	90.4	9.2
Barbados	2,000	0.9	< 0.1
Belarus	19,000	0.2	< 0.1
Belgium	638,000	6.0	< 0.1
Belize	< 1,000	0.1	< 0.1
Benin	2,259,000	24.5	0.1
Bermuda	< 1,000	0.8	< 0.1
Bhutan	7,000	1.0	< 0.1
Bolivia	2,000	< 0.1	< 0.1
Bosnia-Herzegovina	1,564,000	41.6	0.1
Botswana	8,000	0.4	< 0.1
Brazil	204,000	0.1	< 0.1
British Virgin Islands	< 1,000	1.2	< 0.1
Brunei	211,000	51.9	< 0.1
Bulgaria	1,002,000	13.4	0.1
Burkina Faso	9,600,000	58.9	0.6
Burma (Myanmar)	1,900,000	3.8	0.1
Burundi	184,000	2.2	< 0.1
Cambodia	240,000	1.6	< 0.1
Cameroon	3,598,000	18.0	0.2
Canada	940,000	2.8	0.1
Cape Verde	< 1,000	0.1	< 0.1

Cayman Islands	< 1,000	0.2	< 0.1
Central African Republic	403,000	8.9	< 0.1
Chad	6,404,000	55.7	0.4
Channel Islands	< 1,000	0.1	< 0.1
Chile	4,000	< 0.1	< 0.1
China	23,308,000	1.8	1.4
Colombia	14,000	< 0.1	< 0.1
Comoros	679,000	98.3	< 0.1
Congo	969,000	1.4	0.1
Cook Islands	< 1,000	< 0.1	< 0.1
Costa Rica	< 1,000	< 0.1	< 0.1
Croatia	56,000	1.3	< 0.1
Cuba	10,000	0.1	< 0.1
Cyprus	200,000	22.7	< 0.1
Czech Republic	4,000	< 0.1	< 0.1
Denmark	226,000	4.1	< 0.1
Djibouti	853,000	97.0	0.1
Dominica	< 1,000	0.2	< 0.1
Dominican Republic	2,000	< 0.1	< 0.1
Ecuador	2,000	< 0.1	< 0.1
Egypt *	80,024,000	94.7	4.9
El Salvador	2,000	< 0.1	< 0.1
Equatorial Guinea	28,000	4.1	< 0.1
Eritrea	1,909,000	36.5	0.1
Estonia	2,000	0.1	< 0.1
Ethiopia *	28,721,000	33.8	1.8
Faeroe Islands	< 1,000	< 0.1	< 0.1
Falkland Islands (Malvinas)	< 1,000	< 0.1	< 0.1
Federated States of Micronesia	< 1,000	< 0.1	< 0.1
Fiji	54,000	6.3	< 0.1
Finland	42,000	0.8	< 0.1
France	4,704,000	7.5	0.3
French Guiana	2,000	0.9	< 0.1
French Polynesia	< 1,000	< 0.1	< 0.1

Country	Population	%	%
Gabon	145,000	9.7	< 0.1
Gambia	1,669,000	95.3	0.1
Georgia	442,000	10.5	< 0.1
Germany	4,119,000	5.0	0.3
Ghana	3,906,000	16.1	0.2
Gibraltar	1,000	4.0	< 0.1
Greece	527,000	4.7	< 0.1
Greenland	< 1,000	< 0.1	< 0.1
Grenada	< 1,000	0.3	< 0.1
Guadeloupe	2,000	0.4	< 0.1
Guam	< 1,000	< 0.1	< 0.1
Guatemala	1,000	< 0.1	< 0.1
Guinea	8,693,000	84.2	0.5
Guinea Bissau	705,000	42.8	< 0.1
Guyana	55,000	7.2	< 0.1
Haiti	2,000	< 0.1	< 0.1
Honduras	11,000	0.1	< 0.1
Hong Kong	91,000	1.3	< 0.1
Hungary	25,000	0.3	< 0.1
Iceland	< 1,000	0.1	< 0.1
India	177,286,000	14.6	10.9
Indonesia	204,847,000	88.1	12.7
Iran	74,819,000	99.6	4.6
Iraq *	31,108,000	98.9	1.9
Ireland	43,000	0.9	< 0.1
Isle of Man	< 1,000	0.2	< 0.1
Israel	1,287,000	17.7	0.1
Italy	1,583,000	2.6	0.1
Ivory Coast	7,960,000	36.9	0.5
Jamaica	1,000	< 0.1	< 0.1
Japan	185,000	0.1	< 0.1
Jordan *	6,397,000	98.8	0.4
Kazakhstan	8,887,000	56.4	0.5
Kenya	2,868,000	7.0	0.2
Kiribati	< 1,000	< 0.1	< 0.1
Kosovo	2,104,000	91.7	0.1
Kuwait *	2,636,000	86.4	0.2
Kyrgyzstan	4,927,000	88.8	0.3

Laos	1,000	< 0.1	< 0.1
Latvia	2,000	0.1	< 0.1
Lebanon *	2,542,000	59.7	0.2
Lesotho	1,000	< 0.1	< 0.1
Liberia	523,000	12.8	< 0.1
Libya *	6,325,000	96.6	0.4
Liechtenstein	2,000	4.8	< 0.1
Lithuania	3,000	0.1	< 0.1
Luxembourg	11,000	2.3	< 0.1
Macau	< 1,000	< 0.1	< 0.1
Madagascar	220,000	1.1	< 0.1
Malawi	2,011,000	12.8	0.1
Malaysia	17,139,000	61.4	1.1
Maldives	309,000	98.4	< 0.1
Mali	12,316,000	92.4	0.8
Malta	1,000	0.3	< 0.1
Marshall Islands	< 1,000	< 0.1	< 0.1
Martinique	< 1,000	0.2	< 0.1
Mauritania	3,338,000	99.2	0.2
Mauritius	216,000	16.6	< 0.1
Mayotte	197,000	98.8	< 0.1
Mexico	111,000	0.1	< 0.1
Moldova	15,000	0.4	< 0.1
Monaco	< 1,000	0.5	< 0.1
Mongolia	120,000	4.4	< 0.1
Montenegro	116,000	18.5	< 0.1
Montserrat	< 1,000	0.1	< 0.1
Morocco *	32,381,000	99.9	2.0
Mozambique	5,340,000	22.8	0.3
Namibia	9,000	0.4	< 0.1
Nauru	< 1,000	< 0.1	< 0.1
Nepal	1,253,000	4.2	0.1
Netherlands	914,000	5.5	0.1
Netherlands Antilles	< 1,000	0.2	< 0.1
New Caledonia	7,000	2.8	< 0.1
New Zealand	41,000	0.9	< 0.1
Nicaragua	1,000	< 0.1	< 0.1

Niger *	15,627,000	98.3	1.0
Nigeria *	75,728,000	47.9	4.7
Niue	< 1,000	< 0.1	< 0.1
North Korea	3,000	< 0.1	< 0.1
Northern Mariana Islands	< 1,000	0.7	< 0.1
Norway	144,000	3.0	< 0.1
Oman *	2,547,000	87.7	0.2
Pakistan	178,097,000	96.4	11.0
Palau	< 1,000	< 0.1	< 0.1
Palestinian territories*	4,298,000	97.5	0.3
Panama	25,000	0.7	< 0.1
Papua New Guinea	2,000	< 0.1	< 0.1
Paraguay	1,000	< 0.1	< 0.1
Peru	< 1,000	< 0.1	< 0.1
Philippines	4,737,000	5.1	0.3
Pitcairn Islands	< 1,000	< 0.1	< 0.1
Poland	20,000	0.1	< 0.1
Portugal	65,000	0.6	< 0.1
Puerto Rico	1,000	< 0.1	< 0.1
Qatar *	1,168,000	77.5	0.1
Republic of Congo	60,000	1.6	< 0.1
Republic of Macedonia	713,000	34.9	< 0.1
Reunion	35,000	4.2	< 0.1
Romania	73,000	0.3	< 0.1
Russia	16,379,000	11.7	1.0
Rwanda	188,000	1.8	< 0.1
St. Helena	< 1,000	< 0.1	< 0.1
St. Kitts and Nevis	< 1,000	0.3	< 0.1
St. Lucia	< 1,000	0.1	< 0.1
St. Pierre and Miquelon	< 1,000	0.2	< 0.1
St. Vincent and	2,000	1.7	< 0.1

the Grenadines			
Samoa	< 1,000	< 0.1	< 0.1
San Marino	< 1,000	< 0.1	< 0.1
Sao Tome and Principe	< 1,000	< 0.1	< 0.1
Saudi Arabia *	25,493,000	97.1	1.6
Senegal	12,333,000	95.9	0.8
Serbia	280,000	3.7	< 0.1
Seychelles	< 1,000	1.1	< 0.1
Sierra Leone	4,171,000	71.5	0.3
Singapore	721,000	14.9	< 0.1
Slovakia	4,000	0.1	< 0.1
Slovenia	49,000	2.4	< 0.1
Solomon Islands	< 1,000	< 0.1	< 0.1
Somalia	9,231,000	98.6	0.6
South Africa	737,000	1.5	< 0.1
South Korea	75,000	0.2	< 0.1
Spain	1,021,000	2.3	0.1
Sri Lanka	1,725,000	8.5	0.1
Sudan *	30,855,000	71.4	1.9
Suriname	84,000	15.9	< 0.1
Swaziland	2,000	0.2	< 0.1
Sweden	451,000	4.9	< 0.1
Switzerland	433,000	5.7	< 0.1
Syria *	20,895,000	92.8	1.3
Taiwan	23,000	0.1	< 0.1
Tajikistan	7,006,000	99.0	0.4
Tanzania	13,450,000	29.9	0.8
Thailand	3,952,000	5.8	0.2
Timor-Leste	1,000	0.1	< 0.1
Togo	827,000	12.2	0.1
Tokelau	< 1,000	< 0.1	< 0.1
Tonga	< 1,000	< 0.1	< 0.1
Trinidad and Tobago	78,000	5.8	< 0.1
Tunisia *	10,349,000	99.8	0.6
Turkey	74,660,000	98.6	4.6
Turkmenistan	4,830,000	93.3	0.3

Turks and Caicos Islands	< 1,000	< 0.1	< 0.1
Tuvalu	< 1,000	0.1	< 0.1
Uganda	4,060,000	12.0	0.3
Ukraine	393,000	0.9	< 0.1
United Arab Emirates*	3,577,000	76.0	0.2
United Kingdom	2,869,000	4.6	0.2
United States	2,595,000	0.8	0.2
U.S. Virgin Islands	< 1,000	0.1	< 0.1
Uruguay	< 1,000	< 0.1	< 0.1
Uzbekistan	26,833,000	96.5	1.7
Vanuatu	< 1,000	< 0.1	< 0.1
Vatican City	< 1,000	< 0.1	< 0.1
Venezuela	95,000	0.3	< 0.1
Vietnam	160,000	0.2	< 0.1
Wallis and Futuna	< 1,000	< 0.1	< 0.1
Western Sahara	528,000	99.6	< 0.1
Yemen *	24,023,000	99.0	1.5
Zambia	59,000	0.4	< 0.1
Zimbabwe	109,000	0.9	< 0.1
Asia-Pacific	**1,005,507,000**	**24.8**	**62.1**
Middle East-North Africa	**321,869,000**	**91.2**	**19.9**
Sub-Saharan Africa	**242,544,000**	**29.6**	**15.0**
Europe	**44,138,000**	**6.0**	**2.7**
Americas	**5,256,000**	**0.6**	**0.3**
World Total	**1,619,314,000**	**23.4**	**100.0**
* = Arab	**440,324,000**		

* * *

Rightly Guided Caliphs (Section #5)

After Muhammad died in 632 CE the Muslim community needed a new leader. A leader of a Muslim community would become known as a caliph. Following Muhammad's death, the debate began over who was to take over leadership of the community.

Caliph Abu Bakr:
After much discussion the community elders elected Abu Bakr as the new leader. He was Muhammad's closest friend and companion. He was among the first people to embrace Islam. Abu Bakr: "Obey me as long as I obey God and His messenger, If I disobey God and His messenger you are free to disobey me". Abu Bakr's appointment was not without detractors. Others felt that Muhammad's son in la Ali should be chosen successor so that leadership would remain within Muhammad's family. After just years of leadership Abu Bakr fell ill and died in 634 CE (Some say he was poisoned). Omar was chosen to succeed him as the next caliph of the Muslim state.

Caliph Omar:
Omar had embraced Islam after initially denying and persecuting those who joined Muhammad in the early days. He was tough and disciplined and was well respected for always telling the truth. During Omar's ten years in office, the borders of the Islamic state greatly expanded. Peace treaties were signed in Damascus and Jerusalem. As the message of Islam spread the Muslims defended themselves against aggression but did not use force to convert others to the faith. Omar was assassinated in 644 CE by a non Muslim who had a grudge against him on a personal matter.

Caliph Uthman:
The community leadership elected Uthman to become the third caliph of Islam. Uthman was also a merchant known for his generosity, integrity and kindness. He was married to Muhammad's daughter, Ruqaiyah; when she passed away he married another of Muhammad's daughters, Umayyad Kulthum. During his years of leadership, Uthman made great achievements in pushing the borders against the Persian and Byzantine Empires, and establishing Muslim rule in what is now Libya and parts of Eastern Europe. Uthman also led an effort to preserve the text of the

Quran and it remains in its original form today. Muslims representatives from Egypt accused Uthman of favoritism toward his own family, the Umayyad clan. Uthman was murdered and his killers were never prosecuted.

Caliph Ali:
Following Uthman's death, the Prophet Muhammad's son in law Ali was chosen to be the next caliph. It further increased the rift between Sunni and Shi'a Muslims. This split began as apolitical difference of opinion over who should assume leadership of the Muslim community. The Shi'a believed that leadership should remain in Muhammad's family (Later named Shiite). The Sunni believed that the most qualified for the job should be selected from among the community (later named Sunnis). One of Uthman's relatives, Mu'awiyah was a powerful governor in Syria. He and others opposed the selection of Ali as the new leaders.

Ali was the young first cousin of Muhammad, who grew up in his household and later married Muhammad's daughter Fatima. Together they had two children, Hassan and Hussein. He was one of the first to embrace Islam in the family. Ali took over the caliphate reluctantly and led the Muslim community from his base in Kufa (Iraq). the conflict with Mu'awiyah continued to fester. The two sides battled in 657 CE. In 661 Ali was killed and his son Hassan was proclaimed the next caliph. However Hassan deferred to Mu'awiyah.

The first four caliphs of Islam Abu Bakr, Omar, Uthman and Ali were among Muhammad's closest companions. They are therefore known as the Rightly Guided Caliphs of Islam.

The Umayyads:
As the leadership of the Muslims community passed to Muawiyah what became known as the Umayyad Dynasty began. The center of Umayyad rule was in Damascus (Syria).
During Muawiyah's rule, the division between the Sunni and Shi'a Muslims continued to grow. Ali's second son Hussein tried to win the caliphate from the Umayyads but he was killed in a battle at Karbala (Iraq). He is still mourned by Shi'a Muslims in observances that mark the anniversary of his death.

Islam continued to spread from China and Russia to North Africa and Spain crossing cultural and linguistic boundaries to unite people into a common community of faith.
Others accused the caliphs of being lavish and self serving in the middle of the 18th century a rebellion began to unfold that would bring down the Umayyad dynasty. Control of the Muslims empire fell to descendants of the Prophet's uncle, Abbas.

The Abbasids:
When the Abbasids took over they moved the capital of the Muslim empire from Damascus to Baghdad. They created written manuals that codified government procedure, a postal service, and a banking system. The Islamic civilization reached its peak during the reign of Harun al Rashid (786-809 CE). The massive intellectual achievements that developed during the Abbasid period became the hallmark of what came to be called the Golden Age of Islamic civilization. Baghdad became a center for knowledge and research, literature and science. The world's first universities (Baghdad).
Studies of astronomy, medicine, mathematics and alchemy. The translated scientific works from the Greek and introduced many original ideas and innovations. The scholarly work that was done during this period helped propel Europe out of the Dark Ages, and preserved ancient knowledge for later generations. At this time, the Islamic world was the cradle of civilization (The Golden Age).

***

Ruling Families in the 19th & 20th Century (Section #6)

THE OTTOMAN SULTANS
Selim III, 1789-1807
Mustafa IV, 1807-8
Mahmud II, 1808-39
Abdulmecid I, 1839-61
Abdulaziz, 1861-76
Murad V, 1876
Abdulhamid II, 1876-1909
Mehmed V Resad, 1909-18
Mehmed VI Vahideddin, 1918-22
Abdulmecid II, recognized as caliph but not sultan, 1922-4

THE KINGS OF SAUDI ARABIA
'Abd al-'Aziz, 1926-53
Sa'ud, 1953-64
Faysal, 1964-75
Khalid, 1975-82
Fahd, 1982-

THE DYNASTY OF MUHAMMAD 'ALI IN EGYPT
Muhammad 'Ali, *Vali* (governor) of Egypt, 1805-48
Ibrahim, *Vali*, 1848
'Abbas I, *Vali*, 1848-54
Sa'id, *Vali*, 1854-63
Isma'il, Khedive, 1863-79
Tawfiq, Khedive, 1879-92
'Abbas II Hilmi, Khedive, 1892-1914
Husayn Kamil, Sultan, 1914-17
Fu'ad I, Sultan, then King, 1917-36
Faruq, King, 1936-52
Fu'ad II, King, 1952-3

THE 'ALAWIS OF MOROCCO
Sulayman, Sultan, 1796-1822
'Abd al-Rahman, Sultan, 1822-59
Muhammad, Sultan, 1859-73

Hasan I, Sultan, 1873-94
'Abd al-'Aziz, Sultan, 1894-1908
'Abd al-Hafiz, Sultan, 1908- 12
Yusuf, Sultan, 1912-27
Muhammad V, Sultan, then King, 1927-61
Hasan II, King, 1961-

***

Twelver Shi'a (Section #7)

Twelver or Imami Shi'a Islam (Athnā'ashariyyah or Ithnā'ashariyyah) is the largest branch of Shi'i (Shi'a) Islam. Adherents of Twelver Shi'ism are commonly referred to as *Twelvers,* which is derived from their belief in twelve divinely ordained leaders, known as the Twelve Imams and their belief that the Mahdi will be none other than the returned twelfth Imam that disappeared and is believed by Twelvers to be in occultation. Approximately 85% of Shi'a are Twelvers, and the term *Shi'a Muslim* as commonly used in English usually refers to Twelver Shi'a Muslims only.

Twelvers share many tenets of Shi'ism, with related sects, such as the belief in Imams, but the Isma'ili and Zaydi Shi'i sects each believe in a different number of Imams and for the most part, a different path of succession regarding the Imamate. They also differ in the role and overall definition of an Imam.

The Twelver faith is a majority in countries like Iran, Iraq, Azerbaijan, Bahrain and Lebanon. Alevis in Turkey and Albania and Alawis of Syria also regard themselves as Twelvers, but hold significantly different beliefs from mainstream Twelver Shiites." The Twelver faith also forms a large memory in India, Pakistan, Afghanistan, Nigeria, Tanzania, Kuwait, Qatar, UAE and Saudi Arabia. Smaller minorities of Twelver also exist in Oman, Yemen, Egypt, Sudan, Kenya, Ghana, Senegal, Indonesia, Malaysia and in many other countries of the world, including Europe and the Americas.

Alternative names:
The Twelvers are also known by other names, each connoting some aspect of the faith.

- The *Shi'ah* (or Shi'a) is commonly used as a synonym for "Twelvers" since this branch comprises the majority group of Shi'i Islam.
- *Ja'fari* refers to Twelvers to the exclusion of the Isma'ili and Zaydi ("Fivers"). This term refers to the majority Twelver school of jurisprudence (a minority school, the Akhbari, also

exists). It is attributed to Ja'far al-Sadiq, who the Twelvers consider to be their Sixth Imam. The founders of the Sunni Hanafi and Maliki schools of jurisprudence narrated Hadith from Ja'far al-Sadiq.
- *Imami* is a reference to the Twelver belief in the infallibility of Imams, this term is used specifically for the Twelvers.

Overview:
Twelvers believe that the descendants of the Islamic prophet Muhammad through his daughter Fatimah and his son-in-law 'Ali are the best source of knowledge about the Qur'an and Islam, the most trusted carriers and protectors of Muhammad's *Sunnah* (traditions) and the most worthy of emulation.

In particular, Twelvers recognize the succession of 'Ali, Muhammad's cousin, son-in-law and the first man to accept Islam (second only to Muhammad's wife Khadijah), the male head of the Ahl al-Bayt or "people of the [Prophet's] house" and the father of Muhammad's only bloodline) as opposed to that of the caliphate recognized by Sunni Muslims. Twelvers also believe that 'Ali was appointed successor by Muhammad's direct order on many occasions, and that he is, therefore, the rightful leader of the Muslim faith.

Although 'Ali is widely accepted by Muslims in general to be the fourth successor to the Caliphate after Uthman, for the Shi'ah, however, he is the first divinely sanctioned "Imam," or divinely appointed spiritual leader after the Prophet Muhammad. The seminal event in Shi'ah history is the martyrdom in 680 CE of 'Ali's son Husayn, who led an uprising against the, illegitimate to them, caliph. For the Shi'ah Husayn came to symbolize resistance to tyranny.

Regardless of the dispute about the Caliphate, Twelvers recognize the religious authority of the Twelve Imams, also called *Khalifah Ilahi*.

Theology
Shari'ah: Religious law:
The Ja'fari derive their Sharia, or religious law, from the Qur'an and the *Sunnah*. The difference between Sunni and Shi'a Sharia results from a Shi'a belief that Muhammad assigned 'Ali to be the first ruler and the

leader after him (the *Khalifah* or steward). Moreover, according to Shi'a, an Imam or a Caliph cannot be democratically elected and has to be nominated by God, Sunnis believe that their Caliphs were popular and had greater vote so they were made caliphs. This difference resulted in the Shi'a:

1. Following Hadith from Muhammad and his descendants the 12 Imams.
2. Not accepting the "examples", verdicts and *ahadith* of Abu Bakr, Umar and Uthman ibn
    Affan (who are considered by Sunnis to be the first three Caliphs).
3 Attributing the concept of the *masum* "infallibility" to the Twelve Imams or The
    Fourteen Infallibles (including Muhammad and his daughter Fatimah) and accepting the examples and verdict of this special group.

Main doctrines:
Twelvers believe in the Five Pillars of Islam, as do Sunnis, but categorize them differently. Twelver beliefs include the following:

Principles of Faith *(Usul al-Din)*:

- Tawhid (Oneness): The Oneness of God
- 'Abdallah (Justice): The Justice of God
- Nubuwwah (Prophethood): God has appointed perfect and infallible prophets and messengers to teach mankind the religion (that is, a perfect system of how to live in "peace" ("submission to God")).
- Imamah (Leadership): God has appointed specific leaders to lead and guide mankind – a prophet appoints a custodian of the religion before his demise.
- Qiyamah (The Day of Judgment): God will raise mankind for Judgment – the Day of Resurrection

Ancillaries of the Faith *(Furu' al-Din)*:

- Salat (Prayer) – meaning "connection", establish the five daily prayers, called *namaz* in Persian and Urdu

- Sawm (fast) – fasting during the holy month of Ramadhan, called *ruzeh* in Persian
- Hajj (Pilgrimage) – performing the pilgrimage to Mecca.
- Zakat (Poor-rate) – charity. *Zakat* means "to purify".
- Khums ("Fifth" of one's savings) – tax
- Jihad (Struggle) – struggling to please God. The greater, internal Jihad is the struggle against the evil within one's soul in every aspect of life, called *jihad akbar*. The lesser, or external, jihad is the struggle against the evil of one's environment in every aspect of life, called *jihad Asghar*. This is not to be mistaken with the common modern misconception that this means "Holy War". Writing the truth (*jihad bil Qalam* "struggle of the pen") and speaking truth in front of an oppressor are also forms of jihad.
- Commanding what is just
- Forbidding what is evil
- Tawalla – loving the Ahl al-Bayt and their followers
- Tabarra – dissociating oneself from the enemies of the Ahlu l'Bayt

The concept of Imams:
The Twelve Imams are the spiritual and political successors to Muhammad, in the Twelver or *Ithna Ashariya* branch of Shi'a Islam. According to the theology of Twelvers, the successor of Muhammad is an infallible human individual who not only rules over the community with justice, but also is able to keep and interpret the Sharia and its esoteric meaning. The prophet and imams' words and deeds are a guide and model for the community to follow; as a result, they must be free from error and sin, and must be chosen by divine decree, or *nass*, through Muhammad.

It is believed in Shi'a Islam that 'Aql, a divine wisdom, was the source of the souls of the prophets and imams and gave them esoteric knowledge, called Hikmah, and that their sufferings were a means of divine grace to their devotees. Although the Imam was not the recipient of a divine revelations, but has close relationship with God, through which God guides him, and the imam in turn guides the people. The Imamat, or belief in the divine guide is a fundamental belief in Shi'i Islam and is based on the concept that God would not leave humanity without access to divine guidance. According to Twelvers, there is always an Imam of the Age, who is the divinely appointed authority on all matters of faith and law in the Muslim community. Ali was the first Imam of this line and in the Twelvers' view, the rightful successor to the Prophet of Islam, followed by male descendants of Muhammad (also known as Hasnain's) through his daughter Fatimah. Each Imam was the son of the previous Imam, with the exception of Husayn ibn Ali, who was the brother of Hasan ibn Ali. The twelfth and final Imam is Muhammad al-Mahdi, who is believed by the Twelvers to be currently alive, and in hiding.

List of Imams:

Number	Name (Full/Kunya)	Title (Arabic/Turkish)	Birth-Death (CE/AH)	Importance
1	Ali ibn Abu Talib Abu al-Hassan	Amir al-Mu'minin (Commander of the Faithful) Birinci Ali	600-661 -23-40	
2	Hasan ibn Ali Abu Muhammad	al-Mujtaba Ikinci Ali	624-680 3-50	

3	Husayn ibn Ali	Sayed al-Shuhada	626-680	
	Abu Abdillah	Üçüncü Ali	4-61	
4	Ali ibn al-Hussein (Zayn al-Abidin)	Al-Sajjad, Zain al-Abedin	658-9 - 712	
	Abu Muhammad	Dördüncü Ali	38 - 95	
5	Muhammad ibn Ali (Muhammad al-Baqir)	Al-Baqir al-Ulum (splitting open knowledge)	677-732 57-114	

	Abu Ja'far	Besinci Ali	
6	Ja'far ibn Muhammad (Ja'far al-Sadiq) Abu Abdillah	Al-Sadiq (the Trustworthy) Altinci Ali	702-765 83-148
7	Musa ibn Ja'far (Musa al-Kadhim) Abu al-Hassan I	al-Kazim Yedinci Ali	744-799 128-183
	Ali ibn Musa (Ali ar-Ridha)		765-817

8	Abu al-Hassan II	Al-Rida, Reza Sekizinci Ali	148-203	
9	Muhammad ibn Ali (Muhammad al-Taqi) Abu Ja'far	al-Taqi, al-Jawad Dokuzuncu Ali	810-835 195-220	
10	Ali ibn Muhammad (Ali Naqi) Abu al-Hassan III	al-Hadi, al-Naqi Onuncu Ali	827-868 212-254	
11	Hassan ibn Ali (Hasan al-Askari) Abu Muhammad	al-Askari Onbirinci Ali	846-874 232-260	
	Muhammad			

12	ibn al-Hassan (Muhammad al-Mahdi)	Al-Mahdi, al-Qa'im, Hidden Imam, al-Hujjah	868-unknown
	Abu al-Qasim	Onikinci Ali	255-unknown

The Shi'a Imams are seen as infallible. It is an important aspect of Shi'a theology that they are not prophets *(Nabi)* not messengers *(Rasul)*, but instead carry out Muhammad's message. While Sunni Muslims view all religions and groups that accept prophets or messengers after Muhammad to be heathen or heretical Shi'a Muslims do consider the Imams to be higher in rank than all the prophets and messengers except Muhammad.

The role of Imam al-Mahdi:
Muhammad al-Mahdi

In Twelver eschatology, Muhammad ibn Hasan ibn 'Ali, or al-Mahdi (transliteration: Mahdi, also Mehdi, "Guided One"), is the twelfth Imam and the Mahdi, the ultimate savior of mankind and prophesied redeemer of Islam. Twelvers believe that the Mahdi has been hidden by God (referred to as The Occultation) and will later emerge to change the world into a perfect and just Islamic society alongside Jesus (Isa) before the *Yaum al-Qiyamah* (literally "Day of the Resurrection" or "Day of the Standing"),

Shahada: Declaration of faith

- [I testify that] there is no god (ilah) but Allah and [I testify that] Muhammad is messenger of Allah.

In usage the occurrence of *'ashadu' an* "I testify that" are very often omitted.

Twelvers, along with Sunnis, agree that a single honest recitation of the Shahada in Arabic is all that is required for a person to become a Muslim according to most traditional schools.

Though this form of the Shahadah is recited daily by other Shi'a sects such as the Nizari Ismailis, Twelvers view it as *Mustahabb* (recommended), but not *Wajib* (obligatory).

Salat/Namaz: Prayer
Ghusl and Wudu
There are minor differences between Sunnis and Shi'a in how the prayer ritual is performed. During the purification ritual in preparation for prayer (which consists of washing the face, arms, feet, etc. and saying of some prayers), the Shi'a view wiping the feet with wet hands as sufficient, as opposed to some of the Sunnis who consider complete washing of the feet necessary.

During prayer, it is the Ja'fari view that it is preferable to prostrate on earth, leaves that are not edible or wood, as these three things are considered purest by Muhammad in Hadith specifically mentioning *Tayammum*. Hence many Shi'a use a small tablet of soil (a mixture of earth and water and often taken from the ground of a holy site) or wood during their daily prayers upon which they prostrate.

The Ja'fari consider the five daily prayers to be compulsory, though the Ja'fari consider it acceptable to pray the second and third prayer and the fourth and fifth prayer, one after the other during the parts of the day where they believe the timings for these prayers to overlap. The other three Sunni schools allow this consolidation of daily prayers only while travelling or under some other constraint.

Khums: One-fifth tax
Khums is the Arabic word for one fifth (1/5). In Islamic legal terminology, it means "one-fifth of certain items which a person acquires as wealth and which must be paid as an Islamic tax". According to Shi'a, the items eligible for Khums are referred to as *Ghanima* in the Qur'an. The Arabic and Ghanima has two meanings:

- "spoils of war" or "war booty"

- gain or profit

The Sunni translate this word exclusively as "war booty" or "spoils of War". The Twelvers hold the view that the word *Ghanima* has two meanings as mentioned above, the second meaning is illustrated by the common use of the Islamic banking term *al-ghunm bil-ghurm* meaning "gains accompany liability for loss or risk".

Mut'ah: Temporary marriage *"Nikah Mut'ah"*
Nikāḥ al-Mut'ah, Nikah el Mut'a Arabic: also *Nikah Mut'ah* literally, "marriage of pleasure"), or *sighah,* is a fixed-time marriage which, according to the Usuli Shi'a schools of Shari'ah (Islamic law) is a marriage with a preset duration, after which the marriage is automatically dissolved. It is the second form of Islamic marriage (Nikah). However, it is regarded as *Haram* (prohibited) by Sunnis. This is a highly controversial *Fiqh* topic; Sunnis and Shi'a hold diametrically opposed views on its permissibility.

Calendar:
Twelver Shi'a, celebrate the following annual holidays:

- Eid ul-Fitr, which marks the end of fasting during the month of Ramadan and falls on the first day of Shawwal.
- Eid al-Adha, which marks the end of the Hajj or pilgrimage to Mecca, starts on the 10th day of Dhu al-Hijjah.

The following holidays are observed by Twelvers Shi'as, unless otherwise noted:

- The Mourning of Muharram or Remembrance of Muharram and Ashurah for Shi'a commemorates Imam Husayn ibn Ali's martyrdom in the Battle of Karbala. Imam Husayn was grandson of Muhammad, who was killed by Yazid ibn Muawiyah, the second Caliph of the Umayyad Caliphate (and the first one by Heredity). One group of Sunni Scholars have deemed Yazeed to be a kaafir (e.g. Sunni Scholar Ibn Jauzi in Wafa al-Wafa, another has stated he was a Fasiq (transgressor), a Fajir (one that commits debauchery) and a drunkard. Yazeed considered Nikah (marriage) with mothers and sisters to be permissible and drank

alcohol". Ashurah is a day of deep mourning which occurs on the 10th of Muharram. Sunnis also commemorates Imam Husayn ibn Ali's martyrdom, but little different from Shi'as.
- Arba'een (Arabic word for forty (40)) commemorates on 40th day of Imam Husain's martyrdom
- (40th day is an auspicious day for any deceased as per Islam) remembering the suffering of Imam Husayn and his household, the women and children. After Husayn was killed, they were marched over the desert, from Karbala (central Iraq) to Shaam (Damascus, Syria). Many children (some of whom were direct descendants of Muhammad) died of thirst and exposure along the route. Arba'een occurs on the 20th of Safar, 40 days after Ashurah.
- Milad al-Nabi, Muhammad's birth date, is celebrated by the Shi'a on the 17th of Rabi' al-awwal, which coincides with the birth date of the sixth imam, Ja'far al-Sadiq.
- Mid-Sha'aban is the birth date of the 12th and final imam, Muhammad al-Mahdi. It is celebrated by Twelvers on the 15th of Sha'aban. Many Shi'a fast on this day to show gratitude.
- Eid al-Ghadeer celebrates Ghadir Khum, the occasion when Muhammad announced Ali's imamate before a multitude of Muslims. Eid al-Ghadeer is held on the 18th of Dhu al-Hijjah.
- Al-Mubahila celebrates a meeting between the Ahl al-Bayt (household of Muhammad) and a Christian deputation from Najran. Al-Mubahila is held on the 24th of Dhu al-Hijjah.

Martyrdom of Imam Husayn:
The death of the grandson of Muhammad and the son of Ali, Husayn ibn Ali on the Tenth of Muharram – known as Ashura – plays a significant role in Twelver theology. This day is annually commemorated with grief and sorrow; some participate in ritual beating of their chests, as some believe this is a form of expressing the helplessness that comes from a practical inability to have helped Husayn and his small troop of 72 family and supporters. Some hit themselves as a form of emotional and love for the *ahlulbayt* and their sacrifice and martyrdom. In most nations with significant Shi'a populations, one can observe large crows in processions grieving over Husayn's death. The events of Ashura tell a story of a leader fighting against an oppressive tyrant, Yazid, whom

seized power and had committed atrocities against the people of the empire that he had inherited.

Notable scholars:
List of Shi'a Muslim scholars of Islam

- Mulla Sadra
- Muhammad Baqir Majlisi
- Muhammad ibn Ya'qub al-Kulayni
- Al-Shaykh al-Saduq
- Al-Shaykh Al-Mufid
- Shaykh Tusi
- Nasir al-Din al-Tusi

Guardianship of the Jurisprudent:
Traditionally Twelver Shi'a Muslims consider 'Ali ibn Abi Talib and the subsequent further eleven Imams not only religious guides, but political leaders, based on a crucial Hadith where Muhammad passes o his power to command Muslims to Ali. Since the last Imam, Muhammad al-Mahdi, went into "occultation" in 939 and is not expected back until end times, this left Shi'a without religiously sanctioned governance. In contrast, the Ismaili Imams did successfully gain political power with the Fatimid Caliphate. After the fall of the Fatimid Caliphate Ismaili Shi'ism started to lean towards secular thought.

The first Shi'a regime, the Safavid dynasty in Iran, propagated the Twelver faith, made Twelver's law the law of the land and patronized Twelver scholarship. For this, Twelver ulama "crafted a new theory of government" which held that while "not truly legitimate", the Safavid monarchy would be "blessed as the most desirable form of government during the period of awaiting" for Muhammad al-Mahdi, the twelfth imam.

Historically, Zaidi and Ismaili Shi'a imams functioned as both religious and political leaders, but later after the fall of the Fatimid Caliphate the Ismaili imamate became a secular institution. In general, Twelver Shi'a historically remained secular.

This changed with Iranian Revolution where the Twelver Ayatollah Khomeini and his supporters established a new theory of governance for the Islamic Republic of Iran. It is based on Khomeini's theory of guardianship of the Islamic jurist as rule of the Islamic jurist and jurists as "legatees" of Muhammad.

The Supreme Leader must be an Islamic jurist.

Twelvers The Fourteen Infallibles:

Muhammad – Fatimah – and
   The Twelve Imams:
Ali – Hasan - Husayn
al-Sajjad – al-Baqir – al-Sadiq
al-Kadhim – al-Rida – al-Taqi
al-Naqi – al-Askari – al-Mahdi

Concepts:
Fourteen Infallibles
Occultation (Minor – Major)
Akhbar – Usul – Ijtihad
Taqleed – 'Aql – Irfan
Mahdaviat

Principles:
Monotheism
Judgment Day – Justice
Prophethood – Imamate

Practices:
Prayer – Fasting – Pilgrimage
Charity – Taxes – Jihad
Command Justice – Forbid Evil
Love the family of Muhammad
Dissociate from their

Enemies

Holy cities:
Mecca – Medina
Najaf – Karbala – Mashhad
Samarra – Kadhimayn

Groups:
Usuli – Akhbari – Shaykhi
Nimatullahi – Safaviya
Qizilbash – Alevism
Alawism
Bektashi – Tabarie

Hadith collections:
Peak of Eloquence – The Psalms of Islam – Book of Fundamentals – The Book in Scholar's Lieu – Civilization of Laws – The Certainty – Book of Sulaym ibn Qays – Oceans of Light – Wasael ush-Shia – Reality of Certainty – Keys of Paradise

Shi'a terms:
- Shi'a Islam
- Moderate Shi'a
- Real Shi'a
- Shi'a of Ali
- Shi'a of Uthman
- Shi'a of Mauqiyah

Shi'a Twelver Hadith:
Mut'ah
Hadith of Umar and Mut'ah
Hadith of the Twelve Successors
Hadith-e-Thaqalayn
Death of Fatima

Hadith of Mut'ah and Imran ibn Husain
Hadith of Muhammad's inheritance
Hadith of the Pen and Paper

*

The Shiah Imams (Twelvers):

Shiah Islam developed sophisticated theology regarding the succession and leadership of the community via divinely appointed 'imams', who were descendants of the Prophet. After Muhammad's death, those who supported Ali believed that succession should be via the Prophet's male descendants" as he had no surviving sons, this would be through his daughter Fatimah's marriage to Ali. The Shiah imams, of whom there are 12 in total, are all descendants from Fatimah and Ali's marriage.

Shiah historical development:
Shiah Islam is a highly organized branch of the faith, which, unlike Sunni Islam, has a clergy. A central tenet of Shiah thought is that authority must be lawfully and divinely vested in leaders.
For Shiahs, the term 'imam' refers to those of Muhammad's descendants who are believed to have been divinely designated by God as the Prophet's heirs. Each imam appointed his successor before his death and Shiahs believe that he was inspired by God in this choice.

Dissension was therefore viewed as a religious act. After Ali's death, his followers turned their attention to his son Hassan, and recognized him as imam. Hassan was very quietist, whereas his brother Hussain, the third imam, became a pivotal public figure in the development of Shiah Islam with his martyrdom at Karbala in 680. After Karbala, the Sunni-Shiah divide took on further theological shape.

Theology of the Shiah:
As prophethood was now closed, Shiahs asserted that God would guide humankind through divinely appointed imams. Imams are therefore viewed by Shiah Muslims as *ayat-Allah*, signs of God's mercy, and as *hujjat-Allah*, proof of God. Shiahs also believe that these imams were

created from the same light as Muhammad and Fatimah, thereby making them *masum*, sinless and hence infallible.

Eleven imams lived earthly lives. However, since the death of the 11th, the 12th imam is believed by Shiahs to have gone into hiding, or occultation (*ghaybah*), as a child, to reappear at an apocalyptic time near the ending of the world. Shiahs have their own Hadith collections of the teachings of the imams, which explain the Quran's esoteric meanings, and the Prophet's life example.

Different branches of Shiah Islam developed because of disputes over the persona of the imams. The Twelvers evolved largely in urban Iraq and believe in the 12 imams listed above. The Ismailis lived in rural North Africa, leading to the formation of the Fatimid dynasty in Egypt. They believe Ismail ibn Ja'far was the rightful seventh imam. Zaydis, the third largest Shiah group, are found mainly in Yemen.

The Twelve Imams
1. Ali (d. 660)
2. Hassan (d. 670)
3. Hussain (d. 680)
4. Ali Zayn al-Abidin (d. 712)
5. Muhammad al-Basqr (d. 743)
6. Ja'far al-Sadiq (d. 765)
7. Musa al-Kazim (d.799)
8. Ali al-Rada (d. 818)
9. Muhammad Jawad al-Taqi (d. 835)
10. Ali Hadi al-Naqi (d. 868)
11. Hassan al-Askari (d. 874)
12. Muhammad al-Mahdi (went into hiding 941)

Shiah pilgrimages:
Iran and Iraq are key places of pilgrimage for Shiahs. Iraq contains holy shrines in Karbala, Najaf and Samarra, while Iran has Mashhad and the centers of Shiah learning at Qom. The world's principal pilgrimage site is the same for Shiah and Sunni Muslims: Makkah in Saudi Arabia, the destination for the *Hajj,* which is compulsory once n a lifetime for all able-bodied Muslims who can afford it. Like their Sunni counterparts,

Shiah Muslims travel to the Great Mosque and make seven circuits of the sacred *Kaabah*.

Karbala and Najaf:
After Makkah and Madinah, the most sacred place for Shiahs is Karbala in Iraq. Karbala is the site of the battle in which Hussain ibn Ali, grandson of the Prophet, was killed on 10 Muharram 680. Around one million Shiahs travel as pilgrims to Karbala to commemorate his death in the month of Muharram. South-east of Karbala is the holy Shiah city of Najaf, site of the tomb of Ali ibn Abu Talib, the first Shiah imam. Pilgrims visit the Imam Ali Mosque and the Wadi as-Salam, a cemetery nearby that contains the graves of many holy men of the Shiah faith. Najaf is also a great center of Shiah scholarship.

Samarra:
Another center for Shiah pilgrims in Iraq is the city of Samarra, which was the capital of the Sunni Muslim Abbasid caliphate (833-92). It contains the extraordinary Great Mosque of Samarra, built by Caliph al-Mutawakkil (reigned 847-61). Pilgrims visit a shrine marking the place at which Al-Mahdi was last seen before his occultation. Samarra is also the site of shrines to the 10th and 11th imams, Ali al-Hadj al-Naqi and Hassan al-Askari. The mosque once had a dazzling golden dome, 68 meters (223 feet) across, and two golden minarets each 36 meters (118 feet) tall but both dome and minarets were destroyed in bomb attacks attributed to Sunni militants in February 2006 and June 2007.

Mashhad and Qom:
In Iran, the principal pilgrimage destination for Shiah Muslims is the city of Mashhad. It contains the shrine of Ali al-Rida, the eighth Shiah imam, who is said to have been poisoned by Abbasid caliph al-Ma'mun (reigned 813-33) and is viewed as a martyr. The tomb of Abbasid caliph Harun al-Rashid (reigned 786-809) stands opposite the shrine to Ali al-Rida.

Qom, the principal center for Shiah scholarship in the world and the place where Ayatollah Khomeini trained, is another Iranian pilgrimage site for Shiahs. According to tradition, the 12thm and hidden, imam, Muhammad al-Mahdi, miraculously appeared at the mosque and pilgrims there make intercessions to him at a sacred well, from which it is said he will one day emerge.

***

Islam's great accomplishments (section #8)

Science in the medieval Islamic world, also known as **Islamic science** or **Arabic science**, is the science developed and practiced in the Islamic world during the Islamic Golden Age (c.750 CE – c.1258 CE). During this time, Indian, Asyriac, Iranian and especially Greek knowledge was translated into Arabic. These translations became a wellspring for scientific advances, by scientists from the Islamic civilization, during the Middle Ages.

Scientists within the Islamic civilization were of diverse ethnicities. Most were Persian, as well as a great number of Arabs, Moors, Assyrians, and Egyptians. They were also from diverse religious backgrounds. Most were Muslims, but there were also some Christians, Jews and irreligious

The religion of Islam was founded during the lifetime of the Islamic prophet Muhammad. After his death in 632, Islam continued to expand under the leadership of its Muslim rulers, known as Caliphs. Struggles for leadership of the growing religious community began at this time, and continue today.

During the Umayyad Caliphate, the Islamic empire began to consolidate its territorial gains. Arabic became the language of administration. The Arabs became a ruling class assimilated into their new surroundings across the empire, rather than occupiers of conquered territories.

The civilization in the Muslim world:
Through the Umayyad and, in particular, the succeeding Abbasid Caliphate's early phase lies the period of Islamic history known as the High Caliphate. This era can be identified as the years between 692 and 945, and ended when the caliphate was marginalized by local Muslim rulers in Baghdad – its traditional seat of power. From 945 onward until the sacking of Baghdad by the Mongols in 1258, the Caliph continued on as a figurehead, with power devolving more to local Amirs.

During the High Caliphate, stable political structures were established and trade flourished. The Chinese were undergoing a revolution in commerce, and the trade routes between the lands of Islam and China boomed both overland and along the coastal routes between the two civilizations.

The wars and cultural divisions that had separated peoples before the Arab conquests gradually gave way to a new civilization encompassing diverse ethnic and religious backgrounds. This new Islamic civilization used the Arabic language as transmitters of culture and Arabic increasingly became the language of commerce and government.

Over time, the great religious and cultural works of the empire were translated into Arabic, the population increasingly understood Arabic, and they increasingly professed Islam as their religion. The cultural heritages of the area included strong Hellenic, Indic, Assyrian and Persian influences. The Greek intellectual traditions were recognized, translated and studied broadly. A new era of high culture and innovation ensued, where these diverse influences were recognized and given their respective places in the social consciousness.

Culture in the High Caliphate:
The pious scholars of Islam, men and women collectively known as the ulama, were the most influential element of society in the fields of Sharia law, speculative thought and theology. Their pronouncements defined the external practice of Islam, including prayer, as well as the details of the Islamic way of life. They held strong influence over government, and especially the laws of commerce. They were not rulers themselves, but rather keepers and upholders of the rule of law.

Conversely, among the religious, there were inheritors of the more charismatic expressions of Christianity and Buddhism, in the Sufi orders. These Muslims had a more informal and varied approach to their religion. Islam also expressed itself in other, more esoteric forms that could have significant influence over public discourse during times of social unrest. New trends and new topics flowed from the center of the Baghdad courts, to be adopted both quickly and widely across the lands of Islam.

Apart from these other traditions stood *falsafa*; Greek philosophy, inclusive of the sciences as well as the philosophy of the ancients. This science had been widely known across Mesopotamia and Iran since before the advent of Islam. These "sciences" were in many ways contrary to the teachings of Islam and the ways of the **Adab**, but were nonetheless highly regarded in society. The ulama tolerated these outlooks and practices with reservation. Some *Faylasufs* made a good living in the practices of astrology and medicine.

Evolution:
In the zoology field of biology, Muslim biologists developed theories on evolution which were widely taught in medieval Islamic schools. John William Draper, a contemporary of Charles Darwin, considered the "Mohammedan theory of evolution" to be developed "much farther than we are disposed to do, extending them even to inorganic or mineral things." Ideas on evolution were widespread among "common people" in the Islamic world by the 12th century.

The first biologist to develop a theory of evolution was al-Jahiz (781-869). He wrote on the effects of the environment on the likelihood of an animal to survive, and he first described the struggle for existence. Al-Jahiz was also the first to discuss food chains and was also an early adherent of environmental determinism, arguing that the environment can determine the physical characteristics of the inhabitants of a certain community and that the origins of different human skin colors is the result of the environment.

Medieval Science in the Muslim World:
The roots of Islamic science drew primarily upon Iranian, Indian and Greek learning. The extent of Islamic scientific achievement is not as yet fully understood, but it is extremely vast.

These achievements encompass a wide range of subject areas; most notably:

- Mathematics
- Astronomy
- Medicine

Other notable areas, and specialized subjects, of scientific inquiry include:

- Physics
- Alchemy and chemistry
- Cosmology
- Ophthalmology
- Geography and cartography
- Sociology
- Psychology

The **House of Wisdom** is referred to the University of Gundeshapur of Persia which was the first university in history. Gundeshapur was evidently transformed into a library after the Arab's Muslim conquest of Persia and used as a translation institute in Abbasid-era Baghdad, Iraq. It was a key institution in the Translation Movement and considered to have been a major intellectual center during the Pre-Islamic Persia. The House of Wisdom (Gundeshapur) was a society took over by Caliph Harun al-Rashid and culminating under his son-al-Ma'mun, who reigned from 813-833 AD and is credited with its institution. Majority of its Persian books were burned and/or thrown into the Euphrates river after the Muslim conquest of Persia (Iran) believed by most historians to be simply because of Umar's intentions to replace the Persian Language with Arabic language for Islam to settle. As Persia (Iran) lost its borders, Gundeshapur based in today's Baghdad continued to be under the Arab rule from the 9th to 13th centuries; the university eventually became abandoned and destroyed.

During the reign of al-Ma'mun, observatories were set up and the House was an unrivalled center for the study of humanities and for science in medieval Islam, including mathematics, astronomy medicine, alchemy and chemistry, zoology and geography and cartography. Drawing on Persian, Indian and Greek texts – including those of Pythagoras, Plato, Aristotle, Hippocrates, Euclid, Plotinus, Galen Sushruta, Charaka, Aryabhata and Brahmagupta – the scholars accumulated a great collection of world knowledge and built on it through their discoveries. Baghdad was known as the world's richest city and center for intellectual development of the time and had a population of over one million, the largest in its time.

Foundation and origins:
In the Abbasid Empire, many foreign works were translated into Arabic from Greek, Chinese and many other languages like Sanskrit. Large libraries were constructed, and scholars persecuted by the Byzantine Empires were welcomed. Works were also translated at the Academy of Gundishapur, during the Muslim conquest of Persia.

In 750, the Abbasid dynasty replaced the Umayyad as the ruling dynasty of the Islamic empire, and in 762, the caliph al-Mansur (reigned 754 – 775) built Baghdad and made it his capital (the previous capital having been Damascus). Al-Mansur founded a palace library, modeled after the Sassanid Imperial Library.
Many manuscripts and books in various scientific subjects and in different languages were translated in the House of Wisdom.

Under Al-Ma'mun:
Under the sponsorship of caliph al-Ma'mun (reigned 813 – 833); it seems that the House of Wisdom took on new functions related to mathematics and astrology. The focus also shifted from Persian to Greek texts.

At that time, the library was directed by the poet and astrologer Sahl ibn Haroun (d. 830); the other notable scholars associated with the library are Muhammad ibn Mūsā al-Khwarizmi (780–850), the Banu Musa brothers (Mohammed Ja'far ibn Musa, Ahmad ibn Musa, and al-Hasan ibn Musa), Sind ibn Ali and Yaqub ibn Ishaq al-Kindi (801–873). Christian scholar Hunayn ibn Ishaq (809–873) was placed in charge of the translation work by the caliph. The most renowned translator was the Sabian Thabit ibn Qurra (826–901).

The House of Wisdom flourished under al-Ma'mun's successors al-Mu'tasim (reign 833–842) and al-Wathiq (reign 842 – 847), but declined under the reign of al-Mutawakkil (reign 847–861), mainly because Ma'mun, Mu'tasim, and Wathiq followed the sect of Mu'tazili, while al-Mutawakkil followed orthodox Islam. He wanted to stop the spread of Greek philosophy which was one of the main tools in Mu'tazili theology.

The House of Wisdom eventually acquired a reputation as a center of learning, although universities as we know them did not yet exist at this time — transmission of knowledge was done directly from teacher to student, without any institutional surrounding. Maktabs soon began to develop in the city from the 9th century, and in the 11th century, Nizam al-Mulk founded the Al-Nizamiyya of Baghdad.

Destruction by the Mongols:
Along with all other libraries in Baghdad, the House of Wisdom was destroyed during the Mongol invasion of Baghdad in 1258. About 400,000 manuscripts were rescued by al-Tusi before the siege, which he took to Maragheh.

*

Notable scientists:
In medieval Islam, the sciences, which included philosophy, were viewed holistically. The individual scientific disciplines were approached in terms of their relationships to each other and the whole, as if they were branches of a tree. In this regard, the most important scientists of Islamic civilization have been the polymaths, known as *hakim* or sages. Their role in the transmission of the sciences was central.

1. **Abbas ibn Firnas** (810-887) was an Andalusian scientist, musician and inventor. He developed a clear glass used in drinking vessels, and lenses used for magnification and the improvement of vision. He had a room in his house where the sky was simulated, including the motion of planets, stars and weather complete with clouds, thunder and lightning. He is most well known for reportedly surviving an attempt at controlled flight.

2. **Al-Battani** (850-922) was an astronomer who accurately determined the length of the solar year. He contributed to numeric tables, such as the Tables of Toledo, used by astronomers to predict the movements of the sun, moon and planets across the sky. Some of Battani's astronomic tables were later used by Copernicus. Battani also developed numeric tables which could be used to find the direction of Mecca from different locations. Knowing the direction of Mecca is important for Muslims, as this is the direction faced during prayer.

3. **Al-Farabi:** (870-950) was a rationalist philosopher and mathematician who attempted to describe, geometrically, the repeating patterns popular in Islamic decorative motifs. His book on the subject is titled *Spiritual Crafts and Natural Secrets in the Details of Geometrical Figures*.

4. **Al-Ghazali (Algazel):** (1058-1111), Abu Hāmed Mohammad ibn Mohammad , known as **Algazel** to the western medieval world, born and died in Tus, in the Khorasan province of Persia (modern day Iran) was a Persian Muslim theologian, jurist, philosopher and mystic.

Ghazali has sometimes been referred to by historians as the single most influential Muslim after the Islamic prophet Muhammad. Others have cited his movement from science to faith as a detriment to Islamic scientific progress. Besides his work that successfully changed the course of Islamic philosophy – the early Islamic Neoplatonism developed on the grounds of Hellenistic philosophy, for example, was so successfully refuted by Ghazali that it never recovered – he also brought the orthodox Islam of his time in close contact with Sufism.

School affiliations:
Al-Ghazali contributed significantly to the development of a systematic view of Sufism and its integration and acceptance in mainstream Islam. He was a scholar of orthodox Islam, belonging to the Shafi'i school of Islamic jurisprudence and to the Asharite School of theology. Ghazali wrote more than 70 books on Islamic sciences, Philosophy and Sufism.

5. **Al-*hakim*:** (996-1021) was most often a poet and a writer, skilled in the practice of medicine as well as astronomy and mathematics. These multi-talented sages, the central figures in Islamic science, elaborated and personified the unity of the sciences. They orchestrated scientific development through their insights, and excelled in their explorations as well.

6. **Al-Idrisi:** (1100-1166) was a Moroccan traveler, cartographer and geographer famous for a map of the world he created for Roger, the Norman King of Sicily. Al-Idrisi also wrote the Book of Roger, a geographic study of the peoples, climates, resources and industries of all

the world known at that time. In it, he incidentally relates the tale of a Moroccan ship blown west in the Atlantic, and returning with tales of faraway lands.

7. **Al-Khwarizmi**: (780-847) was a Persian mathematician, geographer and astronomer. He is regarded as the greatest mathematician of Islamic civilization. He was instrumental in the adoption of the Indian numbering system, later known as Arabic numerals. He developed algebra, which also had Indian antecedents, by introducing methods of simplifying the equations. He used Euclidian geometry in his proofs.

8. **Al-Razi**: (854-925/935), Abu Bakr Zakariya, was a Persian born in Rey, Iran. He was a polymath who wrote on a variety of topics, but his most important works were in the field of medicine. He identified smallpox and measles, and recognized fever was part of the body's defenses. He wrote a 23-volume compendium of Chinese, Indian, Persian, Syriac and Greek medicine. Al-Razi questioned some aspects of the classical Greek medical theory of how the four humors regulate life processes. He challenged Galen's work on several fronts, including the treatment of bloodletting. His trial of bloodletting showed it was effective; a result we now know to be erroneous.

9. **Al-Tabari**: (838-923), Abu Ja'far Muhammad ibn Jarir was a prominent and influential scholar, historian and exegete of the Qur'an from Tabaristan, modern Mazandaran in Persia/Iran. Al-Tabari founded his own Madh'hab which is usually designated by the name Jariri. He memorized the Qur'an at seven, was a qualified religious leader at eight and began to study the prophetic traditions at nine.

A major teacher in Rayy was Abu Abdillah Muhammad ibn Humayd al-Razi, who had earlier taught in Baghdad but was now in his seventies. Among other material, ibn Humayd taught Jarir Tabari the historical works of ibn Ishaq, especially *al-Sirah*, his life of Muhammad. Tabari was thus introduced in youth to pre-Islamic and early Islamic history.

Tabari then travelled to study in Baghdad under ibn Hanbal, who, however, had recently died (in late 855 or early 856). There he met a number of eminent and venerable scholars.

In his late twenties he travelled to Syria, Palestine and Egypt. In Beirut he made the highly significant connection of al-Abbas b. al-Walid b. Mazyad al-'Udhri al-Bayruti (c.169-270/785-6 to 883–4). Tabari arrived in Egypt in 253H (867), and sometime after 256/870 returned to Baghdad. Tabari never married. He died in Baghdad on February 17, 923.

Works:
He did not hesitate to express his independent judgment *(ijtihad)*. He was very much opposed to religious innovation. In general Tabari's approach was conciliatory and moderate, seeking harmonious agreement between conflicting opinions.

The first of the two large works is generally known as the *Annals* (Arabic *Tarikh al-Tabari)*. This is a universal history from the time of Qur'anic Creation to AD 915 and is renowned for its detail and accuracy concerning Muslim and Middle Eastern history. Tabari's work is one of the major primary sources for historians.

10. **Al-Tusi:** (1201-1274), Nasir al-Din, was a Persian astronomer and mathematician whose life was overshadowed by the Mongol invasions of Genghis Khan and his grandson Hulagu. Al-Tusi wrote an important revision to Ptolemy's celestial model, among other works. When he became Hulagu's astrologer, he was furnished with an impressive observatory and gained access to Chinese techniques and observations. He developed trigonometry to the point it became a separate field, and compiled the most accurate astronomical tables available up to that time.

11. **Al-Zahrawi**: (936-1013) was an Andalusian surgeon who is known as the greatest surgeon of medieval Islam. His most important surviving work is referred to as al-Tasrif (Medical Knowledge). It is a 30 volume set discussing medical symptoms, treatments, and mostly pharmacology, but it is the last volume of the set which has attracted the most attention over time. This last volume is a surgical manual describing surgical instruments, supplies and procedures. Scholars studying this manual are discovering references to procedures previously believed to belong to more modern times.

12. **Al-Zarqali**: (1028-1087) was an Andalusian artisan, skilled in working sheet metal, who became a famous maker of astronomical equipment, an astronomer, and a mathematician. He developed a new design for a highly accurate astrolabe which was used for centuries afterwards. He constructed a famous water clock that attracted much attention in Toledo for centuries. He discovered that the Sun's apogee moves slowly relative to the fixed stars, and obtained a very good estimate for its rate of change.

13. **Banu Musa brothers**: (803-873) Ja'far-Muhammad, Ahmad and al-Hasan were three Persian sons of a colorful astronomer and astrologer. They were scholars close to the court of caliph al-Ma'mun, and contributed greatly to the translation of ancient works into Arabic. They elaborated the mathematics of cones and ellipses, and performed astronomic calculations. Most notably, they contributed to the field of automation with the creations of automated devices such as the ones described in their Book of Ingenious Devices.

14. **Harun al-Rashid:** (763-809) (English: Aaron the Upright, *Aaron the Just*, or *Aaron the Rightly Guided*) was the fifth Arab Abbasid Caliph that encompassed modern Iraq. He ruled from 786 to 809, and his time was marked by scientific, cultural and religious prosperity. Art and music Hamd o Na'at also flourished significantly during his reign. He established the legendary library Bayt al-Hikma ("House of Wisdom").

Since Harun was intellectually, politically and militarily resourceful, his life and the court over which he held sway have been the subject of many tales: some are factual but most are believed to be fictitious. Among what is known to be fictional is **The Book of One Thousand and One Nights,** which contains many stories that are fantasized by Harun's magnificent court and even Harun al-Rashid himself.

Life:
The Barmakids were a Persian-Tajik family which dated back to the Barmak of Magi, who had become very powerful under al-Mahdi. Yahya had aided Harun in obtaining the caliphate, and he and his sons were in high favor until 798, when the caliph threw them in prison and confiscated their land.

Harun became caliph when he was in his early twenties. On the day of accession, his son al-Ma'mun was born, and al-Amin some little time later: the latter was the son of Zubaida, a granddaughter of al-Mansur (founder of the city of Baghdad); so he took precedence over the former, whose mother was a Persian slave-girl.

It was under Harun ar-Rashid that Baghdad flourished into the most splendid city of its period. Tribute was paid by many rulers to the caliph, and these funds were used on architecture, the arts and a luxurious life at court.

In 796, Harun decided to move his court and the government to Ar Raqqah at the middle Euphrates. Here he spent 12 years, most of his reign. Only once he returned to Baghdad for a short visit. It was close to the Byzantine border.

Due to the *Thousand-and-One Nights* tales, Harun al-Rashid turned into a legendary figure obscuring his true historic personality. In fact, his reign initiated the political disintegration of the Abbasid caliphate.

Al-Rashid virtually dismembered the empire by apportioning it between his two sons al-Amin and al-Ma'mun (with his third son, al-Qasim, being belatedly added after them). After the death of Harun al-Rashid, civil war broke out in the empire between his two sons, al-Amin and al-Ma'mun.

Harun made the pilgrimage to Mecca several times, e.g., 793, 795, 797, 802 and last in 803. Al-Rashid sent embassies to the Chinese Tang dynasty and established good relations with them. He was called "A-lun" in the Chinese T'ang Annals. In 808, Harun went to settle the insurrection of Rafi ibn Leith in Transoxania, became ill, and died.

15. **Hunayn ibn Ishaq**: (809-873) was one of the most important translators of the ancient Greek works into Arabic. He was also a physician and a writer on medical subjects. His translations interpreted, corrected and extended the ancient works. Some of his translations of medical works were used in Europe for centuries. He also wrote on medical subjects, particularly on the human eye. His book *Ten Treatises on the Eye* was influential in the West until the 17th century.

16. Ibn al-Haytham (Alhazen): (965-1040), Abu 'Ali al-Hasan ibn al-Hasan was a Muslim scientist and polymath described in various sources as either Arab or Persian. Alhazen made significant contributions to the principles of optics, as well as to physics, astronomy, mathematics, ophthalmology, philosophy, visual perception, and to the scientific method. He also wrote insightful commentaries on works by Aristotle, Ptolemy, and the Greek mathematician Euclid.

He is frequently referred to as ibn al-Haytham, and sometimes as al-Basri after his birthplace in the city of Basra. He was also nicknamed *Ptolemaeus Secundus* ("Ptolemy the Second") or simply "The Physicist" in medieval Europe.

Born circa 965, in Basra, present-day Iraq, he lived mainly in Cairo, Egypt, dying there at age 74. Overconfident about practical application of his mathematical knowledge, he assumed that he could regulate the floods of the Nile. After being ordered by Al-Hakim bi-Amr Allah, the sixth ruler of the Fatimid caliphate, to carry out this operation, he quickly perceived the impossibility of what he was attempting to do, and retired from engineering. Fearing for his life, he feigned madness and was placed under house arrest, during and after which he devoted himself to his scientific work until his death.

17. Ibn al-Haytham (965-1040) was an Egyptian scientist who worked in several fields, but is now known primarily for his achievements in astronomy and optics. He was an experimentalist who questioned the ancient Greek works of Ptolemy and Galen. At times, al-Haytham suggested Ptolemy's celestial model, and Galen's explanation of vision, had problems. The prevailing opinion of the time, Galen's opinion, was that vision involved transmission of light from the eye, an explanation al-Haytham cast doubt upon. He also studied the effects of light refraction, and suggested the mathematics of reflection and refraction needed to be consistent with the anatomy of the eye.

18. Ibn al-Jazari: (1136-1206), Badi'al-Zaman Abu al-'Izz Isma'il was an Arab or a Kurdish Muslim polymath: a scholar, inventor, mechanical engineer, craftsman, artist, and mathematician from Jazirat ibn Umar (current Cizre), who lived during the Islamic Golden Age (Middle

Ages). He is best known for writing the *al-Jami Bain al-'ilm wa al-Amal al-nafi' fī Ṣinā'at al-ḥiyal* (*The Book of Knowledge of Ingenious Mechanical Devices*) in 1206, where he described fifty mechanical devices along with instructions on how to construct them.

Biography:
Like his father before him, he served as chief engineer at the Artuklu Palace, the residence of the Mardin branch of the Turkish Artuqid dynasty which ruled across eastern Anatolia as vassals of the Zangid rulers of Mosul and later Ayyubid general Saladin.

Some of his devices were inspired by earlier devices, such as one of his monumental water clocks, which were based on that of a Pseudo-Archimedes. He also cites the influence of the Banu Musa brothers for his fountains, al-Asturlabi for the design of a candle clock, and Hibat Allah ibn al-Husayn (d. 1139) for musical automata.

He used the crankshaft with a connecting rod in two of his water-raising machines: the crank-driven Saqiya chain pump and the double-action reciprocating piston suction pump. His water pump also employed the first known crank-slider mechanism.

According to Encyclopedia Britannica, the Renaissance inventor Leonardo da Vinci may have been influenced by the classic automata of al-Jazari.

19. Ibn al-Nafis: (1213-1288) was a physician who was born in Damascus and practiced medicine as head physician at the al-Mansuri hospital in Cairo. He wrote an influential book on medicine, believed to have replaced ibn-Sina's *Canon* in the Islamic world – if not Europe. He wrote important commentaries on Galen and ibn-Sina's works. One of these commentaries was discovered in 1924, and yielded a description of pulmonary transit, the circulation of blood from the right to left ventricles of the heart through the lungs.

20. Ibn Ishaq al-Kindi: (801-873) was a philosopher and polymath scientist heavily involved in the translation of Greek classics into Arabic. He worked to reconcile the conflicts between his Islamic faith and his affinity for reason; a conflict that would eventually lead to problems with his rulers. He criticized the basis of alchemy and astrology, and contributed to a wide range of scientific subjects in his writings. He worked on cryptography for the caliphate, and even wrote a piece on the subject of time, space and relative movement.

21. **Ibn Khaldun:** (1332-1406) (Arabic: Abu Zayd 'Abdu r-Rahman bin Muhammad bin Khaldun Al-Ḥaḍrami), was an Arab Tunisian historiographer and historian who is often viewed as one of the forerunners of modern historiography, sociology and economics.

He is best known for his *Muqaddimah* (known as Prolegomenon in English), which was discovered, evaluated and fully appreciated first by 19th century European scholarship, although it has also had considerable influence on 17th-century Ottoman historians like Ḥajjī Khalifa and Mustafa Naima who relied on his theories to analyze the growth and decline of the Ottoman empire. Later in the 19th century, Western scholars recognized him as one of the greatest philosophers to come out of the Muslim world.

Biography:
Generally known as "Ibn Khaldun" after a remote ancestor, he was born in Tunis in AD 1332 (732 A.H.) into an upper-class Andalusian family, the *Banū Khaldun*. His family, which held many high offices in Andalusia, had immigrated to Tunisia after the fall of Seville to Reconquista forces around the middle of the 13th century. His brother, Yahya Ibn Khaldun, was also a historian who wrote a book on the Abdalwadid dynasty and who was assassinated by a rival for being the official historiographer of the court.

In his autobiography, Ibn Khaldun traces his descent back to the time of Muhammad through an Arab tribe from Yemen, specifically Hadhramaut, which came to Spain in the eighth century at the beginning o the Islamic conquest. Even in the times when Berbers were ruling in Al-Andalus, the reigns of Almoravids and Almohads, the Ibn Khalduns did not reclaim their Berber heritage."

Education:
His family's high rank enabled Ibn Khaldun to study with the best teachers in Maghreb. He received a classical Islamic education, studying the Qur'an which he memorized by heart, Arabic linguistics, the basis for an understanding of the Qur'an, Hadith, Sha'aria (law) and Fiqh (jurisprudence). He received certification (Ijazah) for all these subjects.

The mystic, mathematician and philosopher, Al-Abili of Tlemcen, introduced him to mathematics, logic and philosophy, where he above all studied the works of Averroes, Avicenna, Razi and Tusi. At the age of 17, Ibn Khaldun lost both his parents to the Black Death, an intercontinental epidemic of the plague that hit Tunis in 1348-1349.

Ibn Khaldun, therefore, decided to move to Granada. At al-Khatib's instigation, Ibn Khaldun was eventually sent back to North Africa. He lived there for over three years under their protection, taking advantage of his seclusion to write the *Muqaddimah* "Prolegomena", the introduction to his planned history of the world. In 1378, he returned to his native Tunis. There he devoted himself almost exclusively to his studies and completed his history of the world. Under pretense of going on the Hajj to Mecca – something a Muslim ruler could not simply refuse permission for – Ibn Khaldun was able to leave Tunis and sail to Alexandria.

Last years in Egypt:
In 1401, under Barquq's successor, his son Faraj, Ibn Khaldun took part in a military campaign against the Mongol conqueror Timur, who besieged Damascus. Ibn Khaldun spent the following five years in Cairo completing his autobiography and his history of the world and acting as teacher and judge.

Works:
Following a contemporary Arab scholar, Sati' al-Husri, the Muqaddimah may be read as a sociological work: six books of general sociology. Ibn Khaldun was first brought to the attention of the Western world in 1697. Since then, the work of Ibn Khaldun has been extensively studied in the Western world with special interest.

22. **Ibn Rushd:** (Averroes) (1126-1198), 'Abu l-Walīd Muhammad bin Ahmad, was an Andalusian Muslim polymath; a master of Aristotelian philosophy, Islamic philosophy, Islamic theology, Maliki law and jurisprudence, logic, psychology, politics, Arabic music theory, and the sciences of medicine, astronomy, geography, mathematics, physics and celestial mechanics. He was born in Córdoba, Al Andalus, modern-day Spain, and died in Marrakesh, Morocco. His school of philosophy is known as Averroism.

Ibn Rushd was a defender of Aristotelian philosophy against claims from the influential Islamic theologian Ghazali who attacked philosophy so it would not become an affront to the teachings of Islam.

Biography:
Ibn Rushd's education followed a traditional path, beginning with studies in Hadith, linguistics, jurisprudence and scholastic theology. Throughout his life he wrote extensively on Philosophy and Religion, attributes of God, origin of the universe, Metaphysics and Psychology. It is generally believed that he was perhaps once tutored by Ibn Bajjah (Avempace). His medical education was directed under Abu Ja'far ibn Harun of Trujillo in Seville. Ibn Rushd began his career with the help of Ibn Tufayl ("Aben Tufayl" to the West), the author of *Hayy ibn Yaqdhan* and philosophic vizier of Almohad king Abu Yaqub Yusuf who was an amateur of philosophy and science. It was Ibn Tufayl who introduced him to the court and to Ibn Zuhr ("Avenzoar" to the West), the great Muslim physician, who became Averroes's teacher and friend. Averroes's aptitude for medicine was noted by his contemporaries and can be seen in his major enduring work *Kitab al-Kulyat fi al-Tibb* (Generalities) the work was influenced by the *Kitab al-Taisir fi al-Mudawat wa al-Tadbir* (Particularities) of Ibn Zuhr. Averroes later reported how it was also Ibn Tufayl that inspired him to write his famous commentaries on Aristotle.

Averroes was also a student of Ibn Bajjah ("Avempace" to the West), another famous Islamic philosopher who greatly influenced his own Averroist thought. However, while the thought of his mentors Ibn Tufayl and Ibn Bajjah were mystic to an extent, the thought of Averroes was purely rationalist. Together, the three men are considered the greatest Andalusian philosophers. Averroes devoted the last 30 years to his philosophical writings.

Works:
Averroes's works were spread over 20,000 pages covering a variety of different subjects, including early Islamic philosophy, logic in Islamic philosophy, Arabic medicine, Arabic mathematics, Arabic astronomy, Arabic grammar, Islamic theology, Sharia (Islamic law), and Fiqh (Islamic jurisprudence). In particular, his most important works dealt with Islamic philosophy, medicine and Fiqh. He wrote at least 67 original works, which included 28 works on philosophy, 20 on medicine, 8 on law, 5 on theology, and 4 on grammar, in addition to his commentaries on most of Aristotle's works and his commentary on Plato's *The Republic*.

His most important original philosophical work was *The Incoherence of the Incoherence* (*Tahafut al-Tahafut*), in which he defended Aristotelian philosophy against al-Ghazali's claims in *The Incoherence of the Philosophers* (*Tahafut al-falasifa*).

23. **Ibn Sina (Avicenna)**: (908-946) was a Persian physician, astronomer, physicist and mathematician from Bukhara, Uzbekistan. In addition to his master work, The Canon of Medicine, he also made important astronomical observations, and discussed a variety of topics including the different forms energy can take, and the properties of light. He contributed to the development of mathematical techniques such as casting out nines.

24. **Jabir ibn Hayyan**: (738-813) was an alchemist who used extensive experimentation and produced many works on science and alchemy which have survived to the present day. Jabir described the laboratory techniques and experimental methods of chemistry. He identified many substances including sulfuric and nitric acid. He described processes including sublimation, reduction and distillation. He utilized equipment such as the alembic and the retort. There is considerable uncertainty as to the actual provenance of many works that are ascribed to him.

25. **Omar al-Khayyam**: (1048-1131) was a Persian poet and mathematician who calculated the length of the year to within 5 decimal places. He found geometric solutions to all 13 forms of cubic equations. He developed some quadratic equations still in use. He is well known in the West for his poetry (Rubaiyat).

26. **Rumi:** (1207-1273), Jalal ad-Din Muhammad, and popularly known as Mevlana in Turkey. was a 13th-century Persian Muslim poet, jurist, theologian, and Sufi mystic. *Rūmī* is a descriptive name meaning "Roman" since he lived most of his life in an area called "Rûm" (then under the control of Seljuq dynasty) because it was once ruled by the Eastern Roman Empire. He was one of the figures who flourished in the Sultanate of Rum.

It is likely that he was born in the village of Wakhsh, a small town located at the river Wakhsh in Persia (in what is now Tajikistan). His birthplace and native language both indicate a Persian heritage. Rumi's family traveled west, first performing the Hajj and eventually settling in the Anatolian city Konya (capital of the Seljuk Sultanate of Rum, in present-day Turkey). This was where he lived most of his life, and here he composed one of the crowning glories of Persian literature which profoundly affected the culture of the area.

He was buried in Konya and his shrine became a place of pilgrimage. Following his death, his followers and his son Sultan Walad founded the Mevlevi Order, also known as the Order of the Whirling Dervishes, famous for its Sufi dance known as the Sama ceremony.

Rumi's works are written in the New Persian language. It reinforced the Persian language as the preferred literary and cultural language in the Persian Islamic world. Rumi's importance is considered to transcend national and ethnic borders. His original works are widely read in their original language across the Persian-speaking world. Translations of his works are very popular in other countries. His poems have been widely translated into many of the world's languages and transposed into various formats. In 2007, he was described as the "most popular poet in America."

When the Mongols invaded Central Asia sometime between 1215 and 1220, Baha ud-Din Walad, with his whole family and a group of disciples, set out westwards. Rumi encountered one of the most famous mystic Persian poets, 'Attar, in the Iranian city of Nishapur, located in the province of Khorasan. 'Attar immediately recognized Rumi's spiritual eminence. He saw the father walking ahead of the son and said,

"Here comes a sea followed by an ocean." He gave the boy his *Asrārnāma*, a book about the entanglement of the soul in the material world. This meeting had a deep impact on the eighteen-year-old Rumi and later on became the inspiration for his works.

From Nishapur, Walad and his entourage set out for Baghdad, meeting many of the scholars and Sufis of the city. He became an Islamic Jurist, issuing fatwas and giving sermons in the mosques of Konya. He also served as a Molvi (Islamic teacher) and taught his adherents in the madrassa. It was his meeting with the dervish Shams-e Tabrizi on 15 November 1244 that completely changed his life. From an accomplished teacher and jurist, Rumi was transformed into an ascetic. On the night of 5 December 1248, as Rumi and Shams were talking, Shams was called to the back door. He went out, never to be seen again.

Rumi spent the next twelve years of his life in Anatolia dictating the six volumes of this masterwork, the *Masnavi*, to Hussam. In December 1273, Rumi fell ill; he predicted his own death and composed the well-known *ghazal*, which begins with the verse:

> "…How doest thou know what sort of king I have within me as companion? Do not cast thy glance upon my golden face, for I have iron legs".

Rumi died on 17 December 1273 in Konya; his body was interred beside that of his father, and a splendid shrine, the *Yeşil Türbe* (Green Tomb, today the Mevlana Museum), was erected over his place of burial. His epitaph reads: "…When we are dead, seek not our tomb in the earth, but find it in the hearts of men".

Poetic works:
Rumi's major work is the *Maṯnawīye Ma'nawī* (*Spiritual Couplets*), a six-volume poem regarded by some Sufis as the Persian-language Qur'an. It is considered by many to be one of the greatest works of mystical poetry. It contains approximately 27,000 lines of Persian poetry.

27. **Sinan Pasha:** (1491-1588) Ottoman's greatest architect. In his 97 years he built 131 mosques and over 200 buildings over the

Empire. His most famous work is the Sulaymaniye Mosque in Istanbul where Suleiman the Magnificent is buried.

28. **Thabit ibn Qurra**: (835-901) was a Sabian translator and mathematician from Harran, in what is now Turkey. He is known for his translations of Greek mathematics and astronomy, but as was common, he also added his own work to the translations. He is known for having calculated the solution to a chessboard problem involving an exponential series.

***

Islamic Charities & Organizations (Section #9)

Alhambra Productions
467 Saratoga Ave, Suite 460
San Jose, CA 95129
Phone 408-244-1402
www.sandalaproductions.com

Al-Haramain Foundation
(Charity – declared a terrorist organization)

Amana Mutual Funds Trust
Saturna Capital Headquarters
1300 N State St
Bellingham, WA 98225
Phone 360-734-9900
Fax 360-734-0755
www.amanafunds.com

American-Arab Anti-Discrimination Committee
1732 Wisconsin Ave NW
Washington, DC 20007
Phone 202-244-2990
Fax 202-333-3980
www.adc.org
adc@adc.org

American Muslim, The
www.theamericanmuslim.org
tameditor@aol.com

American Muslim Alliance
39675 Cedar Blvd, Suite 220 E
Newark, CA 94560
Phone 510-252-9858
Fax 510-252-9863
www.amaweb.org

civilrightsforall@sbcglobal.net

American Muslim Council
AMC National
1005 W Webster, Suite 3
Chicago, IL 60614
Phone 773-248-3390

AMIDEAST
1730 M Street NW, Suite 1100
Washington, DC 20036-4505
Phone 202-776-9600
Fax 202-776-7000
www.amideast.org
inquiries@amideast.org

ArabNews.com – Internet Resource Only
Online Contact Form Only

Arab World and Islamic Resources and School Services
PO Box 174
Abiquiu, NM 87510
Phone 510-704-0517 – Audrey Shabbas, Workshop Information
Fax 505-685-4533 – Rahmah Lutz, Order Fulfillment
www.awaironline.org

Benevolence International Foundation
(Charity – declared a terrorist organization)
No contact information

Center for Cross Cultural Understanding
PO Box 724
Dalton, GA 30720
www.aljazeerah.info
editor@ccun.org

Council on American-Islamic Relations – New York
475 Riverside Drive, Suite 244
New York, NY 10115

Phone 212-870-2002
Fax 212-870-2020
www.cair-ny.org
alatif@cair.com – Aliya Latif, Civil Rights Director
fali@cair.com – Faiza N. Ali, Community Affairs Director

Council on Islamic Education
PO Box 20186
Fountain Valley, CA 92728-0186
Phone 714-839-2929
Fax 714-839-2714
www.cie.org
info@cie.org

Freedom House Center for Religious Freedom
Hudson Institute
1015 15th St NW, 6th Floor
Washington, DC 20005
Phone 202-974-2400
Fax 202-974-2410
www.hudson.org
info@hudson.org

Graduate School of Islamic and Social Sciences
45150 Russell Branch Pkwy, Suite 303
Ashburn, VA 20147
Phone 571-223-0500
Fax 571-223-2544
www.cordobauniversity.org/gsiss
cordoba@siss.edu

Hariri Foundation Lebanon Relief Fund
7501 Wisconsin Avenue, Suite 715
Bethesda, MD 20814-3602
Phone 301-656-1666
www.haririfoundationusa.org
mailbox@haririfoundationusa.org

Hifz Nation

Yusuf Ziya Kavakci Institute
Good Tree Academy
P O Box 850994
Richardson, TX 75085-9859
Phone 214-306-6174
www.hifznation.com
www.goodtreeacademy.org
info@goodtreeacademy.org
Attn. Imam Zaid Shakir

IANT Qur'anic Academy
Islamic Association of North Texas
Dallas Central Mosque
PO Box 850273
Richardson, TX 75085
Phone 972-231-5698 Ext. 103
Fax 972-231-6707
www.quranicacademy.org
info@quranicacademy.org

Institute of Islamic Information and Education
PO Box 410129
Chicago, IL 60641-0129
Phone 773-777-7443
Fax 773-777-7199
www.iiie.net
light@iiie.net

International Institute of Islamic Thought/
Association of Muslim Social Scientists
500 Grove St, Suite 200
Herndon, VA 20170
Phone 703-471-1133
Fax 703-471-3922
www.iiit.org
iiit@iiit.org

International Islamic Relief Organization
PO Box 14843

Jeddah
21434
Saudi Arabia
Phone 966-2-6512333
Fax 966-2-6518491
www.iirosa.org

Iraq.net – Internet Resource Only
No contact info

Iraq Action Coalition
7309 Haymarket Lane
Raleigh, NC 27615
Fax 919-846-7422
www.leb.net/~iac
IAC@leb.net

Islam101.com – Internet Resource only
Online Contact Form only

Islamic Art and Architecture Organization
829 Bethel Road #140
Columbus, OH 43214
www.islamicart.com

Islamic Assembly of North America
3588 Plymouth Rd
Ann Arbor, MI 48105
Phone 734-528-0006
www.iananet.org

Islamic Circle of North America
ICNA Relief
166-26 89th Avenue
Jamaica, NY 11432-9772
Phone 1-866-354-0102 / 718-658-7028
www.reliefonline.org
info@reliefonline.org

Islamic Food and Nutrition Council of America
777 Busse Hwy
Park Ridge, IL 60068
Phone 847-993-0034
Fax 847-993-0038
www.ifanca.org

Islamic Information Center of America
PO Box 4052
Des Plaines, IL 60016
Phone 847-541-8141
Fax 847-824-8436
www.iica.org
info@iica.org

IslamiCity – Internet Resource
PO Box 4598
Culver City, CA 90231-4598
Phone 310-642-0006
www.islamicity.com
icinfo@islamicity.com

Islamic Society of North America
PO Box 38
Plainfield, IN 46168
Phone 317-839-8157
Fax 317-839-1840
www.isna.net

Islamic Texts Society
Independent Publishers Group
814 N Franklin St
Chicago, IL 60610
Phone 312-337-0747
Fax 312-337-5985
www.its.org.uk
frontdest@ipgbook.com

Islamic Training Foundation
PO Box 204
Sparks, NV 89432
Phone 702-784-6824
Fax 702-355-0393
www.islamist.org
beekun@scs.unr.edu

Kinder USA
P O Box 224846
Dallas, TX 75222-9785
Phone 972-664-1991
www.kinderusa.org

KindHearts: Charitable Humanitarian Development
Dept. AE/VA, PO Box 23310
Toledo, OH 43623-09965
Phone 866-546-3478
www.kind-hearts.org

Latino American Dawah Organization
(Online Only)
www.latinodawah.org

Life for Relief and Development
17300 W. 10 Mile Road.
Southfield, MI 48075
Phone 248-424-7493
Fax 248-424-8325
www.lifeusa.org
life@lifeusa.org
Attn. Dr. Khalil Jassemm, President & CEO

Long Island Muslim Society/Islamic Center of Long Island
835 Brush Hollow Road
Westbury, NY 11590
Phone 516-581-5893 (Habeeb Ahmen)
Fax 516-982-3460 (Mohammed Saleh)

Middle East Council
Foreign Policy Research Institute
1528 Walnut St, Suite 610
Philadelphia, PA 19102
Phone 215-732-3774
Fax 215-732-4401
www.fpri.org
fpri@fpri.org

Middle East Institute
1761 N St NW
Washington, DC 20036-2882
Phone 202-785-1141
Fax 202-331-8861
www.mei.edu
information@mei.edu

Middle East Outreach Council
Lisa Adeli – Outreach Coordinator
University of Arizona
845 N Park Ave, Room 470
Tucson, AZ 85721
Phone 520-621-7904
Fax 520-621-9257
www.meoc.us
adeli@email.arizona.edu

Middle East Policy Council
1730 M Street NW, Suite 512
Washington, DC 20036
Phone 202-296-6767
Fax 202-296-5791
www.mepc.org
info@mepc.org

Middle East Research and Information Project
1500 Massachusetts Ave NW, Suite 119
Washington, DC 20005
Phone 202-223-3677

Fax 202-223-3604
www.merip.org

Middle East Studies Association
University of Arizona
1219 N Santa Rita Ave
Tucson, AZ 85721
Phone 520-621-5850
Fax 520-626-9095
www.mesana.org
sbs-mesa@email.arizona.edu
Attn. Amy Newhall, Executive Director

Minaret of Freedom Institute
4323 Rosedale Ave
Bethesda, MD 20814
Phone 301-907-0947
www.minaret.org
mfi@minaret.org

Muslim American Society, The
1325 G St NW, Suite 500
Washington, DC 20005
Phone 202-552-7414 / 703-642-6165
http://muslimamericansociety.org
info@masfreedom.org

Muslim Council of Britain
PO Box 57330, London E1 2WJ
Phone +44 0-845-262-6786
Fax +44 0-207-247-7079
www.mcb.org.uk
admin@mcb.org.uk

Muslim Public Affairs Council
110 Maryland Ave NE, Suite 210
Washington, DC 20002
Phone 202-547-7701
Fax 202-547-7704

3010 Wilshire Blvd #217
Los Angeles, CA 90010
Phone 323-258-6722
Fax 213-258-5879
www.mpac.org
contact@mpac.org

Muslims for Humanity
Helping Hand-USA
12541 McDougall St
Detroit, MI 48212
Phone 888-808-4357 / 313-279-5378
Fax 313-366-0200
www.hhrd.org

Muslim Student Association
PO Box 13930
Fairlawn, OH 44334
www.msanational.org

Muslim Women's League
3010 Wilshire Blvd, Suite 519
Los Angeles, CA 90010
Phone 626-358-0335
Fax 213-383-9674
www.mwlusa.org
mwl@mwlusa.org

**National Council on Islamic Affairs /
American-Arab Relations Committee**
230 E 44th St, suite 3F
New York, NY 10017
Phone 212-972-0460

New School, The
PO Box 10520
Oakland, CA 94610-9991
Phone 510-456-9709

**New York University Center for Dialogues:
Islamic World—U.S.—The West**
194 Mercer St, 4th Floor
New York, NY 10012
Phone 212-998-8693
Fax 212-995-4091
www.centerfordialogues.org
info@centerfordialogues.org

SAAR Foundation, The
555 Grove Street
Herndon, VA 20170

Safa Trust, Inc.
555 Grove Street
Herndon, VA 20170
Phone 703-464-8999

Saudi Arabian Cultural Mission
2600 Virginia Ave NW
Washington, DC 20037
www.sacm.org
sacm@sacm.org

Saudi Joint Relief Committee
(Charity – declared a terrorist organization)

Saudi Red Crescent Society
Al Sahafa
11129 Riyadh
Saudi Arabia
Phone 966-489-2556
Fax 966-489-2225
www.srcs.org.sa

Startec Global Communications
7361 Calhoun Place, Suite 520
Rockville, MD 20855
Phone 301-610-4300

Fax 301-610-4301
www.startec.com
customercare@startec.com

Taibah International Aid Association
Formerly located in Virginia
(Declared a terrorist organization)

United Association for Studies and Research
PO Box 1210
Annandale, VA 22003-1210
Phone 703-750-9011

Uruklink.net – Internet Resource Only
Washington Institute for Near East Policy
1828 L St NW, Suite 1050
Washington, DC 20036
Phone 202-452-0650
Fax 202-223-5364
www.washingtoninstitute.org

Washington Report on Middle East Affairs
1902 18th St NW
PO Box 53062
Washington, DC 20009
Phone 202-939-6050
Fax 202-265-4574
www.wrmea.com

World Assembly of Muslim Youth
PO Box 8096
Falls Church, VA 22041
Phone 703-820-6656
Fax 703-783-8409
www.wamy.org
support@wamyusa.org

Zakat Foundation of America, The
PO Box 639
Worth, IL 60482
Phone 708-233-0555 / 1-888-925-2887
Fax 708-233-0339
http://zakat.org
info@zakat.org

***

Bibliography and recommended reading (Section #10)

A Brief Illustrated guide to understanding Islam
(I.A. Ibrahim)
ISBN 9960-34-011-2

After the Prophet:
The epic Story of the Shi'a-Sunni split in Islam
(Lesley Hazleton)
ISBN 978-0-385-52393-6

A History of God
(Karen Armstrong)
ISBN 0-345-38456-3

A history of Iraq
(Charles Tripp)
ISBN 0-521-55404-7

A history of the Arab Peoples
(Albert Hourani)
ISBN 1-56731-216-0

American encounter with Islam
(Anjun Mir)
ISBN —???

American Islam:
The struggle for the soul of a Religion
(Paul M. Barrett)
ISBN 0-374-10423-9

American Jihad: Islam after Malcolm X
(Steven Barboza)
ISBN 0-385-47011-8

American Muslims: The new generation
(Asma Gull Hasan)
ISBN 0-8264-1279-3

A Peace to End All Peace:
The fall of the Ottoman Empire and
the creation of the modern Middle East
(David Fromkin)
ISBN 13-978-0-8050-8809-0

Approaching the Qur'an: The early revelations
(Translated by Michael Sells)
ISBN 1-883991-30-7

Arabs: A narrative history
from Muhammad to the present
(Anthony Nutting)
Library of Congress 63-19899

Arabs: Journeys Beyond the mirage
(David Lamb)
ISBN 0-394-54433-1

Beyond belief
(V.S. Naipanl)
ISBN 0-375-50118-5

Chronology of World History
(G.S.D. Freeman-Grenville)
ISBN 901-72067-4

Churchill's Folly:
How Winston Churchill created modern Iraq
(Christopher Catherwood)
ISBN 0-7867-1351-8

Complete Idiot's guide to the Gulf War
(Charles Faco)
ISBN 0-02-864324-0

Complete Idiot's guide to understanding Islam
(Yahiya Emerick)
ISBN 0-02-864233-3

Complete Illustrated guide to Islam
(Raana Bokhari and Dr. Mohammad Seddon)
ISBN 13-978-1-84681-512-6

Concise Encyclopedia of Islam
(H.A.R. Gibb and J.H. Kramens)
ISBN 0-391-04116-9

Conqueror of the world:
The life of Ghengis-Khan
(Rene Groussel)
LCCC 66-26935

Crusade: Chronicles of an Unjust War
(James Carroll)
ISBN 0-8050-7703-0

Crusade:
The untold story of the Persian Gulf War
(Rick Atkinson)
ISBN 0-395-60290-4

Crusades: A history of armed
pilgrimage and Holy War
(Geoffrey Hindley)
ISBN 0-7867-1105-1

Crusades: A very short introduction
(Christopher Tyerman)
ISBN 978-0-19-280655-0

Crusades: The illustrate history
(Thomas F. Madden, Editor)
ISBN 0-472-11463-8

Disarming Iraq
(Hans Blix)
ISBN 0-375-42302-8

Dungeon, Fire and Word
(John J. Robinson)
ISBN 0-87131-657-9

Early Islam
(Desmond Jizward)
Library of Congress 67-27863

Empires, wars, and battles
(T.C.F. Hopkins)
ISBN 13-978-0-7653-0327-1

Encyclopedia of world history
(Market house Books, LTD) Oxford Univ. Press
ISBN 0-19-860223-5

Europe in the High Middle Ages
(William Chester Jordan)
ISBN 0-670-03202-6

Everything understanding Islam book
(Christine Huda Dodge)
ISBN 13-978-1-58062-783-2/8

Faith and Power: The politics of Islam
(Edward Mortimer)
ISBN 0-394-51333-9

Fighting for the Cross
(Norman Housley)
ISBN 978-0-300-1188-9

Fourth Crusade and the sack of Constantinople
(Jonathan Phillips)
ISBN 0-670-03350-2

Full Circle:
Escape from Baghdad and the return
(Saul Silas Fathi)
ISBN 978-0-9777117-8-9

Genghis Khan
(R.P. Lister)
ISBN 8128-1247-6

Genghis Khan and the making of the modern world
(Jack Weatherford)
ISBN 0-609-80964-4

Genghis Khan: Conqueror of the world
(Leo De Hartog)
ISBN 0-7607-1192-5

God's battalions
(Rodney Stark)
ISBN 978-0-06-158261-5

God's Crucible:
Islam and the making of Europe
(David Levering Lewis)
ISBN 978-0-393-06472-8

God's War: A new history of the Crusades
(Christopher Tyerman)
ISBN 978-0-674-02387-1

Heroes and Holy places
(Dr. Kaled Abou El-Fadl)
ISBN 1-59084-704-0

Historical Atlas of Islam
(Malise Ruthven and Azim Nanji)
ISBN 0-674-01385-9

Historical dictionary of Islam
(Ludwig W. Adamec)
ISBN 0-8108-3962-8

History of the Jews & Israel
(Saul Silas Fathi)
ISBN 978-0-9777117-3-4

History of the Mongols
(Bertold Spuler)
ISBN 0-88029-271-7

History of the world: In photos
(Britannica)
ISBN 13-978-1-57912-583-7

Holy Qur'an
(S.V. Mir Ahmed Ali)
ISBN 978-0-940368-9

Holy warriors
(Jonathan Phillips)
ISBN 978-1-4000-6580-6

In search of Genghis Khan
(Tim Severin)
ISBN 0-689-12134-2

Inside Islam
(Reza F. Safa)
ISBN 978-0-88419-4163

Inside Islam:
The faith, the people, and conflicts...
(Edited by John Miller and Aaron Kenedi)
LCCC 2002-1007-40

In the path of God
(Daniel Pipes)
ISBN 0-465-03451-9

Introducing Islam: The basics
(Dr. Khaled Abou El-Fadl)
ISBN 1-59084-697-4

Iraq's last Jews
(Edited by: Tamar Morad,
Dennis Shasha, and Robert Shasha)
ISBN 13-978-0-230-60810-8

Islam
(Jean Mathe)
ISBN —???

Islam
(Matthew Gordon)(Oxford)
ISBN 0-19-521885-x

Islam: A brief history
(Paul Lunde)
ISBN 0-7894-8797-7 / 1-4053-0404-9

Islam: A short history
(Karen Armstrong)
ISBN 0-679-64040-1

Islam and revolution
(Imam Khomeini)
ISBN 0-933782-04-7

Islam and terrorism
(Mark A. Gabriel)
ISBN 0-88419-884-7

Islam and the Jews
(Mark A. Gabriel)
ISBN 0-88419-956-8

Islam and the West
(Norman Daniel)
ISBN 1-85168-043-8

Islam & world peace
(M.R. Bawa Muhayaddeen)
ISBN 0-914390-30-9 / 0-914390-25-2

Islam: An Illustrated history
(G.S.P. Freeman-Grenville and Stuart C. Munro-Hay)
ISBN 0-8264-1417-6

**Islam: Discover the faith, culture,
and history that have shaped the modern world**
(Kitty Blount, Editor)
ISBN —???

Islam explained
(Tahar Ben Jelloun,
Translated by Franklin Philip: French)
ISBN 1-56584-781-4

Islam: Religion, history and civilization
(Seyyed Houssein Nasr)
ISBN 0-06-050714-4

Islamic Fundamentalism
(Dr. Khaled Abou El-Fadl)
ISBN 1-59084-703-2

Islam in America
(Jane I. Smith)
ISBN 0-231-10966-0

Islam in the world
(Malise Ruthven)
ISBN 13-978-0-19-530503-6

Islam: Opposing viewpoints
(David Bender and Bruno Leone;
Paul A. Winters, Editor)
ISBN 1-56510-247-9

Islam: Opposing viewpoints
(David M. Haugen, Susan Musser,
and Kacy Lovelace) – Editors
ISBN 978-0-7377-4526-9

Islam: Religions and religious movements
(Mitchell Young, etc.)
ISBN 0-7377-2571-0

Islam: The religion and the people
(Bernard Lewis)
ISBN 0-13-223085-2

Islam today
(Akbar S. Ahmed)
ISBN 1-86064-257-8

Islam: World religions – Revised edition
(Matthew S. Gordon)
ISBN 0-8160-4401-5

Jihad: The trail of political Islam
(Anthony F. Roberts)
ISBN —???

Judaism and the world's religions
(David Bamberger)
ISBN 0-87441-461-x

Key to understanding global history
(James Killoran and Stuart Zimmer)
ISBN 1-882422-40-6

Khubilai Khan: His life and times
(Morris Rossabi)
ISBN 0-520-05913-1

Last Crusaders:
The Hundred-Year Battle for the center of the world
(Barnaby Rogerson)
ISBN 978-1-5902-286-9

Legacy of Jihad:
The Islamic Holy War and the fate of non-Muslims
(Edited by Andrew G. Boston, M.D.)
ISBN 978-1-59102-307-4

Lord of the Horizons:
A History of the Ottoman Empire
(Jason Goodwin)
ISBN 0-8050-6342-0

Lost Centuries: 1145 – 1453
(Sir John Bagot Glubb)
ISBN —???

Meaning of the Holy Qur'an
(Abdullah Yusuf Ali)
ISBN 0-915957-76-0

Middle East: A brief history
(Bernard Lewis)
ISBN 0-684-80712-2

Middle East and South Asia
(Malcolm B. Russell)
ISBN 978-1-935264-04-0

Middle East for Dummies
(Craig J. Davis, Ph.D.)
ISBN 0-7645-5483-2

Militant Islam
(G.H. Jansen)
ISBN 0-06-012202-1

Muhammad
(Deepak Shopra)
ISBN 978-0-06-178242-8

Muhammad: A biography of the Prophet
(Karen Armstrong)
ISBN 0-060250014-7

Muslim – 100
(Muhammad Mojlum Khan)
ISBN 978-1-84774-0069

Myths and legends of the ancient Near East
(Fred Gladstone Bratton)
ISBN —???

My years inside radical Islam
(Daveed Gartenstein-Ross)
ISBN 13-978-0-58542-551-8

No God but God
(Geneive Abdo)
ISBN 0-19-512540-1

Osman's dream:
The history of the Ottoman Empire
(Caroline Finkel)
ISBN 13-978-0-465-02306-7

Ottoman centuries:
The rise and fall of the Turkish Empire
(Lord Kinross)
ISBN 0-688-03093-9

The Oxford dictionary of Islam
(John L. Esposito)
ISBN 0-19-512558-4

Oxford Encyclopedia of the modern Islamic world
(John L. Esposito)
ISBN 0-19-506613-8

Oxford Illustrated history of the Crusades
(Jonathan Riley-Smith)
ISBN 978-0-19-285428-5

Palestine: Peace, not Apartheid
(Jimmy Carter)
ISBN 13-978-0-7432-8502-5

People of the First Crusade
(Michael Foss)
ISBN 1-55970-414-4

Pocket Timeline of Islamic civilization
(Nicholas Badcott)
ISBN 13-978-1-56656-758-9

Qur'an
(Tarif Khalid)
ISBN 978-0-670-020-23-2

Revolt on the Tigris
(Mark Etherington)
ISBN 0-8014-4451-9

Saddam Hussein
(Efraim Karshtinari Routsi)
ISBN 0-02-917063-x

Saladin
(Andrew S. Ehrenkrutz)
ISBN 0-87395-005-x

Saladin in his time
(P.H. Newby)
ISBN 0-88029-775-1

Saladin: The politics of the Holy War
(Malcolm Cameron Lyons and D.E.P. Jackson)
ISBN 0-521-22318-x

Saladin: The Sultan and his time
(Hannes Mohring)
ISBN 978-0-8018-8991-2

Secrets of the Kingdom
(Gerald Posner)
ISBN 1-4000-6291-8

Silent no more:
Confronting America's false images of Islam
(Paul Findley)
ISBN 1-59008-000-9

Sleeping with the devil
(Robert Baer)
ISBN 1-4000-5021-9

Soldiers of the faith
(Ronald C. Finncane)
ISBN 0-312-74256-8

Spirit of Allah: Khomeini & the Islamic Revolution
(Amir Taheri)
ISBN 0-917561-04-x

Spread of Islam
(Michael Rogers)
ISBN 0-7290-0016-8

Standing alone in Mecca
(Asra Q. Nomani)
ISBN 0-06-057144-6

The American encounter with Islam
(Anjun Mir)
ISBN 1-59084-699-0

The American Muslim teenager's handbook
(Dilara Hafiz, Yasmine Hafiz, Imran Hafiz)
ISBN 978-1-4169-8578-5

The Arabs:
A narrative history from Muhammad to the present
(Anthony Nutting)
LCC 63-19899

The Arabs: Journey beyond the mirage
(David Lamb)
ISBN 0-394-54433-1

The CIA World Factbook
(Central Intelligence Agency)
ISBN 978-1-60239-727-9

The complete idiot's guide to the Gulf War
(Charles Faco)
ISBN 0-02-864324-0

The complete idiot's guide to world religions
(Brandon Toropov & Father Luke Buckles)
ISBN 0-02-864208-2

The complete illustrated guide to Islam
(Raana Bokhari & Dr. Muhammad Seddon)
ISBN 978-1-84681-512-6

The complete idiot's guide to understanding Islam
(Yahiya Emerick)
ISBN 0-02-864233-3

The crisis of Islam:
Holy War and unholy terror
(Bernard Lewis)
ISBN 0-679-64281-1

The Crusades
(Thomas Asbridge)
ISBN 978-0-06-078728-8

The Crusades
(Zoe Oldenbourg)
ISBN - ???

The Crusades:
A history of armed pilgrimage and Holy War
(Geoffrey Hindley)
ISBN 0-7867-1105-1

The Crusades: A very short introduction
(Christopher Tyerman)
ISBN 978-0-19-280655-0

The Crusades through Arab eyes
(Amin Maalouf)
ISBN 0-8052-4004-7

The Crusaders in the Holy Lands
(Meron Benvenisti)
LCC 70-1800293

The Crusades through Arab eyes
(Amin Maalouf)
ISBN 0-8052-4004-7

The decline of the Ottoman Empire
(Alan Palmer)
ISBN 0-871-754-0

The Devil's Horsemen
(James Chambers)
ISBN 0-689-10042-3

The enigma of Iraq
(James B. Mayfield)
ISBN 1-4196-0956-4

The essential Koran: The heart of Islam
(Thomas Cleary, translator)
ISBN 0-06-250196-8

The essential Middle-East
(Dilip Hiro)
ISBN 0-7867-1269-4

The everything Koran book
(Duraa Anwar)
ISBN 1-59337-139-X

The everything understanding Islam book
(Christine Huda Dodge)
ISBN 978-1-58062-783-2/8

The fight for Jerusalem
(Dore Gold)
ISBN 978-1-59698-029-7

The Fourth Crusade: And the sack of Constantinople)
(Jonathan Phillips)
ISBN 0-670-033350-2

The glorious Qur'an
(Dr. Syed Vickar Ahmed, translator)
ISBN 978-1-879402-96-6

The great religions
(Richard Cavendish)
ISBN 0-668-04929-4

The Heirs of Muhammad
(Barnaby Rogerson)
ISBN 978-1-58567-896-9

The Holy Qur'an
(Abdullah Yusuf Ali, translator)
ISBN 81-7435

The Holy Qur'an
(S. V. Mir Ahmed Ali)
ISBN 978-0-940368-9

The Holy Qur'an: The final Testament
(S. V. Amir & Agha H. M. M. Pooya)
ISBN 978-0-940368-85-9

The House of Saud
(David Holden & Richard John)
ISBN 0-03-043731-8

The inner journey
(William C. Chittick, Editor)
ISBN 978-1-59675-017-3

The Iranians
(Sandra Mackey)
ISBN 0-525-94005-7

The Islamic threat: Myth or reality?
(John L. Esposito)
ISBN 0-19-507-184-0

The Israelites
(Leonard Beder)
ISBN 978-0-9789565-0-9

The Jews of Arab lands
(Norman A. Stillman)
ISBN 0-8276-0198-0

The Jews of Islam
(Bernard Lewis)
ISBN 0-691-054-19-3

The Jews of Spain
(Jane S. Gerber)
ISBN 0-02-911574-4

The key to understanding global history
(James Killoran & Stuart Zimmer)
ISBN 1-882422-40-6

The Koran
(N.J. Dawood, translator)
ISBN 0-14-044558-7

The legacy of Jihad:
Islamic Holy War and the fate of the Non-Muslims
(Andrew G. Bostom, MD)

ISBN 978-1-59102-307-4

The lost centuries: 1145-1453
(Sir John Bagot Glubb)
LCC 67-22280-54072

The meaning of the Holy Qur'an
(Abdullah Yusuf Ali)
ISBN 0-915957-76-0

The Middle-East and South Asia
(Malcolm B. Russell)
ISBN 978-1-935264-04-0

The Middle-East: A brief history
(Bernard Lewis)
ISBN 0-684-80712-2

The Middle-East for Dummies
(Dr. Craig S. Davis)
ISBN 0-7645-5483-2

The Mongol Empire
(Michael Prawdin)
LCC 55-10925

The Mongol mission
(Christopher Dawson)
LCC 55-10925

The Muslim Jesus:
Sayings and stories in Islamic literature
(Tarif Khalidi)
ISBN 0-674-00477-9

The Muslim-100
(Muhammad Mojlum Khan)
ISBN 978-1-84774-00609

The Muslim World
(Geoffrey Orens)
ISBN 0-8242-1019-0

The Ottomans
(Andrew Wheatcroft)
ISBN 0-670-84412-8

The Ottoman centuries:...
(Lord Kinross)
ISBN 0-688-03093-9

The outline of history
(H. G. Wells)
ISBN - ???

The Oxford dictionary of Islam
(John L. Esposito)
ISBN 0-19-512558-4

The Oxford Encyclopedia of the modern Islamic world
(John L. Esposito)
ISBN 0-19-5066-13-8

The Oxford illustrated history of the Crusades
Jonathan Riley-Smith)
ISBN 978-0-19-285428-5

The Persian Gulf crisis
(Steve A. Yetive)
ISBN 0-313-29943-9

The Qur'an: A biography
(Bruce Lawrence)
ISBN 978-0-87113-951-1

The rise of Islamic Fundamentalism
(Phillip Marguilies)
ISBN 0-7377-2985-6

The rise of the Taliban in Afghanistan
(Neamatollah Nojumi)
ISBN 0-312-29402-6

The Shi'a revival
(Vali Masr)
ISBN 978-0-393-06211-3

The spirit of Allah:
Khomeini and the Islamic Revolution
(Amir Taheri)
ISBN 0-917561-04-X

The spread of Islam
(Michael Rogers)
ISBN 0-7290-0016-8

The sword and the Scimitar:
The saga of the Crusades
(Ernie Bradford)
ISBN 399-11375-4

The Timetable of History
(Bernard Grun)
ISBN 0-671-24988-6

The truth about Muhammad
(Robert Spencer)
ISBN 978-1-59698-028-0

The two faces of Islam
(Stephan Schwartz)
ISBN 0-385-50692-9

The ways of the Sufi
(Idries Shah)
LCC 71-926-15

The world of Ottoman art
(Michael Levey)
ISBN 0-684-14850-1

The world's religions
(Huston smith)
ISBN 0-06-250799-0

Toward understanding Islam
(Abul A'La Mawdudi)
ISBN 1-883591-01-05

Toward understanding the Qur'an (5 Vol.)
(Sayyid Abul A'La Mawdudi)
ISBN 0-86037-205-7

Tulips, Arabesque & Turbans:
Decorative arts from the Ottoman Empire
(Edited by Yanni Petsopoulos)
ISBN 0-89659-279-0

Turkish reflections: A Biography of a place
(Mary Lee Settle)
ISBN 0-13-917675-6

Understanding Iraq
(William R. Polk)
ISBN 978-0-0607-6469-2

Warriors of God
(James Reston, Jr.)
ISBN 0-385-49561-7

Warriors of the Prophet: The Struggle for Islam
(Mark Huband)
ISBN 0-8133-2780-6

War without End
(Dilip Hiro)
ISBN 0-415-28801-0

What went wrong?
(Bernard Lewis)
ISBN 0-19-514420-1

When Baghdad ruled the Muslim World:
The rise and fall of Islam's greatest dynasty
(Hugh Kennedy)
ISBN 0-306-81435-8

Who Are the Muslims?
(Dr. Khaled Abou El-Fadl)
ISBN 1-59084-701-6

Wisdom's journey:
Living the spirit of Islam in the modern world
(John Herlihy)
ISBN 978-1-933316-64-2

Who Speaks for Islam?
(John L. Esposito and Dalia Mogahed)
ISBN 978-1-59562-017-0

World history for Dummies
(Peter Hangen)
ISBN 0-7645-5242-2

Worriers of God
(James Reston Jr.)
ISBN 0-385-49561-7

Worriers of the Prophet: The struggle for Islam
(Mark Huband)
ISBN 0-8133-2780-6

End******End

Saul Silas Fathi's books & ISBN #'s:

1. Full Circle: Escape from Baghdad and the return
   ISBN# 978-0-9777117-8-9

2. History of the Jews and Israel
   ISBN# 978-0-9777117-3-4

3. Islamic leaders, their biographies & accomplishments
   ISBN# 978-0-9777117-5-8

4. Glossary of Arabic terms
   ISBN# 978-0-9777117-4-1

5. Arab-Islamic groups and organizations
   ISBN# 978-1-62620-377-8

Saul Silas Fathi
27 Broadlawn Drive
Central Islip, NY, 11722-4616
fathi@optonline.net
www.saulsilasfathi.com

***

Books by Saul Silas Fathi

ISBN# 978-0-9777117-8-9

ISBN# 978-0-9777117-3-4   ISBN# 978-0-9777117-5-8   ISBN# 978-0-9777117-4-1

www.saulsilasfathi.com

www.ingramcontent.com/pod-product-compliance
Lightning Source LLC
Chambersburg PA
CBHW022101150426
43195CB00008B/225